BOOKS BY THE AUTHOR

How You Can Become Financially Independent
    by Investing in Real Estate

How To Manage Real Estate Successfully —
    In Your Spare Time

COURSES BY THE AUTHOR

Lowry/Nickerson Seminar
Creative Real Estate Financing
Successful Real Estate Management
Business Opportunities — Cash Flow & Profit
Foreclosures and Distressed Property

How to Manage Real Estate Successfully- in Your Spare Time

by Albert J. Lowry, Ph.D.

Simon and Schuster, New York

This publication is designed to provide accurate authoritative information with regard to the subject matter covered. It is sold with the understanding that the publisher is not engaged in rendering legal, accounting, or other professional advice. If legal advice or other expert assistance is required, the services of a competent professional person should be sought.

. . . From a Declaration of Principles jointly adopted by a Committee of the American Bar Association and a Committee of Publishers and Associations.

Copyright © 1977 by Dean V. Ambrose as Trustee
All rights reserved
including the right of reproduction
in whole or in part in any form

Published by Simon and Schuster
A Division of Simon & Schuster, Inc.
Simon & Schuster Building
Rockefeller Center
1230 Avenue of the Americas
New York, New York 10020
SIMON AND SCHUSTER and colophon are registered trademarks
of Simon & Schuster, Inc.

Manufactured in the United States of America

8 9 10 11 12

Library of Congress Cataloging in Publication Data

Lowry, Albert J.
How to manage real estate successfully—in your spare time.

Edition for 1977 published under title: How to successfully manage real estate—in your spare time.
1. Real estate management. I. Title.
HD1394.L68 1979 658'.91'33333 78-27861
ISBN 0-671-24829-4

CONTENTS

II. SO YOU'RE THE NEW MANAGER   21

III. THE HUMAN SIDE OF PROPERTY MANAGEMENT   33

XII.   THE RENTAL DOCUMENT   163

XIII. RECORD-KEEPING CAN BE EASY   175

XV.   COPING WITH COSTS   237

FOREWORD

Your second career — or your first — can start with this book.

At any age from your teens to your seventies, you can begin managing real estate part-time for an owner of one or more rental houses, or of a small apartment property.

Wherever you are in America, you can find hundreds of owners who need someone to manage residential property for them. Census figures show that more than five million new multi-unit residential structures went up in the 1960s; probably as many more have already been built in the 1970s. Currently, for every two apartment buildings rising in the central cities, one is rising up just outside them. And how many older apartment buildings are still flourishing? The number is beyond counting. But they all need managers to collect the rent, fill the vacancies, see that maintenance and repairs are kept up — and perhaps do considerably more, if an owner or manager is profit-minded.

As you learn the business, you can begin to manage more or bigger properties. Your income will grow.

What will you do with that extra income? If you want a career, you may well decide to invest some of your money in property which you can manage for yourself. You will then be in business — your own boss.

Independence! What a wonderful sound that word has.

What a thrill to think of working for yourself instead of someone else — to have the incentive of profits instead of a fixed salary. How pleasant to stop worrying about company politics.

The most persistent and widespread of all dreams in America, from its founding until today, has been the dream of making money in a business of one's own, with no limit on potential profits.

Maybe you've thought that such a dream was unattainable for you. Or maybe you're wedded to the security of a salaried position. If so, stop and reflect for a moment.

As an employee in a business organization, you've naturally expected — or at least hoped — that your pay would keep rising, maybe permanently until retirement. Once upon a time, there was some truth to this notion. Many people did struggle along at lower salaries in the early and middle years of their lives, then burst into the high-pay brackets in their late forties or fifties or even sixties.

No more. A whole new earnings pattern is emerging in U.S. corporate life. After a gradual rise, salaries tend to spring upward in the late thirties and mid-forties, then subside. When someone loses a job after 45 — you must know dozens of acquaintances to whom this has happened — he or she is forced to accept a lower salary somewhere else. One statistical study of the earnings of 50-year-old executives showed that more than half of them were making *less* than they had at 44. Another analysis of 55-year-olds indicated that most were even lower-paid than they had been at 50.

Even those who win promotions may find themselves faced in their fifties with the enormous costs of putting children through college. Then too, taxes and inflation — or the new life-style that goes with the promotion — may gobble up the whole salary increase, leaving the same penny-ante bank balance and a gnawing worry about what will happen if the job disappears.

Nothing kills ambition and energy more surely than the feeling of being un-rewarded for great effort. But there are people — even quite elderly people — who manage their careers intelligently enough to surmount these obstacles. In their spare time they learn to carry on a successful business of their own.

For most of these people, the business is managing real estate which they buy with small down payments. This is the best kind of business: a family-owned business. It isn't a get-rich-quick business, but it's probably safer than any other, because you needn't be on hand all the time in order to profit. Residential real estate generates a steady stream of income, and can be resold or traded (normally at a plump profit) when you choose.

Without taking serious risks, with no special connections or elaborate educa-tion or big bankroll, you or any other ambitious person can enter into this profes-sion of building(s) owner-manager in whatever part of the country you wish. You can realistically expect to earn a decent living from it, and eventually to achieve financial independence through it, or even grow rich if you choose to apply your-self energetically.

This can be done. You can do it. Believe me, I know. I've done it myself and I've trained others to do it.

My relation to property management isn't academic or second-hand. It is intimate. I still work at it for at least a few hours each week, and have done so for the past 15 years.

I was raised in an orphanage; then went from one odd job to another. After working for years without getting anywhere financially, I began to discover that people like me were making money by owning and managing modest duplexes and fourplexes. How and why did they buy these properties, I wondered. I looked into it, and was amazed at what I learned:

1.   You can buy real estate for less cash outlay than most things. A down payment of 15% or less may be enough. And the mortgages are long-term, not short-term, debts.

2.   Payments on mortgages aren't payments at all. They are forced savings, because they build up your equity in the property. Except for the interest (which is tax-deductible against your other income), you're paying the money to yourself. This makes real estate mortgages a good way to invest savings and build your net worth.

3.   Real estate is a valuable tool for many kinds of tax-saving, cash-raising, estate-planning, trading, and investing maneuvers. You can do a lot of wheeling and dealing with it. It is flexible enough for a wide range of personal investment needs and tax problems. It is the best possible collateral for loans; even banks accept it readily.

4.   People used to think that buying real estate was an outrageously risky gamble. It isn't. Land and dwellings are limited in quantity. People are multiplying. Competition for land use keeps pushing values higher.

Because of these conditions, real estate prices have risen almost continuously for centuries.

5.   As soon as you hold title to a little property, Uncle Sam and inflation can almost buy more for you if you manage it correctly. In addition to the cash flow from rentals and the profits from selling, real estate saves you taxes through depreciation. This whipsaw effect enables you to deduct the *cost* of real estate as depreciation; then pocket most of the property's *appreciation* as a capital gain when you sell.

When I understood these facts, I began putting a few hundred dollars into small residences. Naturally, I handled the renting, rent-collecting, and upkeep myself; I couldn't afford a manager to do it for me. So I learned about managing, from the basement up.

I found that efficient management could bring in extra income for very little extra money. And every extra dollar in rental income could be worth $10 in resale value. Within a few years I knew that owning and managing apartments — especially older apartments — was the prudent way to make big profits on small investments of time and money. So I went at it full-swing. By 1970, I was wealthy enough to buy and sell supermarkets.

Buying, reselling, and exchanging real estate can be a fascinating pursuit, and a way of making your money grow quite rapidly if you want to keep expanding. I've taught people how to do it in three-day seminars all over the country, as well as in my 1977 book published by Simon & Schuster, *How You Can Become Financially Independent By Investing In Real Estate.*

But there isn't time in the seminars, nor space in the book, to say much about one aspect of realty investment that struck me repeatedly: the financial advantages of making sure a property is well managed while you own it.

Again and again I established a good stream of income from houses and apartments while I managed them myself, only to see the income dwindle and the resale value shrink when I turned them over to less experienced management. Good property managers are surprisingly hard to find. Many managers I hired made costly mistakes, because property management isn't taught correctly and isn't thoroughly explained in manuals I could find.

So you might say I've written this book in self-defense. I want to give it to my managers, to teach them the methods that will maximize profits. As they learn these methods, I think they'll go on to become owner-managers themselves.

I hope you will too, if you're a manager now, or if you're thinking of becoming one. You may be one of the thousands of potential money-makers in America, walking around undiscovered by anyone, including themselves. When you read this book and begin to understand the possibilities in well-managed real estate, it may awaken the dynamo that has been hiding inside you all along.

Or maybe you're an owner now, relying on others to manage property for you. If so, you're already aware that the value of a building lies in its earning power — but maybe you're not aware how much this earning power can be augmented by an efficient, knowledgeable, and likable manager.

This book will help you choose managers with the right personal qualities. And then it will help you manage your managers after you hire them. You'll know the right ways and wrong ways of going about each part of their job. You'll know in detail what they should and shouldn't be doing. Remember, being a trusting person has nothing to do with good business sense.

Maybe you'll decide to take over the job yourself. That's one way of putting money in your pocket.

Another way, of course, is to buy a copy of this book for each of your managers.

Then they'll know what you expect of them, and how to fulfill your expectations. If you pay them a percentage of the gross, as many owners do, they'll increase their own earnings as well as yours.

Of course, when they learn to be expert managers, they may eventually leave you to become owner-managers for themselves. But you can always hire more managers and buy more copies of this book, can't you?

I   *Should You Be Managing?*

YOU'RE ALREADY MANAGING PROPERTY, in a limited sense, if you own even a one-family house. You're keeping records for tax purposes and probably for budget purposes. You're writing checks for insurance, utilities, supplies, and maybe umpteen other expenses like mortgage payments, lawn care, swimming pool care, and so on, far into the night. You're making decisions about repairs, maintenance, improvements. And you're either contracting with people to keep the place in livable condition (or luxury condition) and supervising them, or you're doing the work yourself. All this is part of property management.

And if you own a house that you rent out, probably you're into property management a few steps deeper. You try to make the property more valuable (assuming that you have the money-making instinct that a property manager needs). You collect rent. You cope with complaints. You try to keep occupants happy. You set rent levels. You make decisions about leasing or renting terms. All this, too, is part of the work of a property manager.

Some owners of rental houses arrange to turn these chores over to someone in a realty office, but they find that most management decisions are still up to them. Sometimes they also find that their manager is inept or dishonest, and that their property would have brought them more income if it were better managed.

NOW YOU HAVE BIGGER PROPERTY TO MANAGE, we'll assume, or you wouldn't be reading this book. Perhaps you've been hired as a manager. Perhaps you've bought a multi-family dwelling or an apartment house. Conceivably, you're owner or part owner of some of those imposing 50-unit or 500-unit or 1,000-unit complexes that have become familiar landmarks in our lifetime.

This book is for you if you're either (a) wondering how to manage a certain piece of residential income property, or (b) wondering how to judge the performance of the manager. In other words, it is a manual for the professional manager, for owners who supervise them, and for owners who do their own managing.

MOST OWNERS KNOW NOTHING ABOUT MANAGING, and don't seem to care. It's sad to see how many supposedly smart investors treat their rental property as if it were a needless cluster of cottages in Nowheresville. They are totally absentee hands-off owners, blithely assuming that the place and its occupants will take care of themselves under the guidance of an all-wise and true-blue manager. "No news is good news, so long as the money keeps rolling in," these owners think.

For all they know, their possession may be fraught with hazards and nuisances that violate the law and leave them open to horrendous damage suits. It may be dangerously under-insured — or loaded with extra insurance. All sorts of hidden costs and scandalous waste may be eating away at future profits. Managers may be secretly enriching themselves at the owners' expense, or may be antagonizing occupants and employees and neighbors and building inspectors and policemen and Lucifer knows who-all else.

OWNERS ALSO MISMANAGE

Strange as it seems, property owners who are intelligent, hard-working, and successful in their own businesses and professions are nevertheless prone to costly mistakes in the management of their residential income properties — even when their properties are multi-building apartment complexes. A *Business Week* survey indicates that 40% of owners with $25,000-or-over incomes try to do their own bookkeeping and tax work and use cut-rate assistance; only 10% of them ever check the background of contractors, vendors, suppliers or property managers before spending big money through them.

"We spend millions to plan, finance, build and promote our projects," says Ed Coleman, research director for the National Apartment Association. "Then, like half-wits, we turn them over to a group of untrained, incompetent, insolent and lazy paranoids who consider tenants personal enemies to engage with in hand-to-hand combat."

Coleman's lament doesn't apply to you, surely, or you wouldn't be reading this book. The chances are you're wondering why the property you own or manage (or both) isn't a far more bountiful income-producer than it is at the moment. You want to learn how it can be managed for optimum results. This book will tell you.

Incidentally, pronouns can be confusing, so let's try to untangle the obscurity right now. Throughout this book, the pronoun "you" will mean you as manager or owner-manager or owner, whichever you may be; the sentence and paragraph in which "you" is used will help you see which identity is particularly being addressed at the moment.

And when the book uses the pronoun "he" or "his" in mentioning either an owner, manager, resident, visitor, employee or the like, this usage is merely to save space. To be fully correct, the book should say "he or she" and "his or hers" in all such situations, since there are plenty of female owners and managers and so on. In fact, there are also plenty of husband-wife teams who do very well as owners or managers or both; so to be entirely accurate, the book should say "he and/or she," but this doesn't make for smooth reading. So, whenever you encounter the masculine term, please take for granted that the book's intent is to refer to both sexes.

IF YOU'RE A HIRED MANAGER, the book will enable you to be a highly professional substitute for the owner, just as the lawyer and accountant apply their specialized skills in the owner's best interests. Your goal — to sum up a complicated job in eight words — is to produce the highest possible net operating income.

That is, you are supposed to find ways to make the property bring the owner the maximum amount of money after operating expenses are paid. We're talking long-term net, of course — not short-term. Only a foolish owner would judge your success by the cash that comes to him in a few months; by spending no money on repairs or upkeep, you might produce a flood of "profit" temporarily, but it would have to pour out again later to pay for the deferred maintenance (or would cause a costly drop in the resale value of the property, as well as an exodus of residents). A good budget, expertly followed, is what we should want. We'll get into this in great detail when we reach Chapter 14.

Some owners would like their property manager to do more than produce maximum net operating income. They would also like him to maximize the cash flow — which is net operating income minus debt service (payments on the mortgage). But the owner's debt is entirely out of the manager's supervision. As manager, you're like the captain of a ship. The captain's prime concerns are the safety of the ship and the people on it. If the ship owner is in financial trouble, the captain can try to save money, but not when it begins to endanger the ship or the people. You'll be doing all that can rightfully be expected if you keep the expenses to a prudent minimum, and collect all the rent the building should produce.

This book will sum up for you the operating secrets learned by others in many years of practical experience. By following its rules, you'll grow faster in a talent-scarce profession. The resident manager is almost a newcomer to the realty business — a successor to the old-time janitors and "building superintendents" and often as inept as they were. Even professional management firms don't always do a good job; some have done such poor jobs that otherwise sound investments have been forced into foreclosure. Because good managers are hard to find, bigger and better-paid jobs constantly open up for them.

THE FIRST STEP ON THE CAREER LADDER in property management may be as a trainee in a management firm, or as a summer janitor or weekend rental agent. The next step would probably be as a maintenance worker in a sizable apartment complex, then as a maintenance supervisor, and then as a resident manager.

The successful management firms advance their people fast. Someone who makes good as resident manager of a small property is likely to find himself, within the next four years, supervising the managers of several hundred properties. By the time you've spent ten years in the business, you can be the chief officer in charge of 10,000 or 20,000 apartment units, with rents totalling millions of dollars, and your salary plus incentive fees and bonuses can be $40,000 or up into six figures.

FREE LANCE MANAGING, instead of working in a firm, can be even more lucrative in the long run. Your income may not be high on your first few jobs, but you'll soon know so much about how to make properties profitable that you'll want to buy one and manage it yourself. Later you can branch out, buying more properties, because you'll know how to make sure that their resident managers do a good job. Your story may be like that of the $7,800-a-year mailman, mentioned in several books, who bought and managed a two-family house and within two years was owner-manager of properties worth $400,000.

IF YOU'RE AN OWNER, this book will help you either in do-it-yourself managing or in keeping tab on the manager. For your first venture, you probably shouldn't try to manage anything bigger than a duplex, especially if you're occupied elsewhere full time at a good rate of income. Managing takes more hours than you might imagine; you may have to deal with a crisis at any hour of the day or night. If you own a fourplex or larger, your time could be better used in your full-time business than in managing the property; better hire a manager, because this book will enable you to supervise him intelligently, even if you can't spare more than a few hours a week.

IF YOU'RE AN OWNER-MANAGER of a sizable building, probably you're retired from other work or are occupied only part-time. In such cases, maybe you should be managing, and maybe you shouldn't. It depends on your aptitude and wishes.

WHAT IT TAKES TO MANAGE

Lots of people buy a building, happily intending to manage it themselves in their spare time, only to discover that the work is harder and more complicated than they expected. Managing even a newly-built duplex may take time and know-how. If too little work is done, the duplex dwindles in value. At a minimum, the must-be-done chores include collecting the rent, keeping the place in good condition, ordering supplies, paying the bills, and renting apartments when they're vacant.

Having bought such a property, you shouldn't decide to manage it unless you can face the bother that comes with midnight calls to complain about a noisy party or a stuffed toilet; unless you have a passion for neatness and an eye for what should be done in the way of maintenance and repairs and redecoration; unless you're good at salesmanship, so that you can sell the right people on renting; unless you're used to acting decisively when problems arise; and unless you're energetic enough to stay on top of numerous details of shopping, paperwork, personal relations and the other facets of apartment managing. (Glance through this book's table of contents, if you haven't already done so, to glimpse the range of managerial responsibilities.)

In addition to everything else, you or your spouse should be handy at simple maintenance like fixing faucets, repairing electrical switches, doing small paint and carpentry jobs and the like. A manager who may be perfect in every other way can still drain the property's profits if he has to call in outside artisans every time a minor emergency arises.

PRACTICAL EXPERIENCE WILL HELP

It isn't necessary for you to live in your rentals to manage them, but if you're the right type it's a good idea for several reasons. One reason is that it will keep costs down. (We'll get to the question of managers' compensation in a minute.) Another reason is that if you manage your first property, at least, you'll acquire more know-how than if you never tried your hand at it.

Reading this book should help a lot. But without practical experience, you'll need to keep referring back to the book to remind yourself what questions and suggestions you should put to your hired manager. Your progress toward bigger profits will be faster if you can supplement the book with first-hand experience; the lessons are remembered more vividly that way. A quick glance or a few words of conversation can tell volumes to an owner who has learned by managing.

Amateur husband-and-wife teams have been successful resident managers of properties as big as 30 units — especially when they are also owners — because managers' senses are marvelously sharpened by having their own money in the property. However, as your experience and holdings expand, you'll eventually find that you should delegate all basic chores to employees, and concentrate on overall supervision.

WHAT SHOULD YOU PAY FOR MANAGEMENT?

If we assume that you own a small apartment house, a percentage of rental income typically kept by a manager can eat up most of your net income. With larger rental properties, everything increases — potential gains and losses and the time and expertise needed to manage. One of California's prominent experts in property management has a stock answer when asked how much he pays resident managers. He says, "As much as my budget will allow."

YOU'RE LIKELY TO GET ABOUT WHAT YOU PAY FOR. First you'd better decide how much you want your manager to do. Inexperienced owners think one manager is much like another. Far from it. One manager will go into apartments and fix toilets for residents, cut the grass, keep the books, put ads in the newspapers to rent vacant apartments. Another may even clean and repaint the vacated apartments himself. Still another won't do a thing but collect rents and make bank deposits. Maybe you can plan on handling some of the work yourself.

BEFORE LOOKING FOR A MANAGER, write a detailed job description so you'll know exactly what kind of manager you need. In other words, write a list of everything you want your manager to do.

At the head of your list should be the showing and renting of apartments. This is really the name of the game. A property's net income soon dwindles if the manager can't fill vacancies promptly with desirable occupants. Many managers are expert handymen and neat record-keepers, but are no good at meeting strangers, sizing them up, and convincing the right ones that they ought to move in. Such managers think it's enough to hand any prospect a key and say, "It's apartment 2-B upstairs. Go take a look. I think the owner wants $170 a month for it." This is not showing vacancies. The right way to do it will be covered in detail in Chapter 10.

Even if you own only a fourplex, you need someone on the site who can show vacancies — someone with a pleasant personality and an instinct for salesmanship. Theoretically, you can turn this over to a management firm or a real estate office. But they don't always have someone available to hurry over and show a vacancy. Potential renters won't wait around. They want to see the apartment right now, and either rent it or not rent it on the spot.

YOUR BEST SOLUTION IN SMALL PROPERTIES may be to arrange with an occupant to show vacancies (if you do, be sure to have the occupant study Chapters 9, 10 and 11 of this book). Pick whoever seems most pleasant and intelligent. Call that person an "assistant manager," for a compensation of perhaps $25 off the monthly rent. For that much, the assistant might also do small chores like sweeping balconies and walkways, turning on sprinklers, vacuuming the halls, replacing burnt-out bulbs, straightening up the trash can area, and other light housekeeping. You shouldn't expect much more. For $25 or even $50 a month rent reduction, you won't get anyone who'll prepare vacancies to be rented, place ads, make disbursements, arrange for major maintenance work, or take other managerial responsibilities. These jobs will have to be done by you in your spare time, or delegated to a property management firm.

However, your assistant manager might help with rent collections under your supervision or someone else's. The best system for this is to provide a monthly set of envelopes addressed to you or the management company. About two days before rents are due, the assistant drops one of these envelopes into each resident's mailbox. The resident need only put the rent into the envelope, stamp it and mail it.

You won't need more on-the-spot help than this, even in a property as big as 12 units, providing you or an outside firm will do the rest of the managerial job from a distance. In a building of 10 or 12 units, about half a month's rental allowance would be the normal compensation. You could pay separately, item by item, for other jobs such as painting or plumbing, if your on-site person can do these.

Most people who are willing to manage full-time won't consider a position that doesn't provide them at least a free apartment. This means the building should be 16 or 20 units or more. Above 20 units, you'll need to pay a certain amount of cash in addition to the free apartment in order to keep a good manager on the premises. The manager of a 40-unit complex may get $125 per month in addition to the free apartment.

Why do we say that 16 units is the point at which you need a resident manager?

For economic reasons, if you have a 10-unit property and the manager occupies one unit free, you cut your maximum possible rental income by one-tenth. At that rate, you can hardly hope to clear a profit. But if you give your manager one-sixteenth of your monthly gross, you have a chance. You have a considerably better chance if one-twentieth is the share.

In fact, seasoned investors often figure on paying a professional resident manager about 5% of the month's gross (figured on the basis of a free apartment plus cash), which, of course, is one-twentieth. Likewise, property management company fees are usually 5%, starting with a minimum of $100 a month. At that minimum, your building should gross $2,000 a month to justify a management firm.

A FLAT PERCENTAGE rather than a fixed sum is the common way of compensating management, whether the work is done by a company or by a resident manager. The percentage varies from 4% to 7% or even more, depending on the responsibilities and ability of whoever does the job. Obviously, an all-round manager is worth a higher percentage than one who phones a plumber whenever a washer needs replacing.

THE DO-IT-ALL MANAGER ISN'T ALWAYS A BARGAIN, however. Assuming that he's great at showing apartments and getting along with people — the two most vital parts of his job — he may be only average at cleaning vacant apartments and getting them in shape for re-renting, which also is quite important. If he does the cleaning, then it's awkward for the owner to tell him that his cleaning job wasn't good enough, and that the apartment must be re-cleaned before the manager will be paid. If you use an outside service, then holding up payment is enough leverage to get a better job done quickly.

Whatever percentage you choose for the manager, be sure to figure it in monies actually collected that month, not on the "scheduled" rents. This gives your manager an incentive to make collections and fill vacancies — and a penalty if he doesn't do so.

AN INCENTIVE BONUS, above the fixed percentage, more than pays for itself. The national average for apartment vacancies is 5%, so you'd normally include a 5% loss factor in your budget. You can explain this to your manager, and tell him that whenever the property is more than 95% rented, you'll share the excess with him half-and-half.

The owner of a 24-unit complex worked out a slightly more complicated plan. It was in an area where turnover was considerably higher than the national average; most complexes always had four or five vacancies. The owner told his manager, "Each month that you have 23 units rented, you get a $25 bonus. And whenever the 24th unit is rented, you keep half its rent." The apartments rented for $95, so the manager could pick up an extra $72.50 per month by keeping the complex fully rented. She seldom failed to do so.

SHOULD YOU HIRE A MANAGEMENT FIRM?

IF YOUR PROPERTY IS TOO FAR AWAY TO VISIT REGULARLY, you have only two choices: find a resident manager you can trust implicitly, or turn the management over to a professional firm.

If you're a novice in the business, probably you don't know anyone with whom you feel confident about hiring as a manager, so you'll have to shop around for a management firm. Even if you're not a novice, the firm may be preferable to a manager. Good managers are hard to find, while good firms often save you far more than the fee they charge.

The company will install its own resident manager if the property is big enough to require this. It will decide on the manager's compensation, which it will include in its fee. So in this case, its total fee might be 6% or 7% of the total rents collected (and of any other miscellaneous collections). In low-income rentals where collections come hard, the firm might charge you as much as 10% of collections.

If you want major improvements made in your property, the firm can arrange with contractors to do the whole job under its supervision, for an extra fee of 5% to 10% of the cost of the improvements.

IF THE PROPERTY IS SO BIG that full-time maintenance workers and office workers are needed, these too will be hired by the company. It can afford to do this without increasing the percentage it charges, because the percentage will amount to a handsome sum in a big development. Nevertheless, some firms charge an extra 1% or 2% if the budgeting and accounting duties are complicated.

The advantages of using a management firm lie in its professional expertise and equipment. Presumably, it already has everything needed to cope with the normal duties of apartment management. It may be making continuous surveys that help it figure how much rent to charge. It knows how to compare your property with similar properties, and make whatever adjustments are needed to bring yours into line. It gets the economies of quantity buying. It is familiar with city, county and state regulations, and with the people who enforce them. It should know the best cleaning and maintenance materials and how to get the best prices. It should be alert to every possible way of enhancing the value of your property.

THE DISADVANTAGES are that some firms aren't really as expert as they claim to be, and that it's temptingly easy to pad your bills if you are inexperienced or far away. So check as closely as you can.

The first thing to do in checking on a prospective firm is to ask for the names of properties it manages. And the second thing, of course, is to talk to those owners, by long distance phone if need be, and try to find out how good a job the firm has done for them.

Even a small realtor may manage property as a sideline. This may be the only professional management you can get if your property is smaller than ten units: big firms aren't geared to handle just a few units. Try to hire a small firm whose principals use the letters C.P.M. (for certified property manager) after their names. To get this designation, they must have years of experience in managing properties, and must pass certain examinations and practical tests. Even so, a C.P.M. may be good or bad as in any other profession.

QUESTIONS TO ASK A MANAGEMENT FIRM

A firm, or an individual professional, presumably knows all facets of the hour-by-hour and room-by-room care that an apartment house needs. You can check by asking test questions.

IF YOU HAVE A SMALL PROPERTY that rents to people in the middle or lower-middle income brackets, here are questions you can ask during a chat with someone who claims to be able to give your property professional management:

"If you need to evict a resident, how fast can you do it legally?" (The answer in California and most other states should be "18 to 30 days, as a practical matter.")

"Who can serve a legal notice on the resident?" (Answer: Anyone over 21 and not a party to the action.)

"How much would an unlawful detainer action cost?" (Answer: From $85 to $275.)

"If I want to lay new carpet in one of my units, what kind would you recommend and how much would it cost?" (Answer: Nylon; $6 to $9 a yard.)

"There's a leak in the ceiling of one of my apartments from the bathroom upstairs. Have you any idea what the likeliest causes might be?" (Answer: A leaking tub drain seal, or overflow seal, or shower pan.)

IF YOU HAVE A SOMEWHAT LARGER PROPERTY, or one that rents to higher-income people, you need a professional who can answer questions like these:

"After you show someone a vacant apartment, what do you do next?" (Answer: Ask if the prospect will fill out an application and make a deposit.)

"Do you investigate a prospect before renting?" (Answer: Should ask for references and check them; should also check with the credit bureau. You'll see why when you get to Chapter 11.)

"Am I supposed to withhold taxes from a resident manager's cash salary?" (Answer: Yes, usually.)

"During what hours is a manager covered by workmen's compensation insurance?" (Answer: All around the clock, night and day, as a resident.)

"One of my residents is complaining about lack of hot water. What do you think the cause might be?" (Answer: Probably the thermostat is defective, or the pilot light has blown out.)

"What kind of paint do you recommend using on interior walls?" (Answer: Latex.)

"If an apartment is vacated and I have to get it repainted, how long should it take? It's about 500 square feet." (Answer: Eight to 10 hours, plus an extra hour or two for cabinets and doors.)

ONE WAY TO GET A BIG MANAGEMENT FIRM — or an experienced full-time resident manager — for your small apartment building is by arranging to share the cost with the owner of another building (or several other buildings) adjacent to you or across the street. Such properties might easily be managed by one resident, or one firm, for the usual fee of the percentage of rents collected. It requires a little extra bookkeeping to allocate disbursements to the separate buildings and separate owners, but otherwise it's almost as easy as managing one good-sized property. The only pitfall: if the resident manager lives in one building, he may feel more loyal to it, and rent its vacancies before the other's.

HOW TO HIRE A MANAGER

Assuming that you'll personally supervise your resident manager, here's how to go about hiring one.

BUY A CLASSIFIED AD in the local paper, preferably the Sunday edition. It might read:

> COUPLE WANTED to manage
> 20-unit apt. house. No children
> under school age. Pay $125 mo.
> plus $157 unfurnished 2-bdrm.
> apt. Should be experienced in
> management and maintenance.
> Box 000.

If your apartments have special features that might attract higher-quality candidates – air conditioning, swimming pool, sauna or whatever – be sure to mention these in the ad. Don't give your address or phone number; glancing through letters is much faster than interviewing.

Your ad would normally run under Help Wanted, but in a tight rental situation you might try running it under Apartments For Rent. Anyhow, writing the ad isn't as important as judging the replies.

PICK OUT THE GOOD LOOKING ANSWERS. Look for letters that show some indications of salesmanship and enthusiasm, because these are the qualities a manager needs most. Neatness is important too; a sloppy-looking letter bespeaks a sloppy manager. Usually, a couple is better than a single person. The cost is the same, but you get double coverage. Married people are less prone to travel than singles.

Experience isn't essential, if you'll be supervising. Training your own manager can pay. It's better to coach an eager applicant than to struggle with a jaded professional who has been soured by unhappy experiences, and who may be constantly objecting. "That's not how we did it in the last place I worked." Experience sometimes breeds bad habits such as taking kickbacks from suppliers and maintenance people, quarreling with residents, shirking chores, neglecting rent collections, and so on.

VISIT THE HOMES of applicants whose letters impress you. Phone them and ask if you can come to see them. Your unspoken purpose, of course, is to take a look at their housekeeping. In your building, most prospective renters will visit the manager's apartment, and the impression they form will have much to do with whether they want to live in the building.

Never hire sight unseen, even if you can't make a home visit. The applicants' personalities are more important than their housekeeping. Regardless of other qualities, a manager with an unpleasant personality or unkempt appearance won't do a good job.

SPELL OUT THE MANAGER'S DUTIES in detail during the interview. You can ask questions like these:

"Do you expect to stay on the premises most of the time? Will anyone else in your family be able to show apartments and do other small urgent jobs that may come up while you're away for an hour or so?"

"Would you expect to keep the halls and yard clean as part of your duties? Are you willing to handle small manual jobs like picking up around the trash area, changing light bulbs, checking hot air filters?"

"When an apartment is vacated, would you expect to do the cleaning and repainting yourself, or hire outside help?"

"Can you move furniture if necessary? Can you mow the lawn and trim the shrubbery?"

These may not be the right questions in your case. You may know of a handyman who'll come in for odd jobs. You may plan to hire a gardener. The point is, you should know exactly what you do expect of your manager, and make sure the prospect knows too. He may have some disability that would prevent doing something you want done. Or he may resent being asked to tackle menial chores like removing grease from carports. The way to avoid dissension is to get all these details settled during the interview.

A MANAGER SHOULD BE COMPATIBLE WITH RESIDENTS in his building. He should "fit" but not mingle. If it's a building with older retired people, a sixty-ish manager will understand them better than a younger applicant, who in turn would be preferable to an elderly manager in a building full of young couples.

Age isn't the only yardstick, of course. The manager's education, economic status, and social background should approximate those of the residents.

Likewise, if your building accepts families with children, the best manager is likely to be someone who also is raising a child or two. However, managers whose children are under school age may not be able to show vacant units, so this is an exception to the rule. Children up to three years old can't be left alone for long, nor hauled to an apartment showing. Unless both parents are part of the management team, you'd better steer clear of anyone with very young children.

REFERENCES ARE A MUST. And you must check them. Give your prospective manager an application form like one of the samples shown on the next few pages. (The bigger the job, the more elaborate the form.) Tell him he will be bonded, and ask if there is any reason why he could not be bonded.

IF YOUR AD DOESN'T BRING FORTH THE RIGHT APPLICANT, there are other places to try. Your local police or fire department may be willing to let you put a card (worded like the ad) on the bulletin board — and it could bring you an application from a dependable married couple. There are advantages to having a policeman or fireman, with a good wife, as your management team.

Managers in other buildings can often suggest a good prospect — or may themselves be looking for better places. Apartment associations often have employment bureaus or reference lists of potential resident managers. Local realtors often know of someone.

SIGN A CONTRACT with your manager immediately. A new manager should take charge on a trial basis. But once he has proven himself, you want him to be permanent — so you need a contract. A sample is shown on Page 17.

MANAGING A RESIDENT MANAGER

DON'T TEMPT YOUR MANAGER with lax supervision or loose accounting methods. Managers have been known to try to supplement their incomes by fleecing unwary tenants with fictitious fees, double rents, ballooned deposits, security payments, key charges, unrefunded deposits. Of course, the owner doesn't lose any legitimate income. And the victims may never discover that they are cheated. But sooner or later, someone always finds out, and spreads the word — and it's the owner whose reputation suffers. He may be held financially responsible, too. Don't let any of this happen to you.

MAKE SPOT CHECKS without warning. Drop in and say, "Will you give me the key to that vacant apartment? I want to see what we can do to make it more rentable." You just might find furniture and clothes in an allegedly empty unit. This may mean that the manager is collecting rent while reporting it as vacant. Or it may mean that he is letting friends or relatives live there at no cost.

DOUBLE-RENTING is harder to spot. Sometimes an occupant must vacate unexpectedly in the middle of a renting period. (Military orders, a job change, unexpected illness and various other contingencies can cause this.) The manager points out to such occupants that they are legally supposed to give 30 days' notice, but under the circumstances, he won't hold them to it. They are so grateful that they don't even think of asking for any refunds. The manager re-rents the apartments the same month, collecting double rent which he doesn't report. Since no vacancy shows up on the monthly summary, the owner won't know unless he keeps track of leases or rental agreements by name.

EMPLOYMENT APPLICATION

1. Applicant's Name_____ Age _____
   Address_____ Phone (home)_____(work)_____
   Married   (yes)___ (no)___ No. in Family_____
                                                            (Adults)   (Children)

   Social Security No. _____

2. Job Desired_____
                      (Res. Mgr., Engineer, Porter, Elevator Oper., Janitor, Charwoman, etc.)
   Desire Quarters   (yes)___ (no)___

3. Present Employer's Name _____ Phone_____
                                 (Real Estate firm or Owner)

   Address _____
   Name of Supervisor or Res. Mgr. _____ Phone_____
   How long employed at present job_____Salary_____
                                                               (week or month)

   Reason for leaving _____
   Explain Duties _____
   _____
   Previous Employer's Name _____ Phone _____
   Name of Supervisor or Res. Mgr. _____ Phone_____
   How long employed? From_____To_____ Salary_____
                                                               (week or month

   Reason for leaving _____
   Explain duties _____
   _____

4. Check either "yes" or "no" to each of the following:
   a. Can you make minor plumbing repairs   (yes) _____ (no)_____
   b. Can you make minor electrical repairs   (yes) _____ (no)_____
   c. Can you do any painting   (yes) _____ (no)_____
   d. Can you do any plastering   (yes) _____ (no)_____
   e. Are you familiar with air conditioning system (yes) _____ (no)_____
   f. Are you familiar with oil burner operation   (yes) _____ (no)_____
   g. Are you familiar with automatic stoker operation (yes) _____ (no)_____
   h. Are you familiar with hand-fired furnace operation (yes) _____ (no)_____
   i. Are you familiar with steam heating systems   (yes) _____ (no)_____
   j. Are you familiar with hot water heating systems (yes) _____ (no)_____
   k. Do you hold a D.C. Engineering license   (yes) _____ (no)_____
       If answer is "yes," what class   _____
   l. Are you a licensed elevator operator   (yes) _____ (no)_____
   m. Do you operate a switchboard   (yes) _____ (no)_____

5. Attach any additional papers, letters of recommendation, etc., to this application.

   Interviewed by _____ First Impression _____

   Use reverse of this application for references investigation findings.

   If applicant is hired, file this sheet in Owner's file.

RESIDENT MANAGERS EMPLOYMENT APPLICATION

(Please print or type the following information)

PERSONAL INFORMATION

Name (husband) _____
                        Last   First   Middle

_____
        Social Security No.   Age   Date of Birth

Name (wife's) _____
                        Last   First   Middle

_____
        Social Security No.   Age   Date of Birth

Present Address _____
                        Street   City   State

Your Phone_____ Landlord's Home & Phone No. _____

Physical Description (husband) _____
                        Height   Weight   Eye Color   Hair Color

Physical Description (wife)_____
                        Height   Weight   Eye Color   Hair Color

Handicaps or Physical Defects _____
_____
_____

Present Employment (husband)_____
                                        Name of Company

_____
                                Address

_____
                Position   Years Employed

Name of Supervisor _____ May we Contact your Employer?_____
If so, phone number_____

Present Employment (wife) _____
                                        Name of Company

_____
                                Address

_____
                Position   Years Employed

Name of Supervisor _____ May we Contact your Employer?_____
If so, phone number _____

Children _____ Ages_____ Others expected in near future (yes)_____ (no) _____

EMPLOYMENT APPLICATION — PAGE 2

Other Dependents _____ Friends or Relatives in our Employ? (yes)____(no) _____
                                    If yes, explain _____
                                    _____

Estimate roughly your net worth (total assets in real estate, stocks, etc., less total liabilities, loans
or other obligations): $_____

EXPERIENCE AND EDUCATION:

SCHOOLS: High School Graduate (yes)___ (no)___   Year___ City _____
                                                  State _____
Other Training Courses _____
College(s) Attended _____ No. of Years, Degrees _____

Prior Management Experience:

No. of Units	How Long	Reference	Phone No.
No. of Units	How Long	Reference	Phone No.
No. of Units	How Long	Reference	Phone No.

Check either "yes" or "no" to each of the following:

Can you make minor plumbing repairs   (yes)____(no) _____
Can you make minor electrical repairs   (yes)____(no) _____
Can you do any painting   (yes)____(no) _____
Can you do any plastering   (yes)____(no) _____
Are you familiar with pool maintenance   (yes)____(no) _____
Are you familiar with apartment furnace operations (yes)____(no) _____
Are you familiar with steam heating systems   (yes)____(no) _____
Are you familiar with hot water heating systems   (yes)____(no) _____
Are you a licensed elevator operator   (yes)____(no) _____
Have you operated a switchboard   (yes)____(no) _____

REFERENCES:

Give below the names of two persons not related to you, whom you have known at least one year:

Name _____Address _____ Business_____

_____ Years Acquainted _____

Name _____Address _____ Business_____

_____Years Acquainted _____

Bank Reference — Checking _____
                          Name   Account No.   Address

                          _____
                                              City

14

EMPLOYMENT APPLICATION — PAGE 3

Bank Reference — Savings _____

_____

Credit Reference: Name _____ Address _____

City _____

Credit Reference: Name _____ Address _____

City _____

Credit Reference: Name _____ Address _____

City _____

Are You   Previous
Bondable? _____ Bonding _____

Ever Been Arrested? _____ For What? _____ When? _____

In Case of Emergency, Notify _____

DATE _____   SIGNATURE(S)

_____

_____

Attach any additional papers, letters or recommendations, etc., to this application.

EMPLOYMENT APPLICATION

Date _____

Name _____ Phone No._____

Address _____

Position
Desired _____ Salary
Expected _____ Could Report
For Work On _____

Soc. Sec. No._____ Driver's License No._____

Date of Birth _____ Sex _____ Weight_____ Height _____

Are You a Citizen of the U.S.? _____ Alien Reg. No. _____

Marital Status (single, married, widowed, separated, divorced)_____

Husband's or Wife's Name _____ Place of
Employment _____

Dependents (give name, relationship and date of birth) _____

_____

Physical Defects or
Chronic Ailments _____

In Case of Emergency, Notify _____ Phone No. _____

Address_____ Relationship_____

PREVIOUS EMPLOYMENT
(Including U. S. Military Duties)

Present Employer	Job Held, Duties		Date Hired
Address	Rate of Pay	Reason Left	Date Left
Last Employer	Job Held, Duties		Date Hired
Address	Rate of Pay	Reason Left	Date Left
Previous Employer	Job Held, Duties		Date Hired
Address	Rate of Pay	Reason Left	Date Left
Previous Employer	Job Held, Duties		Date Hired
Address	Rate of Pay	Reason Left	Date Left
Previous Employer	Job Held, Duties		Date Hired
Address	Rate of Pay	Reason Left	Date Left

EDUCATION

Name of School	Address	Attendance Dates From	Through	Did You Graduate	College Degrees

Major and special study
and/or trade training _____

_____

Special Skills in trade or other trades (If
clerical, give shorthand and typing speeds, etc.) _____

_____

_____

Membership in Technical or Professional Societies

_____

_____

_____

PERSONAL REFERENCES

Name	Address	Telephone No.	Occupation

Signature _____

- -

This space NOT to be filled in by Applicant

Interviewed by _____ Date _____

Remarks _____

_____

Starting Date _____ Classification _____ Grade _____ Salary or Rate _____ P/R No. _____

Dept or Job No. _____ OK to Hire _____ Approved by: _____

Authorized Signature

RESIDENT MANAGER'S EMPLOYMENT CONTRACT

Parties, Purpose

With respect to the following covenants _____

(herein referred to as Owner) or his duly appointed agent_____

hereby agree to employ _____

(herein referred to as manager) to rent, lease, operate and manage the Owners property commonly designated as _____

_____ exclusively.

The terms herein set forth are for the period of _____ beginning

on the_____day of _____ 19____, and ending on the_____day of

_____ 19____ .

Renewal Termination

and thereafter for annual periods unless on or before sixty (60) days prior to the date last mentioned, or on or before thirty (30) days prior to the expiration of any such renewal period, either party herein shall notify the other in writing of an intention to terminate this agreement in which case that agreement may be terminated prior to the last mentioned date.

Vacancy

In the event of cancellation of this agreement, the Owner reserves the exclusive right to demand vacancy within seven (7) days of a notice which shall show reason for such dismissal. Manager hereby agrees to said covenant waiving any rights conflicting in manager's residence lease.

Compensation

Owner agrees to compensate manager at an hourly rate of $_____ with the understanding that manager's weekly hours of employment are limited to_____ hours, and/or other such compensation or rental allowance shall be as follows:

_____

_____

Manager agrees to Owner's standard residence lease or rental contract, payment of deposits, etc., with respect to employment residency and all provisions therein not conflicting with this contract.

Day of rest and vacation provisions shall be as so stated hereafter: _____

_____

Handling of funds

Manager hereby promises complete honesty and willingness of disclosure secured by the maintaining of a bondable position, and further agrees to the handling of any and all funds or assets in the following prescribed manner:

_____

_____

No expenditures in excess of $_____will be made without previously obtaining the Owner's permission.

Duties

Manager agrees to, and affirms a complete understanding of, the assigned duties and order of conduct pertinent to employment. An outline of such obligations and functions is/may hereby be accepted as part of this contract by addendum(a).

Signed with knowledgeable understanding:

_____   _____
          Owner or Agent   Manager

Date: _____   Date: _____

CLEANING AN APARTMENT may be done adequately in the manager's opinion but not in the owner's. Only by checking will the owner discover that the vacant apartments aren't really clean enough to rent in a competitive market.

CHECK YOUR MANAGER'S ATTITUDE TOWARD VISITORS by making an arrangement with another owner. Each of you visit the other's premises, posing as a prospective renter, and ask to look at a vacancy. See how you're received, and report it to the other owner. You may be shocked to hear that your units are shown by flashlight, or that your manager tells visitors, "Can you come back later? I'm sort of busy now."

These reciprocal spot checks can also tell you whether your manager's living quarters are presentable. Or you can find this out through your own drop-in visits — especially during a lunch hour, or a weekend, or in the evening. Your visits should be friendly, and leisurely enough to encourage a good manager to offer suggestions about operational matters. Of course, you don't want to visit so often that your manager feels harassed or spied on. Once or twice a month may be enough.

CHECK WITH OCCUPANTS TOO, particularly those who pay rent by cash. You can say, "We're doing routine bookkeeping, and for some reason our books don't quite balance. Could I please see your rent receipts?" It's possible that these will be for larger amounts than shown on the receipts the manager turned over to you; he has quietly raised rents and pocketed the difference, making out false receipts for your benefit. Or he may do this with cleaning fees, security deposits and other miscellaneous collections. He can charge the occupant one amount and report another. Such tricks are impossible if you use one of the systems for receipts explained in Chapter 13.

CHECKING ON A MANAGEMENT COMPANY

THE MONTHLY REPORT from your professional management firm can tell you more than it's intended to, if you know what to look for. The essence of managing your management company is checking this report.

The report is supposed to give a breakdown of the property's income and expenses — its operating costs and capital outlays and any other disbursements, as well as monies received from any sources. How detailed is it?

BEWARE OF BROAD CATEGORIES. You don't want a report that says $318 was spent for "maintenance and repairs." You should be told exactly what work was done and where.

Even if the report indicates an amount was spent for "painting apartment," it isn't specific enough. Which apartment? Was it completely painted, or just certain walls? Who was the painter? How does his bill compare with previous painting bills? Where are the cancelled checks to him? If anything seems suspicious, you (or someone representing you, if you can't do it yourself) should go and look at the apartments allegedly painted. It's not uncommon to find that some of the specified apartments haven't been painted at all.

Landscape maintenance is the category which is easiest of all to fake. How can you tell whether the reported work was done, and whether the price was reasonable? Only by close supervision, insistence on details, and an occasional unexpected spot check.

DEMAND A COMPLETE BREAKDOWN of every category. (A really good firm provides this automatically, without being asked. It knows that if your property is to be re-sold — for which the firm would be the logical broker — all prospective buyers and lenders will want to look at thorough records.)

A LEDGER SHEET ISN'T A BREAKDOWN. It merely shows rents collected, rents overdue, and vacancies — or sometimes just total dollars of income. You should be told which apartments are vacant, how long they've been vacant, how much rent was collected from each resident, and how many dollars were laundry income, vending machine income, garage income and so on. Management firms, like resident managers, may be tempted to rent out garages or carports separately for cash, or forget to report these, unless an owner keeps them on a tight rein.

A monthly ledger sheet, or a vague tabulation of broad categories, means that your property isn't well managed. Insist on details, in writing. Then scan for discrepancies, or for expenses unsupported by bills and receipts. You'll soon learn to spot the signs — if there are some — that your people are making a little something extra off you in operating the property. Chapters 13 and 14 will give you more ideas about what to look for, and how to spot suspicious numbers.

WHEN YOU MUST GET RID OF A MANAGER or a management company or some employee, try offering two weeks' pay for leaving the premises within 24 hours. This gives the departing miscreant little chance to spread the word to sympathetic residents — and adequate incentive to spend his time packing instead.

The worst thing you can do is delay. As soon as you see that discharge is necessary, take over personally if you possibly can while hunting a replacement. If this isn't possible, find a replacement as fast and quietly as you can. Then give the employee a written notice of termination. Keep his service record, and a notation of what caused you to discharge him, as protection against any legal complications.

REMEMBER THESE BASIC POINTS:

* *Much property is mismanaged. There's a widespread need for good managers of residential real estate.*

* *If you're looking for a manager, start by writing detailed job specifications.*

* *About 5% of the month's gross is a normal rate of pay. An incentive bonus above this can more than pay for itself.*

* *If you're an absentee owner, better put your property in charge of a management firm. But check closely.*

* *In finding a manager whom you'll supervise, you can tell a lot by the quality of written answers to a classified ad. Make visits to the homes of applicants who seem best qualified.*

* *Sign a contract with a manager. Keep making occasional spot checks without warning.*

* *In reading reports from a management firm, insist on complete breakdowns of all reports of monthly operations. A monthly ledger sheet, or a vague tabulation of broad categories probably means that the firm isn't doing a good job.*

II *So You're the New Manager*

Maybe yesterday you took title to a property you intend to manage personally. Or maybe yesterday you were appointed to manage someone else's property. Presumably, there'll be a few days yet before you officially go on the job.

But your job will be easier if you size it up in advance. It may hold some hidden surprises. Forewarned is forearmed.

Throughout this chapter, we'll assume there has been a change of ownership as well as management. If you're coming in to replace a manager under the same ownership, a few parts of the following won't apply, but most will.

MAKE A PRELIMINARY VISIT

FAMILIARIZING YOURSELF WITH THE PROPERTY and its needs must be high on your agenda, even before you move in. Personally, your owner (perhaps with your help) made a thorough inspection before buying. But now you'll want to look into smaller details.

For example, do you know whether the roof will leak during the rainy season? As soon as possible, you'd better go up on the roof with a hose and wet it down. If there are leaks in any upper apartments, you should get them fixed while the weather is still dry. Roofers will be busy once the rains start.

Plan to reduce the property's liability exposure quickly by replacing any outside light bulbs that have burned out; repairing any cracks in walkways or stairs or driveways where someone might stumble and get hurt; making sure the front and back gates are latched securely, if there is any "attractive nuisance" such as a swimming pool, so that no child can wander in; trim back any rosebushes or hedges that stick out enough to scratch someone; perhaps put up a bumper guard on building corners exposed to car traffic, to save yourself expensive repair jobs.

After a quick inspection tour of areas that are open to the public, your next step is to familiarize yourself with the apartments themselves, and their occupants. The outgoing manager can help you do this. Presumably, she (or he) is still on the premises. If so, you should drop in for a friendly social call.

Try to arrive unannounced, because part of your purpose is to check up on the current operation of the property. But don't act snoopy. Play the role of the eager-to-learn novice, not the hardboiled inquisitor.

The manager presumably knows that you're to be the incoming manager. If not, you'll begin by explaining this as you introduce yourself. You can add that you're there to learn from the previous management. Normally, the outgoing manager will be glad to teach you; it's human nature to enjoy playing the roll of mentor to an earnest pupil.

The best time for your visit is Saturday or Sunday, and the next best time is early some weekday evening — because one of the unmentioned purposes of your visit is to get a look at the occupants, and more of them are likely to be home during weekends and evenings.

During the first few minutes with the outgoing manager, you can mention that you hope to get acquainted with residents on this visit — so could you see an up-to-date list of them? With this in mind, your next step, immediately, is to say, "I'm also interested in the vacant units. Let's take a look at them now and talk about what I might do to get them rented." (You should already know, from the owner's closing statement, how many vacancies supposedly exist.)

HOW DO THE VACANT UNITS LOOK? It just might be that the manager will reluctantly show you a vacancy where you'll see clothes or other signs of occupancy. No doubt the manager's explanation will be, "They're moving and they promised they'll have everything out tomorrow." But the true explanation is likely to be either that friends or relatives of the manager are staying there rent free, or that the manager is collecting the rent in cash and reporting it as vacant.

However, the average manager will immediately open up all vacancies for you. This is a reassuring sign of honesty. You're not really so concerned at the moment about how to fill them; there'll be time enough for that in a week or two. So just make a quick once-over.

Are the vacant apartments clean and ready for showing to prospects? If not, what will be done to put them in shape immediately? (Presumably, the new owner, you or your boss — made sure there was a clause about this in the sales agreement.)

Do the vacant apartments — or any of the others — contain leaky faucets, pipes, showerheads, or toilets? If so, they should be fixed immediately, to cut down your first month's water bill. Leaks are more costly than you might think. A slowly dripping faucet drains off 15 gallons a day. A 16th-inch hole will let a hundred gallons dribble out. A leaky toilet can waste even larger amounts. Yet, you can stop most leaks with a washer that costs a few cents.

What about the apartments' heating equipment? The units still may be chilly — and running up high heating bills — if there are cracks that let the air leak through. Maybe you need insulation, weatherstripping, and/or storm sashes. Tightly fitted storm windows and doors can warm up leaky apartments and so can weatherstripping that keeps out drafts around the edges of doors and windows. If heating bills have been too high in this building, such caulking can more than repay its cost.

Where are the thermostats that control heating and air conditioning? Make sure they're not placed where temperatures fluctuate widely, such as near the door, or near a window where sunlight comes in.

Unless you live in a mild climate, heating will be this property's third largest expense, exceeded only by interest payments and taxes. In most apartment properties a bundle of money goes up in smoke needlessly, because a heating system can lose one-fifth of its efficiency merely through poor adjustment.

Therefore, after you've finished visiting individual apartments (or perhaps before you start), you'll want to check the building's central heating system, if it has one. Let's consider it now, even though we still haven't finished our imaginary tour of apartments with the previous manager.

Forced air heating systems usually include filters that get clogged, thereby reducing the amount of heat that comes through. Some managers don't even know that their heating plants have filters, so when the filters are clogged, the occupants turn the heat up high and still don't feel warm enough. Take a look at this property's system. Somewhere in the unit, usually near the base, you'll see a wide slot. It contains a slide filled with fiberglass or metal mesh. Is it dirty? If so, you should clean it when you take charge, or replace it with a new one from a hardware store.

If the building burns gas as a fuel, make a mental note to find out whether the control is correctly set, as soon as you come on the job. The burner's efficiency depends on air and fuel being mixed in correct proportions. The setting can be quickly adjusted by a furnace repairman or by the utility company serviceman, who may do it without charge.

Oil burners are more complicated. Not only must air and fuel be mixed properly, but valves and screens must be kept clean. Periodic cleaning and adjustment by a professional are essential to keep them working well.

Having finished this side trip to the heating system, let's get back to the individual apartments. In each unit there may be safety hazards that you should notice, and should press to get eliminated even before you take over, if possible. If an accident happens in a few days before you take charge, the lawsuit will probably be your headache.

Is there a frayed carpet that could hook someone's heel? Are any floors slippery or splintery? Is there a lock that turns hard? A balky lock is a safety hazard because it may be on the verge of jamming so completely that no key will open it. You can imagine the consequence if the manager is showing the apartment to someone and an air current slams the door, imprisoning them inside. Or if there's a fire in the unit (yes, fires can start in — or spread to — a vacant apartment) and the door into it won't open.

Alright, you've had a quick look-see through each apartment which the outgoing manager says is vacant. You did this as soon as you arrived, because you wanted to forestall, if possible, any non-paying tenants from eliminating clues to their presence.

WHAT THE OUTGOING MANAGER CAN TEACH YOU. So now what's your next move during this first get-acquainted tour? Probably to ask the manager to show you her daily and weekly routines, like checking the garbage collection areas and the water level in the boiler, and testing the chemical content of the swimming pool water. Care of the laundry room, vending machines, and other facilities that may be on this agenda.

Then ask if she'll show you how to take care of minor foul-ups, such as how to unstick the garbage disposals. Find out where the power and gas cutoffs are for each apartment, and how to turn them off. Find out where the master water valve is, and make sure it's labelled conspicuously. Is there a fuse box or main switch box, or circuit breaker? Is there other equipment (fire extinguishers, even an emergency flashlight or candle) that would be important if something went wrong suddenly?

In the course of this briefing, you'll probably be taken into the basement. It's an area you need to know all about. Look for telltale water stains on the floor, on the inside of the foundation wall, and on any boxes stored there. If nothing is stored there, you can be pretty sure there was serious flooding at some time in the past.

Look for wall cracks and for warped or sagging wooden members. (These aren't likely to call for immediate action, but to forestall trouble in the long run, you should have an expert look at these signs of future trouble soon after you take charge.) Make sure you know what you need to know about the heating equipment and the air conditioning, if any.

As your next step, you might say to the manager, "I'd like to be ready for emergencies before they happen. If there should be trouble with plumbing or wiring or the roof, do you have a list of companies that give quick service when you call? . . . If I need a handyman on a few hours' notice, do you know of a good reliable one?" Write down all such information, and save it to put in the Operations File you'll soon be starting.

WHAT TO ASK OCCUPANTS. Now for the most important part of your visit.

You say to the manager, "I'm going to call on every occupant personally. Can I borrow your rent schedule? And a list of other payments credited to each person, like damage deposits, cleaning deposits, key deposits, final month's rent? . . . And I'll need your inventory of appliances and furnishings that are part of the building's property." (If your owner was astute, he collected all this information before the sale was closed, and you already have it in hand. If not, you'll have to push hard for the most complete information you can get.)

You're beginning a vital check-up procedure. Many owners don't keep good records. Sometimes they don't know what deposits they've collected from residents, especially from those who have been there for several years. Residents often don't know either. Part of your job is to resolve discrepancies with the old management, and make sure it fulfills its obligation as stated in the sales agreement, before you take over.

Refrigerators and other fixtures were probably figured into the sales price. Won't it be embarrassing if someone says to you next year, in moving out, "These drapes and lamps and the refrigerator are mine, and I'm taking them with me."? You need to know, now, who owns what.

The only way to be sure is to get an itemized list from the seller; then get a signed confirmation from each occupant. Mimeographed blank copies of the Confirmation Form should be in your briefcase when you make your first visit.

Now, papers ready but concealed, you go from door to door. You flash your friendliest smile as you explain to tenants that you're the new manager, and that all deposits they've made are being transferred to their credit under the new management. "That's why I'd like to have you complete this Confirmation Form," you finish, producing the form.

This is also the time to chat a little with each person about any "special arrangements" he or she may have with the manager. (Before you start calling on occupants, you should make a point of asking the outgoing manager if there were any special arrangements. Now you're double-checking.)

Don't be surprised if it turns out that fewer apartments are occupied than the new owner thought when he bought. Unless he checked closely, it would have been easy to fool him. For example, maybe he relied on mailboxes as the indicators of which units were occupied. If so, he was inexperienced. Resident managers usually know that mailboxes with empty name slots give a bad impression to prospective occupants (as well as to prospective buyers of the property). So they often leave the former occupant's name on the box until the unit is re-rented.

An owner who wants to cheat a buyer can inflate the rental income in ways that are hard to detect unless you talk to the occupants. He can make all sorts of private agreements that may or may not show up on the leases or rent rolls.

Examples: Maybe an occupant received a gift of furniture or a brand new suit as an inducement to move in, and gets a similar gift every Christmas. Maybe he has an understanding that his last month's rent will be free. Maybe he pays $150 a month rent but gets $20 worth of liquor or medicines or groceries every month, chargeable to the owner's credit card.

Or maybe the manager has been cheating the owner, collecting higher rents than are shown on the records, and pocketing the surplus. You won't know until you ask each occupant how much he pays, and check it against the records. The same might be true of cleaning deposits — a sly manager can charge the occupant $50 and report $40 received. This is a temptation in buildings where people pay cash rather than by check.

If an outgoing owner and manager have over-stated the net income from a building, a new owner can seek a court judgment against them for damages, and maybe punitive damages for fraud. So your duty is to protect the interests of your employer — the new owner — by spotting discrepancies quickly. If the fraud is flagrant, he may be able to cancel the purchase and get his money back.

Presumably, you won't continue any "side deals" made with occupants by the previous management. If some of them threaten to move out, don't panic. There are plenty of ways to re-rent vacant apartments, as you'll see later in this book.

CHECK THE RECORDS. Read the leases, if any. You may find that some occupants are renting on a month-to-month basis. They may claim later that they have an oral lease — which is binding up to one year, under some state laws. Ask the outgoing manager about any "oral leases" — and any promises to make future improvements in certain apartments. Now is the time to check. Later he (or she) may be hard to locate.

And read the records of rent receipts. If any occupants are behind in their payments, you have a problem. The farther behind they are, the more incentive they have to skip out without paying. Do the manager's records show where they're employed, so you can trace them if necessary?

You'll want to make clear, in your first chat with a slow-paying resident, that the new owner's policy is to require rents to be paid in advance, promptly on the date due. You can explain that the owner must make his own mortgage payments exactly when due, so it's essential for him to receive the rents on time.

While you're chatting with occupants on your door-to-door tour, you can say something like this: "There are two other things I'd like to do — either now, or later if you prefer. I'd like to go through the apartment with you and look at anything that may need repair. Secondly. I'd like to check over this inventory with you, so I can be sure I know which items belong to you, which to the building."

If the previous manager didn't keep inventories of the contents of all apartments, that was poor management. Tenants will be able to claim that various furnishings are their own property. You'll have to take their word for this, unless you find very similar furnishings in other apartments.

But at least make sure that *you* compile, with the occupant's help, an itemized list of everything that he agrees belongs to the suite. And get his agreement on its current condition — new, soiled, frayed or whatever. Have him sign it. Explain that you'll file it so he and you can re-check it together when he moves out. This fixes in his mind the fact that he's responsible.

Be especially careful to find out about each set of drapes. It's likely that some occupants have replaced the building drapes with their own, and nobody knows where the old ones are. If the building was sold as fully carpeted and draped, the seller must make good for the missing drapes.

It's also a good idea to make your own list of each tenant's major personal belongings — television sets, beds and so on. This might be important later, if you seek a judgment against some tenant who seems likely to decamp without paying. The list might also be important if there's a fire or burglary, and a tenant wants you to pay for non-existent "valuable art works" or the like.

FACING THE TROUBLE-MAKERS. In your get-acquainted rounds you may find an occupant who won't let you in to inspect the apartment. This is understandable the first time. He may be entertaining a guest he prefers not to introduce. His apartment may be so untidy that he doesn't want anyone to see it. Or he may be doing something he hates to interrupt, like baking a cake or watching television. So okay.

But if he refuses to set any time when he'll show you the apartment, and if he waxes angry at your offer to go in and do the inventory alone when he's not there, then you know his apartment is either badly damaged or very dirty. Better plan on asking him to move. You can expect your cost of putting his rooms in shape to be far higher than any normal damage deposit, but the sooner you get it done, the better. He may do worse damage if he stays, and he already may be obnoxious to other residents.

Occupants may probe a little, on your get-acquainted visit, to see what type you are. A few exceptional ones may jump on you with a long list of complaints. Think of them as your customers, and your guests. Your income (and to some extent, your peace of mind) depends on keeping them feeling as friendly as possible. There can be snarling residents but there should never be a snarling manager.

Listen carefully to their complaints, and look sympathetic. Take copious written notes. Just an attentive attitude will probably make them feel better, while a cold skeptical air can only worsen matters at this stage. If someone wants a little extra care, a little understanding, why not give it to him? Isn't this the way you treat guests in your home?

But use good judgment in deciding which complaints deserve action. When you see that they are trivial or exaggerated, you can say something non-commital like, "Of course, I'm not the manager yet. But as soon as I take charge, I'm going to get all necessary maintenance work done as fast as I can, and I'll give priority to the most urgent problems."

Occasionally a pugnacious occupant sets out to browbeat a new manager. He says his apartment is falling apart, and he's going to move unless the manager does this and that and so on. To someone who is too threatening or demanding, your best response is to smile sadly and say, "I see what you mean. The property could certainly be improved a lot if I had an unlimited budget. But there may not be enough cash coming in to pay for all the work you're suggesting. If you're really determined to move out, please be sure to give me the legal written notice so I can arrange for someone else to move in."

No matter what, don't fire back the logical retort, "How come you've stayed here so long with a manager who didn't give you any of these things?" You can win the argument but make an enemy. Contrariwise, don't try to placate this type by giving him what he asks. Like Hitler, he'll keep coming back with new demands. Just be friendly but firm. He'll either subside or move. If he moves, he would have moved anyway as soon as he made a demand that you didn't meet.

Some tenants' complaints may be justified. If they're seriously inconvenienced because of malfunctioning plumbing, electricity, heating, air cooling or anything else which affects their hour-to-hour living, this is your chance to be a hero. Get the malfunction fixed that very day if you can, even though you're not yet the manager-in-residence. Either pressure the old manager, or, if this doesn't work, call a repairman on your own initiative.

Just be sure to verify with your own eyes that the trouble is serious. Everyone tends to exaggerate, and most grievances aren't as bad as described. "Water flooding the whole place," usually turns out to be only a partially-clogged drain. A non-flushing toilet may need only a manual adjustment or a new piece of hardware costing a few cents. If you're handy at household repairs, as most small property managers must be, you'll see at a glance how to solve most toilet problems without the costly ministrations of a plumber. "Roof leaking all over the living room" may be true, but the reason may be that an attic window is broken or was left open. Less urgent trouble, described by an occupant as just arising that day, may have existed for months past. So don't be stampeded.

WILL RENTS BE RAISED? Occupants have probably heard some time ago that the property has changed owners. They're bound to be uneasy, even suspicious and resentful.

Resistance to change is built into human nature. People fear the unknown. In a residential building they fear an unknown management. The likelihood of a rent increase is uppermost in their minds. Beyond this are fears that the new management will be unpleasant to deal with, will let the place go to hell, or, conversely, will make it a bedlam with unwanted "improvements."

All these fears make your first contact with each occupant especially important. At least you can convince everyone that you're not a grouch or a cold fish. Try to show how likable and reasonable you are, how intent on giving more than just adequate service. Every good businessman knows that it's worth extra trouble to keep customers happy, because winning new customers is harder and costlier than holding the present ones. These apartment dwellers are your customers. Some may ask you openly if changes — especially rent boosts — are planned. What should you say?

That depends. If the building obviously needs improvement, and the owner plans to improve it, you can mention his plans — but be brief. Don't prattle on about details. The more you say, the worse it will sound to the type of resident who hates to be in the midst of a clutter of workmen, ladders, ropes, buckets and other entanglements and disturbances.

On the other hand, if the owner doesn't plan any work except urgent repairs in individual apartments, whether you should say this depends on the condition of the property. If it's shabby, you'd better just say that you don't know whether the owner has made any plans yet. But if it's good looking, you might as well announce that no immediate changes are in prospect; this will please everyone who's content with the place as it is, and that may include the entire roster.

Any talk of improvements will heighten fears of a rent increase, and stir some occupants to look for apartments elsewhere. What you say about rents depends on what you and the owner have decided upon, if anything.

If he has already studied the situation thoroughly and decided for the time being that he'll keep rents where they are, or raise them only as he re-rents units, you can answer frankly, "The owner has no plans to raise your rent." Presumably, he (or you) has found that comparable apartments are renting at the same or lower levels than yours, so competitive conditions won't justify a boost.

On the other hand, the new owner may plan to upgrade the building and fatten its rental income, thereby heightening its resale value. This is the most profitable strategy in retail investment. So if you think there's any possibility of this happening, you'd better just say, "Of course, costs are going up everywhere, but I don't know what the owner's plan are. He may not have given any consideration to increases."

Even if you know for sure that an across-the-board raise is coming soon, this isn't the time or place to announce it. Wait until you're on the job. Later in this book you'll see how to handle whatever rent increases are advisable.

DO YOUR KEYS WORK? One last tip about this first tour of the premises. Get the manager to give you the master key, and take it with you; also her spare keys to each unit, if possible. Ask each occupant's permission to make sure that the keys work. At apartments where no one answers your knocking, just test the key without opening the door. (You must be extremely careful about tenants' privacy; more on this later.)

You may find that an occupant has changed a lock. Generally, the owner and manager have a right to enter an apartment when necessary to safeguard it; so, after you're on the job, you'd better take up the matter with the resident, and ask him to provide you with a duplicate key. This may already be covered in the lease or rental agreement, if the previous owner was smart and knowledgeable. So much for your first visit.

Now you know your way around the premises. You haven't met all the occupants, unless your luck was phenomenal, but you've met some of them. You've probably become aware of a few problems. And you've done what you could to avert being caught off guard by any existing situations. Now you're ready for the other preliminaries which can get you well started before you take charge.

PREPARATORY PAPER WORK

In some places an apartment owner and/or manager needs a business license. If so, maybe the previous management's license can be transferred, or you may need to get a new one. You can find out by telephoning city hall. Now is the time to do it, before you move in.

Now is also the time to prepare a mailing to all occupants. Unless there are dozens of them and you have no facilities for personalizing a mass mailing, you'd better get a personal letter typed for each occupant, because a personal letter seems much pleasanter than a form letter.

YOUR INTRODUCTORY LETTER. At the very least, you can mimeograph the letters, leaving blank lines so you can type in "Dear Mr. Woozis." And at the bottom you can jot a personal note, one for those you met and another for those you did not meet during your get-acquainted tour — something like:

— This is mostly for residents I missed last Sunday.

— Glad you were in and we had a chance to get acquainted.

As for the letter itself, it can be brief or chatty, depending on the type of building. If the property is a low-rent place with a business-first, no-nonsense owner who is determined not to spend a nickel more than he must, a brief letter like the following should be preferable:

Dear Mr. _____ :

This is to inform you that the (name of property) has been purchased by (name of owner) and I will become the manager on (date).

Will you kindly fill out the enclosed form for my records, and let me have it back within five days? Later I'll send you our standard rental agreement for your signature.

Rent for your apartment should reach me on or before the first of each month. If you pay by check, you can either drop it in my mailbox, slide it under my door, or hand it to me personally.

Cordially yours,

I.M. NEWMANAGER

A longer, warmer letter is preferable if you'll be managing a fairly high-grade operation. Here's a sample:

Dear Mr. _____ :

This letter is to introduce me as the new manager of the _____ _____ Apartments. I'll be living here in Apartment _____, and I'll make a point of meeting you soon. My telephone number is _____ _____.

Meanwhile, I want to assure you that I'll do my best to keep this a pleasant and comfortable place to live. I'll always be looking for ideas to improve its operation, and your suggestions will be welcome.

The new owner is Mr. _____. (He, she, they) is/are *very* pleased to own this property. It was purchased because it is unusually well-built and attractive — with residents who obviously thought likewise since they chose it as their home.

Our immediate plans are to make it even more attractive by (painting the exterior? — improving the landscaping? — redesigning the lobby? . . . If the owners have no plans to improve the property as a whole, obviously you'll omit this paragraph. Instead, you may want to substitute something like the following paragraph.)

The owners aren't contemplating any major changes in the immediate future. If and when they consider doing something that will affect you, I'll keep you informed ahead of time.

I plan to visit with each resident to check the apartment for any necessary maintenance work — especially plumbing or electrical. This work will be scheduled in the near future, with priority to the most urgent problems. The owners and I plan to maintain this property so that everyone living here can be proud of it. We appreciate our residents and respect their rights to live in a well-kept property. We'll do everything in reason to continue a pleasant relationship for years to come.

I am authorized to collect the rent checks. They should be made payable to _____. They can be dropped in my mailbox, slipped under my door, or handed to me personally, just so they reach me on or before the first of each month.

Cordially,

I.M. NEWMANAGER

You can enclose an inventory of whatever furnishings and appliances in the apartment are the property of the new owner, and ask the occupant to sign and return a copy, if you didn't get this done during your preliminary visit. Ditto for the lease, if there is one, and rental agreement.

This mailing should be timed to reach the occupants no later than the day you move in. Meanwhile, you still have other matters to attend to.

CHECK THE INSURANCE COVERAGE. If the property has changed hands, probably the new owner has already been in touch with his insurance agent to make sure that adequate insurance is in force. But don't take this for granted. Don't relax even if he tells you, "Oh, sure, my agent has us covered."

Many amateur realty investors are notoriously ignorant and neglectful about insurance. One of their common mistakes it to assume that they're covered as soon as the seller transfers the existing policy. What they don't know is that the insurance company hasn't the least legal obligation to honor that transfer until the moment their authorized representative has signed the assignment.

Usually, this assignment is merely mailed to the company for assent as a routine matter, taking a week or more. In the interim, if the property burns down or if someone brings suit because of loss or injury there, the new owner can be wiped out — even though the insurance policies are made out and dated as of the day he took title. The insurance company is legally free to shrug its corporate shoulders and say, "Sorry, our contract is to protect the previous owner, not the new one." This may not be altogether ethical, but some companies are carefree about "moral obligations" so long as the law can't touch them.

Sure, there's only a once-in-a-lifetime chance that anything serious will happen during the ten days or so between the time the agent transfers the insurance and the time the company officially consents to the transfer. But why take even a long chance of a catastrophic loss? Better urge your boss, the owner, to call his insurance agent this very hour. Maybe the company's assent can be expedited. If not, the only safe course is to get interim coverage despite the extra cost.

Another common error among apartment owners is to overlook Workmen's Compensation Insurance. How well covered is your owner?

Even if you, as manager, are getting only a reduction in rent — no cash wages at all — and you break your leg while hurrying to answer the phone in the line of duty, the owner may be liable for major damages. You are legally his employee. The same is true of any occupant who is hurt while doing any work around the place, if there's an understanding that it will save him a little rent money.

Most owners don't understand who is legally classified as an employee. There are many more "employees," legally speaking, than the payroll shows.

A kid next door who comes in to do a few chores occasionally, not directly supervised and not bound by any requirement to put in specific hours, is nevertheless an employee in the eyes of the law. If he cuts himself with the pruning shears, your owner or insurance company will probably have to pay if a clever lawyer brings a damage suit.

Owners often think, too, that employees of a service company are not the owner's worry in case of injury, since the owner isn't hiring them or paying them. That's only true if the service company carries Workmen's Compensation. If it doesn't — and many small outfits don't — the apartment owner can be held liable for the roofing company employee who falls off the roof, the window washer who makes a mistake from a high window, or the floor waxer who gets punctured by a rusty nail. Exterminators, painters, once-a-week gardeners, washroom service companies and the like are in this category.

So beware! The company may tell you, "Why, naturally we've got insurance." It may even give you a written contract guaranteeing to hold the owners harmless if there's an accident. Or it may show you its ad in the yellow pages warranting that the company is fully covered. None of this will avail the owner if he's sued.

The owner — or you, as his representative — has the obligation of *seeing* the certificate of insurance that the company *says* it has. Nothing else will do. So, if any work is being done on the premises before you move in, you or the owner ought to check as soon as he takes title. His potential loss from liability claims is unlimited.

Another often-neglected type of insurance coverage is for "Non-Owned Auto." Suppose you, as manager, drive to a store to buy some paper — even before you move into the manager's quarters — and you're involved in an accident. The owner may be liable because you work for him. In fact, even when you're not on a mission for him, someone might claim you were, and might sue him because they figure he's wealthier than you are.

The premium for non-owner auto coverage is so small — maybe $20 a year — that insurance companies and agents seldom bother to solicit it. But it can be added to the apartment building liability policy. Do the owner a favor — and maybe yourself — by advising him to add it.

These are the most urgent and often-overlooked points. However, many other insurance questions are just as important. They're discussed in detail in the chapter on expenses. Maybe you should read that whole section before you go on the job. From the hour he takes title, every big property owner is a sitting duck for damage suits, and judgments are getting bigger every year.

YOUR FIRST DAYS ON THE JOB

Now you're in residence. Fully responsible. In full charge. What should you do first?

Before anything else, post notices of your name and apartment number, and probably your phone number, so that residents know how to get in touch with you. Laws of most states require that if an apartment building has three or more units, the manager's name and address must be prominently posted in *two* conspicuous places. One of these places should be at the mailboxes. Another must be in the elevator, if there is an elevator. In fact, if there are several elevators, your name must be posted in each.

Your phone number is something that every occupant will want. It might be important to an elderly person living alone, in case of illness or accident. You can visualize all sorts of situations where someone might be unable to go outside to look for your phone number at the "prominent place" where it's posted. So why not give every resident a card showing your number? Handing out these cards is another good excuse to visit everyone, or at least the occupants whom you missed on your preliminary reconnaissance — and it's important that you visit everyone for purposes of inspection and inventory, as we saw earlier in this chapter.

During your first few days, you should make a point of being visible much of the time — smiling, introducing yourself, shaking hands, asking, "Is your apartment alright? Anything I can do?" First impressions are crucial, so put your best foot forward. Take time to chat with any residents who seem inclined to chattiness. If they feel you're friendly and interested, they'll be easier to deal with.

A new restaurant tries to give extra-attentive service and generous portions during its first weeks, in order to build repeat business. In the same way, you can build good relations by taking pains at the outset to show everyone that you're prompt and efficient in dealing with service requests. Of course, you can't put in new drapes for a tenant the day she asks for them. But you can start arranging for them, even without waiting to be asked. If you observe that her drapes will need replacing anyway before you can re-rent the apartment if she moves out, you might well give her an immediate promise of new ones, and let her know when to expect them.

Most occupants probably won't ask for anything more than small favors — fixing a leaky tap or sticking door, cleaning windows, checking a TV aerial. You can make a lasting impression by doing these things within the hour if possible, even though it means postponing weightier matters. Good service is the major reason why people spend money in an establishment. If at first they're pleased by your service, they'll be more likely to make allowances for you later on.

Your routine first visit to occupants whom you haven't met can be handled more smoothly now than when you were touring the premises unannounced. Unless you're deeply suspicious of an occupant, it's best not to knock on the door unexpectedly and ask to come in. Instead, you can telephone first, introduce yourself, and say something like, "Sometime I'd like to stop by and say hello, and also to look at the installations in your apartment to see if they'll need servicing soon. I also want to leave you my card with the telephone number, so you can call whenever you have any request or complaint. Will it be convenient if I drop in a little later this evening? Or would Saturday be better?"

MAKE FRIENDS BEFORE YOU NEED THEM. In the days to come, there'll be many occasions when you may be amazed to see how much more easily a difficulty can be ironed out if you're on friendly terms with someone whose cooperation you need. The sooner you establish good realtionships with everyone around you, the easier your job will be in the future.

While your relations with residents are especially important, your standing with neighbors, tradespeople, public authorities, trade associations, and whoever else you meet can be important, too. An old saying warns, "There are no little enemies." Don't give anyone cause to make a career of getting even with you. Be nice to that surly delivery boy. He could be a big shot a few years from now.

Just on general principles, you should get acquainted with the mailman, policemen on the beat, managers of other apartments in the block, suppliers you'll be buying from. Your neighbors to right and left of you — and perhaps abutting the property in the rear — can make life easier or harder for you, depending on what they think of you. So, It's good business to introduce yourself to neighbors, and perhaps do a few small favors to cement relations if you think of anything appropriate.

Sooner or later you'll probably need an attorney who is well versed in real estate law — who knows the exact procedures for getting judgments against deadbeats or evicting them, what you can and cannot say in advertising your apartments, what should be said in leases, and the like. If your owner doesn't already have such an attorney, don't wait until a crisis arises to hunt for the right one. Find him now. The realty board can probably suggest names, and so can the apartment owners association.

Look ahead to tax-filing time. The property's tax return will be fairly complex. The owner will be counting on you to provide him all the data, and perhaps to file the return. You'll probably need a good CPA who can advise you on questions of depreciation credit, allowable deductions for operating expenses, various ways of treating income. Why not find the right man now, and have him help you set up your books?

In short, try to foresee every troublesome thing that might happen, and try to have a "contingency plan" to meet it, just as military commanders supposedly do. Find the people with special expertise or special connections before you need them. Get on a friendly footing, so they'll be glad to give you prompt attention when the contingency arises.

This has been a long chapter — to help you through a big change in your life. Having done all the things suggested here, you should be well started.

REMEMBER THESE BASIC POINTS:

* *Just before taking charge of a property, try to make a preliminary visit unannounced. Familiarize yourself with the property as much as possible.*

* *Try to get the outgoing manager to teach you how the property is being managed.*

* *Call on each resident personally. Have each one fill out a Confirmation Form showing which fixtures and accessories are personally owned. Ask if anything needs repair. Listen sympathetically to complaints.*

* *Check the leases and the records of rental payments. If anyone is behind in rents, press for immediate payment.*

* *Send an introductory letter to all residents.*

* *Check the insurance coverage.*

* *During your first days on the job, make a point of being visible.*

* *Take pains to be prompt in handling service requests.*

* *Establish good relations with tradesmen, public authorities, and others whose cooperation you may need.*

III *The Human Side of Property Management*

You are now operating a money machine. The more smoothly it purrs along, the more money it will make. But there's an odd fact about this particular kind of machine; if and when it sputters and wobbles and backfires, its basic trouble won't be mechanical, but human.

PROPERTY MANAGEMENT IS PEOPLE MANAGEMENT, in other words. A manager can be shrewd in money matters, and can be the world's handiest jack-of-all-trades at repairs and maintenance, without bringing in good profits unless he gets along well with people.

Apartment dwellers who dislike the manager can cause trouble in many ways that cut down the cash from the money machine. Quite often they can and will move out.

Whenever someone moves out, you must spend time and money for cleaning, painting, carpeting, or whatever else must be done to put the apartment in condition for the next occupant. It means time — and maybe money — spent in finding the next occupant.

Each move means extra paperwork for you. It means wear and tear on stairs and corridors as furniture comes in and out. Most important of all, it means that the property's income from rents is smaller each day that the apartment is vacant.

So, one of the big facts of life for apartment managers is that high turnover puts a serious crimp in their money machine. Strive for low turnover (unless at first you happen to inherit a property full of bad actors who must be cleaned out and replaced with better people). The amount of money the property clears next year can be doubled or halved, depending on your success in keeping it fully rented to good tenants.

Your personality and efficiency will make or break the property — will determine how fully rented it is, and how well the residents behave. Most people respond well when they think they're treated well. So, your most important task is to convince the residents that you're treating them well.

To you, the apartments are a business. But to the people who pay rent, an apartment is a home, a place to be comfortable, a place to socialize, maybe a place to raise a family. They're likely to feel strongly about it.

They are your customers — the most important people in your business. They aren't dependent on you; your income depends on them. They aren't interruptions of your work; they are the purpose of it. Your relations with them will determine your success in the property management business.

A very few will be bothersome no matter what you do. One in a hundred is a born trouble-maker who causes financial loss through damage to property, who annoys neighbors wherever he lives, who cheats and steals whenever he can get away with it. Your only remedy for him is firmness. Sometimes you may have to carry firmness to the point of getting rid of him. There are many ways to do this, as you'll see in the next chapter. But don't be too quick to decide someone must go. Try to work around him as a farmer plows around a stump; combine firmness with friendliness if you can.

You'll learn to distinguish between occasionally troublesome people who can be pacified and the chronic nuisances who can't. Nearly everyone is unreasonable at times, but most of us gentle down when handled diplomatically. Diplomacy is the biggest part of your job.

Did you hold a position of authority before you became an apartment manager? If so, you probably were accustomed to running things as you chose, without questions or explanations. And maybe you're saying to yourself now, "If I took time to be diplomatic with everyone in my apartment building, I'd go crazy."

Well, in this business, you'd better take time to be diplomatic all day, every day, or you won't go far. And, in fact, you'll find that diplomacy is fun. It's an art. Mastering any art brings deep satisfaction.

WHAT DO MOST HUMAN BEINGS REALLY WANT? Even the cranky ones who take so much of your time have the same underlying desires as the nice ones. Do they want the removal of minor grievances (which is what most of their complaints are about)? Or do they want something deeper, which they never put into words?

Basically, they all want to feel important, according to psychologists.

Lajos Egri, a Hungarian dramatist who knew a great deal about human nature, once analyzed real estate dealings and pointed out, "Everyone's importance is a relatively unstable commodity. Therefore if a realtor can indirectly convey to clients that they are being treated in a special fashion, something extra automatically is added to the realtor's service. The little things that you don't have to do, but do, are the ones that count."

Mr. Egri was expressing the basic fact that everyone is chiefly interested in himself. We all like to talk about ourselves. So, we like people who pay attention to us, who bolster our self-esteem, who act friendly toward us. Contrariwise, we instantly dislike those who hurt our pride by paying insufficient attention to us, or by acting unfriendly.

Dolly Madison was the most popular hostess in America — and not because she served the best ice cream. Someone once asked, "Dolly, why is it everybody loves you?" And Dolly answered, "Well, I love everybody!" And this sums up a secret of success in apartment management.

UNENTHUSIASTIC? THEN ENTHUSE! Few of us can force ourselves to love everybody. But we all can build up our interest in other people. How? Just by taking a little extra care in dealing with them. When we concentrate on them as puzzles to be solved, even the ornery ones become interesting.

Shakespeare advised us, "Assume a virtue if you have it not." He went on to imply that the habit of assuming it will build the virtue; pretense will become sincerity. By acting as if we like people, we really do begin to like them. Here's how the great psychologist, William James of Harvard, analyzed it:

> Action and feeling go together; and by regulating the action, we can indirectly regulate the feeling. Thus the sovereign voluntary path to cheerfulness, if our cheerfulness be lost, is to sit up cheerfully and to act and speak as if cheerfulness were already there.

The same is true of friendliness, which property managers need above all else. Keep acting friendly until it becomes part of you. If you need an incentive to do this, just remember that happy people in your apartments will make money for you.

FIVE KEYS TO KEEPING THEM HAPPY

SERVICE WITH A BROAD GRIN is a technique every good apartment manager learns. Show pleasure at every chance to help an occupant. When he asks for something — or complains about something — let him see that you're eager to hear all about it, eager to do what you can to satisfy him. Never ever let him feel that he's a nuisance.

Don't let him know the solution to his complaint is routine, if it is; let him feel you went out of your way to help. He'll consider himself a valued resident if he sees that you understand his problem and really care about it. And you do want him to feel valued, don't you?

People react to your facial expression. Whenever a resident approaches you, put on a smile, even if — or especially if — you're sure there's a complaint coming. A smile says, "I like you. You make me happy. I'm glad to see you." It usually wins a smile in return.

THE VOICE THAT WINS is a friendly voice. This is especially important on the telephone, where you do most of your business, and where the caller gets his entire impression of you from the sound of your voice. When people phone to ask about a vacancy, all it takes is a gruff tone or a flat and bored tone to discourage them from coming to look at the apartment.

THE SWEETEST SOUNDS IN THE LANGUAGE are the sounds of a person's own name. So, call people by name whenever possible. Hotel bellboys and restaurant waiters know that remembering names is a way to win votes. You can enhance your own success with the same technique.

TAKE AN INTEREST in whatever interests an occupant. There's no surer way to make people like you than to pay them the compliment of interest in their hobbies, their experiences, their opinions. When you discover their favorite subject, bring it up the next time you meet them, and they'll expand like flowers in the sun. Whatever you do, avoid turning the talk toward your own interests. For example, if someone mentions an accident, you'd blunder by saying, "My son had an accident just like that," and babbling on about your son.

If you listen well, and respond well, people will talk freely to you. Their talk will sometimes give you advance warning of a problem before it arises. Make a point of chatting with each tenant regularly — if only to ask, "Is everything the way you like it? Any problems in your apartment?"

Most times, you can do this casually, as you happen to meet a resident around the grounds or in a corridor. But you should check off his or her name in a little private list you're keeping. And those whose names aren't checked should get a casual visit from you or at least a friendly phone call every month or so.

When occupants begin to realize that you take an active interest in their comfort, the atmosphere will become friendly. You'll find it easy to spot small troubles and remedy them. But when you begin your visits, don't be surprised if people are suspicious.

The lower the occupant's income, the greater the suspicion. People without much money have painful problems of health, education, and family relations as well as finances. Many times the resident head of the household is a lone woman with several small children. Because of past experiences with tough owners and troublesome neighbors, many of these women worry about the motives of a manager who asks questions. Why is he here? Who is he looking for? Is he snooping to see how good a housekeeper I am, or how many people are living in my apartment, or how much damage I've done?

But you may also find a few residents with leadership ability. If you win their trust and good will, they can help you build rapport with other residents. Through them you can get many residents involved with cooperative projects. As you learn to understand their fears and worries, you can help them have a more secure and comfortable home.

SAY THANKS as often as you can, or bestow a little praise, which amounts to the same thing. "What a pleasure it is to have a satisfied resident such as you," you might say, or " . . . one who always pays so punctually," or ". . . one who takes such good care of his home." Also watch for chances to lather on a little praise and encouragement among employees, tradesmen, and others with whom you must cope — especially the disagreeable ones.

It should go without saying that all the above techniques must be more than sham. You must back them up with genuine helpfulness. No amount of sweet talk and smiling theatrics will keep a resident quiet when his roof leaks or his plumbing malfunctions. If you mentally put yourself in his place, and consider how you'd feel, you'll find it easy to dedicate yourself to making this building a comfortable, happy home for its occupants.

INFORMATION PLEASE. A regular newsletter is a helpful idea if your property has more than a few residents. The bigger the property, the greater the need for a newsletter to nurture friendly feelings. You want residents to think of you as a person and a friend — not some distant bureaucrat raking in their rent money.

People like recognition. They like to feel they're an important part of the property. They like to know what's going on and why things are happening. You can use your newsletter to keep them informed of new arrivals and departures, of the future paint job or the problem with the laundry room. You can make sure they know how taxes (or wage rates, or utility charges, or contractors' fees) affect the rent they pay and the service you provide. What better way is there of keeping residents aware of everything you do for them?

Your newsletter should come out on some regular schedule, but this isn't strictly necessary. What is important is that you rush out an immediate bulletin if there is news which residents should know quickly.

Don't delay. You don't want to be in the position of one manager of a high-rise whose residents came home one evening to find a note posted in the elevator asking them not to park their cars in a certain area of the garage because repair work would be going on. This meant they had to go back and move their cars. "Why couldn't you have sent this notice to everyone a day ahead, so we could have parked properly in the first place?" they asked the manager. He had no answer.

Nor would you like to be another manager who neglected to inform residents that locks would be changed on a certain day. When a burly workman knocked on doors to do his lock-changing job, some people took him for a thug and refused to let him in.

In short, communicate! It's a vital part of your job.

And listen for feedback. A perceptive hearing can go a long way to soften the wrath — sometimes justifiable — of a frustrated group of occupants.

WHAT YOU SHOULD DO FOR OCCUPANTS

Good service, plus a little coddling now and then, will keep you free of serious troubles with the great majority of apartment-renters. Here's what they're entitled to expect in the way of service.

GOOD HOUSEKEEPING. They expect you to keep the property in good condition at reasonable expense. "Lack of good housekeeping and proper maintenance" is the most common cause of occupants' complaints, according to surveys by apartment associations. Maintenance — especially preventive maintenance, which means the kind of upkeep that heads off breakdowns before they happen — will get a whole chapter later in the book.

If you neglect to make repairs after a resident tells you of the need, legal remedies are available to him. He can hire someone to make the repairs and deduct the cost from his next month's rent. Or he may move out, and have no further liability, regardless of any lease he may have signed.

We've already seen the value of a quick response in keeping residents happy after they ask that something be fixed. But, of course, this doesn't mean you should say, "I'll get it fixed right away," if you're the least bit uncertain that you can do so. Suppose you find that a needed part won't be available for ten days. Your belated explanation won't satisfy the resident. He'll only remember that you made a promise which you didn't keep.

Usually, your best response, when you get a complaint, is to say, "I'll check into it right away," and be as good as your word. If it's something you can't fix yourself, get an expert out to look at it within the hour, if possible. This in itself will make the complainer feel considerably better, because he's probably had sad experiences with slow-moving managers elsewhere. After you and the repairman examine the problem and decide what will be done, tell the resident your plan, and explain that it shouldn't take long if the necessary equipment and technical manpower are available.

Some residents tend to dramatize complaints. Don't let them stampede you. If a refrigerator doesn't work, a resident may envision all her food spoiling and may think you should deliver a new refrigerator within the hour. Keep calm and figure out some less expensive way of pacifying the lady, perhaps by finding emergency storage for a few perishables while the refrigerator is being fixed.

THINK OF THE OCCUPANTS' PROBLEMS AS YOURS, whether or not they affect your own comfort and convenience. They'll certainly affect your income in the long run.

Suppose a mother has no place to put her three-year-old child while she is at work. A hobbyist has no space in his apartment for a work bench. A widow, who likes to garden, can't find any nearby patch of ground where she can experiment. "Those are no worries of mine," a mediocre manager might say. But a bright manager would seek ways to help those occupants.

He might try to get a day care center organized, if there are many working mothers nearby. He might create a workshop for hobbyists out of storage space, by adding electrical outlets and good lighting, and installing a work bench. He might also designate a certain section of the property as a garden for the use of residents. Such measures would make the property more attractive to prospective residents, and would certainly help to hold the present occupants.

KEEP ALERT FOR MINOR NUISANCES, AND CORRECT THEM. In one case, the nuisance was a faucet on a ground-floor laundry room. Children in the building used the faucet to fill their pails; they also used it to fill balloons for water fights. The balloons often burst in the laundry room, creating a mess for occupants who used it. The manager knew better than to try to reform the juvenile cutups. Instead, he had a faucet installed in the play yard. The children used it to the hearts' content without flooding the laundry room. End of nuisance.

ATTRACTIVE NUISANCES, as lawyers and judges call them, are another potential problem for the residents and neighbors — and possibly a big lawsuit for you. Part of your job as manager is to keep the property as safe as possible. A well-known legal concept requires every owner to take special precautions in keeping children away from anything attractive which may be dangerous to them or others. A swimming pool is an obvious example. If it is unfenced (or even fenced, but with an easily-opened gate) and unsupervised by a lifeguard, then the owner and manager risk liability if a trespassing child wanders in and drowns.

A GOOD MANAGER IS PREPARED FOR EMERGENCIES. If his property has a swimming pool, he at least knows how to give artificial respiration, and he knows how to summon a fire department inhalator squad.

If an occupant loses his apartment key or locks himself out, there will be someone available day or night to open the door with a passkey. If a fire breaks out, the fire department number is posted in places where everyone can see it quickly — and the manager has an up-to-date list of all tenants and their phone numbers so he can call them immediately if necessary.

The manager knows where all the plumbing shut-offs are. He makes sure that they are conspicuously labeled — and that tenants know how to use them in emergencies. He keeps a handy list of reliable plumbers, electricians and other service people who might be needed on short notice. Such precautions sometimes save thousands of dollars by holding down the damage.

THE RIGHT TO PRIVACY is important to occupants, and they expect you to respect this right. Don't walk into their apartments without advance permission. Never use your passkey except by prearrangement with an occupant, or in case of dire emergency. When using it, even if you feel sure nobody is inside, always ring the doorbell, knock loudly, and then call the occupant's name several times with the door open, before you step inside (leaving a notice on the door that you were inside). You can never be sure that a resident hasn't returned unexpectedly a few moments ago and gone straight to bed, or into the bathtub. Managers have been sued when they blundered into such situations.

The best relationship between you and the residents is one in which you respond immediately to a resident's call — presuming the resident is being reasonable — but otherwise isn't seen or heard. This is not a social relationship. Residents don't expect you to organize parties for them or drop in at their suites for cozy chats.

In fact, if you get on partying terms with them, you'll find it much harder to be firm when the occasion demands. On the other hand, you can't very well decline invitations to occupants' parties, particularly during holidays. If you go, your best bet is to accept one beverage if offered, be pleasant in an unobtrusive way (not as the life of the party, nor as teller of lengthy stories) and depart early.

PEACE AND QUIET are partly your responsibility. Residents expect you to discourage other residents from being overly noisy, especially in the late evening and early morning. Sometimes you really will have to act as a silencer, but it's usually better tactics to suggest to occupants that they themselves mention the matter lightly to a noisy neighbor. Usually, he'll apologize and be quieter thereafter. But if you intercede with him, his reaction is likely to be "What's wrong with those crabby neighbors? I wasn't making that much noise." He may secretly think that you're the crab, and that his neighbors didn't really complain.

Sometimes a whole group of occupants get together loudly, to the annoyance of peace-loving neighbors. This could cause civil war within the property, if it happens often. It's up to you to find the leader of the noisemakers and offer him a friendly suggestion about a couple of residential developments for real swingers, where rules are more liberal and nobody objects to noise. Would they like to move to one of these congenial locations? If so, you'll be glad to help make arrangements. Thus encouraged, the swingers may move en masse, to the relief of everyone else on your premises. The vacancies will cost you money in the short run, but your money machine will produce more in the long run.

Occupants have a right to expect you to act when someone disturbs them repeatedly and seriously. But some kinds of disturbances may be serious to the complainer without being grounds for drastic action by a manager. For example, a crying baby. Unless your house rules forbid children, you can't expect the parents to silence their infant or move out. And what should you do about a barking dog? Again, the answer is easy if pets are taboo under house rules, but if you permit occupants to keep pets, you'll have a hard time deciding how many barks add up to a public nuisance.

You may also get an occasional protest about the length of a resident's hair, or style of dress, or choice of language. Someone may indeed find someone else's life-style so obnoxious that he'll move out rather than tolerate it, but in these liberated days there aren't many managers who find it good business to try to oust anyone for mere unconventionality. This just points up the fact that you should be extra prudent in renting to people in the first place; try to screen out types who may offend your long-established residents.

WHAT YOU SHOULD EXPECT FROM OCCUPANTS

The list of do's and don'ts can be almost endless, depending on the type of property you're managing. We'll get to the occupancy agreement and the house rules a few chapters farther along. Meanwhile, some general observations are in order.

SAFETY PRECAUTIONS — especially against muggers and burglars — are an obligation of occupants as well as management. Depending on conditions in your neighborhood, you may have to ask everyone to take unusual care. For example, out of innocent politeness, residents often hold a building entry door open for a stranger on their heels. In one case, this allowed a drug addict to get into a lobby where he shot and robbed someone.

Perhaps you'll want to emphasize getting to know one's neighbors; having strangers identify themselves before letting them into an apartment; reporting suspicious characters; taking precautions in the laundry room; keeping garage doors and other exits closed.

KEEPING THE PEACE. You should expect residents to be considerate of one another. Anyone living above someone else needs to realize that he disturbs the people below by using the garbage disposer, dishwasher, or vacuum cleaner during normal sleeping hours — say, from 11 p.m. to 7 a.m. — or to take a shower or tub bath during those hours, since the water pipe is in the bedroom wall of those beneath him.

We needn't give much space to the problem of noisy radio, stereo, and TV sets. If a set can be heard in nearby apartments, it's too loud. Occupants will usually speak to an offender themselves, but if this doesn't suffice, they'll complain to you, and it's up to you to act promptly but tactfully.

You should expect residents to be at least a little discrete in inviting company. Most people give occasional parties and bend the walls. There are birthdays, engagements, weddings, poker games, and those extra-special parties to celebrate a divorce. If your building is a tower complex, only three or four neighbors will be disturbed, and they probably won't protest much because they know they too might give such a party. But you can ask all party-givers to advise you in advance, so you can tell any complaining tenants that the noise isn't caused by a drunken orgy, but just a special happy occasion —and that the host has promised you it will be all over by 1 a.m.

On the other hand, if your building is small, everyone in it will hear party noise. You still can't expect occupants to refrain from partying. But you can insist on advance notice, and on a promise to close at 1 a.m. If the uproar continues after this hour, you'd better remind the hosts of their promise; otherwise, the police will soon be at their door, even if they've invited the whole building, because the building across the street will have made the phone call.

INDIVIDUAL VISITORS are usually none of your business, even if they move in for awhile. A resident has a right to invite out-of-town relatives to stay several days. The children of a divorced resident can come in periodically — even though it's an adults-only building — but it would be nice if you're advised beforehand. As for the bachelor whose "sister" stays overnight, or the couple living together under separate names, it's not your job to supervise their morals. But it may become your job if a lady entertains a series of male guests at hourly intervals, or if marijuana fumes get thick in the halls.

SAFETY AND SANITATION, though mainly your responsibility, are partly up to occupants, too. You should expect them to obey municipal ordinances, at the very least. Obviously, you can't let them strew garbage around, in or out of their rooms. Nobody can hurl baseballs or ride skateboards.

On the other hand, you can't snoop inside apartments to see whether the style of housekeeping meets your approval. Only when something smells bad, or insects begin to swarm, or other signs of unsafe behavior become noticeable, can you take the matter up with occupants. You should be able to screen out most slobs during the rental negotiations; they're often easy to spot.

What isn't so easy to detect is the alcoholics, drug addicts and people who smoke in bed. They can be menaces to themselves and everyone else — but until they actually cause an emergency, you may not be aware of their bad habits. About all you can do is to keep alert for the first signs of potential trouble, and investigate them diplomatically.

WHEN AN OCCUPANT INTENDS TO LEAVE, you have a right to expect advance notice. Probably you should provide every resident with a form headed NOTICE OF INTENTION TO VACATE (you'll find a sample in Chapter 4) with blanks to indicate the departure date, and perhaps the reason for leaving, as well as a forwarding address. This form should make clear that in signing it the resident authorizes you to show the premises to prospective tenants by appointment.

When you receive such a notice, no doubt you'll want to give the occupant instructions about defrosting and cleaning the refrigerator, removing trash, turning in keys, and doing whatever else you think should be required.

SIMPLE HONESTY in business dealings is, of course, your number one expectation from each resident. You expect their rent to be paid promptly, and their checks to be good. This brings us to one of the most important subjects in this book.

THE SCIENCE OF COLLECTING RENT

SLOW-PAY OCCUPANTS can be a serious problem — especially those who are well-behaved in all other ways. The "slow but good" type leads the list of delinquent renters because he knows that the manager figures he is good for the money. This type gradually assumes the right to postpone payments as he chooses. In effect, he's borrowing money without paying interest; he's expanding his own purchasing power at the expense of the property owner.

Once he's settled into the rut of paying late, he may deepen it, paying later and later. Eventually, he may try to use an accumulated past-due balance to wangle a rent reduction from you, or to get you to make unnecessary improvements in his apartment. The longer he can put off paying, the more incentive he has to skip out without paying at all. He may even feel reckless about damaging the premises.

Maybe he's not the type to try to take such advantage of you; maybe he's nothing worse than a habitual late payer. Even so, you'd better be firm. If you're easy with two or three residents, word gets around, and soon many are paying only when they feel like it. They'll give excuses, of course, like, "There wasn't anyone in the office . . . My check was late. . . My mother is sick." Or they'll give you a check they've "forgotten" to sign.

His delays are plausible, except that they're familiar because so many residents use the same tactics. The fact remains that the average person will pay the rent ahead of all other bills unless:

— the manager is seldom around;
— the manager is careless and lenient about collections;
— the manager is slow in responding to maintenance requests;
— the manager never thanks or compliments residents for paying promptly.

In short, a list of rent delinquencies is a sure sign of a poor manager.

About the only resident on whom you can go easy is someone who has paid regularly for years; then suddenly runs into temporary trouble such as illness. If he frankly tells you what the trouble is, sometimes you can work out a plan for him to pay monthly rent in weekly installments. This is where your judgment of character is crucial. When younger people have chronic problems in paying, you'd better counsel them to find a smaller apartment at lower rent.

It's risky to tie up capital in overdue rent accounts, because you can't postpone paying the property's current expenses. If the owner can't make his mortgage payment on time, he gets socked with penalty charges. Besides, you need some of the rent money to meet the cost of services you provide. So, you're jeopardizing the whole financial structure of a rental property by slow collections. It's important to keep everyone paying rent on schedule. How can you do this?

TRAIN AN OCCUPANT WELL when you first get him, and you'll have less trouble. People pay as they're trained to pay. You should mention when rent is due and payable at least three times: when a prospective renter fills out the application, when you notify him he's been accepted, and when you hand him the lease for signing.

REMINDERS ARE IMPORTANT. Some managers put a note in each mailbox, or under each door: "Tomorrow is the day when rent is due." At the end of the next day, where payment isn't in, they follow up with another note, phone call, or personal visit. Sometimes humor makes this easier: "I don't care if you're late with the rent, but the bank does."

To nudge a few residents who are still late after two days, you can hang reminder cards in highly visible colors on their apartment doors — glowing green perhaps on the third day; bright orange on the fifth. Embarrassment at having neighbors notice these cards will give offenders a powerful push toward on-time payments.

Another way of using visual psychology in your own office, where most residents drop in occasionally, is to keep a sheet headed DELINQUENT RENTS in big letters next to your receipt book on your desk — but keep names or apartment numbers out of sight, because too many people can read them upside down, and you don't want to cause anyone too much humiliation. Or you might keep a box of small red flags from your stationer beside the card index of residents. These clues to your serious concern about late payments will be talked about on the grapevine.

At the end of the third day you definitely should visit a delinquent resident to pick up his check. If he makes excuses, explain pleasantly that you just can't afford to pay his rent for him, which is what he's asking you to do when he stays without paying. Mention the building's expenses you must meet. Suggest he borrow the money from someone he knows. Maybe he'll reply, "I can't borrow because I can't get credit." Then you can point out, "If your credit isn't good enough for a bank or loan company, how can it be good enough for me? I'm not even in the business of lending money . . . I'd hate to ask my lawyer to start the three-day eviction proceedings, but I won't have any choice unless you can pay up within the next 48 hours. Non-payment is legal grounds for eviction, you know."

This is strong medicine. Use it only when a resident says flatly that he can't pay for awhile. It will usually convince him that he can't stall. (The legal process for getting him out is explained in the next chapter.) Such a showdown will seldom be necessary if you've educated residents about their responsibilities. Nearly everyone will find the money or move out voluntarily. Only a hard-core deadbeat will hang in there for actual court-ordered eviction.

LATE CHARGES help get residents into the habit of punctual payment. The first managers who tried this system added a $5 charge when the rent was five days overdue. This speeded up some slowpokes, but it actually slowed down others still further; they realized that they would still owe only the extra $5 if they waited until the 15th. Once they incurred the late charge, they decided to use their money quite awhile longer before paying the rent.

So managers changed to a plan that added $1 per day, not applicable until after the fifth day of delinquency. This meant that residents were allowed five days' grace, but were charged $6 extra when rent was paid on the sixth day, or $7 on the seventh, and so on.

The late charges were controversial for some time. A few residents felt that such a charge was illegal, and refused to pay it. Some judges upheld the charge in small claims courts; others threw it out. But now, with so many big retailers hitting their credit customers with late charges, the controversy seems to have died down. And managers often waive the charges when a resident lets them know ahead of time that his payment will be a few days late.

A painless way — indeed, a pleasant way — of imposing late charges can be gradually installed as new residents move in. You can set their rent high enough to cover a late charge; then give a discount for paying on time. Some owners give Blue Chip (redemption) stamps to all residents who pay on or before the due date.

ANOTHER WAY OF APPLYING FRIENDLY PRESSURE on someone who falls behind is to make a pleasant phone call: "Hello, this is the manager. Just calling to find out when it will be convenient to show your apartment. Will this afternoon be okay?" The usual response is, "What do you mean, show the apartment?" "As you haven't paid the rent, I presume you're moving." This may bring quick payment, if you have the right personality and know your people.

WHEN A CHECK BOUNCES you should phone the bank (if it's a local bank) and ask whether the check will clear now. If the answer is yes, hurry to the bank and cash it. If the answer is no, go see the resident. If he says that the check should clear now, you can say, "Have you made a deposit today? I called the bank, and they said there are insufficient funds."

Be wary of accepting checks on out-of-town banks. If one is rubber, you won't know for several days. Occasionally, someone who plans to defraud you will play this little game to gain time. No law forces you to accept checks for rent. You can insist on cash if you suspect you're being conned.

You'd better put a resident on a cash-only basis the first time a check is returned, even if it clears when re-deposited. Or you can impose a $3 charge for a returned check; after all, the owner's account is charged by the bank.

ASSIGNMENT OF PERSONAL EFFECTS is a compromise that sometimes clears up a deadlock. One manager, trying to help a resident who lost her job and fell two months behind in rent, knew she owned her own furniture. Because she was jobless, she couldn't get a loan on her furniture, even though it was free of any lien or mortgage.

When the manager asked if she would assign the furniture as security, the resident said, "I'll do better. I'll sell it to you." This wiped out the rent debt. The owner was happy because now he had a furnished apartment, which was easier to rent in that particular district. The resident was happy because she avoided the burden of moving and storage costs; she moved in with a friend during her temporary unemployment.

But, obviously, the people who give you bad checks or have to sell their furniture to pay rent are likely to cause worse problems than the ordinary need of getting people to be prompt in their business dealings. This brings in a whole different area of management work: problem people. There are certain major types of problem people whom you should learn to recognize. In the next chapter, we'll consider them and see how to deal with them.

REMEMBER THESE BASIC POINTS:

* *Happy residents make money for you. Try to stay on cordial terms with ever-one in your building. Remember that they like to be noticed.*

* *Show friendliness and enthusiasm. Say thanks often.*

* *Keep residents informed about potential problems, and about plans for changes. A newsletter may be a good way to do this.*

* *Whenever you get a complaint, say, "I'll check into it right away," and do so. If repairs are indicated, get them done as soon as possible. If there'll be a delay, tell the resident.*

* *Prepare for foreseeable emergencies.*

* *Respect residents' privacy. When using a passkey, even if you think no one is inside, always knock loudly, call the resident's name, and leave the door open when you enter.*

* *Insist on residents being considerate of one another.*

* *Train them to pay rent on time. Late charges, or discounts for paying promptly, can help.*

IV *Problem People and How to Handle Them*

Tact and good service, plus big dollops of personal charm, aren't always enough to keep everything smooth between you and a resident. As a manager, you'll meet some peculiar, puzzling people. They'll test you out, to see whether or not they can handle you. As you get a reputation for being able to handle *them*, you'll be tested less. The better you handle people, the more you prosper.

It's important to distinguish between the harmless occupant who may inadvertently cause trouble and the continuously difficult people who wreck your plans, make other residents unhappy, and cause serious financial losses. These chronic trouble-makers fall into certain categories. You'll meet them again and again (especially if you're not perceptive in screening prospective tenants, a technique we'll consider in a later chapter). Here they are:

MR. HARD NOSE seldom is satisfied for long. Give him a royal suite with red plush carpet, and he'll grump that the elevator is too slow. A quiet, peaceable, long-time resident sometimes changes gradually into a Hard Nose as he grows older, especially when he's retired and has less to do.

For example, you may see a change come over a retired plumber. At first he just asks you to fix a leaky faucet in his kitchen. As you change his washer, you chuckle silently at such a request from an expert plumber. But as he gets better acquainted with you — or as he gets older and crankier — his complaints escalate, even though you may have been improving service and operations ever since you took charge.

Let's say someone spills oil in the parking area. It gets tracked into Mr. Hard Nose's apartment. Thereupon he demands that you replace the carpeting. Soon you find he is cornering every resident in the building and griping about you (or about them).

Try as you will to please him, he stays sour. His talk makes other residents wonder if you're doing a poor job with the building. So, you go to see him, and pleasantly explain what you're doing to improve the operations of the building. No use. Next day you see another resident trying to escape from Hard Nose. Face it; you'll have to get rid of him.

MRS. BUSY BODY pays rent on time, obeys rules, keeps her apartment spotless. A perfect tenant? Far from it. You've just received 30-days notice that another resident, a young divorcee, intends to vacate. Her reason: everyone in the building knows whom she entertains and when, her occasional overnight guest. Mrs. Busy Body delights in spreading the news. Your building has become a whispering gallery of gossip, much of it malicious, and most of it started by Mrs. Busy Body. She sees all and tells all. She must go — or other residents will.

MR. AND MRS. SWINGER. You checked their credit and employment record; everything in order. When they move in you notice their attractive furniture. But one night they come home very late. You hear them — and so do many others, because the Swingers have several guests in tow, laughing and talking at top decibels.

They turn up the stereo until the walls shake. You ask them to tone it down. They graciously comply. But at dawn their guests' stentorian farewells awaken the whole building again. Later you corner Mrs. Swinger and read the riot act. She apologizes prettily, explaining that the guests were important brass from her husband's company.

Every week or so the Swingers raise pandemonium, while your phone rings all night with complaints. It's just a question of time until someone tells you, "Look, I like parties too, but this is ridiculous. If you can't cool it, I'm moving."

Even by calling police you fail to quell the bedlam more than intermittently, so one resident after another decides to vacate. The Swingers should be in a building full of other swingers. Having broken your house rules about noise, they've violated the lease. You must give them written notice to stop or vacate.

ROY REBEL is an angry college student, or at least he's around the campus incessantly, organizing protest marches and sit-ins and picket lines. He's a street-corner lawyer who hates the Establishment and takes pains to flout every rule. He infuriates other residents by parking his car across their stalls, propping open a fire door so his buddies can walk in from the alley, drinking wine at poolside and leaving broken bottles there.

Roy thrives on the rage of neighbors. He rages back at them. He's ever ready for long debates. He says you're plotting to violate his rights. Again, your only recourse is the notice to quit (which is covered in detail later in this chapter).

MISS DEMEANOR seems gentle, pleasant, and artistic in a far-out way. Unwisely, you rent her an upper-floor apartment. The couple underneath come home one evening to find water seeping through the ceiling onto their furniture, drapes, clothing, and stereo set. You thump on Miss Demeanor's door. No answer. Entering, you see such havoc that your senses reel.

It isn't a waterbed that caused the flood; your rules forbid waterbeds in upstairs apartments, and this rule at least is intact. But in the bathroom a faucet has been left running into a plugged basin. The bathroom is flooded, the hallway carpet is soaked, and rivers are spreading through the living room and bedroom.

The bedroom, incidentally, has been painted purple by Miss Demeanor. Her guests have ruined the parlor walls with crude collages. Other walls are pocked with holes from oft-moved pictures. The dinette is plastered from floor to ceiling with travel posters glued on and covered with shellac. As your head droops in grief, your eyes see the new carpet streaked with paint drippings and wine stains. You'll not only have to evict Miss Demeanor, but sue her for the cost of rehabilitating her apartment and the one beneath.

THE SLICKSTER FAMILY arrives in a costly new car and asks for a two-year lease. They've just arrived from Atlanta, they say. Advance deposit? Mr. Slickster flourishes a wad of American Express money orders. Identification? Well, that is a slight problem. He left his credit cards in his attache case at the Superluxe Motor Inn. "But I'll give you a few local references," he proposes, "and come back this afternoon to pick up the key."

Phoning the Superluxe, you learn that the Slicksters are indeed registered from Atlanta, having checked in five days ago. You reach two of the local references by phone, and they recommend him heartily. So you give him a key to the apartment when he returns that afternoon and pays the remaining deposit.

When the rent falls due, he says he's sorry he overlooked it, but he's waiting for his commission check to arrive from Atlanta. He's obviously a man of some consequence, so you decide not to press him. During his third free month in your building, you reluctantly realize that you've been cheated by a professional deadbeat. You'll never get a dime. Evict. And pray for better judgment when the next artful dodger comes your way.

MR. PASSAWAY is a problem only because he lies dead in his room, and you have no idea whom to notify. Somehow, when he signed the lease, you neglected to get names of any relatives or close friends. Should you make a quick search of his apartment for papers that will give you a clue? Not on your life. That's against the law. Normally, you could at least call the doctor who attended his last illness, and try to saddle him with the responsibility for disposing of the corpse. But Mr. Passaway had no doctor, as far as you know.

Call the coroner. He'll summon a mortician; then search the apartment — and probably seal the door. If he doesn't, you should. It's your responsibility to fend off even family members until you're shown a document certifying someone as executor or administrator of Passaway's estate. There's a good reason for this. Many old or bedridden people hoard cash and other valuables in the apartment. So, you dare not begin to clean, refurbish, or show the apartment until its contents have been officially tabulated for probate and moved to storage by some court-appointed person.

GETTING THEM OUT

In Chapter 3 we described all the steps in extracting rent from slow-pay residents. None of these steps will work, of course, when you're confronting a hard-core no-pay deadbeat. Your only recourse in such situations is to evict, just as it's your only recourse with people who may pay their rent but are chronic trouble-makers in other ways.

A manager who lets residents fall behind in rent will soon find them farther behind. When they owe two months' rent, the amount looks astronomical to them. They may realize that it is easier to skip out than to catch up on payments — or they may decide to see how long they can hold out in the apartment without paying anything at all. By the same token, slobs seldom reform. If they continue to be nuisances after the first warning, the longer you wait to dispossess them, the more trouble they'll cause.

Owners hesitate to start evicting a tenant because it is costly and troublesome, when done the legal way. Sometimes they accept part payment, in the vain hope that the rest will be forthcoming soon. Or sometimes they postpone action when a non-paying resident says something like, "We'll pay you the full month when my husband gets paid this Friday." If these are new occupants, or if you've had previous difficulties in collecting from them, you'd better stand firm. Evict.

Maybe you can allow a little leeway if the family has a past record of reliability. Even then, don't accept any vague assurance like, "I'll take care of it as soon as I can." Insist on a clear promise of the day when payment is to be made. The day should be no more than five days in the future.

And there must be an implied threat of immediate action if the promise is broken. You can say pleasantly, "On the understanding that you'll definitely make full payment this Friday, I'll hold off on legal action until then." But don't delay another day if the money isn't forthcoming at the promised time. Make up your mind that the occupant must leave. And take action to get him out.

BUYING OUT AN UNDESIRABLE OCCUPANT is often the simplest and cheapest solution to the problem, even though you may hate the idea of throwing good money after bad.

You'll actually save money, as well as time, when a deadbeat or an obnoxious resident accepts your offer of $50 cash for vacating the apartment and giving you the keys. Your cost of evicting him will be at least double that amount, and sometimes much more when you must hire an attorney and go to court. In addition, figure how much rent you'll lose before the legal machinery moves the occupant out.

Some owners do more. They offer to pay the first month's rent for an occupant in a new location, to rid themselves of him. If you make such an offer, take precautions to see that your tenant doesn't just pocket your cash and stay put. This may seem like a dirty trick to play on some other apartment manager, but if he doesn't care enough to check the applicant's past record, why should you play guardian angel?

If the prospective new landlord does call you and ask for a reference, of course your only ethical behavior is to give a truthful answer. You won't get rid of the undesirable occupant, but your conscience won't bother you either. However, there are legal reasons for watching your language. Use vague terms like, "The tenant didn't live up to the standards we set for occupancy." That way you're safer from slander suits.

WHEN YOU'VE RENTED TO AN UNDESIRABLE and you can't buy him out, the first step in evicting him is to serve a written three-day notice, which is essentially a threat: "Do this or get out." It is commonly used when someone is in arrears in rent, although it can be amended to read, "Three-day notice (or legal number of days in your state) to shut off loud noise after 10 p.m. or leave," or the like. (Often this is headed PAY OR QUIT NOTICE, but the word "quit" confuses many occupants, so you may want to use clearer language.)

The usual causes for eviction are actual violation of the lease, such as non-payment of legally due rent, or creating a nuisance, or violating other house rules which a resident signed a promise to obey.

The three-day notice always gives the recipient an alternative to moving. It implies that if he meets your demand, he is entitled to stay. This is almost the only kind of notice that you can personally hand to the occupant, or fasten to his door, or mail to him as a last resort. Other legal papers must be served by a third party.

If you want to give an occupant no alternative to moving out, you can send a 30-day "Notice of Termination of Tenancy" with or without reason if the tenant is on a month-to-month basis. If he has a current lease, you can use a 30-day "Notice to Quit for Violation of Covenant." Or you can wait until the lease expires and then refuse to renew it, which means he then has no legal right to stay.

Sometimes occupants ask why they are being ordered to move. Your best answer is that the notice is being given "as provided by state law for the purpose of securing possession of the apartment." You needn't give any other reason. It's prudent to avoid argument, even if the tenant knows the reason for the notice. You'll only embitter him further if you enter into a debate.

There's only one thing worse than going through the unpleasantness and expense of evicting a deadbeat or trouble-maker, and that is the unpleasantness and expense of *not* evicting him. So, make up your mind to get it over with as quickly and smoothly as you can.

Unless you choose the longer route of the 30-day notice with no alternative, use a form like the samples shown on the following pages. The form must say exactly how much is owed, and for what specific period of time (give the dates). It must specify

THREE DAYS' NOTICE TO PAY RENT OR VACATE

TO: _____ TENANCY IN POSSESSION.

You are hereby required to pay within_____ after the service on you of this notice, the rent of the premises hereinafter described, and of which you now hold possession, said rent now amounting to the sum of $_____ from _____ to _____ .

Or to Deliver Possession of the said premises within the said three (3) days to:

_____

who is hereby authorized to receive possession thereof, or any rent due or unpaid from you, or Owner shall institute legal proceedings against you to declare the forfeiture of the lease or tenancy agreement under which you occupy the herein below described property and to recover possession of said premises and damages.

The undersigned elects to, and does declare a forfeiture of your lease or tenancy agreement by reason of the aforesaid nonpayments.

Said premises are situated in the City of_____ , County of_____ , State of_____ , and described address as follows:

_____

_____

_____

_____   _____
Dated   Signed by Owner

PROOF OF SERVICE OF _____ NOTICE

I hereby certify that I served the_____NOTICE on

_____ , on the herein named tenant in possession.

I declare under penalty of perjury that the foregoing is true and correct.

DATED: _____ , 19____
at_____ , _____
                                                  State

_____
Signature of Server

NOTICE TO PAY RENT OR MOVE OUT

To_____
                                    Tenant in Possession

You are hereby notified that you are required within three days after this notice is served upon you, either:

     (a) To pay the rent due for the premises, consisting of housing accommodations herein-after described, of which you now hold possession, amounting to the sum of $_____
_____ Dollars ($_____) and including the _____ day of _____ 19____ ; or _____

     (b) To surrender and deliver up possession of said premises to the undersigned.

If you fail to do so, legal proceedings will be instituted against you to recover possession of said premises with treble rents and such other damages as may be allowed by law.

The Owner ( ) Manager( ) hereby elects to declare the forfeiture of the agreement under which you hold possession of said premises.

The rent for said premises is $_____ per month, on a tenancy from month-to-month, said rental month beginning on the_____ day of each calendar month. Said rent is due for said premises from _____19____ to _____19_____ .

The ground upon which your eviction from said premises will be sought is non-payment of rent.

Said premises are known and described as _____ No._____
                                              Apartment/Room/Suite

in the _____ designated by No. _____
            Name of Apartments

Street, _____ California.

                      _____
                                     Owner

                      _____
                                  Manager

the exact premises. It must be dated. It must be signed, preferably by the owner, but if necessary, by you as the owner's agent.

If you give the three-day notice for non-payment of rent, it must offer the choice of paying the back rent or losing the right to live there, besides being liable for all past due rent. In the extremely unlikely event that the resident pays the full amount due within the three days, you must accept. Then he is back in good standing and doesn't lose his occupancy rights. However, once the three-day period has passed, he can't stop the eviction by paying unless you or the owner consent to this, as provided by law in your state.

You're entitled to serve notice on the very first day the rent becomes overdue, or any day from then on. (In other words, if rent is due May 1, the notice can be served May 2.) Occasionally, it shocks a long-delinquent resident into paying at once; usually it doesn't. Sometimes he moves out; sometimes he tells you, "I'll need more than three days to find another apartment." But don't weaken. You shouldn't serve notice of any kind unless you're determined to follow through. Your residents will soon catch on to empty threats.

Service can be a hard task sometimes. Legally, it must be served by someone not a party to the lease or the implied rental contract — which means the owner can't serve it. But most people don't know about this obscure legal point. It would only arise if the occupant decided to put up a legal battle, and had been served by the owner rather than the manager.

Anyway, to be safe, you and a friend of yours should go and hand the notice to the occupant, so that your friend can sign an affidavit certifying that the three-day notice was properly served. The notice must be personally delivered to the resident. (The same procedure is required if you give the 30-day notice.)

If the notice is served personally, he's stuck with it, even though he refuses to touch it. You can see him through the window and wave it at him and say, "You're served," or "This is for you." That's good enough. If either husband or wife comes to the door and kicks away the notice when you drop it at their feet, you've still served it legally. Even if you catch him coming out of a bar, and he sees you and turns and runs, you can throw it after him and it's a good valid service.

Many delinquent occupants go into hiding, and you can't catch them to make personal service unless you wait for hours or days. Don't bother. There's a much easier way, known as the "mail and nail" method of service.

Just take the notice to the front door, or adjacent to it in a conspicuous place, and send another copy by certified mail. The law assumes that he's been served notice when the first copy is posted on the door, providing the other copy does arrive later.

THE NUISANCE TENANT can be served with a three-day notice similar to the one given to non-paying people. If the occupant hasn't lived up to a condition of a lease, has broken house rules, has committed a public or private nuisance, or has misbehaved in various other ways, he can be served.

However, your notice should specifically state the reason for dispossessing him — and it should be a substantial one, not just some trivial breach of promise. "The law hates forfeitures," as judges say, and a court won't uphold an eviction and forfeiture of a lease because of a minor infraction.

Furthermore, any eviction because of the race, religion, national origin, or sex of a resident is against the law; so is an eviction as revenge for having reported a housing violation to the authorities or having organized other residents to take organized action against the owner. An owner can't use legal grounds for eviction as a subterfuge to hide his unlawful prejudice. So be careful. (Also check the chapter in this manual on Tenant Power.)

NEVER TRY TO EVICT WITHOUT LEGAL PROCESS. Some owners and managers seem to think that by serving the three-day notice and getting no response, they can simply put the tenant out the door. Not so. You may be sued if you enter his premises without permission; if you remove a door, or change the lock, or cut off utilities or seize his possessions, or lay hands on him. If the lease says differently, the lease is void, in most states.

There are certain states — notably, New York, New Jersey, Pennsylvania, Massachusetts, and a few others — which allow an occupant to be physically moved out with no court hearing and no action by a peace officer. But even in those states, if you, as owner or manager, do it yourself, you can only use reasonable force at reasonable times, and you can't commit a breach of the peace. Moreover, you run the risk of a lawsuit for heavy damages if you cause any harm to the occupant's personal belongings, or if you cause any injury — even mental injury, like humiliation — to the tenant or any member of the family. So, you'd better check first with a good real estate lawyer, who'll probably advise you against such steps, even in localities where they seem to be legal.

SOMETIMES YOU CAN TALK PEOPLE OUT THE DOOR, if you're willing to wait 30 days for them to move. First, prepare a 30-day written notice in a form like the sample shown below. Then, brace yourself for any of many different reactions from your target: tears, tirades, calm defiance, maybe even violence. Make up your mind you won't waver, no matter what the reaction is. Then go to the resident's door and ask if you can come in for a brief business discussion.

30-DAY NOTICE
OF TERMINATION OF TENANCY

To _____ or any persons in possession of the property located at

_____

_____

NOTICE IS HEREBY GIVEN that your tenancy of the above described premises is terminated as of_____ , and you are hereby required to quit and deliver up possession of the premises to the undersigned on or before said date.

This is intended as 30 days' notice to terminate said tenancy.

DATED_____19_____ .

_____
Manager

_____
Apartments

Keep chitchat to a minimum. Be polite but definite, and get to the point quickly. Tell the resident that you want to rent his apartment to someone else. Don't be drawn into discussing why. You can just say, "The state law provides this procedure for securing possession of the apartment." Or you can say the owner has decided to remodel. You don't have to give a reason with a 30-day notice if the occupant is on month-to-month rental; the owner is entitled to his property whenever he sees fit. (If the resident has an unexpired lease, use a 30-day "Notice to Quit for Violation of Covenant" and be ready to prove in court, if need be, that he violated the terms of the lease.) Where rent controls are in force, the situation is more complex; see an experienced lawyer.

After you've told the resident you want him to move, you can say something like this:

"Now, Mr. Doe, we can handle this one of two ways. Either you can give me a written notice that you're leaving, or I'll have to give you an official Notice of Termination of Tenancy. It will be much better for you if you give me notice. Then my records won't show that you were asked to move. If I have to give you the notice, this will become part of your permanent record.

"We're members of the Apartment Owners Association. Any negative information on our residents is recorded in a central file. Do you see why your record will look much better if it shows that the notice came from you?"

Here's where a variety of reactions may arise. Unless violence seems to impend (in which case you leave, of course), just stay calm and polite. Explain the legal steps that can force him out. Review the reasons why he should give notice. Insist that he write it out while you're there with him. (See sample shown on the following page.)

If he won't do this, hand him your 30-day notice, and follow through with the necessary legal steps to be explained in a moment. Where the problem is chronic slow pay, refuse to accept any partial payment. And even after accepting full payment, insist on giving the 30-day notice. You've already made a firm decision to get rid of this person.

Avoid all friction if you can. Some managers get so emotional in these unpleasant situations that they cause themselves needless trouble by overplaying the tough guy, berating and harassing outgoing occupants. Play it cool. Anyone who has been ordered out of an apartment is likely to feel belligerent. After the 30-day notice (and, of course, after a 3-day notice), you'll be wise to dodge further discussion. The big idea is to get rid of this problem as peaceably as you can. This can best be done by staying clear of it.

YOU CAN RAISE AN UNDESIRABLE'S RENT as another way of pressuring a trouble-maker (but not a deadbeat) to leave. This avoids the unpleasant interview involved in the "get out" notice just described. The occupant can save face, telling everyone he preferred to move rather than pay the higher rent. The only way he can fight a rent raise, usually, is by not paying. Check this method with your attorney.

But if he doesn't pay, he may be able to stall you for another few months before being evicted. He may even pay the raise for awhile, continuing to cause trouble in the meantime, until he finds another apartment. So, you'll have to decide whether you want to force the issue by serving notice, or gamble on greasing the skids with a rent raise. If you choose the latter plan, make the raise as stiff as you dare without giving him grounds for a public outcry that he's being persecuted.

YOU CAN GET COURT HELP, if a resident won't move after receiving your notice to do so. The legal procedure is quick. It's called an "unlawful detainer" or "summary dispossess" action.

NOTICE OF INTENTION TO VACATE BY TENANT

TO: _____ DATE: _____

Dear Sir:

You are hereby advised that the undersigned will vacate the premises located at

_____ on_____.

This is a definite vacating date, and you are hereby authorized to show the premises to prospective tenants by appointment if you so desire. I understand that the giving of this notice does not relieve me of any liability that I may have under my present rental agreement, and I am complying with the State of _____ law requiring a written 30-day Notice.

New forwarding address: _____

_____
Tenant Sign

_____
Tenant Sign

(Please read your Rental Agreement regarding Security, Deposits, Refunds.)

Don't be afraid to go to court if necessary. It's simpler than you think. And you'll very seldom have to do it. The legal phrasing of a 3-day notice, posted on the door and sent by registered mail, almost always frightens people into moving. Not one resident in a hundred will force you to the final resort of having him ejected by a constable or a deputy sheriff. But just in case you ever run into the determined opponent who stretches the law to the limit, here are the legal steps for getting someone out.

Eviction suits, or unlawful detainer actions, as they are called in most states, are usually handled by an attorney. But the average attorney moves rather slowly, and every day you lose in this situation is a day's rent lost, plus whatever additional damage the occupant may do to the apartment while he holds out. Younger attorneys tend to be faster-moving, and more willing to follow a knowledgeable client's instructions without needless palaver. So, pick your lawyer carefully for this action.

Give him a copy of the lease, if the occupant has one. Give him a copy of the 3-day notice. Give him the affidavit from your server that the notice was served. Tell him, "Ask for an unlawful detainer judgment — today if possible."

Many attorneys don't know that you can get a judgment by affidavit in most judicial districts. If your attorney isn't sure, insist that he phone the court clerk and find out. The point is that if the court permits judgment by affidavit, you can sometimes hand your requested judgment to the court clerk at 11:30, and he'll step into the judge's chambers and get him to sign it while eating lunch. By 1:00 you may have a judgment in hand.

This means you've filed suit against the occupant. That is, you've requested a court writ for possession of your premises — and usually for money as well, either as damages or back rent.

Now a court summons must be served on him. After receiving it, he'll have five days (in most judicial districts) to file an answer if he chooses to fight you in court. **THE RESIDENT MUST PERSONALLY RECEIVE THE COURT SUMMONS.** You don't handle this as easily as you did your 3-day notice; the mail-and-nail process isn't enough now. And if a man and wife occupy the apartment, you'd better try hard to serve the man and wife both; some courts won't evict if only the woman is served, because the man is the head of the household.

For all you know, the person who rented the apartment from you may have left town and sublet the apartment to a pal who, in turn, has sublet to someone else, so there's someone in your building whose name you don't even know. Therefore, have your summons made out in the name of the original occupant or "John Does I, II, and III." Then you can slip it to whoever is in actual residence.

Sometimes you'll have to hire a process-server to stake out the apartment, at $4 or $6 an hour, and he may have to sit up all night to catch the resident sneaking in or out at 5 a.m. Whatever it takes, you must get a personal service.

YOU HOPE THE RESIDENT WILL MOVE OUT OR DO NOTHING after the unlawful detainer summons is served on him. It requires that he file a reply in court. If he doesn't do so, he is in the position of not opposing your suit, and the court will probably issue a default judgment against him, if you ask for it.

Suppose your papers are served on Wednesday, the day before Thanksgiving. In that case, the period of days starts on Friday, since holidays don't count. Friday is the first day. Saturday and Sunday don't count because the court is closed. Monday is the second day; Tuesday the third. If this should be a three-day summons (which it usually is, since courts recognize that a non-paying tenant holding possession of an owner's property can mean serious loss for the owner), the resident has until midnight Tuesday to file a reply. If it's a five-day summons, he has until midnight Thursday. At the end of that time you can start action to obtain your judgment.

This three or five days of waiting is a crucial period. During that time, the occupant can do several things to cause trouble for you. He can smash up the property, for which you'll have to try to collect damages later. Or he can fight you legally.

He probably can't wage a winning legal fight, which takes brains or money or both. If he has enough money to hire a private attorney, he probably has enough brains not to get into a scrape like this in the first place. But for the moment, let's suppose he goes to an attorney and says, "I've got this legal paper. It was served on me yesterday. What should I do about it?"

The attorney will look at it and say, "Hmm, unlawful detainer. Why does the owner want you out?"

He's wondering if the resident is being railroaded out in reprisal for getting you in trouble with fair housing or civil rights authorities, or something of that kind. If so, he may grab the case. But we're assuming that there's no such factor in the case — that this resident either hasn't paid his rent or has made a flagrant nuisance of himself. Once he ascertains this by questioning the resident, the attorney will say, "If I were you, I'd get out of there real fast." He'll see little chance of winning in court — or of collecting a fee.

But let's say that instead of going to a private attorney, this particular resident seeks out someone who'll help for free. He may have heard that he can get help in almost any predicament by going to his welfare worker or his local chapter of his ethnic association, or maybe his labor union. The chances are he'll go to a welfare worker.

The worker may tell him something like, "Well, gee, yes, I can see things have been pretty tough for you and your six kids, and I know you've been almost out of your mind with pain because of your toenail. So, I'll see what we can do for you. I'll call that landlord. Maybe I can induce him to let you stay, and work out an agreement so there'll be no more trouble."

One reason the welfare worker may do this is to avoid the extra work of finding a new place for his "client" to live. This would mean processing voluminous paperwork, and providing enough money for the first payment at the new apartment. So, he'd rather see his client stay put.

He may telephone you: "I see you served poor Joe Whoozis with an eviction notice. I think we can work this out amiably. We can arrange it so you won't have any more trouble."

If this happens, you should sympathize and emphathize with the social worker. Don't be cast in the role of the hard-hearted landlord who's railroading a poor man brave enough to stand up for his rights. Just quietly explain, in factual detail, the troubles you've had with this tenant.

Be nice. Tell him you understand his agency's problems, and you admire the work it does for deserving people, and you want to help him. You want him to know the facts before he goes out on a limb in court. The chances are he'll decide not to bother putting up a fight this time.

Even if he does put up a fight, there'll be an immediate trial. Unlawful detainer actions are given priority on court calendars. Be ready with your evidence to prove that the tenant gave you ample cause to evict him. If you do this, you should get an immediate judgment.

IF THE RESIDENT DOES NOTHING, at the end of the three- or five-day waiting period, you fill out a second set of papers asking for a default judgment. In essence, you've requested two things: possession of your premises, and a court order that the occupant pay some money to cover whatever back rent and compensation for damages to the apartment are due you. You'll probably never collect the money, but sometimes the judgment is a good tool to use in negotiating.

Take these papers to the clerk of the court. Some states require court appearances by the owner, or by the owner's lawyer. But in California and many other states there can be a judgment by affidavit — which means that you submit a notarized affidavit, swearing to certain things, and the court grants a judgment without further ado, if the defendant in your lawsuit hasn't responded within the time granted.

What you get — assuming that you comply with whatever rules apply — will be a judgment for the writ of possession and a writ of execution. It's usually a single form. Once you have it in hand, you can take it to your county sheriff or city marshal, and ask him to execute it by physically evicting the occupant of your apartment.

However, it's a good idea to show the paper to the occupant first, to convince him that an officer of the law will move him out forcibly, while all the neighbors watch. At this point, he is likely to leave in a hurry, saving you a sizable fee for the marshal's services.

But let's assume he holds out to the bitter end. In that case, you go to the lawman who will insist not only on the writ, but also on a stipulated amount of cash in hand — usually about $50 per room — to pay for the possible picking up, moving and storage of the tenant's furniture and belongings. Until you put the cash in his hand, he won't go to the apartment.

With money in one hand and writ in the other, the officer will go out within a few days — whenever he has time — to post the writ on the door. The family is thereby warned that it had better be out soon, or the final step will be taken. The marshal will return with a moving van, the furnishings will be carried out, and the tenants will be physically ejected if necessary. They can't plead illness or pregnancy or any other excuse; the court has ordered them removed willy-nilly.

IF A TENANT SKIPS without paying rent, or paying for damage he did, you take legal steps similar to those we've just seen. You get a court judgment against the vanished deadbeat. After 30 days you can sell certain of his belongings at a public sale. Call the newspapers to arrange for the necessary public notice, which must be published two weeks in advance. However, most states prohibit you from selling the furniture, bedding, refrigeration, or other necessities. About all you can sell, usually, are jewelry, furs, and art objects — unlikely to be found in the average skip's apartment.

At least you can sit down, have a drink, and congratulate yourself on getting rid of a bad resident. Then you'll need to consider certain problems: how to dispose of whatever he left behind; how to take possession, and how to find him in order to sue.

Taking possession is your first problem. Are you sure he really has abandoned the apartment? Just because the rent is overdue and he hasn't been seen for some time, you can't assume that he won't be back.

You're pretty safe if he's taken everything out. Then you can assume abandonment, clean the apartment, and rent it to someone else. But if it still contains anything of value, you must go through certain legal formalities, varying slightly from state to state.

Usually, you must wait until the rent is two weeks overdue. Then you must send a "notice of belief of abandonment" to the renter at his last known addresses — his place of work, if you know it, as well as his home address in your apartment building. Your attorney will help with this. Then you must wait another fortnight or so, to see if the renter responds. After that, you can go ahead, storing whatever the tenant has left behind and selling it — or destroying it, if you can certify that you believe it to be worth less than $100.

This is fairly slow and complicated, but it's a big improvement over older laws in California and elsewhere, which required owners to hold abandoned property for six months before starting the machinery for public sale.

The best way to find a missing occupant is through the rental application which you had him fill out — if you knew your business — before he got a key. It gave the name of his nearest relative or friend, a permanent home address, his place of employment, and so forth.

Another way is to ask at the post office. For a $1 fee you can get his forwarding address, if he left one. Or you can send a letter to the old address (your own building) writing on the outside of the envelope, "Forwarding Address Requested." The post office will respond, unless its rules have changed since this was written.

A third way is to call your apartment owners association. It subscribes to a credit agency which can do skip tracing for you. If your missing tenant is an expert dodger of debts, none of these techniques will work, and you'll probably never see him again. But if he's new at the game, you may locate him — in which case you can use the courts to try to collect what he owes you.

TO SUE FOR BACK RENT, you can file a claim in either municipal court or small claims court. The latter is cheaper and quicker, and you don't need a lawyer.

However, it's open to you only if the rental agreement is month-to-month, and if you're suing for no more than $500 (the limit may vary a little in different states). You can file this suit at the same time you file your eviction suit or unlawful detainer action, in California and many other states. The judge may give you a judgment for the back rent the occupant owes you, without ordering him evicted; or he might grant the eviction order but no money; or he might grant both. Your attorney can advise you whether it's a good idea to try this double-barreled action, especially if he knows the habits of the particular judge you'll be facing.

Small claims court procedures are deliberately informal, and the rules of evidence are relaxed. Both sides simply tell their stories to the judge. He wants facts, not arguments. He'll ask questions, and usually make his decision immediately.

Your first step in suing is simply to swear out a complaint before the court clerk. He sends your debtor a summons by registered mail. If there's no response, the court will give you a judgment — which you will collect, if necessary, by court order, and so on.

It's hardly worth the trouble, unless you're going after someone to show other residents that you mean business, or unless your target is long-established at his place of employment, so that you may be able to attach part of his salary or other assets without finding that he's vanished overnight.

All in all, bad occupants can cause you enormous trouble, cost you money, and waste your time. It's better to get good occupants. How can you do this? That's what we'll consider in the next chapter.

REMEMBER THESE BASIC POINTS:

* *Continuously difficult residents should be given notice to move.*

* *If a single resident dies, call his doctor or the coroner. Make sure the apartment is sealed as soon as the body is removed. You can't do anything to the apartment until a court-appointed person tabulates the contents and removes them to storage.*

* *Offering an undesirable resident cash to leave is often the simplest, cheapest, fastest way to get him out.*

* *The first step in legal eviction must be to serve a three-day notice. If you want to give the resident no alternative to moving, you send a 30-day notice.*

* *Don't be drawn into discussions of why you want someone to move. Avoid friction as much as possible.*

* *If a resident doesn't move within the specified time, after notice has been served, get an unlawful detainer judgment from a court. You can get it by affidavit in most places.*

* *The next step is a court summons, which the resident must personally receive. At the end of the several-day waiting period, fill out papers asking for a default judgment, and take them to the court clerk. Show the judgment to the resident. If he still doesn't move, you must pay cash to a marshal who will evict the resident.*

V *What Kind of Occupants Are Best?*

The word "tenant" seems to be going out of style. Some people who live in rented property would apparently prefer to be called occupants or residents or lessees. At least there's a theory that they would.

This is in line with the trend to calling a janitor or caretaker a "custodian" because the word seems to have more dignity. Likewise, the word "landlord" is a no-no nowadays because it seems to imply that the owner is lording it over poor serfs who live on his land.

Such niceties of phraseology probably don't matter to the majority of people living in apartments. They often think of themselves as tenants, and don't mind being called such. But let's assume that some people feel demeaned when they are called tenants. As manager, you certainly don't want to offend anyone in your apartments, do you? Therefore, in line with your broad general policy of seeking pleasant relations with everyone upon whom your job depends, probably you can sacrifice the short handy word "tenant" and replace it with the more cumbersome "occupant" or "resident."

HOLD ONTO THE GOOD OCCUPANTS YOU HAVE

Any "good" occupant — one who pays rent on time and causes no trouble — is a golden asset to an owner and a manager. As manager, your work is easier when the building is fully rented, because then you don't have to spend time or money seeking new occupants.

Surprisingly, many owners and managers ignore the cost of constant turnover. They seem to think it's unavoidable, like a certain amount of bad weather each year. They take pride in re-renting their apartments quite promptly, quite often! Some of them even say, "No tenant is going to tell me how to run this property. If they move out, so what? I can always rent to someone else."

They never stop to figure what it costs to rent to someone else.

The owner who has a vacancy paints the vacant apartment; gives a thorough cleaning to oven, range, tile, cabinets, shelves, glass and so on; has the rug shampooed or perhaps replaces it. The wear and tear caused by moving out and in is an invisible expense that reduces the value of the apartment in the long run. There are the paperwork costs of preparing a lease, setting up files, running a check on applicants' records, perhaps buying advertising space to induce prospective renters to come and look at the apartment, as well as the time spent in showing it to the prospects. There is also the loss of rent payments during the time the apartment is vacant.

When you add up the visible out-of-pocket expenses and the invisible losses of income, you can see how much better off financially an owner is when you prevent a move-out. As manager, you are better off, too. When you keep a present occupant, you know just what you have; a new occupant is a question mark.

So, when you have good occupants, do your best to hold onto them — even though you might have to redecorate their apartment.

It's strange how this idea horrifies some owners and managers. Yet, no owner is dismayed at the thought of redecorating a vacant apartment to attract a new resident. This contrast irritates the five-year occupant, who hasn't had his apartment painted since he moved in. Aren't you better off spending the same money to keep him happy?

Let's say you offer to redecorate the apartment of everyone — wild thought! — who has been living in the building for two years or more. If you do, they'll stay for another two or three years at least. Managers who have made this offer say that some occupants don't take them up on it until a year or so later, because they don't want the disturbance of moving furniture and having painters in. Meanwhile, with the offer available to them, they aren't angry when a vacancy is redecorated. And they aren't looking for another apartment because of a pinchpenny attitude by the present management.

Most occupants move because their apartments need repainting; the drapes are dirty and threadbare; the shower door is cracked; the kitchen linoleum is wearing through. The only way they can get a freshly refurbished apartment is to move to another building. Ironically, the unit they move into was probably vacated by someone else because it needed repainting and new drapes!

Think about the arithmetic. What will it cost to redecorate an apartment before it becomes vacant? Maybe you'll spend $120 for decorating and $40 for shampooing the carpets, a total of $160. But these costs can be spread over a two-year period. So figure your cost at $80 for a year. On a $250 a month apartment, if it were vacant for two weeks while you had it thoroughly fixed up to attract a new renter, you'd lose $125 in rent money alone. Isn't it better to spend $80 to prevent a $125 loss?

Or let's think about a thornier problem. Suppose you're in danger of losing several of your occupants because an apartment building up the street has installed more modern kitchens than yours. You can't afford to redo your kitchens.

Here again, by spending a little money now, you may prevent losing more later. Rather than let a tenant move, why not propose that he select a new appliance, and you'll go halves with him on the purchase? (Agreement should be reached that when he eventually moves, ownership of the appliance will revert to the apartment.) Let him pick out anything from a catalog — a self-cleaning oven, a self-defrosting refrigerator, whatever he wants. He'll take good care of it because he's paying for half of it. And he won't leave because he's put some of his own cash into the kitchen. Furthermore, he's probably better off financially than he would be to incur the cost of moving — and probably of bigger rent payments in the new location. And you're money ahead because the apartment is not vacant.

You've also protected yourself against complaints from other occupants, because you can offer them the same deal. You'll be keeping the people you want to keep. That's always more profitable than finding other people to replace them.

WHAT ELSE CAN YOU DO TO REDUCE TURNOVER and keep occupants happy? Maybe you can provide special maid service by the hour. Maybe you can make a vacant apartment available on weekends to visitors from out of town, so an occupant won't have to hunt up some other place for them to sleep. Maybe your office can be a service point for delivery of packages or messages. Maybe you can provide a portable hair dryer and other appliances which occupants might like to borrow. Maybe you can turn empty space into a permanent storage facility. Maybe you can keep an extra TV or radio on hand for occupants to use when theirs blow out an hour before a show they've been counting on catching. Maybe you can provide a special car wash and repair area.

Here's another thought. If you're managing apartments that need improvements which your owner can't afford, maybe some of your occupants will do the work. Quite often someone may be glad to repaint his apartment if you will provide the paint. (The cost of the paint is a tax deduction for the owner — and he's not required to report the value of the free labor as income or gain.) Just be sure the resident is covered by your workman's compensation insurance, in case he has an accident while he's doing the work.

Maybe a bathroom or kitchen needs modernizing. If you make a deal with the occupant, whereby he pays for the modernizing and you deduct it from his rent, the owner gets an immediate tax benefit — because he collects less rent on which he'll be taxed.

The owner also gets other tax benefits from such arrangements. Let's say a contractor tells you the work will cost $1,200. And the owner figures that the remaining useful life of the building is 16 years. If the cost of the work is paid from the property's money, the depreciation deduction for it will average $75 a year over the 16-year period. But if an occupant pays for the work, the owner gets a tax savings equivalent to writing off the full $1,200 in one year.

Since the bargain is so advantageous for the owner, he may be willing to sweeten it a little more for a reluctant occupant. Maybe the occupant can be permitted to deduct somewhat more than the cost of the improvement. The owner should realize that the improvement will increase the apartment's rental value later on, as well as its eventual resale value.

Whatever you do, you can't always prevent vacancies. People will move out for unavoidable reasons: illness or death, economic setbacks, a transfer or new job in another city, a need for a larger or smaller apartment.

When these inevitable vacancies occur, it's vital that you fill them with new people who will stay a long time, pay their rent promptly, and cause no trouble. A low turnover rate is the main measure of your success as a manager. Filling vacancies with the right kinds of occupants may be all you need to make your building a smooth-running money machine.

But what are the "right" kinds of occupants? People who are right for one property may be wrong for another. Different types of occupants, like gasoline and booze, don't mix.

So you need to analyze the property, and the surrounding environment, in order to decide what kind of occupants will fit best. No apartment property can have facilities that will satisfy all groups of prospects. When you know which groups you're aiming to please, you can try to adjust the facilities to meet their special standards and desires.

What is it that numerous people in your area look for when they're apartment hunting? What are they willing to pay extra for? Do they prefer pools to barbecue pits? Disposals to wet bars? Is this a neighborhood of families, or single working people, or college students, or who? And why?

Look at the buildings in the district. Is this a luxurious high-rent area? Or a middle-class neighborhood? Or a noisy commercial area? Are any new stores, houses, or apartment buildings going up nearby? (They often make an area more desirable, enabling apartment managers to attract better-paying occupants.)

A quiet neighborhood is worth higher rents to residents. Lower-paying people gravitate toward areas where a major traffic artery slashes through, or where buildings are older and more crowded, or maybe where there's something obnoxious nearby such as abandoned lofts or a freight yard or a river that sometimes overflows. People thereabouts expect to pay low rent because of the disadvantages. Obviously, you can't hope to attract well-to-do families into the finest apartment house if it's next door to a factory or a sports arena or an all-night eatery.

How convenient is shopping? Typical apartment dwellers want a drugstore, a delicatessen, and probably a bank and laundromat and branch post office within walking distance. If a supermarket shopping center is only a few minutes' drive from the neighborhood, this is another plus.

You should make a list of the area's "plus factors" because you'll need to talk about them later when you meet prospective occupants. To do a good selling job, you must be a fountain of information. As you learn, use the information to compile a booklet you can give to residents as they move in.

Is public transportation handy? If so, where will it take people, and how often does it run, and how crowded is it? Are there churches, parks, branch libraries or movie theaters, restaurants and other amenities in the vicinity?

What about schools? How near are they, and how good is their reputation? These are key questions. Fine schools cost money. Apartments in districts served by well-regarded public schools can rent at a premium to families with kids. Partly because of the poor reputations of most big-city school systems, rents often drop sharply inside the city line, even though neighborhoods may seem the same otherwise.

As we'll see later, just because your apartment building happens to be in a less-desirable area, you needn't despair. There are ways to fill your apartments with steady-paying residents, perhaps at a little higher than the prevailing rents, by using ingenuity. But first you must know the area, its bad points as well as its good ones.

We'll assume you've made your analysis of the area. Now you're ready to zero in on the kinds of occupants who'll be your best market.

OCCUPANTS COME IN SEVERAL VARIETIES. There are singles and couples and families, swingers and straights, students and old folks, squatters and empty-nesters, quiet and loud, career people and retired people, and so forth.

Let's consider the different types, what you can expect from them, and which ones fit into which kinds of apartments. Your marketing strategies will depend on the people you aim at.

To begin with, you can group all occupants into two broad categories: renters by choice and renters by necessity.

Those who deliberately choose apartment living are likely to stay longer. They'll cause fewer problems. They'll be more desirable occupants. They'll commit money and energy to making their apartments nice homes.

In this category of renters by choice you'll find career people, settled childless people, empty-nesters (couples whose children have grown and left), and retired senior citizens. They probably don't need the extra space available in a purchased house. Maybe they want the freedom from cutting the grass and sweeping the walks that renting provides. Or maybe they choose to rent because it is the easiest way to live in the area of their choice. In any case, they're satisfied with apartment living — so they won't move unless you make them dissatisfied with a particular apartment.

In the other category, renters by necessity, we find apartment dwellers who don't really want to be in apartments. They rent a place as a short-term substitute for the home they hope to acquire eventually — or sometimes just as a "pad" in which to rest briefly until they feel like moving again, or are forced to move. Military people — stable and reliable though they may be in other ways — fall into this category because they must change locations whenever their orders require it. A student away from home is in this category, too. He or she may need an apartment for a three-month quarter or a ten-month academic year.

There are many others in the same unwilling-renter category. Young families just want a place to stay until they can afford a down payment on a home. Swingers and live-together couples want a place to have fun before eventually settling down. Transient workers want a bed close to their working place until they switch jobs again. These renters tend to feel rootless and uncommitted. They can cause you big problems.

Different kinds of apartment dwellers have different preferences for location. The old saying about birds of a feather will affect them. Swingers attract more swingers. Slobs feel more comfortable among other slobs. Families with school children may try hard to get into an area near a good school — or even near an average school; some families don't want their children in top-quality schools because competition from bright students would be too intense. Contrariwise, childless people may flock into areas far from schools, so studio apartments rent quickly there.

EMPTY-NESTERS would probably be the first choice of any experienced property manager who had complete freedom to pick whatever occupants he wanted. These typically are married couples who spent most of their lives in a single-family home, raising their children, and now have chosen the carefree ways of apartment living.

They are good housekeepers. They invest in furnishings and appliances for their comfort and convenience. They are the most finicky of all renters in their housing decisions — they shop around carefully for the best housing, best services, and best management they can afford, They'll complain if there's too much noise or too little maintenance, but they hate the bother of moving. When they make a choice, they hope to stay for 10 or 20 years.

However, empty-nesters are numerically a small fraction of the prospective apartment-dwelling market. You'll probably need to appeal to other segments of the market in order to keep your building filled.

CAREER PEOPLE are probably the second most desirable type. These can be childless couples, or single men and women. They have a small circle of close friends, and the comfort and status of their apartment will count heavily.

They tend to choose smaller apartments in well-established neighborhoods, located conveniently for their work and for entertainment. Because of their careers, they may move at unpredictable intervals, so they aren't quite as desirable as their elders.

SENIOR CITIZENS, married or single, who are living on retirement benefits are also a desirable group of occupants — if their income is adequate to withstand the erosion of inflation. They tend to prefer small apartments, especially if they're watching their pennies carefully. They live quietly, pay promptly, and take good care of apartments.

They may not be able to afford the location they would really prefer, but they'll still be choosy in shopping for a place that meets their basic daily needs. An aging person who lives alone may develop disabilities that will pose problems for you as a manager. Otherwise, these people are a highly desirable segment of the market.

FAMILIES WITH CHILDREN are a big part of the rental market. As the costs of building or buying a single-family home keep skyrocketing, more and more families will probably be forced into apartments against their will. Many managers try to avoid the special problems caused by children — including a family's need for more parking facilities, more storage space, more recreation and play areas, more of almost everything.

On the other hand, some managers gladly take families, and do quite well financially. A family is more stable, less likely to move, than other kinds of occupants. Managers can count on fewer vacancies, slower turnover, less trouble with rent delinquencies and skip-outs, if the families are well chosen. But you'll need a creative management program to steer the energies of youngsters in undestructive directions.

Above all, don't try to mix families and childless couples, or families and singles, in the same building. Separately these groups can be excellent tenants. But mixing a family with other types of occupants will breed trouble because the children need to play outside. They often run up and down stairways and walkways, whooping and squalling, and their noise maddens non-parents.

YOUNG ADULTS make up the biggest segment of the rental market. They may be singles or young newlyweds. In either case, they can be a pain to managers and older neighbors. They are restless and mobile. They tend to stay up later, play the stereo louder, and generally create more uproar.

Usually, they lack experience and judgment — as well as worldly goods. Their jobs may be insecure. In choosing apartments, they tend to be attracted by superficial gimmicks. But many of them expect luxury, having grown accustomed to the life-style that their parents took a lifetime to achieve. Often they earn good money but don't know how to budget, so they're chronically short of cash - which means problems for you in collecting rents.

And yet, some managers prefer young people. A youth usually just sleeps in his abode. He eats out, visits friends, and takes trips on the weekend. He seldom bothers a manager with requests for maintenance or repairs. He may be willing to pay more rent to be where the action is.

Because young apartment-seekers are so numerous, they are a market from which you may be able to fill your building quickly. But they bring with them the likelihood of short occupancies and sudden departures. Nevertheless, you may need them in spite of the turnover among them. There are few markets where managers can keep a sizable property fully rented without this class of occupants.

STUDENTS are the least desirable occupants, as a group — partly because they are so temporary. Because their moods are rambunctious, they can be very hard on a property, causing burdensome maintenance problems. They flock into areas near college campuses, bringing few possessions and less money. If you happen to be managing a property in one of these areas, you may not have much choice of target groups for your marketing; students may be virtually your only possible market. In that case, concentrate on choosing them carefully and starting them right. (See Chapter 7 for suggestions.)

But if you have any choice at all, be cautious of students. Collecting rents from them will be harder. Now that school enrollments are falling, investment properties that rent to students will face more and more vacancies. Only those who specialize in the student market will care to face the problems of dealing with this group.

INCOME LEVEL is an important consideration in planning how to market your apartments. This is a touchy subject, but its broad outlines are clear. In general, white collar and professional people are better prospects than blue collar workers, who in turn, are easier to deal with than low income unskilled workers. To manage low income housing takes far more skill than to manage properties rented to affluent people.

Only limited parts of this book can apply to the difficult art of operating a housing complex for disadvantaged groups.

YOUR TENANT MIX is something you'll have to consider carefully before you start planning how to fill vacancies. If you have a new building to fill, you're fairly free to choose the types of occupants you want. If you have several buildings in one complex, you might rent one building just to unmarrieds, another only to couples, and yet another to families. This mix can work in a multi-building complex, but not in one building. A family doesn't mix well with either singles or the childless couples.

If you choose to have a swinger building, don't try to do any mixing, not even in another building in the same complex. The swingers' life-styles just do not fit with young marrieds in the same project. It will create more problems than you should try to solve.

Assuming that your building is already partially full of desirable occupants, you need to consider these occupants in selecting newcomers to be their neighbors. For example, if you rent to a night worker, he'll want to sleep during the day, and will be unhappy if children play nearby, or if a resident upstairs uses the vacuum cleaner or the hi-fi during the day. On the other hand, day workers and night workers might mix in an all-adult building where everyone goes out to work, since one group is sleeping while the other is away.

A good manager tries to avoid renting too many apartments to people employed by the same company. If a cutback causes heavy layoffs at a company where three of your families work, you may suddenly have three occupants who can't dig up the rent money. It isn't unusual for a 30-unit complex, fully rented, to see six families lose their income overnight if it has rented most of the units to employees of one organization. You'll be much safer if you spread the risk by signing up occupants from a variety of positions and firms.

THE TYPE OF BUILDING can tell you much about what to expect from occupants — and what sort of changes will or won't pay off.

For example, if a building has a mixture of studio apartments and three-bedroom suites, you'll have a hard time making it profitable. Your residents will be different types, with differing needs and desires. Ill-assorted occupants make a building hard to manage and hard to rent. So, you'd better strive for uniformity. Decide in advance on a "profile" of the type of person you'll be trying to bring in to fill vacancies as they arise.

This profile needn't necessarily conform to the people already in your building. Maybe some of those people shouldn't be there. For instance, if the building is five stories high and has no elevators, any elderly people on the upper floors are misplaced. You'd better figure on losing them (or moving them to the ground floor) and look for ways to make the apartments attractive to younger people who can bound upstairs without strain.

Suppose your building has mostly three-bedroom suites. Then its residents are bound to be families with children (which comprise 54% of all metropolitan families). You need to know where the schools are, and how good, so you can discuss them informatively with your prospects. You also need to take into account, in looking at your rent scales, what your probable costs will be for frequent cleaning, painting, and repairing. Children run these bills up. So the question is whether your prospective occupants could and would pay the unusually high rents you'd have to charge.

Suppose they couldn't. Then how can you rent your three-bedroom units? You can't. All-adult families seldom rent even a two-bedroom unit. So, you'd better talk to your owner about remodeling — maybe converting some units into bachelor singles or "studio" apartments, and a few into units which you can advertise as "One bedroom with den . . . One bedroom with music room . . . Bedroom and formal dining room." This strategy sometimes enables smart managers to fill up buildings that were white elephants as multi-bedroom properties.

Let's consider a few of the other choices that may loom ahead as you try to select the occupant profile, or combination of profiles.

Suppose you take over management of a complex of three buildings. One building has six two-bedroom units. The other buildings have a total of 28 one-bedroom units. The complex has a swimming pool surrounded by a patio for outdoor cooking and eating (a layout that is more and more popular in the sunnier parts of the nation). Aside from the pool and patio, there isn't much yard area. Your market analysis shows a need for apartments for singles, for couples, and for families. How do you decide which groups to shoot for?

The lack of a yard or play area is the deciding factor. It forces you to rule out families with children of ages that need to play outdoors. Garages and small balconies won't do for them; neither will the pool and patio, because adults want these for themselves. The only exceptions might be a family with a baby under 18 months, or with a son or daughter older than 15 years. Even so, you should set a limit of one minor per unit.

Never overcrowd an apartment. People want and need space to move around. No matter how compatible a couple may be, they'll soon find a one-room apartment intolerable. Rent studio apartments to singles only.

Suppose a couple applies for a two-bedroom unit, to accommodate twin babies not yet walking. You might rent to them, since the twins could share the same bedroom, leaving a bedroom for the parents. Yet, you ought to turn away another couple with a 17-year-old son and a 16-year-old daughter. Two children of opposite sex couldn't share a bedroom, so one of them would probably sleep in the living room — not a good arrangement for permanent occupants. The family won't stay any longer than the time it takes to find something larger.

What if you have a couple with a child of 15? This is a borderline case. It depends on your judgment of other factors. If you find that the family is an exceptionally good credit risk, and seems likely to be highly desirable in other ways, you might be tempted to say yes. But don't forget that your pool requires an adult in attendance with anyone under 16. You'll want to discuss this rule with the whole family before renting, and make sure there's a clear understanding that the 15-year-old will abide by this rule.

Let's say a couple with a year-old baby asks for a one-bedroom unit. Their credit and reputation are excellent. Should you accept them? Definitely not — no matter how persuasively the young couple may insist that your unit is large enough since "we can place a dividing screen by the crib." They'll be looking for larger quarters within a matter of months.

Yet, you might rent that same unit to a pregnant wife and her husband. A couple can manage quite well in a one-bedroom apartment until the child is nine or ten months old. But when that child begins to walk, the walls close in. You'll soon have a vacancy, because the family will yearn for a larger apartment. The child that is already a year old when you rent the unit will most likely see his parents make a move within six months.

When you rent to families with a small child, you should make one rule very clear at the outset, and should enforce it firmly: children are not allowed in the common areas without a parent in attendance. A toddler alone will scatter litter on the ground, scribble with chalk on the sidewalks, mark up walls with paints or crayons. Of course, there's no guarantee that a parent on the scene will always prevent this, but it can help — and can help you collect from the family if repairs or repainting are needed.

THE MOST PROFITABLE OCCUPANTS are adults who are employed and away from home most of the time, and who have no pets or children. If you can keep your building full while renting to people with this profile, count yourself lucky.

No doubt the world needs kindly apartment managers who accept children and pets because they love them. Such managers are rare, and seldom last long. Cats, dogs, and kids bring grief to managers, and run up the maintenance and repair bills.

Whether a manager accepts children and pets may indicate the rentability of the units, and their profit margin. If units stay vacant otherwise, managers start accepting animals and youngsters. Pressure of competition can force concessions — and acceptance of less desirable lessees is one of these concessions. The more concessions a building must make, the higher its expense.

SHOULD YOUR APARTMENTS BE FURNISHED OR UNFURNISHED? Usually, this depends on market conditions in the area. If the neighborhood is full of students or transients, there's a strong market for furnished units. But if it's a more stable residential area, most prospects prefer to bring in their own furnishings.

Let's say you become manager of a building with some furnished units, some unfurnished. Should you work toward an all-furnished or all-unfurnished building, or try to keep it the way it is? Here are some factors to think about.

Furnished units tend to attract people with few household possessions who tend to move often because they travel light. In Southern California, where there are probably more transients than in any other region, turnover rate in furnished units is more than 100% per year, while it's only 55% in unfurnished apartments. All over the country, you can probably figure on twice as many vacancies in furnished apartments as in unfurnished ones. Worse yet, half your furnishings may wear out in the course of a year.

Despite this higher turnover, furnished properties have some points in their favor. Your cleaning and maintenance costs will probably be lower. Little spots that need repair or touching up are less noticeable.

Then too, if you choose your occupants carefully with a view to their job stability and ability to get along with each other, you needn't necessarily have much turnover. Good choice of occupants can pay off even more profitably in furnished properties than in unfurnished ones.

To repeat: The unfurnished properties will cost you more for cleaning and maintenance. Apartments, like houses, don't show well when empty. Every blemish is more noticeable than it would be if the same rooms were furnished. The discoloration from gas heat is so eye-catching in an empty room that walls generally have to be repainted between occupancies. Also, when people move their furniture in and out, they can hardly avoid denting walls and scarring doors.

This means that the turnover rate becomes even more crucial in managing unfurnished property. Each vacancy means more expense for refurbishing. So, you'll have to concentrate hard on attracting residents who'll stay a long time.

Another factor to think about, when deciding whether to make a change from furnished to unfurnished or vice versa, is how attractive (or ugly) your furnished units will look. Many people shopping for a furnished unit are more concerned with the looks of the furniture than they are with the unit itself. They may stay for years if they feel they're getting good value for the rental dollars.

Therefore, quality furnishings can be a big plus, especially if they're almost new.

They may have a useful life of three to ten years. If your owner plans to resell the property soon, and the furnishings are good enough now to last a few years without showing their age, you can probably keep the building filled — which is extremely important to the owner in proving that the building is a good buy for the next owner.

On the other hand, remember that the rents you can charge for furnished units will begin to shrink as the furnishings deteriorate. So don't count on an easy time in maintaining the profit margin if units are full of furniture that is wearing out notice-ably. You may be smarter to get rid of all such furniture, perhaps by selling it to occupants as they leave.

SHOULD YOU PERMIT PETS? Dogs, cats, lizards, skunks, monkeys, canaries, and hamsters are all pets. They are dirty and may cause damage. Birds flying loose in an apartment can leave a trail behind and can twitter all night. Snakes and small rodents can escape and wend their way into someone else's room. Cats and dogs drop hair, have fleas, carry dirt in from the outside, and scratch drapes and furniture. Even an aquarium can leak, inundating carpets and floors.

The pet population is booming. Three of every five households — a total of 70 million households — keep some kind of pet. Of course, homeowners account for more pets than do renters. But it's estimated that nearly half of all renters own pets. So, if you enforce a "no pets" rule, as some managers do, you're cutting off nearly half your rental market.

Rather than a total ban, you might settle for limitations: no dog or cat over 20 pounds, pets allowed only on the ground floor, no pets except cats and birds (be-cause dogs bark too much, and more exotic pets pose unexpected problems), no pets unless specifically approved by management in advance. It's up to you, depending on how much you can afford to limit your market.

Usually, a better choice is to sort out the dedicated pet owner from the casual owner. The true pet-lover considers the animal a part of the household and will make sacrifices to see to the pet's needs. The casual owner doesn't care much. He won't sacrifice his own comfort or convenience for the pet.

You can quickly find out which type you're confronting by charging more for pets. Some managers charge an extra $5 to $15 per month if an occupant keeps a pet. Others tack on a non-refundable "pet deposit" of, say, $100 or $150.

Neither of these policies is a perfect solution to the problem, because once the owner pays the stated amount, he thinks he has paid for all damage the pet may cause. He doesn't worry about what his animal does to doors, carpets, grass and plants. But at least he'll prove, by making the advance payment, that he thinks a lot of his pet. The casual pet-lovers will either get rid of their animals in order to move in for less rent, or will leave you in peace while they look for an abode that doesn't charge for pets.

A good tactic is to ask the pet owner for an amount to be added to the refund-able security deposit. That way the pet owner has some hope of getting money back if his pet behaves. And if the pet doesn't behave, you have the enlarged deposit to cover the damage. Asking for the extra money is a good way of testing the owner. If he pays it, he'll be careful with his pet.

Another way to spot a true pet-lover is to ask, "Who will take care of the pet when you're out of the apartment?" The dedicated owner has already worked out arrangements; he wouldn't think of leaving his dumb friend uncared for. Casual owners probably don't worry about the matter, and may not realize or care that a dog left alone can be a noisy nuisance.

Still another way to sort out the dedicated from the casual owners is by limiting pets to certain designated areas of the property. For example, if you have several buildings on your property, set aside no more than one-fourth of them — those in the least desirable locations, near a road or vacant lot where owners can run their dogs — for renting to pet owners. The rest of the buildings are then pet-free. In a multi-story building, reserve the lower floors or the least attractive wing for pet owners. It's a good indication when someone accepts the harder-to-rent location for the sake of a pet. (Your rules for pets should be spelled out in the Occupancy Agreement, which we'll consider in detail in Chapter 7.)

As you decide on your own answers to questions like those mentioned in the last few pages, you're hammering out your "profile policy" by which you'll screen prospective occupants, thereby keeping out nearly all undesirables — you hope.

This profile policy will minimize your own emotional snap judgments in saying yes or no to applicants. Most of us tend to prefer people who are like us. Apartment managers and rental agents are likely to judge a rental applicant by whether he would want that person for a personal friend. So they may say, "We won't rent to any families with children because they'll tear up the place and make too much noise." There goes 54% of your market.

"We won't rent to people with pets because they'll soil the carpets." There goes 60% of the market.

"We won't rent to people over 65 because they get sick and die on us," which eliminates another 10% of the market.

"We won't rent to hippies, homosexuals, or unmarried couples because we don't like their morals," and there goes some more of the market.

By the time you finish eliminating groups you don't want, there may be precious few who'll qualify to live in your building. That's alright, if you know how to find those few and persuade them. Just be aware of how you're trimming your market.

Remember, too, that rules for qualifying applicants must always apply equally across the board. You can't show favoritism or inconsistency. There are laws against turning down applicants because of race, nationality, sex, or religion. These are federal laws and they are vigilantly enforced. Don't try to get around them.

On the other hand, you can set your own standards if all these groups have an equal chance to meet them. You may rent exclusively to vegetarians, bald-headed people, deep sea divers, or any other types you choose, so long as you don't discriminate on the basis of race, color, religion, or national origin (or sometimes on the basis of sex, although the courts haven't drawn all the lines yet on the battlefield of women's rights).

Once you decide which groups you will and won't rent to, put the rules in writing, and make sure all your rental agents follow them. That way you'll avoid subjective judgments in accepting or ejecting applicants. You'll also protect yourself against legal skirmishes caused by turning down an applicant for personal reasons.

IF YOUR BUILDING IS ALMOST EMPTY

Bold and imaginative measures can attract steady-paying residents into a property that is run down, in an undesirable location, and has been almost empty for years.

For example, one new manager quickly filled a seedy apartment complex by advertising it as exclusively for cat lovers. "Nobody can move in here without at least one cat, female only," he proclaimed. He knew that many lonely folks like to keep cats, but that few apartments permit them. He scaled his rent according to the number of cats the resident kept. This more than paid for the inevitable damage. He soon had a harmonious, happy group of residents — since nobody complained about anyone else's cats.

In another community, dotted with empty apartments, a manager converted her property's 40% vacancy rate into a long waiting list because she thought herself into the places of her prospects. Most of them were military families; a big military base was nearby. Reasoning that wives of military men hate to get up early to drive their husbands to the base, she leased a bus to take the men to and fro. This didn't cut her profits because she charged extra for her bus service. Families were glad to pay.

A manager of property in a horrendously noisy neighborhood capitalized on this defect by finding tenants who didn't mind noise. He advertised his apartments as "specially designed for tenants with hearing problems." Every unit was equipped with lights that flashed to signal that the phone or doorbell was ringing. He put amplified receivers on telephones. He provided earphones to be plugged into radios and TV sets; alarm clock devices that awakened a sleeper by jiggling a pillow; even a shopping service for those too deaf to do their own shopping. He guaranteed that every resident would be personally alerted in case of a fire in the building. Naturally, he figured the cost of all these extras in setting the rent, which residents paid gladly. The din outside the building never bothered them.

Terry Parker turned a shabby unprofitable building in Texas into a still-shabby but highly profitable haven for nudists. The building's poor location and the 14 apartments' leaks and peeling paint used to repel all prospective tenants. It still is an aesthetic nightmare, and its plumbing and electricity aren't highly reliable. But now, since nudity, nobody notices decor or lack of conveniences. The place has become a sought-after address, with a waiting list of would-be nudists willing to pay premium rents. The waiting list has eliminated the need to spend money on advertising.

Parker had checked with lawyers, and found that nudity is legal on private property, where it isn't accessible or visible to the public. Because his building encircles a central courtyard which holds the swimming pool, all he needed to block it from public view was an eight-foot fence across the entrance.

Parker's hardest job, he found, was persuading the owner to put up $150 for the fence, signs warning of nudity within, and a gate that could be opened only by residents. The residents now sign a standard lease, with an extra clause added, "The signer is not offended by nudity and agrees to inform his guests about the nudity." This proviso was inserted to protect the nudists from complaints to the police by other residents or their guests. If private property is screened from public view, police can't concern themselves with nudity there, unless they receive a complaint from someone within the building.

The chronic problem of juvenile mischief was solved by managers of Chicago's huge low-income housing developments. They found maintenance employees who liked youngsters and were willing to become leaders of Cub packs, Boy and Girl Scout troops for the residents' children. The same strategy might work for owners of smaller buildings in a district where children are a costly nuisance.

So, you see there are countless ways to convert an undesirable property into a desirable one. Occupants who are unwanted in most locations can become ideal occupants in a place that caters to them. If you have a major vacancy problem, use your imagination!

REMEMBER THESE BASIC POINTS:

* *Turnover is costly. Try hard to keep it to a minimum. Make concessions to good residents.*

* *In filling vacancies, analyze the building and its environment to decide what kind of occupants will fit best. Different kinds have different preferences.*

* *If you have any choice, try to select the least troublesome type.*

* *The most desirable residents are adults who are employed, and who have no pets or children.*

* *If you must take pets, ask for an addition to the refundable security deposit.*

* *If your building is run-down, in an undesirable area, you may be able to fill it by catering exclusively to some special class which has trouble finding apartments elsewhere.*

VI *Vacancy Coming? Here's What to Do*

You've been on the job as manager only a week or two, we'll suppose, when you learn that your first vacancy is coming up. One of your occupants gives notice that he'll be moving the first of the month.

This happens occasionally to the best of managers. They all have vacancies now and then, and must find ways to fill them. In this chapter we'll go step by step through the whole series of procedures to be followed from the time you learn of the vacancy until the apartment is completely ready to be rented again.

PUT THE "GOOD" IN GOODBYE. You may be irked by the news that someone is leaving, but don't turn cold and haughty toward the departing resident.

Say you're sorry — and show it by your face and voice. Say something like, "I hope you know how much I've appreciated having you here. Good occupants are rare. If you'll be looking for another apartment elsewhere, I'll be delighted to give you a reference."

Establishing a good mood is important. You'll need cooperation from the outward bound family in the days or weeks before they leave. (They're supposed to give 30 days' notice. But many people don't plan far enough ahead to do this. When they don't, you can't very well force them to stay for the full month, although you can keep the rent money if they paid a month in advance, as is customary. Otherwise, you may have to work out a prorating of the amount due.)

With the mood established, your next question can be, "Will it be convenient if I drop in tomorrow to inspect the apartment with you? I need to see what should be done to get the apartment ready for the next occupant . . . and we need to go over an inventory of the contents of the apartment."

After agreeing on a time for the inspection session, there's another detail you should get straight. Do they intend to move on the last day of the month or the first?

Maybe they'll say, "We figured on staying until our rent was up. Wouldn't that be the first of the month?"

"No, your rent starts the first of each month," you can point out. "A full month covers from the first through the 30th or 31st, inclusive, ending at midnight on the last day of the month. So, if you stay beyond that, additional rent will be due."

This may seem like much ado about almost nothing. What difference does a day make?

Every day could be important if the apartment is in such good shape that you hope to re-rent it within a few days. If a promising prospect can't take possession on the first, you might miss him altogether (unless you offer to pay motel rent for him while he waits). In any case, the sooner you can get the apartment ready to be rented, the less revenue you're likely to lose. Every day it stands empty is money out of the owner's pocket.

Furthermore, if an occupant feels you don't care whether he moves out on the 30th or the first, he may not actually finish moving until the third or the fourth. Other residents will notice this. They'll expect you to be equally lenient with them when they leave. In other words, you'll be setting a precedent that will come back to plague you.

CHECKING OUT THE OLD RESIDENT should include a detailed inspection of the apartment.

Maybe he paid a cleaning or "security" deposit. This is supposed to cover the costs of putting the apartment into rentable condition again after his departure. Therefore, if the apartment is vacated in the same condition as rented (less normal usage), you have a moral obligation to return the deposit — or whatever part of it isn't needed to cover the costs of whatever refurbishing, repairs or replacements are essential.

Some owners and managers take advantage of occupants by keeping the full deposit regardless. This is short-sighted as well as unethical. Sooner or later a resident who got no refund will learn that other people have been getting them from other managers. He'll realize that he was short-changed, and he'll talk about it. Word gets around, to the detriment of sharpshooting apartment owners.

Conversely, some residents leave their units in such bad condition that fixing it up will cost far more than any deposit they paid. In extreme cases, you may have to demand additional payment for damages — with a hint that legal remedies are available to the owner if the payment isn't forthcoming. (You'll need to use your best judgment in such situations. As we saw in Chapter 4, sometimes you can consider yourself lucky just to get rid of a destructive family, without hoping to extract any extra dollars from them.)

Anyhow, you definitely need to inspect the apartment before the resident moves out. You need to discuss with him the repairs that must be made, and their approximate costs. It's a good idea to have an inspection checklist in your hand as you go through the premises with him. You'll find a sample form on the next page.

You also ought to have a checklist of all physical items in the apartment. If it's a furnished apartment, this list will be fairly long. If not, it will cover quite a few items anyhow. Everything removable in the apartment should be listed: drapes, rugs, electric bulbs, shower head, refrigerator and so on. Maybe the occupant put in some of these, and owns them. Fine. Just make sure you and he agree on who owns what — and get it down in writing on the inventory sheet. His signature on this sheet could be important.

Signing such an inventory will deter most residents from removing things that don't belong to them. If it doesn't at least you have their written confirmation of the facts about ownership, and can use it with the police or with your attorney if you decide to regain anything they steal. They can't claim, "it was ours."

As you wind up the inspection visit, you may want to give the occupant some instructions about defrosting and cleaning the refrigerator, removing trash, turning in keys, and doing whatever else you think you can require. Some managers hand out a typewritten sheet, single-spaced, crammed with as many as 20 demands for waxing floors, washing windows, polishing furniture, scrubbing down walls, and generally preparing for a military-style "inspection prior to clearance." Some kinds of occupants will hold still for this. Others won't.

Let's hope that you've had few problems with this particular resident. In that case, your inspecting and inventorying should go smoothly. Why not use the occasion to reinforce your friendly relations with him or her? You never know when a friendly ex-resident can steer other good prospects your way. As we'll see in the next chapter, "referral by resident" is one of the most productive of leads for filling vacancies.

UNIT APARTMENT INSPECTION

Refurbish Apartment No._____

Tenant's Name _____ Address _____ City _____

Ordered By _____ Approved by _____

BATHROOM		FLOORS		CUPBOARDS	
Closet	_____	Strip & Rinse	_____	Shelves	_____
Shelves	_____	Seal	_____	Drawers	_____
Doors	_____	Finish	_____	Under Sink	_____
Mirror	_____	Vacuum	_____	DISHWASHER	
TUB & SHOWER		Spot	_____	Outside controls	_____
Seal	_____	Shampoo	_____	Inside (all parts)	_____
Clean	_____	FURNITURE		GARBAGE DISPOSAL	_____
Walls	_____	Vacuum	_____	Counters	_____
Floors	_____	Spot	_____	Sink	_____
Shower Doors	_____	Remove Marks	_____	Drains	_____
FIXTURES		SERVICE UNITS		Faucets	
Basin	_____	Hot Water Heater	_____	REFRIGERATOR	
Drains	_____	Furnace Unit	_____	Vacuum, Coil-motor	_____
Faucets	_____	Air conditioner	_____	Clean Floor Under	_____
Showerhead	_____	WALLS & CEILING		Inside & Out (all parts)	_____
Counters	_____	Spot	_____		
Exhaust Fan	_____	Wash	_____		
Check Float Level	_____	Paint	_____	PATIO DECK	
Clean Bowl	_____	WINDOWS		Panels	_____
Clean Basin	_____	Clean Screens	_____	Deck	_____
Towel Racks	_____	Doors	_____	Cement	_____
		Door Runners	_____		
		Latches & Locks	_____	OTHER	
IN ALL ROOMS				_____	
CLOSETS				_____	
Shelves	_____	KITCHEN		_____	
Walls	_____	Stove, outside	_____	_____	
Doors	_____	Burners/Reflectors	_____	_____	
DRAPES		Drip Pan	_____	_____	
Dust	_____	Vent	_____	_____	
Clean	_____	Timer Controls & Knobs	_____	_____	
Repair Rods	_____	Clean Oven	_____	_____	
ELECTRIC FIXTURES		Racks	_____	_____	
Light Fixtures	_____	Broiler Pan	_____	_____	
Bulbs	_____	Light	_____	_____	
Switch Plates	_____	Hood Fan Light	_____	_____	
Outlet Plates	_____	Hood Filter	_____	_____	
Check Switches	_____			_____	
TV Outlets	_____			Date _____	

	CONTRACTOR	DATE JOB GIVEN	DATE COMPLETED
Cleaning	_____	_____	_____
Dry Cleaning	_____	_____	_____
Shampoo	_____	_____	_____
Repair	_____	_____	_____
Replacement	_____	_____	_____

Furthermore, you may learn a lot from chatting with outgoing occupants. Why did they originally select this apartment? How did they find out about it? What features have they especially liked? Would they recommend the place to friends? And why did they decide to leave?

Even if they're leaving for unavoidable reasons, such as a transfer to another city, there may have been things they disliked about the apartment. "Would you mind telling me frankly about any disadvantages you noticed," you can ask, "so that I can try to improve?"

To stimulate them, you can ask about specific things. How was the heating and air conditioning? Did you like the kitchen? The bathroom? How about the laundry room? Do you think the building and grounds are kept up well? Did you find the shopping convenient? Is public transportation good?

You need to know the good and bad aspects of your property as seen by those who use it. Then you can improve it so there'll be fewer and fewer vacancies, bigger and bigger cash flow.

You can't depend on your own impression to guide you in making improvements. Things often look different to the resident than they do to a manager. Complaints can help you improve. Yet, some residents may not complain about little things (which sometimes make a big difference) unless you ask. And even then some residents won't say much because they're not the complaining type. But when they're leaving they're less inhibited, and are more likely to give you valuable tips about things that could be improved.

PREPARING FOR THE NEXT OCCUPANT should start as soon as the previous one disappears down the street. Take the key and walk into that vacant apartment with a note pad in hand.

You begin by looking the place over to decide whether any remodeling should be done. Now is your chance to make major improvements — if they'll definitely upgrade the apartment so you can charge higher rent, and if the owner can afford the necessary costs.

KITCHEN AND BATH are the most important areas. They are where remodeling can show dramatic improvements — the kind of improvements that prompt people to pay higher rent.

Women look first at kitchens where they'll spend much of their time. And women make most rental decisions. So this is where you too should look first in thinking about possible improvements.

In most buildings more than a dozen years old, the kitchens are depressingly old fashioned. You may find that shelving should be doubled to bring it up to today's standards. Architects now consider 60 square feet the minimum for kitchen cupboard space, plus 20 square feet of drawer space.

Cabinets may be rusty, and drawers may resist opening. So you consider ripping them out and replacing them. But maybe this would cost so much that you couldn't raise the rent enough to pay for it. (Top rents being charged in the vicinity are your invisible ceiling. You can't raise your rents much above this top, if at all.)

So you may consider other possibilities. You might leave the old cabinets on the top and make some improvements in the counter area. Or you could put in a dishwasher, a range, an attractive refrigerator. You could take the water heater out of the kitchen and put it in a closet. Any of these changes would be worth money to renters.

Sometimes strictly cosmetic improvements in the kitchen will bring the biggest proportionate returns. You'll be wise to spend a little extra to make a kitchen good looking. Colorful wallpaper — plums and apples and cherries in a pattern, perhaps —

is smart and up-to-date on one wall. Or a beautiful picture or mural on a wall will work wonders. Bright cheerful paint is good.

What about microwave ovens, indoor charcoal grills, fancy electric gadgetry? Don't get carried away. Many women don't like electric kitchens. Too many things can go wrong, they say.

What about a garbage disposal unit? People want them unless they are too noisy, as many are. Something like an Insinkerator may be worth considering, despite its expense, because it is very quiet —and durable. You should know the life expectancy of whatever you put in, for appraisers will take this into account later in setting the value of the building.

Now, onward to the bathroom. If you see an ancient tub on spidery legs, or a stained and cracked sink, you'll have to buy replacements unless you figure on poverty-level rent scales. You might tear out the washbasin, and install a little cabinet or chest of drawers under the new one.

A built-in modern medicine cabinet and makeup bar cost little but add much to the next buyer's appraisal of the bathroom. Sometimes you can inexpensively modernize a washbasin by changing individual hot and cold faucets to mixing faucets with chrome handles. Sometimes an up-to-date adjustable shower head over a bathtub, with sliding shower doors, will be worth another $10 a month in rent. A heater, inset into a wall, is also a good bet.

In luxury buildings you might spend thousands to put in sun lamps, heat lamps, a fashionable new sauna. But in renovating older middle-class places, you can't do any of this without pushing your rents far through the invisible ceiling. Go take a look at bathrooms in the highest rent buildings in the neighborhood. Do they have anything that yours lack? If so, these are what you should try to add.

Make your vacant apartment eye-catching and alluring. It is your stock in trade; you are a merchant, and you must package and display your product attractively. So study the apartment through the eyes of prospective renters. Is there color, charm, and homelike appeal? Or is the place drab and tired looking?

FLOORS AND CARPETING are often the most neglected features of an apartment. They show up most conspicuously when the rooms are bare of furniture. If floors are in poor shape, you should cover them with wall-to-wall carpeting. But this won't be enough if flooring is broken and creaky; you'd better get estimates for repairs from a floor contractor.

In most suburban apartments, wall-to-wall carpeting is standard in all living areas (living room, dining room, bedrooms and halls). Carpeting gives your apartment a strong marketing advantage. Few residents want to buy their own apartment carpeting.

Maybe the present carpeting will look okay after you get it shampooed, or at least well vacuumed. But find out how old it is before you decide. The average life of an apartment carpet is three to six years. It should be shampooed at least every year.

If the carpet is badly stained but not worn, think about having it dyed. This may cost only a third as much as replacing it. Call in a carpet expert for help in deciding. If he knows his business, he'll warn you about the pitfalls in dyeing; when a carpet is taken out to be dyed, it shrinks; the cost of picking it up and laying it again must be figured in your total cost; but if the dyeing is done in the apartment, as it should be, dye may get onto the baseboard woodwork, forcing you into a repainting job.

Carpet styles change like other fashions. What is chic today may look ancient next year. So don't make the blunder of buying high-priced long-wearing carpets. Generally, shag carpeting looks better than it really is, and is easy to repair, but doesn't wear well, which may be okay in apartments.

The best carpets are neutral in color. Their patterns are tweed or salt-and-pepper because these conceal wear patterns, burns, and soiling more easily than solid colors. Beware of yellows and celery tones; they look great when they're new, but soon show dirt and wear. Also avoid too-bright colors because they're hard to decorate around.

WALLS AND CEILINGS are likely to show you possibilities — or downright necessities — for improvement. If you find that the paint job, no matter how recent, is in marginal or poor condition, don't hesitate. You'll be money ahead by taking the time and money for fresh paint now, instead of finding after the apartment has stood vacant for a month that its appearance drives prospects away.

The first time you paint, figure on using the same color of paint each time thereafter, so you can do minor touch-ups or a single wall without a complete paint job. Be sure to keep a note of the brand and color of paint used.

Incidentally, painters are more expensive than paint, and sometimes you may be unable to find a painter who'll agree to come soon. So, in exceptional cases, if you're well acquainted with a prospective occupant, you might offer him a free supply of interior paint and a discount on the rent if he'll do the actual painting. Repeat: "In exceptional cases," remember that 19 or 20 prospects will turn away as soon as they see dingy walls. You seldom find one who'll do the painting.

How about the electrical fixtures? Outdated switches and outdated hanging fixtures mark an apartment as archaic. Better replace them. Are there other ancient features like ornate molding or fireplace mantels? (These might be considered quaint and lovable, rather than decrepit, if the rest of the apartment seems bright and convenient.)

Are any window shades or venetian blinds torn or worn? They'll be noticed. Get new ones before you show the apartment.

DRAPES are a special problem. If they've been up for a year, they should go out for cleaning. If the drapery hardware needs repairs, call the drapery man now. Be sure you've installed traverse rods at the windows. If you don't, people will put up their own and take them down when they leave, which means that the constant putting-in and taking-out will damage your walls. Use the double rods that provide for liners when necessary.

Do you have the same kind of drapes in all apartments? They give your building a better appearance from the street. But in some parts of the country, occupants put foil against the windows to ward off heat in summer, while others put newspapers on bedroom windows to keep out early morning sunlight — even when the windows already have drapes. If you have such occupants, you're foolish to worry about trying to keep your building's windows looking uniform.

Drapes have other drawbacks. Transient-type occupants want them (the drapes help them save on furnishings) but don't take good care of them; they get exposed to dirt, snow, and rain because windows are left open. Consequently, the drapes need cleaning all too often, and certainly whenever the apartment is vacated.

The higher-quality resident usually prefers to buy his own drapes. He may resist renting because drapes are included. He knows that drapes provided by an apartment building are almost sure to be second rate; apartment house drapes seldom last longer than four years. And from about the second year onward, they usually don't hang well.

To drape or not to drape? This dilemma points up the importance of knowing your market — of drawing a "profile" of the kinds of people you can reasonably expect to be interested in occupying the kind of apartments you're managing. So, if you don't recall what was said about this subject in Chapter 5, maybe you should look back and review it.

Conditions in your market may dictate that you include drapes. But if your direct competitors don't have them, or if you're upgrading the quality of residents to whom you rent, try to avoid drapes. You'll save both the purchase costs and the maintenance costs, which are high for drapery. In general, residents who'll install their own drapes are more desirable than those who like the drapes included.

DEPRESSING-LOOKING ROOMS can sometimes be made cheery and inviting if you use color cleverly and tastefully. For example, a low ceiling looks higher if the walls are painted darker than the ceiling, or if wallpaper has a pattern of vertical stripes. Contrariwise, too-high ceilings don't seem so remote if the walls are lighter, or if you paint horizontal bands on the walls. Horizontal bands also broaden a small room. So do big mirrors. Papering just one wall can give an inviting effect.

AFTER YOU'VE DECIDED ON IMPROVEMENTS AND REPLACEMENTS, if any — and have arranged for them — your next step, even if you've decided that nothing at all needs remodeling or replacing, is to get every inch of the apartment sparkling clean and in perfect working order.

Numerous managers neglect this. You wouldn't believe how many of them show apartment hunters a musty apartment with stained carpet, unwashed windows, filthy window sills, and walls marked with dirt where pictures have hung. Often, there's dirt on the floor under major appliances. (No mess disturbs a woman quite as much as accumulated dust, slops and spills beneath a sink or heater or some other appliance; even if the rest of the unit is spotless, she's likely to be in a bad mood through the rest of her visit.) Often the refrigerator has food stains, the sink is rust-streaked, the stove is encrusted with debris, and there's insect poison in the cabinets. Sometimes there are dead insects in the bathtub and in light globes, the toilet bowl is stained and dried up, the washbowl has a piece of half-used soap, the medicine cabinet shelves contain rusty razor blades, and the mirror is de-silvered. Maybe there's a fireplace full of old ashes, or a closet littered with bent hangers. As a clincher, bulbs are missing from light fixtures, or the power is off, so the manager has to show the apartment by flashlight.

You may think this is exaggerated. Certainly it won't happen on your premises, if you're the kind of manager for whom this manual is written. But vacant apartments shown by most of your competitors are likely to have some of the glaring faults enumerated in the above paragraph. Their managers always say, "We'll fix it before you move in."

People judge by first impressions. If they'll move into a seedy apartment just because a manager say, "We'll fix it up," what kind of people are they? Prospects who are moving try to "trade up" if they can, and find a better apartment than they had before. If a grimy run-down apartment means moving up, just how bad was their last place? Do you want such people in your building?

CLEANING AN APARTMENT so it will entice prospective residents is a science. You can engage a professional maintenance company to do it, or supervise the part-time handyman around the premises, or do the cleaning yourself as part of your managerial responsibilities. Let's assume that you're going to do it.

You should figure out a detailed plan, but a flexible one. Painters, plumbers, repairmen, maintenance crews and others can't always pinpoint their time of arrival. So you need a plan that enables you to clean intermittently while waiting for them.

Here's an outline that can make your cleaning job faster and more efficient. Apply it to the peculiarities of your own premises.

1.   Immediately start defrosting the refrigerator. Then apply a cleaning compound in the oven.

2.   Inspect every ceiling, wall and floor. Never ignore a squeaky floor; it can be

hellishly annoying. You can fix it with special nails similar to sharp-pointed screws. (Ask any hardware man for them.) Strip any old wax from the floor; then get it freshly waxed. Don't overlook cleaning the baseboards, window sills, ledges, and tops of double-hung sashes.

3. Make sure that all appliances and plumbing are in good working order. Check the toilet, shower, faucets, garbage disposer, dishwasher, blender, heat, air conditioner.

See that the refrigerator has the right number of ice cube trays and that the cabinets are clean inside and out. Pay special attention to the undersink cabinet. There shouldn't be any stains in the sink, any dripping faucets. Check the pilot light in gas stoves and make sure all the burners are clean and working properly.

If the apartment has a fireplace, clean out any ashes; make sure there is a proper screen and that the vent works adequately. You might want to put a couple of logs in the fireplace for a realistic homey look.

Check the latches and locks of all doors. Do they work easily? Do all electric switches work? Is the TV outlet usable?

4. Broom clean every room and closet. Clean and wipe out all cupboards and cabinets. Make sure the cupboard latches work, and the drawers pull out smoothly. (Don't be surprised at what an occupant has left behind. One manager found 150 bricks in a closet of a second floor apartment.) Clear out every last wisp of trash.

5. Now begins the real Mr. Clean treatment, starting with the bedroom or bedrooms. Clean the upper and lower compartments of the wardrobes using hot soapy water, cold turkish towels, and soft cloths. Wash the windows inside and out; then make sure they open and close easily. Wash the sills, venetian blinds, and screens. Clean the light switch and its plate. Clean the light fixtures, and the heater registers.

When you've done all this, the bedroom should be ready for the painter, carpet man and drapery man. After they go, you'll need to clean up once more, naturally. Or you can postpone some of the work listed under items 4 and 5, if they're coming early.

6. The bathroom is next. Clean its window, sill, and screen. Wash the tiles, shower door, soap dish, plumbing fixtures. See if the tub needs caulking. If it does, clean it first, and let it dry for 24 hours before you apply the caulking compound. Look for dripping faucets, stains, or worn out enamel in the tub. The tub and tile grout should be tight and without stains. Clean the toilet and water tank. Replace the toilet seat if it shows worn spots, or if it is peeling. (If you do replace the seat, leave it covered with the plastic container in which it came.) Put in a fresh roll of toilet paper. Put the medicine cabinet and mirror in immaculate condition. Clean the light switch and plate, and the light fixture. Remove lint from the wall heater and polish the chrome. Clean and polish the tile or linoleum, using steel wool soap pads.

7. Now the hall. Clean the windows, sills, blinds and screens. Clean the light switch and plate, the light fixture, the heater register. See that closets and drawers are spotless. Check the door pulls and closers.

8. Next the living room. As in the other rooms, clean windows, walls, blinds and screens, light switches and plates, light fixtures, heater register(s). Check the top of the thermostat for dust. Put the telephone next to the outlet and tie up its cord neatly with ribbon.

9. And at last, the kitchen. Bring your portable radio because you'll be here for several hours. Also bring a six-foot stepladder, which is stronger than a stool.

Get up topside to clean the cupboards and their doors. Clean the breadboard. Check the door pulls for tightness; do they stay closed or swing open? Clean the refrigerator, and leave its doors open to air out the interior. Clean the range and oven. Polish their chrome.

Clean the sink, tile and drainboard. There should be no stains in the sink and no dripping or noisy faucets. Polish the faucets. Clean the diswasher. Check for leaks under the sink, and give the undersink area a thorough cleaning. Clean the hood over the stove, and the fan. Clean the bar, desk and counters. You can clean ceramic tile grouting with a light film of ammonia and an old toothbrush. Wash the linoleum — a small section at a time — being careful to clean next to the baseboards and around the range, oven, and refrigerator.

10.   After you've said goodbye to the painter, carpet man, drapery man, and other maintenance people, move all your cleaning equipment — except your vacuum cleaner, which you'll use for final cleaning of the carpet, lineolum and tiles.

TAKE A MENTAL WALK when you've finished readying the apartment. In imagination, go with a prospect along the route he'll follow to reach the apartment.

What will your prospect see first as he approaches the apartment you want him to rent? (Never forget that renting an apartment is a problem in merchandising. Packaging and display, to appeal to the eye and nose of potential customers, are keys to modern merchandising.)

Start with the front entrance. Look at the sign. Look at the whole building as a visitor sees it from the street. Walk through the parking lot, into the grounds; then into the building — along the hall, into the elevator or up the stairs. Already you've seen enough, probably, to keep your maintenance people busy for some time — sights and smells you wouldn't want a fussy prospect to encounter. You're aiming for someone who is fastidious and tasteful, aren't you? This is the type that usually makes the most desirable resident.

After your prospect has gone through the vacant apartment, if he's still a prospect, he'll want to see whatever amenities are on the premises — laundry room, storage room, garbage chute room, trash can area, hospitality room, swimming pool, or whatever.

As you go through these areas, check the light bulbs to make sure they're not burned out. If possible, there should be a handy switch by each door, so you needn't grope in the dark while the prospect waits. (You weren't counting on showing everything by daylight, were you? Some people do their apartment-hunting in the evening.)

Is your laundry room clean? It should be checked and cleaned often, paying special attention to floors, appliances, ventilators, dryer vents, lighting, and waste receptacles.

How about your storage room? If it's crowded with junk, you can suggest to residents that they stage a "flea market" or "garage sale" to clear out unwanted items. This will get rid of many discarded items that are still usable, and earn money for residents at the same time — while prompting them to get rid of unusable debris in preparation for the sale.

Don't expect every prospect to ignore the garbage chute room which larger buildings usually have. If there's such a room in the building where he is now, he may think of it as a prime pain in the posterior, and may be wondering if yours is similar. Occupants have a tendency to pile garbage behind a door, and stuff up the chute with garbage. The chute door and wall below it may be streaked with accumulated garbage drippings. You can't cure all occupants of misusing the disposal system, so you'll have to make sure your maintenance people clean up the area regularly.

If your building, or some local ordinance, requires that cans and bottles be separated, then you need separate containers for this. They should be kept neat at all times. A trash disposal area can be an eyesore that costs you some good prospects, if you're not meticulous about policing it.

Intensive daily maintenance is needed in your recreational amenities, whatever they are. Otherwise, a visitor will see spills, stains, rips, scratches, cigarette burns and all the other blemishes left by the numerous users of common facilities. Every day, someone must straighten furniture, put away equipment such as pool cues, empty the ash trays, sweep or vacuum the floors, dust the furniture. If there was a big party in the patio the night before a prospective renter comes to call, make sure there's no sign of it when he walks through.

Pay special attention to your swimming pool, if there is one, and to its deck. Outdoor furniture should be clean, in good repair, and neatly stacked during the season — or stowed out of sight at other times. The pool water should be invitingly clean. If the pool is closed for repairs, you should put up a professionally lettered sign that says so and tells the probable date of reopening.

If there is a yard or garden or patio, it should be free of weeds and dead leaves, as well as cigarette butts and the like.

Alright. So now you've finished your mental walk. All the public areas of the property are fit to be seen by a fussy prospect. Your vacant apartment has been thoroughly cleaned. Are you ready now to put up a vacancy sign and show the premises to the first prospect who drops in?

Practically. Just a few small but important details remain to be taken care of.

Check to be sure the vacant apartment smells clean; that the heat and air conditioning are working; that the room temperature is adjusted to a comfortable level. Your checking may reveal that the utilities are turned off. If you have to show a freezing or overheated apartment by flashlight, as some managers try to do, forget it!

A DAILY INSPECTION of any apartment to be shown is essential. This is the only way you can keep it in satisfactory condition.

Here's what may happen otherwise. You may show a prospect into the apartment, and step on a litter of literature that has been slipped under the door during the days or weeks the apartment has been vacant. You are met by stale air, because the place hasn't been aired lately. A dead fly has fallen into the sink. A leaky window has stained a carpet. Get the picture?

If you make a daily inspection, you'll be forced to obtain the key, which is important. You'd be surprised how often a key is missing when a manager or rental agent wants to show an apartment.

The procedure will also remind you to turn on the lights, adjust the heating or air conditioning, or open windows for airing. It will protect you against unpleasant surprises like bugs and leaks.

If you know that your apartment is as perfect as possible whenever you start to show it, you'll feel proud of it, and will talk enthusiastically about it. You'll have the confidence to ask for top rent, and you'll get it. You'll attract high-grade occupants, and you'll be ahead of competition.

Enough said. Now you know the complete set of procedures from the day of a move-out until the apartment is totally ready for re-renting. To sum up the four basic steps, they are: inspecting the apartment to see what it needs; getting it ready; checking to make sure everything was cleaned and repaired; and re-checking daily to make sure everything remains perfect.

REMEMBER THESE BASIC POINTS

* *When you learn that a resident plans to leave, show that you're sorry. Get agreement on a time for you to inspect the apartment, and on the time when the resident will move out.*

* *Go over the inventory with the resident, and get his signature.*

* *Start preparing for the next occupant as soon as the previous one is out. Go through the apartment with note pad in hand, deciding what improvements you'll make. This is your chance to upgrade it so you can charge higher rent.*

* *Give the apartment a thorough cleaning.*

* *When you've finished readying the apartment, take a mental walk through the entire property, seeing it as a prospective renter will. Fix anything you wouldn't want a fussy prospect to encounter.*

* *Until the vacant apartment is rented, inspect it daily.*

VII   *Make Contacts That Rent Apartments*

So you have a vacant apartment, shining and dust-free and ready to be shown. Or maybe a flock of vacant apartments. How do you attract the right kind of people to come and look? There are quite a number of tested techniques. We'll examine them all.

As we do so, we'll also consider their potential for solving bigger-scale problems, along the same line — that is, how to use some of these techniques to pull in prospects by the dozen, as you may need to do if you're managing a property with numerous vacancies, or are seeking to fill up a whole "planned community" built by a developer. Big and little property managers can use similar strategies to attract prospective renters.

HOW TO AVOID SOME COSTLY MISTAKES

FIRST LOOK AT THE RECORDS, if your predecessor kept any, of inquiries and visits by prospects. Maybe these records show why people decided not to rent, or why the manager turned down their applications. Such data could enable you to plan a better program for merchandising the apartments.

For example, suppose the records indicate that many people came to look at your units — and that certain apartments rented quickly, but others stood vacant for long periods. This tells you that something was wrong with those empty apartments (or with the way they were shown; see Chapter 10 on the art of showing apartments). Better investigate now, and make the right improvements if you can. Otherwise, you may waste money in advertising these apartments, or waste time showing them. Usually, it's smarter to fix up a white elephant before putting it on the market.

Here's another example. Suppose the records show numerous telephone inquiries in response to listings or ads; yet, mysteriously few people keeping appointments to see the apartments. What does this tell you?

Probably that whoever answered the phone gave unclear directions for finding the place. Another possibility: maybe the callers were directed clearly, but were given a route that led them past other attractive apartments where they stopped off instead. In either case, you'll want to work out perfectly clear directions that bring prospects to your door with a minimum of distractions.

Do the records show dates and times when prospective renters dropped in or phoned? If so, you can probably find a pattern of busy periods and of lulls. This will help you plan your own timing of contacts, and of advertising if you find ads are needed.

Renting habits vary by location. In some areas there are swarms of apartment-hunters in early spring and early fall. In others, the last half of the month is busier than the first half. Almost anywhere, Saturdays and Sundays tend to be busier than weekdays. Look at your property's records and plan accordingly.

(If there are no records of inquiries and visits by prospects, at least you can keep such records in the future. Set up a weekly inquiry record like the one shown on the following page enabling you to tabulate visits and calls for a week at a time on one sheet. As soon as you start using it, you'll begin to see how useful it is.)

WHERE TO CAST YOUR BAIT

Where are your best prospects? If you can determine this, you can do a better job of scattering the "bait" — making the contacts — that will bring them to you. A good fisherman drops his lures where the fish are biting.

Begin by asking yourself, "If I were hunting an apartment, what would I do first?" And the answer might be, "Probably I'd go out and look around, explore neighborhoods I thought were desirable. I'd watch for signs of apartments for rent . . . If I didn't have time for exploring, I might look first in the newspapers . . . If I were new in the community, I might ask the manager of the motel where I was staying or the Rent-A-Car agency I was using. I might pick up one of those free Apartment Rental Guides available at bus stations and other places. I might stop by the Chamber of Commerce, if the community were small. I might go directly to a real estate broker. I might ask my boss, if I were taking a job in town. I might ask people in my church or service club, if I belonged. I might even ask a friendly employee in a restaurant or gas station."

All these information sources are markets from which new residents may come. Part of your job as apartment manager is to cultivate such sources, as intensively as you think advisable. Let's look at them individually.

ATTRACTING THE DRIVE-BY AND WALK-IN PROSPECTS may be your number one priority. If there are enough of these prospects, attracting them may keep your vacancies filled. In other words, your apartments may be in a location where many passersby see them daily, and you may be able to draw the right people off the street into your rental office.

How can you do this? Mainly, of course, by making the property look attractive. Nice greenery, fresh paint, clean walks and stairways all say, "Come on in." An unkempt looking exterior says the opposite. Your building itself, as seen from the street, is your most important means of contact with prospective renters. It's no use attracting them by other means if they're repelled by their first sight of the property itself.

Looking at various garden-style courtyards, you may wonder what ever happened to American know-how. Many of these yards contain only grass — plus dandelions and crabgrass and cigarette butts and gum wrappers. But at no more cost than you'd need to keep the weeds down, you could build a flagstone walk through beds of petunias and marigolds, or a curbed walkway leading around junipers to a rustic bench. Attractive landscaping will increase occupancy by about 5% on the average.

Of course, you can't wait for new landscaping to fill the vacancies. Just a thorough clean-up is all you may be able to do immediately. But landscaping is something to think about as part of your long-range planning. A nurseryman or landscape gardener will probably be glad to tell you what will grow attractively on the property, and give you an estimate of costs, if he knows you plan to buy plants from him. What you need may cost only a few hundred dollars, plus a monthly payment of $30 to $80

WEEKLY PROSPECT SUMMARY

DATE_____   TO_____

Inquire of each prospect: How did you learn about us?

Sign_____   Tenants_____   Brochure _____
Classified_____   Visitors_____   Flyer_____
Display_____   Business_____   Friend_____

Others_____   Total This Week_____

TYPE OF UNIT WANTED

	STUDIO	EFFICIENCY	1 BR	2 BR	3 BR	TOTAL
Furnished						
Unfurnished						

NUMBER OF DAILY CALLS

MON.	TUES.	WED.	THURS.	FRI.	SAT.	SUN.	TOTAL

WHY PROSPECT DID NOT RENT

Distance from work_____   Transportation _____

Distance from shopping_____   Other_____

Too expensive _____   Qualifications_____

Square footage _____   Children_____

Possession date_____   Pets_____

Someone else _____   Lost rentals, qualified prospects_____

RENTED: Studio   Efficiency   1 BR   2 BR   3 BR   TOTAL

_____   _____   _____   _____   _____   _____

Resident Manager _____

for a gardener — or less, if some of your residents are green thumb types who enjoy tending plants themselves.

At night a well-lit property is as alluring to prospects as candles are to moths. Good lighting spells greater security from crime. It makes residents feel happier and safer. Contrariwise, dark grounds and dim halls look scary; a wandering apartment-hunter won't go near them.

The cost of using a 100-watt bulb for ten hours is only about two cents. So, think now about spending a little on exterior lighting; tonight it might just bring you the prospective residents you need. Your building can cast a friendly glow, advertising itself all night long, highlighting the best features of its exterior and its entrance.

However, even a well-lit property sometimes can't attract many prospects if it is on a dark street. How is the street lighting on your block? Maybe you should check with the utility company or the city engineer's office, and see if a better street light or two can be installed.

SIGNS probably attract more apartment-hunters than any other single business-getting technique. Almost every building has some type of sign. The apartment sign is an important form of advertising — a landmark not only for prospective residents, but also for repair services, delivery people and everyone else who is looking for your building. So it's important. It should be designed and produced carefully and artistically. Get a professional to do the job.

Make sure your sign or signs are always clean, well-landscaped, properly lighted, and visible to people approaching the property; that is, at right angles to traffic, not parallel.

The great majority of apartment signs are a downright detriment to the buildings they represent. Million-dollar complexes sometimes flaunt cheap, worn, dingy signs that make residents ashamed and prospective residents disinclined to walk in. Or sometimes they have perfectly good signs that can't be seen from the street. Either a bad sign or a poorly placed one is a waste of money because it does nothing for your apartments.

Your signs should give a feeling that they belong there, not that they were stuck in as an afterthought. But they shouldn't blend in with the color of the building because this camouflages them so that passing traffic may not notice them. Ask your sign man to design something tasteful that will catch the eye, yet conform to the color scheme and architectural style of your building.

For example, if your building is in the Spanish style, it might have a house-shaped sign reflecting the same motif, with a roof of red tile, suspended from a wrought iron bracket. At night a small light could show up the black or red lettering.

Another possibility — especially for larger buildings or complexes — might be some sort of three-dimensional structure placed prominently in front. It could repeat its message on two or three sides of the sign if traffic flows in several directions.

The permanent message on your sign might itemize some of your facilities, somewhat like this:

EMPASSY APARTMENTS
1 - 2 - 3 Bedrooms   From $175
General Electric Kitchens — Pool and Patio

Admittedly, a prospect driving past may not absorb all these words. But if the sign catches his eye, he may slow down enough to read most of the message. And strollers can read it all, of course. Just be sure your most important information is up where it will be seen quickly.

Before having permanent signs made, you'd better inquire about city or county ordinances regulating them. It would be too bad to install a fine sign and then have to junk it because of some municipal code governing its size and placement.

Once you're sure a sign is right, arrange to have it lighted so it will be working for you after dark. Of course, you don't want anything garish or gimmicky; flashing lights or neon can spoil the home-like atmosphere you're striving to project.

Under the main sign should be hooks on which you can hang smaller signs, removable and interchangeable, advertising vacancies. Apartment-hunters watch for signs that indicate vacancies.

If you have a vacancy, just say, "2 bedroom 2 bath, unfurnished," in big letters that people can read as they pass by in cars. You don't need superfluous words like "apartment for rent."

A few apartment buildings on major boulevards keep almost full by hanging out only a one-word "Vacancy" sign. But these are extreme cases in tight-rental areas. In normal times and places, the sign should be specific about the type of vacancy available, so it will draw only the prospects who seek what you are offering.

And on extra-quiet residential streets where there's little through traffic, the best signs may not pull in any prospects. Even so, a vacancy sign is worth posting, if only because it makes residents aware that an apartment is available; they may bring friends to see it.

A vacancy sign used to be frowned upon, as cheapening the appearance of a building. But now it is generally accepted, because it is seen in so many business locations and at elegant motels. Just be sure it's in a prominent place and professionally lettered, even if you have no permanent sign at all.

"No Vacancy" signs are strictly for overnight stop motels. Good apartment managers never put one up. When all units are occupied, the manager's own apartment can be shown, to give prospects an idea of what the units are like, and people who want to rent can be put on a small waiting list. If your waiting lists get long, this usually means your rent schedule is too low!

There are certain other kinds of signs that should never be used. These include signs put up by property owners or managers who like to behave like top sergeants: KEEP OFF THE GRASS . . . QUIET IS REQUESTED AFTER 10 P.M. . . . DON'T POST MESSAGES ON MAILBOXES, and the like. The effect is the same as if a hotel posted signs in its lobby, "Put cigarette butts in ash trays." You don't want that kind of atmosphere. If you have a specific problem with residents doing something undesirable, or if you need to inform them about some situation, the best way is to distribute typed memos.

Detrimental signs also include those put up by contractors, suppliers, and tradesmen to advertise themselves in apartment developments. Don't allow them. Remove them if they appear. They just add to the clutter and the eyesores, as if you were living in the middle of a marketplace. A few signs may be required by law — swimming pool signs and OSHA (Occupational Safety & Health Administration) posters, for example — but you should post only what the law requires, and avoid everything unnecessary.

DIRECTIONAL SIGNS, posted some distance from the property, are often used by managers of major new apartment complexes, to supplement an advertising campaign that is supposed to bring people out in search of the advertised development. If you do this, put up as many as you can — on telephone poles, trees, fences, or even fixed to small wooden stakes so you can stick them in strategic areas early Saturday morning and pull them out Sunday evening.

These signs can be cardboard, 18″ or 20″ wide, and one foot from top to bottom. If they're too large, the law may not allow them. Remember that their sole purpose is to direct people to your place; don't try to do a selling job, too. Just indicate the name of your apartments and their direction. The signs are useful only if a motorist can read them through the windshield while traveling at the legal speed limit.

One apartment manager in a highly competitive area posted direction signs at every intersection within three miles of his building — some 75 in all. He told a reporter afterward:

"We really didn't know what to expect. In the beginning, nothing much happened. A few prospects did mention that it was easy to find our complex with all the signs on the road. But gradually we found a more important effect; brand recognition. People kept seeing those signs, and our name began to penetrate into their minds. Naturally, we were one of the first places they would visit when they were ready to rent. The response from our newspaper ad improved because people were familiar with our name. There is no doubt that our vacancy factor has been down since we started this program several months ago."

HOW TO BUILD A NETWORK OF VOLUNTEER SALESPEOPLE

Prospects who walk in off the street just because they've seen your signs and liked the looks of your place, may be enough to keep your building fully rented. Even so, you'll find yourself wasting a lot of time on unqualified prospects who don't want what you have or are undesirable. You need to be extremely careful in sizing up these strangers, and checking their references, to make sure you don't get stuck with oddballs, misfits, or other "problem people" to whom we introduced you in Chapter 4. Just one bad guess in renting can be costly.

Instead of trying to guess right among hordes of prospects about whom you know nothing, it's much easier to talk with prospects referred by someone you know. Through this mutual acquaintance, you already have a rough idea of what they're like, since birds of a feather flock together. Likewise, these prospects probably know that your apartments are approximately what they want.

For those and all other reasons (such as the likelihood that one good referral will lead to other good referrals), your first priority in a continuing program for keeping your apartments filled should be to spend some time — and maybe a little money — in encouraging your friends and acquaintances to recommend your apartments to their friends.

FREE ADVERTISING MAY BE THE BEST and fastest way of keeping your building filled, as long as you have only a few vacancies. Word-of-mouth recommendations often are free and unsolicited, if your building deserves them. (However, it's better to pay for every recommendation that produces a rental, unless your apartments are in demand and vacancies are scarce.)

Everyone living in your apartment building is a potential walking, talking advertisement for it. Your best salesmen can be those who know your apartments, live in them and like them. Furthermore, your best prospects are those who get interested because of a recommendation from someone who already lives there.

A friend of a resident is probably the same kind of person as the resident; has probably seen his friend's apartment; probably likes the building; is probably ready to rent. The resident has already done the job of informing and exciting the prospect — which you yourself would have to do with a stranger.

Consequently, you might consider paying a little when such free advertising fills a vacancy. Why not give a reward to any resident whose referral leads to a rental? Remember that a vacancy doesn't cost the owner $20 or $50 — it costs him hundreds of dollars. A quick referral can avert that loss. Your reward for the referral will encourage other residents to spread the word next time a vacancy occurs.

If your development is so big that you need a steady stream of prospects to fill vacancies, make sure all the residents know that you welcome and reward referrals. Put this in writing. Here are a couple of sample letters which you can adapt for your purposes:

Dear Resident:

Maybe you have a friend who is looking for an apartment. We have a vacancy — a two-bedroom upper which rents for $190 a month. (No pets — one child considered.)

Naturally, we'd welcome someone recommended by a preferred occupant such as you. Therefore, if this vacancy is filled through your recommendation, I will be pleased to present you with a $25 gift certificate.

The apartment can be seen now. Please be sure to give me or the manager your friend's name before he looks at the apartment — or better yet, bring your friend in and introduce him — so that you will be credited as the sponsor.

Sincerely, _____ , Owner

*   *   *

WOULD YOU LIKE AN EASY $50 OR $100? Extra cash for a night on the town . . . a new piece of furniture . . . a new suit or dress? It will be our pleasure to give you $50 for each person you recommend to Marina Playa, as soon as the person takes occupancy. We'll send your check that same day. Just be sure to introduce your friend to us on his first visit, or have him tell us you suggested that he visit Marina Playa. The following residents have already received some of this easy money:

Ms. Norma Fitzpatrick   —   Mr. & Mrs. Milton Anderson   —   Ms. Rebecca Nervig

Why not join them?

The more vacancies you expect, the more intensive your referral program should be, especially on your own premises. Set up a bulletin board in the laundry room and post notices about recommendation rewards. Use your residents' newsletter, if you have one, to announce each award as you pay it. You might even drum up a contest to encourage tenant referrals.

In March of 1977 we had a sudden outflow of tenants, many of whom had lost their jobs in the recession. So we announced a little contest. The first tenant to make three recommendations would win a color TV. In addition, there was a special bonus of $100 for anyone making two recommendations.

The tenants really talked it up. They talked to friends, neighbors, anyone they knew, and asked if *they* knew anyone interested in moving into the finest apartment complex in Los Angeles. Some tenants went right to their personnel departments at work and recommended us. Would you believe that one guy was responsible for three rentals in 60 days? This has to be the best promotion we've ever used.

Here are some points that will help you run a profitable program of resident referrals:

1. Don't combine information about the resident referral program with other informational fliers. It might get lost in the garbage.

2. Whenever new residents move in, make sure they receive full information about your rewards for referrals.

3. Keep a copy posted on the resident bulletin boards as a reminder. It should include an up-to-date list of everyone who has received rewards.

4. Distribute reminders every three months or so.

5. People want to know what happens when they send someone to you. Report to them immediately, regardless of the outcome. Even if the prospect didn't rent, this feedback is a courtesy that builds good will and may lead to more referrals.

YOUR AREA IS FULL OF FREE REFERRAL SOURCES. Nearby markets, discount houses, pharmacies, laundromats and other gathering places often have public bulletin boards which carry all sorts of notices about things for sale, for trade, or even for free. These are good places to post a neatly typed card describing the unit you have available, your address and phone number.

In fact, virtually every small merchant and service establishment near you — gas station, barber shop, restaurant, sporting goods store, or whatever — is a potential source of referrals. The people who run these enterprises hear lots of neighborhood news. They want the business of every newcomer, and a good way to get it is by helping a newcomer find a place to live. As you shop, you can tell them about your apartments, and urge them to keep you in mind whenever they hear of a good prospect. If you have brochures or advertising leaflets, you can ask for permission to leave some.

You may decide to do more. You can guarantee that a merchant will sell $50 worth of products every time he refers someone who rents one of your apartments. How can you guarantee this? Simply by giving the new resident a certificate worth $50 in merchandise at the store which referred him to you. You yourself buy the gift certificate from the store and hand it to the resident. Obviously, any retailer will be receptive to such a plan. The plan isn't universally practical, of course, You can't very well give $50 certificates for use in a candy store or barber shop. But it's a great way to steer business to a furniture store, for example, because people often shop for furniture as soon as they rent an unfurnished apartment. Furniture rental places would be good prospects, too — especially the one you deal with if you maintain furnished apartments.

In cases where a gift certificate isn't applicable, you may want to pass the word that a cash gratuity will be forthcoming for any referral that leads to a rental. You should make this known to small hotels and Mom-and-Pop motels because newcomers often stay there first; moving company personnel, because they know of a move before it happens; all delivery people, like milkmen and cleaners, and service people such as those from the telephone company and the gas company.

Show them your premises. Point out the good features. Tell about what you do that makes the property a good place to live. In other words, establish extra-friendly relations and practice your sales talk on the people who come to your property to perform services. They're in contact with countless prospects, and can become good salesmen for you. Be sure to give them leaflets or at least your business card. One card given out in California traveled all the way to South Carolina and returned in the hands of someone else who rented an apartment.

A word about hotel and motel managers. Even though you offer them $50 or

$100 for any residents they may steer to you, they soon forget. They may let your brochures gather dust under a counter. So you need to personalize your program for them, and keep following up.

Make sure that they understand that their referrals must mention their name if they are to get credit. Urge them to stamp their name on your brochure and give it to the prospect, or else send their business card with the prospect. You yourself should make it standard unvarying practice to ask the prospect, "Where did you hear about these apartments?" Otherwise, there'll be cases where a prospect forgets to mention that someone referred him to you, leading to your uncertainty whether to pay a bonus.

Telephone immediately and thank anyone who sends a prospect to you, and let him know the outcome. If the referral turns into a rental, mail your check instantly, or deliver it in person. Somehow the extra speed makes people remember you twice as favorably. Drop in whenever you can to check on the visibility of your brochures, and to refresh the managers' memories.

BIG ORGANIZATIONS CAN SEND MANY PROSPECTS TO YOU. They're always hunting good housing for their transferred employees. Military bases, colleges, hospitals and other institutions are forever compiling lists of apartments to pass out to people coming into the area.

If you take the time to negotiate with them, some of these organizations may go so far as to guarantee rents and good occupants. You needn't operate a big complex in order to do business with a big company; many of their employees prefer to live in smaller apartment buildings. Nor need you limit yourself to soliciting the personnel departments and "housing directors" of the biggest organizations in your vicinity. Satellite companies and small industries may be even better prospects; their personnel need housing, too. Take their personnel directors to lunch and invite them to your building to see what you have to offer.

Big organizations may or may not be worth your time. In some areas they deal exclusively with full-service realty firms which offer a range of services including home sales and mortgage financing as well as apartment rentals. You can find out with a few phone calls.

Some company may need you because it runs six-month or one-year training programs for groups of people who stay in the area only during the training period. If you manage a large enough complex, you might be able to contract directly to provide apartments for the company's whole training group, with the company paying for cleaning and repairs at each move-out. Training directors often prefer to sign up permanently for a block of ten to 30 apartments; it simplifies their housing problems, and of course, can solve your vacancy problems.

Even if all major companies in your area seem to be sewed up by real estate firms, there's no harm in trying to break the monopoly if you're in need of many new residents. You might do this by offering companies a $100 "moving allowance" whenever an employee rents one of your apartments. The company can keep the money as a bonus for sending you an occupant, or can pass it along to the employee as a corporate fringe benefit in reimbursement of moving expenses — or can direct you turn the money over directly to the incoming resident. (The latter seems best to many companies, because if they don't ordinarily pay this fringe benefit, there would be questions about why some employees get a moving allowance while others don't.)

The letter on the following page was used by one apartment-management firm to sign up companies for its referral bonus program.

XYZ Company
Your City

Attention Personnel Director:

May we give $100 to your firm?

We suggest that you pass this $100 on to an employee of your company as a moving expense reimbursement, a fringe benefit offered by *your* firm. As an employee of a select firm in this area, your company personnel are ideal apartment residents. To encourage their residency, we offer to pay directly to your company the $100 in reimbusement of your employee's moving expense when he or she moves to our beautiful MONTEBELLOW HOUSE apartments.

Let us introduce your next apartment-hunting employee to the gracious, spacious, country living at MONTEBELLO HOUSE luxury apartment homes. To introduce an employee to us —

*   Post the enclosed brochure on your company bulletin board;
*   Use the "introductory" cards enclosed and give them to interested employees;
*   Keep this letter handy for future reference.

To register for our $100 gift program, send back the enclosed business reply card today.

Cordially yours, _____ , Owner

When you aim for tie-ups with sizable companies, you'll need a good brochure and some leaflets. (We'll consider these in the next chapter.) And you'll also need to talk informatively and persuasively about your apartments. So make sure you're well prepared when you approach these major prospects.

One point to keep in mind, as you prepare, is that corporations and institutions are concerned about the welfare of their people. They know that burglaries, vandalism, muggings and other kinds of crime are rising in residential areas. So they'll want to hear about safety aspects of your apartments — dead bolts on doors, adequate lighting in halls, alleys and garages, locks on windows, secure storage areas and so on. They may also hope that your development contains recreational facilities that the company may itself lack.

Some companies may have strict policies against recommending housing. But there are avenues through which you may still work out a deal with a few of these companies, if it's important to you. One channel is the employee recreation association, which is always independent of the company; get in touch with the association president and ask his advice on the best way to make your offer known to the membership — which includes almost everybody in the company.

Another possibility is the company credit union, which usually handles all discount offers to employees. It may be glad to get your offer, and since it too is likely to be independent of the company, it can often be persuaded to pass along your literature.

Still another possibility is a labor union, which often hunts housing for members as one of its special services. It doesn't represent salaried employees who are probably your prime prospects — but there may also be a Foreman's Association and/or a Management Club composed of higher-paid people who might be excellent residents. These groups too can use their own judgment about recommendations, independently of the company.

You'll encounter different degrees of cooperation at different companies and from different officials within the same company. Some will distribute your brochure or your discount certificates. Some will let you put a poster on the bulletin board, and will hold certificates in their office for those who ask for them. Some will give certificates only to new employees. Some will handle your literature just as they would a wad of wet Kleenex. Keep trying. You'll find cooperation in unexpected places.

LOCAL APARTMENT MANAGERS WILL REFER PROSPECTS TO YOU if you approach them tactfully.

Go to see them, introducing yourself as manager of whatever apartments you manage. Tell them that quite often you don't have what someone wants in the way of price, size, location, or whatever. "I'd like to be able to refer them to places that would suit their needs," you can continue. "I think your apartments might be just right for some of them. Can you tell me about your rent structure, facilities, and whatever else a prospect should know?"

After they finish talking, you can thank them, promise to send qualified prospects – and then mention casually, almost as an afterthought, that occasionally they too must be unable to help a good prospect. Would they like to be able to refer such people to a non-competitive apartment building such as yours?

Of course they would. By first volunteering to help them, you've soothed their fear of competition.

The key to the success of this program is to tie up with good buildings that aren't similar to yours. If you take children, go to adults-only developments. Go to higher-priced and lower-priced places than yours; larger and smaller ones; those in sharply different neighborhoods – and so on.

Many competent managers are glad to refer prospects whom they can't help. Give them some of your brochures, or at least an information sheet, and explain your policy of paying referral fees. Leave some referral cards with them, and keep in touch.

You can take the initiative in organizing a sort of club of apartment managers with reciprocating referral agreements. Then, if one manager doesn't have the type of unit a prospect wants, he knows of places that do. Someone may want a more elaborate apartment, or a simpler one, or maybe a one-bedroom apartment when there are none available. Whatever he wants, it probably exists in one of the buildings in the group. The manager can enjoy telling the prospect where to find what he needs. It's always a good feeling to play the "nice guy" role. It's also good business in the long run, as any smart manager knows.

As a leading spirit in such a reciprocating group, you're likely to reap more benefits than anyone else – because the other managers probably won't ta▨ trouble as you do to familiarize themselves with other properties. If you▨ your apartments to 20 or 30 managers, left brochures and business cards▨ maybe even brought them out for a tour of your place – you'll be the▨ member best, especially if you're the one that has referred a few prosp▨ So the odds are likely to be 20 or 30 to one in your favor.

REAL ESTATE BROKERS CAN BE PART OF YOUR SUPPLEME▨ FORCE, too. They're primarily interested in selling homes, of course,▨ help you rent apartments if they know that you pay $100 or $15▨

Helping you is actually a logical adjunct to their main business, as y▨ them. Every time they sell a home, the seller becomes a hot prospect▨ rental.

Brokers' work brings them in contact with "empty nester" couple▨ homes because the children have grown up and departed. Empty neste▨ want to be bothered with keeping up a house any longer. They want ap▨

the gardening, housekeeping and other chores are done for them. If your property caters to such people, realtor referrals are a ripe market for you.

Realtors also meet families who arrive in town hoping to buy or rent a house, only to find they can't afford the going rates. These families must hunt apartments instead. Often they have children or pets. Maybe you accept these.

Brokers should know whether you do or don't so they can refer only the right kinds of prospects. Many real estate firms have rental departments. Some of them charge clients $10 or $20 for a list of valuable vacancies. Some charge an owner two weeks' rent for finding a new occupant. But the people in these departments aren't always energetic. You can energize them to some extent by offering higher commissions than they customarily get. Then you can help them along by printing "introductory" cards for them to hand to interested prospects. A supply of rental brochures will also help, particularly if they show the location of your complex on a map.

One property manager printed introductory cards on which a broker could insert the prospective occupant's name. The broker was to give one of these to anyone who sold a home but intended to stay in the vicinity. The card offered the client a move-in gift "since prior home owners make such desirable apartment residents," and the broker was paid $100 whenever a card produced a rental. Thus, the broker could sell a client's home and then offer the same person the extra service of locating an apartment for him, at no charge to the client (but at a profit to himself). A good deal for everyone, including the property manager.

As in all forms of personal contact promotion, you'll need to keep in touch by phone and in person if your realtor referral program is to succeed. You'll gradually learn which brokers will work with you and which ones won't. Drop the deadwood; cultivate the live ones. Make sure your apartments always pop into their minds when they meet someone who'll need an apartment.

GET ON THE RIGHT LISTS

YOUR APARTMENT SHOULD BE LISTED IN THE YELLOW PAGES of the telephone book. However, a simple one-line listing of your apartment development name in boldface type is all you really need. You're entitled to this much free of charge, if your apartment complex is listed as a business telephone in the regular phone directory.

If you like, you can pay a little extra and include the hours when your "rental information office" (if you have one) is open, and an emergency telephone number for the benefit of your own residents who might look for it in the yellow pages.

The main value of the yellow pages is their convenience for delivery people, contractors, friends of residents, and others who are looking for the apartment development but aren't sure of its exact name. Only rarely do prospective renters shop for apartments in the yellow pages. The higher the income and education of the apartment hunter, the less likely he or she is to consult the yellow pages. This being true, you'd be foolish to buy a one inch listing there, or anything larger. You'd be paying for circulation to huge numbers of people who aren't prospects.

LISTING IN OTHER DIRECTORIES may or may not be worthwhile, depending on the size of your property and its budget for advertising — and on how effective the directories are.

"Apartment Rental Guides" are published in many areas. They are usually made up of full-page display advertisements by different developers. You can buy a page for a fraction of what a newspaper ad costs. It can show photos of your facilities together with a complete message about them.

Some of these directories are sold, but most can be picked up free at high-traffic points such as airports, shopping centers, the Chamber of Commerce, moving companies, car rental agencies, hotels and other places. The people who pick them up and read them are almost always in the market.

In some areas, these guides can bring you plenty of prospects; in others, they can't. Unless you happen to have inside information, the only way you can decide whether a page is a good investment is to invest and watch the results.

CLASSIFIED ADS MAY BE FREE in some giveaway "community newspapers," "shopping guides," and other free newspapers. Tests show that these papers are read closely by bargain hunters in some areas. The papers can afford to publish classified ads free of charge because these are good circulation-builders. If listings are available at no cost, why not try them? You've nothing to lose except maybe some time spent talking to unqualified people.

At least four cities in California have a service known as Homefinders Bulletin. Every day it publishes a bulletin of available rentals. Listing is free to property managers and realtors; Homefinders makes its money from a $10 monthly charge to subscribers seeking homes or apartments to rent. The guide itself is comprehensive, usually giving the following information in each listing:

Location	Deposit requirements
Bedrooms	Lease requirements
Bathrooms	Conveniences
Type of dwelling	Restrictions
Rent	Availability date
Furnishings	Address and phone number

If there's such a service in your area, make sure you're listed. It's a fine chance to make your vacancies known to a great many prospective renters.

APARTMENT LOCATOR SERVICES CAN HELP YOU FILL VACANCIES, and you pay nothing until they get results. These services sometimes call themselves rental agencies, free rental services, and the like. You'll find them listed in the yellow pages. They are commercial services that will direct apartment hunters to your property; if a hunter becomes an occupant, you pay the service a fee which is usually two weeks' rent.

Despite their high prices, these services can be profitable to management in areas where the vacancy rate is high. They save a prospect time in shopping around; when the service determines what the prospect wants, it gives him a list of vacancies that meet his needs. What the prospect doesn't realize is that the service will refer him only to apartments from which it will collect a fee.

You'll be smart to maintain friendly relations with these services, and pay them promptly, but use them sparingly. Too many managers become dependent on them, instead of working to develop their own contacts (which cost far less and bring more prospects than the locator services). If a manager has, say, a 50% turnover ratio, he adds significantly to his overhead by using rental agencies. The more he uses them, the less he rents on his own. If you've built up a good network of contacts of your own, the chances are you won't need a locator service except in rare emergencies.

YOU SHOULD BE A CHAMBER OF COMMERCE MEMBER. In a small community, and even in larger ones, the Chamber can be one of your key contacts. Few apartment managers join, so you'll be more in the spotlight.

The Chamber will exhibit your brochure and even some of your promotion literature. When it gets rental inquiries, as it often does from newcomers, it will verbally recommend your property.

The Chamber can help you get acquainted with executives of the corporations and institutions that may steer rentals to you. It can put you in touch with broker and service organizations.

It can also provide you with lists of good prospects, such as people who have recently inquired about moving into the area; executives being transferred in by their employers; retiring executives who want to give up their homes and take apartments; and other prospects to whom you may want to mail brochures or even personal letters.

The staff director of the Chamber is usually informative and helpful. He'll be glad to chat with you at length, giving you a feel for local conditions that may make a difference in your marketing plans.

By cultivating the kinds of contacts mentioned in this chapter, you should fill many vacancies as fast as they occur. One manager of a 36-unit apartment house didn't lose a single day's rent in two years merely because occupants kept referring good prospects, and because she kept in touch with the nearby naval hospital, air base, and chain store headquarters.

Even if you manage a big complex with dozens of vacancies and a high turnover rate, enough good contacts will keep a steady stream of good prospects coming to your door. But you can only generate this stream by intensive, systematic cultivation; going back to all your good sources at regular intervals.

YOU'LL NEED GOOD RECORDS OF YOUR FIELD CONTACTS if you're seeking large numbers of referrals. It isn't hard to set up a good system. Just get a stack of blank 3"x5" cards, and a metal file box with cardboard dividers which will separate your contacts into groups such as other managers, dealer-brokers, institutions, corporations, merchants, and so on.

Samples of contact cards (front and back) are shown below.

FRONT

Type of Contact: _____		
Name _____		
Address _____		Phone No. _____
Date	Person's Name & Title	Result
(4/11/78)	John Smith, Broker	Left brochure & referral letter

BACK

Date	Name	Phone	Rented	Reason for not Renting
(2/4/78)	Al Barnes	263-1411	Yes	
(3/9/78)	Ms. Alice Patience	666-6641	No	Too Small

Review these cards for a few minutes every week. They'll show you the most productive sources, and the ones which need more cultivation. Set up a weekly schedule of old contacts and new contacts, and work at it during part of each week.

IN CERTAIN MARKETS, CONTACTS WON'T DO THE WHOLE JOB. Some areas are overbuilt, creating an over-abundance of available apartments; other areas get hit by business reversals that throw hundreds out of work, causing widespread vacancies. Neighborhoods change.

The average number of prospects needed to rent a unit in a building with moderate rent is four to eight. A luxury building may need 15 or 20 prospects to rent one unit. But there's really no set rule of thumb which tells how long it will take to fill your vacancies. Too many factors are involved.

However, even in a soft market with hundreds of vacancies and cutthroat competition for tenants, some managers continue to prosper by using paid advertising and making it produce rentals.

So, the time may come when you too will need to go beyond referrals and word-of-mouth advertising. That's the time to put money into printed promotion. In the next chapter you'll find how to do it profitably.

REMEMBER THESE BASIC POINTS:

* *Look at the rental records and the inquiry records to determine whether a vacant apartment has been hard to rent. If so, figure out why.*

* *Think first about ways to attract drive-by and walk-in prospects. A good sign may bring them in. Make sure it will be working for you after dark.*

* *Build a network of volunteer salespeople who'll refer prospective renters to you. A friend of a good resident is an excellent prospect. Offer rewards for referrals if you have many vacancies.*

* *Make sure your building is listed in the yellow pages of the phone book. Consider listing in other publications.*

* *Consider joining the Chamber of Commerce.*

* *Keep a card index of all possible referral sources, to help you cultivate them.*

VIII *Salesmanship in Print*

Advertising is often thought of as "salesmanship in print." But that's not what it is when you're advertising apartments for rent.

Salesmanship creates desire; then stimulates you to buy. A good salesman persuades you to do something you originally had no desire to do. First, he catches your attention — maybe with a spectacular demonstration of his product in action, maybe by suggesting that you can become healthier or wealthier, maybe by worrying you with warnings of "iron poor blood" or "hot weather coming." Then he works hard to persuade you. If he succeeds, you do what he suggests.

But the filling of vacant apartments is a problem in merchandising, not advertising. A merchandiser asks, "Who is the customer? What is value for him? What does he need? And how does he buy?" A merchandiser helps you find and buy something you already want. He needn't seek you out as a salesman does. You seek him out.

People who visit rental apartments don't go because someone makes them yearn to rent an apartment. They're already sold on the idea of renting. And they don't read a rental ad because it catches their eye with a cute headline or typographical trick. They're already scanning the apartment-for-rent ads. When they see an ad that describes what they already want, they act without being urged.

In fact, if you try to use printed words to "sell" your apartments, you'll actually weaken your message. For decades people have been so besieged and bombarded by hard-sell efforts from TV, radio, billboards, magazines, newspapers, door-to-door salesmen and junk mail that they automatically discount every sales talk. At the first hint of high pressure, they're on guard and uneasy.

Furthermore, anyone renting apartments is starting with two strikes on him, One, he's a salesman who must sell in order to make money. Two, he's a "landlord" — someone whom "tenants" have traditionally feared because of his feudal power over their lives.

Therefore, when you write an ad or any other message to prospective renters, be factual. They'll read your message hopefully but skeptically. It will succeed if it causes the right prospects to reach for their phones and come out and look at your property. They certainly won't rent an apartment until they've inspected it, no matter how good your ad may be. All the ad can do is help people determine whether your apartment can meet their needs and desires.

PICTURE YOUR PROSPECT BEFORE YOU WRITE

Who is your prospect? Not just anyone who wants an apartment. Your prospect is a particular kind of apartment-hunter, in a particular income range and age range, with special needs and characteristics. What you write should be aimed at this person — and no one else.

The right people, reading your ad, should think, "This sounds like what we've been looking for." The people you don't want or can't accommodate should think, "This isn't for us," so you avoid wasting time with them.

A MARKETING PROFILE, as we saw in Chapter 5, is one of the first tools an apartment manager needs. Probably you used it in deciding how to cut turnover, whether to remodel, what house rules to establish.

Now you need an even more detailed marketing profile, to use in deciding what to say in advertisements. Prepare it by trying to develop answers to these questions:

For what income level are your apartments the logical choice?

For what age group? Married or unmarried? With or without children? What age children, if any? And how many children?

Where are your prospects likely to work? How far are they willing to commute? What kind of work do they do?

What are their social and recreational preferences?

Maybe you can't answer all these questions fully, but do the best you can. The clearer your mental picture of your prospect, the better-aimed your ad will be because it will tell him about features that he wants.

Just be sure your mental picture jibes with the facts. Check it against the group your units have already attracted. In other words, don't get carried away by a theory that your "logical" prospects ought to be young bachelors while the building is full of elderly women, or ought to be artists although it is now occupied by plumbers and welders. Remember the old maxim that birds of a feather flock together.

SLANT YOUR ADS TO YOUR PROSPECTS —to people like those now in the building or in the neighborhood, if they have much in common.

For example, if they are mostly secretaries, your ad might begin, "Working girl's delight, cozy one-bedroom, close to downtown . . . " If they are mainly doctors or lawyers, probably they want solitude after a hectic day, so you might begin, "Secluded two-bedroom, with man-sized den, shag carpeting . . . "

If the neighborhood is full of factory workers, it's probably close to a factory. You could start your ad, "Chrysler plant 10 minutes away . . . " The Chrysler workers who are your prospects will keep reading, whereas they might not get to the end of a sentence that started, "two-bedroom, one bath, no pets, located near Chrysler." If you're near a military base, maybe your logical prospects are service people — who often have young children. An ad slanted to them could say something like, "Safe, secure play area for children, two bedrooms, only minutes to schools and shopping . . ."

WHAT TO PUT IN YOUR ADS

WHAT DO YOUR PROSPECTS LOOK FOR? Many surveys have made clear that, in general, apartment hunters are most interested in the following features in roughly this order:

1. How much is the rent?
2. What part of the city is the apartment in, and what kind of neighborhood?
3. Is there enough living space, storage space and parking space?
4. How big is the apartment complex and what is it like?
5. Is the place clean and attractive?
6. What sort of people live there?
7. What amenities are there — kitchen equipment, carpeting, drapes, heating, air conditioning, vanities, recreational facilities?

Your ad should answer at least the first four basic questions. It can also include whatever information concerning the other three questions you feel will be attractive to your prospect.

However, some of these basic questions may be answered by the classified heading under which your ad appears. Sometimes newspapers put "furnished" and "unfurnished" apartments under separate headings, so there's no need to mention this in your ad. If the apartment is otherwise unfurnished, but does include certain items such as drapes, carpeting, refrigerator or stove, you may want to mention these.

LOCATION IS IMPORTANT — the single most important factor in a resident's choice — but you may not need to emphasize it, because big city papers usually have a geographical breakdown for various parts of the city, grouping them under headings such as "West Oakland," and "East Oakland," and "Central City." Some even divide them into smaller areas, such as "West Chicago, east of Freeway." Where the location is made plain by the classification, you'd waste money by repeating it in your ad.

If there's something special about your location or neighborhood, not immediately obvious from its address or from the geographical classification, this may be a key advantage that should be mentioned within the first few words, such as "north of Woodward," or "Franklin School District," or "Nob Hill suite."

On the other hand, if you're managing a nice building in a rather poor neighborhood, naming the district first might cause some prospects to stop reading. You might better mention closeness to shopping centers or to a park or freeway or school, or whatever other advantages the location offers. The address itself should be given at the end of the ad.

It's important to include travel directions in the ad, if your property is outside the city. Strange as it seems, most ads for suburban garden complexes either don't tell how to find the address or give directions that lead the prospect astray. The manager knows how to get there and forgets an important part of the instructions.

Another possible reason for putting directions in an ad: the most direct route may lead prospects through an ugly neighborhood, or past apartment buildings that compete with yours. Realtors who sell homes make sure to take the prospect along the most pleasant route, even though it's longer. They avoid the dump heap or "massage parlor" three blocks from the house on the shortest route. You should try to do the same.

Make your drive-out instructions unmistakeably clear. Start from a major highway or well-known arterial street, for example, "just south of the junction of Route 6 and Englewood Avenue," or "take U.S.405 to Orchard Boulevard off ramp, go west three blocks to . . . Apartments."

Sometimes a major traffic artery is known by different names in different areas. So if the artery has a route number or highway number shown on maps, you should include this number in the naming of the artery. Identify an exit from an expressway by name and number, after you drive out to make sure these are visible on the expressway. (Maybe you think of the exit as 54th Street because you drive it daily, but the prospect may see only a sign, "Exit 20.")

Also make sure the exit is identified from both directions. Prospects driving from the north may be able to turn off at Exit 20, but there may be a different number from the south — or, worse yet, no south exit.

Tell the prospect which way to turn when he leaves the main artery — east or west — but also right or left if possible, since some people don't carry a compass in their heads. Then continue to guide him along the various streets until he reaches your place. If you manage a large complex and need to rent many apartments, you can reinforce the instructions in your advertising with directional signs and even a billboard, which we'll discuss in detail later in this chapter.

As you do more advertising, you can try variations in your geographical description, and see which pulls the best responses.

Bill Nickerson, the well-known authority on realty investment, tells of a 40-unit apartment house which had 12 vacancies. The manager continuously advertised the apartments as being in East Metropole, an area extending 10 miles from downtown to the city line. But the building was only a block inside the city line, and prospective residents answering the ad for "East Metropole" were disappointed to find it so far out. However, this location was within a block of a desirable residential subdivision incorporated as Cherry Heights. When the apartment manager switched his advertising heading to "Cherry Heights," he filled his apartments quickly with people who wanted to live in that area.

ALWAYS INDICATE THE RENT except perhaps in prestige buildings catering to high-income residents. Some managers are afraid their apartments are over-priced, so they omit mention of the rent, or substitute a coy word like "reasonable." They hope that once the prospect sees the apartment, they can talk him into paying what they ask, or almost that.

This might have worked in the leisurely old days of cheap transportation when people did a lot of comparative shopping before buying, and when they enjoyed haggling over the price of many things they bought. But today a prospective tenant checks the ads for listing in the rental range he can afford. If no price is listed, he usually ignores the ad figuring the the price must be out of line. Why should he bother with it when he can choose among rentals for known amounts?

From studies made by dozens of newspapers and advertisers, there's no doubt that it pays to specify your price, just as in a department store's large display ad. The price draws a larger response from the right prospects, and shuts out time-wasting calls from those who can't afford the rental. However, unless the price is a primary attraction, you needn't feature it prominently.

If you're advertising for a whole building with a variety of vacancies, and don't want to list specific prices, it's alright to use a bottom price, "from $195," or to give a rent range, "from $225 to $480." In fact, the high end of the range adds to the prestige appeal of the property, even though the prospect may be interested only in the low end.

Incidentally, don't try to rent two or more sharply different units (such as studio, one, two and three bedrooms) in the same classified ad. Shooting for more than one group of prospects in one ad is like aiming at several birds with the same shot. If you zero in on one bird, you're likely to hit it. If you aim a shotgun between two, with hopes of getting both, you probably won't hit either one. Surveys show that when two or more apartments are listed, the ad gets poor results. It sounds too vague to be attractive. By taking several small ads, each keyed to a definite kind of prospect, you'll get many more prospects. Remember that each prospect is looking for just one kind of apartment.

ALWAYS SPECIFY THE NUMBER OF BEDROOMS, or the total number of rooms. Apartment hunters look for this essential information before deciding which ads to follow up. If there's ample closet space or convenient parking, these features are worth mentioning. If there are two or more baths, say so. The more space offered, the keener the prospect's interest.

This applies to the space around the unit as well as within it. The size and type of building are important to prospects. Some people want to get away from the big, impersonal, hotel-type building to a small neighborly cluster of bungalows; others want the feeling of safety and seclusion they get in a big building. Therefore, your ad should be as definite as possible: "2-bedroom, 2-bath in an 8-unit custom-built building," or "2-bedroom country apartments with private patios or balconies, swimming pool, lighted tennis courts," or "2-bedroom, nearly 1,000 square feet in full security building, 2 elevators, paneled lobby with settee, garage lockers." Few classified ads spell out the size of the building. Those who do are the ones which fill vacancies fastest.

SHARPENING UP YOUR ADS

PAINT PICTURES WITH YOUR ADJECTIVES and descriptive phrases. Try not to let your ad sound humdrum, as so many rental ads do. If your rooms are big, it's better to write "2 spacious bedrooms," or "elegant king-sized living room," instead of just "2-bedroom," or "large apartment." Other good phrases along this line are "unusually large," "ample," "individual privacy," "flexible living room," and anything else that is vivid, yet accurate. Just as Western Air Lines profitably advertises "leg room" instead of speed, you'll be smart to emphasize roominess if you can truthfully do so.

Romance your prospect a little. Emphasize whatever is favorable. If you have a small apartment, don't say "small 1-bedroom apartment." Advertise a "cozy, homelike apartment," or a "nice apartment with sunny kitchen," or "exceptionally clean apartment with hillside view." Of course, you'd be foolish to fictionalize or exaggerate because people who answer this ad will turn away if they find that it misled them. Don't tell readers about the fine view of the river if they have to look out the bathroom window to see it. There's no use calling a place "quiet," or "luxurious," or "cheerful" if it obviously isn't.

But you do need a powerful, truthful bit of description. Managers have inserted ads that pulled no response, have changed the ad to insert one vivid word, and have received dozens of replies. Probably the one best-pulling word is "redecorated." Here are others that have worked well:

artistic	exclusive	nice	restful
attractive	exciting	patio	secluded
barbecue	executive	peaceful	secure
beautiful	friendly	picturesque	smart
charming	homey	picture window	sparkling
comfortable	lovely	pleasant	sunny
convenient	luxurious	plush	very clean
delightful	modern	quiet	view
desirable	new	residential	

HEADLINE IDEAS that can add power to ads for rental units include:

AUTOMATIC DISHWASHER	HEATED POOL
BEAUTIFUL GROUNDS	INDIVIDUAL PRIVACY
BUILT-IN TV ANTENNA	LUXURY EXTRAS
BUS AT DOOR	NEAR CAMPUS or NEAR SHOPS
CAREFULLY PLANNED	NEAR SCHOOLS
CUSTOM DRAPES or CUSTOM FURNITURE	NEW BUILDING
DECORATOR COLOR SCHEMES	NEWLY PAINTED
	NICE NEIGHBORHOOD
EASY ACCESS TO FREEWAY or EASY COMMUTING	PLAYROOM FOR PARTIES
	PRIVATE GARAGE

ELECTRICALLY EQUIPPED FOR BETTER LIVING	QUIET ADULT LIVING; NO POOL
ELECTRIC KITCHEN	RESERVED PARKING AREAS
ENCLOSED GARAGE	SAFETY; LOCKED ENTRANCES
EXERCISE ROOM	SECURITY PATROL
EXTRA CLOSETS	SECURITY; PLENTY OF LIGHTS AT NIGHT
FENCED POOL	SMARTLY FURNISHED
FOR NEWLY MARRIED COUPLES OR STUDENTS	SOCIAL ACTIVITIES
FRONT & REAR ENTRANCES	SOUND CONDITIONING
GAME ROOM	SPECIAL FOR OLDER COUPLES
GARDEN PATIO	SPECIAL PLAY AREA FOR CHILDREN
GAS KITCHEN	SPECIAL SUMMER RATES
	SPECIAL WINTER RATES
	SPOTLESSLY CLEAN

SMALL ADS PAY BEST. Tests show that the number of responses doesn't increase proportionately with the size of the ad. A one-inch, one-column ad may pull 20 inquiries while the same ad, increased to two column inches, brings no more than 25. You'll get more inquiries by running the smaller ad twice.

One reason for this is that a prospect who sees a big ad is likely to assume that the advertiser has a correspondingly large number of units to rent. People shy away from apartments that seem to be slow-renting or in over-supply. "There must be something wrong with the property or the price, or they wouldn't have to spend so much on advertising," many readers think.

Instinct tells apartment-hunters that if there are any real bargains, these will be in the smaller classified ads. Thus, the smallness of your ad can help create an impression of a rare find.

Hoping to sell you a larger ad, a newspaper advertising department may advise you to use plenty of white space, and large type because it's easier to read. Some apartment managers believe this, and waste money on elaborate ads which get only average results. Don't use white space simply for its aesthetic beauty. The newspaper charges just as much for blank lines as for printed lines. Many a profitable ad is crowded from corner to corner.

And don't be afraid of using the standard newspaper type size for classified ads. When people read the classified columns, their eyes adjust to the small type and they read it easily.

However, if you use many abbreviations, your ad does become hard to read. Avoid all but the most familiar abbreviations — TV, apt., Blvd., Ave., St. — and even these might well be spelled out unless their use will save a whole line when your budget is painfully tight. Numerical figures (2, 3) are alright. But don't expect prospects to decipher such mumbo-jumbo as GD, kit., fpl., tn. ct., or A/C. These may be familiar to people in the business, but they'll slow down anyone else, and they'll look for an easier ad to understand. This is one form of brevity that doesn't pay, even though you'll see it in countless rental ads. Don't take short cuts at the cost of clarity.

Brevity does pay when it leads you to shorten your sentence; use short words instead of long ones, and skip needless words altogether. Clutter is the disease of American writing.

For example, your rental ad needn't say, "$130 per month." The "per month" is needless because the readers know the rent is by the month unless you specify otherwise. "Adults only" uses one needless word. Ditto for "utilities included." To write "1-bedroom with bath" is worse than a waste of two words; it's a damaging blunder, because everyone assumes that an apartment contains a bath. Readers will surmise that if management thinks a bath is a major inducement, the apartment can't be very desirable.

Beware of the long word that is no clearer than the short word: inquire (ask), immediately (at once), numerous (many), approximately (about), vicinity (near), and dozens more. The shorter word saves cost, speeds a sentence and gives it punch.

Beware too of an occasional short word that rubs some people the wrong way. "Kids okay" has a slightly lowbrow tone, suggesting that the manager may be on the crude side. "Children welcome" sounds better to most readers.

IF YOUR UNITS ACCEPT ONLY ADULTS, your ad should say so — unless this is self-evident from the size of the units advertised. A one-bedroom or studio apartment won't draw any inquiries from families with children. But if there are two bedrooms, most readers will assume children are permitted unless your ad says "Adults." (Just the one word is enough. Avoid the unfriendly sound of "No children.")

Conversely, if you do take children, it's seldom necessary to say so. Still, if your ad isn't drawing enough response, you can test by inserting the word "children," to see if the extra encouragement makes a difference.

PETS are forbidden in most furnished apartments, but there's no need to mention the subject in your ad. (The pros and cons of accepting pets were analyzed in Chapter 5.) If you don't permit them, there's time enough to explain this when you're negotiating with an otherwise desirable prospect. Some pet owners will make other arrangements for their animals in order to rent an apartment they like. Some give them away; some leave them at boarding kennels; some lend them to friends or relatives.

SHOULD YOU INCLUDE YOUR TELEPHONE NUMBER in an ad? Experts disagree. Edward N. Kelley, 20 years a property manager, thinks it should be included only if there's a chance that people have trouble finding your property. By phoning, they can get directions.

"Aside from prospects who want drive-out instructions, people who telephone in response to your ad fall into three categories." Kelley writes in *Practical Apartment Management.* "They really aren't serious, but are calling to get an unpleasant duty out of the way . . . They have unrealistic expectations. When they find you don't have washer and dryer connections, they hang up . . . They are fearful of being misled. They don't believe what you say in print and they discount what you say on the telephone . . . If you rely on the telephone, you'll be faced with mostly unfulfilled appointments."

William Nickerson writes, "The phone number is essential for maximum ad response, better than the address, as most tenants want to check by phone before calling in person."

On balance, the best plan seems to be to include the telephone number along with the address at the end of an ad, but try to be as informative as possible in the body of the ad so that prospects will drive out rather than call up for more information. A manager can waste a lot of telephone time with lukewarm prospects.

But when you're experimenting with your first few ads, phone calls can help educate you. An ad gives you no immediate feedback from readers. They can't ask questions, can't even hint whether they like or dislike the apartments you're advertising. But when you talk with prospects, if you pay close attention to what they say and how they say it, and if you ask questions that draw them out, you'll get a feel for how well or poorly you're communicating — and for the attractive and unattractive aspects of the apartment you're trying to rent.

KEEP TAB ON RESULTS

TELEPHONE INQUIRIES — how many and what kind — can be a measure of an ad's effectiveness, especially when combined with a count of the number of prospects who respond to the ad by coming to look at the property. Keep a running tally of these numbers.

The numbers enable you to test differently worded advertisements for the same apartments. If Ad A produces many phone calls but only a few visitors, while Ad B gets fewer phone calls but more visitors, the latter ad is probably a better investment. If A draws more calls than B, and proportionately more visitors, you should put your money on A. If both ads bring a flood of calls, but few visitors, then something is wrong with your ads or your telephone tactics. Answering telephone inquiries is an important part of your merchandising job and will be covered in Chapter 9.

Save copies of every ad, recording the newspapers and dates of publication, costs, number of phone calls and visitors, and final results. Divide the cost of the ad by the number of inquiries, so you'll know your cost per inquiry, which is a key figure in evaluating ads and media. Just because an ad pulls poorly in one appearance doesn't necessarily mean it's a poor ad. Maybe it was a great ad in the wrong paper, or in the right paper on the wrong day. Maybe bad weather kept people from responding.

In most metropolitan areas, one daily paper is the obvious leader in apartment ads. That's the paper to be in. But if you are in a suburban area, you may need to test several papers published nearby. Among these be sure to try the weekly community papers and shopping guides. Sometimes they pull better than the bigger dailies.

Sunday advertising is important. That's the day most prospects are looking. But you should also run one weekday ad — no more. Your weekday ad can be briefer than your Sunday ad because there'll be fewer ads competing against you. Also, someone who looks for apartments during the week is a more serious shopper than a Sunday prospect. Many transferees, who must rent immediately, shop during the week.

After awhile, your records will help you decide when and how to advertise, how much and where. If you're managing a building with continuous turnover, you'll need to advertise constantly. If not, you may need ads only at special times. Either way, your records will help you spend more productively in filling vacancies.

Probably you'll find that classified advertising is the most productive for you. However, a large apartment complex may need some general "institutional" advertising as well, in bigger display ads with pictures and a variety of type sizes. An advertising agency may help you prepare an ad at no cost to you, since agencies often collect a commission from the publisher rather than a fee from the advertiser.

OTHER FORMS OF ADVERTISING

Managers of small and medium-sized apartment properties need no advertising except in the classified columns. However, for the benefit of readers who need other kinds of advertising to attract large numbers of renters into big complexes, let's consider the other possibilities.

BILLBOARDS are sometimes used to promote large new developments. These big signs rent very few apartments. But they do serve a purpose in directing people who are already heading toward the property, and perhaps coax them onward past competing properties. But people can read only six or eight words as they approach the billboard, so your message should be brief.

If you use billboards, it's important to pick good sites — places where many prospects will see them and where simple directions can be given to find your complex. If there's a large military base, hospital or college in the area, it could be a good location for your board. If there's a freeway or a heavily traveled main street, signs alerting motorists where to turn off could be useful.

After you've picked good general locations for your billboards, you must make arrangements for specific spots. Keep these points in mind:

1.   Never put a sign on publicly-owned land. This is especially important around freeways.

2.   Be wary of putting a sign in an area where no other signs are in sight. They may be absent because of a strict ordinance against them.

3.   Your sign should rarely be larger than any other sign nearby. Again, there is probably a reason for their size.

Private property that already has a sign on it is a good prospect. If you see some indication of the owner, ask him what he would charge for letting you put a sign on his property. Often he'll have no idea what to charge, and you may be able to agree on $10 or $15 per month.

Always tell the owner that you take full responsibility for the sign, so if any problem comes up he can get in touch with you personally, and other arrangements can be made when necessary. Often he'll gladly make suggestions about other possible sign locations.

In a case where there's no visible clue to the ownership of land, you may choose to put up your sign anyway and wait until the owner calls you. Under such conditions, your sign had better be inexpensive, for obvious reasons.

Outdoor advertising companies will rent several display sites in rotation. They will design your billboard as part of their service. However, their services are expensive, and their claims must be weighed carefully. If they tell you 10,000 people will see the sign every day, figure it's mainly the same 10,000 going to and from work. They'll soon get used to it and the billboard will lose its impact.

If you rent a rotating series of locations, you may have to take bad sites as well as good ones. Then too, the number of billboard locations is shrinking because of environmental pressures, and this is pushing up rates for remaining sites.

TO GET BARGAIN PRICES FOR SIGNS along major roadways, go to your local tax assessor's office and ask to see the land maps showing your area. From these maps and other property files, you can get names and addresses of owners whose land adjoins important roadways. Write or phone these owners personally, explaining that you'd like to lease a few feet of their land in order to erect a billboard facing the road. Usually, you'll be able to put your signs (made by a local sign maker) in good locations for a fraction of what it would cost through an outdoor advertising company.

Even so, billboards are costly. Only a manager of 50 units or more would find them worthwhile, and even he would probably use them only during the early fill-up period when the property is being advertised in other ways.

WHAT ABOUT RADIO? Don't give it a thought unless you're merchandising a giant complex with hundreds of units which is about to stage a "grand opening." The cost of broadcasting commercials is prohibitively high, even though they may reach hundreds of thousands of people. Few of these people are prospects for your apartments.

Radio is used as a continuing public relations tools by owners of a few vast developments — usually insurance companies and banks. They find that FM radio or even AM radio, if the time and program are well chosen, can cultivate a class of listeners that the management may want, say potential residents of luxury apartments.

The vast Park LaBrea complex of apartment towers in Los Angeles has successfully used a "continental music hall" half hour show to attract a steady trickle of wealthy new renters. But this is a long-term campaign waged by a company that doesn't need quick results.

A few short radio commercials can sometimes attract a flock of people within minutes during a weekend. This is because many radio listeners are in their cars driving around; when they hear of something interesting, they turn their cars in that direction. Unfortunately, this radio-drawn traffic seldom rents. It consists mostly of curiosity seekers who come for whatever giveaways may be offered. Even so, at a grand opening the crowds pulled by radio can help create an atmosphere of excitement and success — which may help convince serious prospects that they'd better rent before all the apartments are taken.

If you buy radio commercials, schedule them to build up from Thursday through Saturday, and taper off by mid-afternoon Sunday. Make sure the times are specified. Many stations have no time available at the period you want. Some may try to make you buy a package of undesirable time slots in order to get the few you want. Sometimes the only station able to sell the times you want are stations that cater to teenage rock music fans who maybe aren't your prime prospects. To avoid these woes, do your time-buying as far in advance as you can — and be careful.

TELEVISION reaches bigger audiences than any other advertising medium, at the lowest cost per thousand viewers. Yet, it is also very costly. You'll need from $500 to $1,000 a week to buy time, plus whatever you spend in producing the commercial. A good TV commercial is expensive to make and must be done expertly to have any effect. Its sounds, sights and colors can be convincing to a captive audience. That's why a few big rental developments use spot commercials as a form of institutional ads.

If you're a big-development manager considering TV, you should know about certain pitfalls. One is the deceptively low rate for commercials late at night, or on Friday and Saturday evenings. The rate is low because the audience is smaller and few of your prospects may be watching.

Another pitfall is buying time on a show that strings a series of real estate commercials together. You need to select a show on which you're the only apartment advertiser. At least you shouldn't be seen in the same hour with two or three similar developments.

NATIONAL PUBLICATIONS can sometimes be used profitably because a few of them — such as *Time*, *Sports Illustrated*, and the *Wall Street Journal*, publish editions which carry local ads for a given city or region. For an apartment manager, ads in national publications can "build an image" over a period of time. The development acquires prestige from the publication. Institutional advertising is probably useful only to luxury apartments.

MEASURE THE EFFECTIVENESS OF VARIOUS MEDIA, in order to avoid wasting a lot of money. Every time a prospect telephones or drops in, he should be asked how he heard about your development. On radio or TV? If so, does he remember the time or the station? From a magazine ad? What magazine? From a billboard? Does he remember approximately where the sign was? By tabulating enough of these responses, you'll be able to figure which media are pulling their weight.

BROCHURES are advertising tools that you can use on selected people at selected times. You arrange for their design, preparation and distribution. You'd better get a professional ad man or art service to help you with the writing and layout. Few printing companies are expert at design or copy writing.

A beautiful glossy booklet may impress you and your friends, but it has only secondary value in renting apartments. Four of every five rentals are made on a prospect's first visit. That leaves the other 20% of renters to be convinced later on, and a brochure can tip the scales with some of these. They visit five or six properties on the same day, can't remember which was which, and need to refer to at least a mimeographed fact sheet — and preferably an illustrated folder — to help them make their choice. Just keep in mind, when planning and budgeting your brochure, that you're creating it for a minority of borderline prospects.

And keep in mind that prospects resist high pressure selling, either in print or orally. They want information, not propaganda. So stick to facts and avoid high-flown language. Brochures should contain:

1. Maps showing the location;
2. Photos of the building and interior;
3. Site plans of the complex;
4. Floor plans for all sizes of units, with dimensions;
5. Complete lists of benefits;
6. Complete street address including city, state, zip code, and telephone number with area code.

The brochure may or may not list prices. If you foresee any need to change prices before printing a new edition of the brochure, they can be left out. Prices probably aren't crucial to your prospects.

Also, leave out any picture or mention of anything that isn't sure to be in your development. The brochure will be saved by renters, and it is an implied warranty. For example, if you mention a sauna bath or show a drawing of one, people will hold this against you if you don't actually provide one. They'll claim that you promised it.

In describing facilities, write in terms of a resident's benefits. Suppose your bathrooms are seven by ten feet, painted in pastels, with overhead lights and large lighted mirrors. Merely stating these facts won't intrigue anyone. Think yourself into a resident's place and write something like this:

— Because this bathroom is so well lighted, it is easy for a woman to apply cosmetics or for a man to shave.

— There is plenty of room for drying after bathing without bumping into the walls.

— The beautiful ceramic tile around the shower area is easily cleaned.

Similarly, if you mention a combination heating and air conditioning unit, you can make the prospect feel the benefits by writing:

— Immediate warmth when you need it, because of the forced air heating system — and comfortable coolness whenever you wish, from the air conditioner.

And when you describe the location of the property, you can point up its benefits with facts like these:

— We're at Lakeshore Boulevard and San Remo Drive with quick access to shopping, business, churches, and schools. Municipal Park, just six minutes away, offers you fishing, swimming, picnic areas, a golf course, plenty of play areas for children, and ample parking.

— We're within 17 minutes of the airport, 12 minutes of downtown. In short, we're conveniently located for virtually everything you might want.

Illustrations should be photographs if at all possible. People don't believe artists' renderings.

Floor plans should be as big as you can show them — at least six by eight inches. The larger the floor plan, the larger the apartment seems to the prospect. If he sees a small floor plan, he visualizes small rooms.

The best page size for a brochure has been found to be 8½" x 11" — the size of a sheet of standard typewriter paper. This size fits conveniently into envelopes, racks, file folders and briefcases. So, it's easy to mail or distribute in other ways. It's also an economical size to print.

POSTCARDS are one more form of supplementary promotion. With a picture of the development and a descriptive sentence or two (as well as the full address, naturally), they can be given to prospects, and can also be used by new residents to notify friends of their change of address.

All these merchandising tools will help keep people aware of the property, will reinforce whatever good things they read or hear about it, and perhaps stimulate them to make a telephone inquiry when they begin to think of moving.

What should happen when people phone to ask about your apartments? We'll see in the next chapter.

REMEMBER THESE BASIC POINTS:

* *People who read rental ads are already sold on the idea of renting. Don't waste money and space on persuasion. Stick to the facts.*

* *Highlight the facts that will appeal to the specific prospect you seek. Indicate the rent and location, and the number of rooms, as well as any special attractions.*

* *Emphasize roominess if you truthfully can.*

* *Strive for vivid descriptive phrases.*

* *Keep ads as small as you can without using unfamiliar abbreviations. Short words and sentences are best.*

* *Keep a record of inquiries pulled by your ads.*

* *In filling up a big development, billboards and local editions of national magazines are worth considering. Brochures are often needed.*

* *Every time a prospect phones or drops in, ask how he heard about your property. Tabulate the answers to evaluate the effectiveness of the various advertising media you use.*

IX *Come Hither on the Phone*

How's your telephone technique?

This is an important question. The telephone may be more important than anything else in your business. If you use it badly, it may kill many chances for rentals, no matter how attractive your apartments are. If you use it well, it may multiply profits by enabling you to fill vacancies much faster than you could otherwise.

People judge by first impressions. Those who get their first impression of you by phone may never come near you if they don't like what they hear. But if they do like what they hear, they may consider renting one of your apartments in preference to others on their list. Not realizing this, many managers make blunders on the phone that they would not make face to face. The result: goodbye prospect.

Filling a vacancy usually takes three steps:

1. A prospect hears of your place, or reads about it, and gets interested enough to . . .
2. Telephone for more information, which whets his desire enough to . . .
3. Come to see it in person.

If you short-circuited the second step by poor telephone tactics, your advertising and referral contacts are nullified.

So, it's crucial for you to make a good impression via phone. You can easily do this, encouraging the right people to come to you, by using a few simple techniques when the telephone rings.

WHAT'S WRONG WITH THESE CONVERSATIONS?

First of all, let's consider some common mistakes so you can avoid them. We'll start with this imaginary situation.

An apartment manager (let's call him Joe Bungle) places a fairly good ad for one of his vacant apartments. So his phone rings. Here's his side of the conversation:

"Hello? . . . Yeah . . ."

"An apartment we advertised today?" (To his wife) "Josephine, what's in the paper today? A one-bedroom? Whereabouts? . . . Yeah, ma'am, I think we've got an unfurnished single, upstairs . . . "

"The rent? Wait a minute . . . It rents for one-eighty."

"Well, I guess I could tell you more about it, but we're eating right now. You better call back — or why don't you come out and look at it?"

"Where? The address is right there in the ad, 1280 Maple . . . Listen, lady, just ask directions at any gas station. Everybody in town knows where Maple is . . . Okay, suit yourself, it's up to you." Bungle hangs up.

No manager could make that many mistakes in 60 seconds, you think? Probably not. A caller wouldn't stay on the line long enough for Bungle to say all the things we've quoted. Nevertheless, the dozen or more blunders in this fictitious conversation are all typical. Countless managers commit some of these crudities whenever they answer the phone.

There is a type of manager who lives in a type of dream world, imagining that would-be renters are swarming all around and that vacancies will be filled automatically. Phone calls annoy him. He figures that people need him more than he needs them, so it doesn't matter if he's rude.

You're not such a manager, or you wouldn't be reading this manual. But it's well for you to be aware that the type does exist, because some day — if you own several properties, or if you become a supervisor in a property-management firm — you may find yourself supervising people like Joe Bungle — which means you'll lose money because of apartments standing vacant for weeks at a time.

One owner, Richard Haber, tells of a discovery he made after his resident manager had reported that a classified ad was bringing a surge of telephone inquiries. The manager went on, "But most of them just don't come down to the apartments. You know how people are — they're all looking to rent in June and it's only March."

This sounded odd to Haber. Why were so many people calling, yet so few coming to look? He decided to test the telephone tactics of the manager's wife, who usually answered the phone.

"My secretary phoned and pretended to be looking for an apartment," Haber recalled. "It was a disaster. Here's how the conversation went:

Mrs. Horan, the renting agent: "Hello."

"Hello. I saw your ad in the paper. My husband and I are interested in renting a one-bedroom apartment. Do you have anything available?"

Mrs. Horan mumbled, "I believe we have a one-bedroom apartment."

"What is the rent?"

"Two-ten."

"Can we come to see it this afternoon? How would I get there?"

"We're at 1395 East Meadow Lane. Greenleaf Apartments is just a mile south of the Richmond Shopping Center. Our renting office closes at six."

"I couldn't believe this conversation," Haber said. "Mrs. Horan had given an exhibition of the worst possible telephone technique. Within 15 days after I corrected the situation, we rented five apartments. I strongly suggest that every apartment owner test his sales office to make sure their telephone technique is satisfactory."

Maybe Mrs. Horan's way of coping with telephone inquiries wasn't really the worst possible. At least she gave some directions for finding the apartment. And she didn't use quite as offensive phrases as Joe Bungle did. But this is the best we can say for her. She missed every chance to make a good impression.

There are many, many of these chances. If you were Richard Haber, what would you have told Mrs. Horan to do to "correct the situation," as he put it? Let's review what happened, and what should have happened, but didn't.

GETTING READY FOR THE PHONE TO RING

First of all, Mrs. Horan — like other apartment managers — should have made thorough preparations for the phone calls that the ad was expected to bring.

When the morning edition of the paper was delivered, she could have turned to the Real Estate section, looked under the heading, "Apartments for Rent, Unfurnished," and found the ad. She could have cut out, not just the ad for her own vacancy, but the column that included all similar ads. She could circle hers with a marking pen, and take a few minutes to notice how her vacancy compared with the others for price, location and features.

Her telephone would be conveniently located on a desk or table with pencils and an "Inquiry Record" like the one shown on Page 116. With it would be a street map to help her tell prospects how to reach the property from any direction. Prestigious landmarks and intersections would be marked, so she could mention these in routing a prospect along an attractive approach. Her map should be mounted on heavy cardboard to keep it flat and readable, as well as to keep it from getting mislaid or torn. If any prospect were likely to go by bus to see the apartment, the bus route should be marked in ink.

How about you? Do you make such preparations?

Let's go on to see what else Mrs. Horan — and you or any manager — should do before a conversation, and during it.

Talking with a likely renter is no time to rely on sudden inspirations or ad libs. The telephone conversation should be well designed. That is, the manager should know in advance what she wants to say, with a written checklist of the main points she should mention and with answers already jotted down for the questions likely to be asked by callers.

If there's any chance a prospect will want to know about the location of nearby churches, shopping centers, bus lines, recreational facilities, schools or the like, a handy tabulation of these should be near the phone. As for the checklist of points to be covered, it could include:

1.   Attractive features of the premises — such assets as pool, patio, security arrangements, pleasant neighborhood, and whatever else might appeal to callers.

2.   The benefits of the unit itself.

3.   Key facts to be obtained from the caller — which we'll get to in a moment.

Pencil in hand, the manager should check off each point during the conversation to be sure she talks about everything vital before a good prospect hangs up. Obviously, Mrs. Horan did none of this.

Although the Inquiry Record should be near the phone, the manager probably won't touch it during the conversation. It is for the tabulation of all calls during a given week. So, she'll mark it up later. As she talks on the phone, she should be filling out a smaller blank — a separate one for each caller.

The manager will save this blank as a memory-refresher just before (and during) the face-to-face conversation she hopes will come later. Under "Special notes" she can jot down details that may help her understand the prospect's background and needs: maybe his accent, his job, where he's from; possibly even background noises during the conversation, or side talk with other family members — anything that could be significant.

In addition to these preparations, Mrs. Horan, or whoever it is, should make sure that the telephone will be kept as free as possible for incoming calls; that everyone else thereabouts will let her be the one to answer; and that she'll do her best to stay close enough to answer by the second ring, at least during hours when call-ins are likely. (Many apartment hunters hang up after the third or fourth ring. They may be checking a long list of ads, with no time to waste on advertisers who seem slack. But if a manager makes a good impression, they may skip calling some of the others, and come immediately to look at the apartment.)

```
┌─────────────────────────────────────────────────────────────┐
│                      INQUIRY RECORD                          │
│                                                              │
│  NAME _____ DATE _____    │
│                                                              │
│  Where did you learn about the apartment?_____    │
│                                                              │
│  Size wanted_____ Furnished?____ Unfurnished?__    │
│                                                              │
│  Price $_____ Is it right?_____     │
│                                                              │
│  Date needed _____ Children_____ Pets_____    │
│                                                              │
│  Reason for moving _____     │
│                                                              │
│  Special notes _____     │
│  _____      │
│                                                              │
│  When will you come to see the apartment? _____      │
│                                                              │
└─────────────────────────────────────────────────────────────┘
```

DON'T SAY HELLO

Some advertisers answer the telephone with "Yes?" in a challenging voice. Some merely say, "Hello," which usually sounds languid and bored. Others with military training bark out their last name and nothing else when they pick up the phone.

No such response is especially encouraging to a caller who's hoping to find a pleasant apartment under good management.

PUT A SMILE IN YOUR VOICE. Have you ever noticed how different a person sounds when he smiles compared to when his face is blank or scowling? Try it yourself right now. Say something such as "Vernon Apartments – can I help you?" while smiling. Now frown as you say the same thing. Hear the difference? It's surprising how that smile comes through. So does the frown, unfortunately.

You may be good looking, well-groomed, smartly dressed. But the caller can't see this. Nothing "shows" except your voice and words. You'll be visualized as glum or sunny or sloppy, according to what you project across the telephone wires. Callers are attracted and put at ease by a pleasant response. They're repelled by a harsh or indifferent way of answering. That's why your very first words on the phone can make a major difference in the number of callers who come and see the unit.

Accordingly, before you pick up the phone, put a smile on your face. Do it automatically the instant you hear the phone ring.

Instead of saying, "Hello," or something equally unprofessional, it's far better to answer by saying, "Good morning, Vernon Apartments – can I help you?" or you might say, "This is Mrs. Jones of the Vernon Apartments," or "Vernon Apartments, Mrs. Jones speaking."

Whatever you say, don't drop your voice at the end of your response, because the effect has a grim finality, rather like, "That's all." Your last syllable should have a cheery upward lilt that projects your smile – a rising inflection, almost as if you were singing. It makes you sound inviting, alert, happy that the stranger is calling.

YOUR TELEPHONE PRESENCE CAN BE PLEASANT if you do four simple things enabling the other person to understand you more easily:

1. Speak directly into the phone. Too many people have a habit of turning their heads or leaning back and gazing at the ceiling, or hunching over the desk, while they speak. If you do this, your voice fades, so the listener has trouble hearing you. He

may need to ask you to repeat, which annoys him. If you fade badly, he may wonder if you're paying attention, or if you're even on the line. Project your voice into the mouthpiece all the time and you'll be heard more clearly. The mouthpiece should be about an inch from your lips.

2.   Keep an even volume. The telephone is designed to carry your voice at its natural volume and pitch. Speak loud enough to be heard, but not too loud. Don't blast one minute and whisper the next, as if you were a crystal radio in a thunderstorm. Some people don't hear as well as others, so you must adjust your volume up or down to accommodate them. But when you get your voice to the right level, keep it there, while varying the expression of your voice to bring out the meaning of what you say.

3.   Adjust your speedometer. Someone who speaks too slowly (as President Johnson sometimes did) can be a bore. But one who jabbers too fast (as President Kennedy occasionally did) can be hard to follow. The ideal is to speak at a moderate understandable speed, between 120 and 160 words a minute. If you find people saying, "Wait, tell me that again," you're probably talking too fast. This is a common fault among business people.

4.   Be distinct. Don't mumble or slur your words. It sounds lazy to say "gunna," "Sadday," or "wunnaful." Keep things out of your mouth because if you're chewing gum, drinking coffee, even smoking a pipe or cigarette, this can be "heard" on the phone.

In fact, it's almost impossible to speak clearly when your lips, tongue or jaw are trying to do something else at the same time. If you have a habit of gnawing a pencil or biting your nails, don't do it when you're on the phone. The best way to avoid annoying people with indistinctness is to form a habit of taking everything away from your mouth as you reach for the phone.

These are the four rules for keeping your voice clear. Now how about the words you use? They're even more important.

GOOD WORDS ARE GOOD BUSINESS. Use simple straightforward language. Avoid slang, because some people dislike it or may not understand it. And go easy on technical jargon. Common trade terms like "studio apartment . . . grout . . . down time . . . turnover rate. . . hold harmless clause . . . lessor . . . lessee . . . mid-rise . . . utility pass-through . . . base rent . . . water balance" may baffle someone who isn't in your business.

For the same reason, you'd better not show off fancy words that happen to be in your vocabulary. "It's a prepossessing apartment," or "I'll facilitate your entry," or "Your call is fortuitous," could ruin your relations with a caller. He might misinterpret your meaning or just be mystified.

Be polite. Sprinkle your talk with courteous words and phrases: "Please . . . thank you. . . would it be convenient . . . you're certainly welcome . . . I'd be very happy to . . . I'd really appreciate it if . . ."

Never interrupt. Even more important, steer clear of expressions that sound bossy or negative: "You can't . . . you'll have to . . . I'm pretty busy . . . can't you . . . you'd better . . . I don't think . . . wait a minute . . . you don't understand . . . what did you want to know?"

Be specific. Steer away from vague words and phrases like, "Something or other . . . and so forth . . . more or less . . . sort of . . . pretty much . . . I guess . . . and that kind of stuff."

Get rid of speech mannerisms that may grate on people's nerves. Probably you know people who keep saying, "y'know . . . y'know" until you clench your teeth to keep from groaning – or "I mean," or "like," or "really," or "and-uh" and "well er. . . " There are innumerable annoying vocal habits. One reporter monitored a Hubert Humphrey television interview, and counted 31 "I b'lieve's" in 40 minutes. That's a lot of b'lieving, y'know?

DRAMA IN THREE ACTS

Once the telephone conversation is under way, the real drama begins. There'll be three acts. Or to be exact, you'll try to do three things in succession, perhaps with some overlapping or interminglings:

1. You'll try to determine whether any of your vacancies are suitable for the caller. That is, you'll "qualify the prospect," as salesmen call this process.

2. If the prospect qualifies, you'll talk about apartment features that should please him.

3. You'll try to arrange a definite appointment for the prospect to look at the apartment.

Let's analyze these three acts separately.

FIRST YOU SCREEN CALLERS – tactfully and pleasantly – to make sure that the wrong ones don't waste their time and yours by visiting the premises.

For example, when someone needs a larger apartment than you're offering, or wants certain features that you don't have – such as a swimming pool, perhaps, or a locked garage – there's no use stringing out the conversation. Or if a caller can't move in for two weeks, and you're trying to rent the apartment at once, he's not a hot prospect. You can take his name and phone number just in case – but don't encourage him to visit until you see whether you can do better with someone else during the intervening two weeks. Likewise, if the apartment is too far from a caller's working place, or obviously doesn't suit some other need or desire, the sooner you both know this, the better.

The prospect's own questions and remarks will often disqualify him, but more often you'll have to do some questioning yourself. Let's see some ways you might go about it. Here's a sample telephone dialogue.

Manager: Good morning, Nirvana Apartments.

Prospect: Hello, I'm calling about a one-bedroom apartment.

Manager: Yes, indeed, we advertised a vacancy this morning. It's just been redecorated – very attractive. I'm glad you called about it. Do you need it right away?

Prospect: In about two weeks.

(This was the first screen-out point. If a prospect says this, and you're trying for immediate rental, there's no need for the rest of the dialogue.)

Manager: Is this apartment just for you?

Prospect: No, it's for my wife and myself.

Manager: Fine. We are an adult complex. (Here was the second screen-out point.) By the way, my name is . . . May I ask your name and where you read about our apartment?

Prospect: My name is Carl Hunter. I saw your ad in the *Tribune*.

Manager: Are you new to our area, Mr. Hunter, or do you live close by? (Third screen-out question.)

Prospect: I'm living at the Gehenna Towers, here in the city.

Manager: I've heard that's a nice place. I imagine you've already given your 30-day notice since you need an apartment in two weeks. (Fourth screen-out question. Indirectly, you're probing into his reason for moving, since it could be a reason you would not want him.)

Prospect: That's right. I've been transferred to the new shopping center, so we'll need an apartment near it in two weeks when I start work. (Fifth screen-out point. If he were unemployed or working in a low-pay job, you might not want him.)

Manager: Although the ad didn't mention it, I expect to have two or three vacancies soon. The rents vary according to the location. Do you have a certain amount in mind that you're budgeting for an apartment? (Sixth screen-out point.)

Prospect: We're looking for an apartment around $175 to $190.

Manager: Fine, Mr. Hunter, I have an apartment that you'll probably like very much. Would it be convenient —

Prospect: Are there tennis courts at your apartments, or nearby? My wife and I like to play every week. (Seventh screen-out point, this time volunteered by the prospect. A lack of tennis courts would screen him out.)

At any stage in this conversation, if you realize that the prospect isn't a good match for your vacancy, then you'll need to end the talk as pleasantly as you can. You might say something like, "Mr. Hunter, it looks as if we don't have what you want because . . . " and explain that your place is unsuitable because of lack of facilities, or the wrong price range, wrong location, rules against children, or some other factor. Maybe you can refer him somewhere else, as suggested in Chapter 7. This could make him so grateful that he'd later refer someone else to you.

SECONDLY, YOU DO SOME SELLING as you answer the prospect's questions. Just keep your salesmanship factual and low-key because the prospect doesn't want to be urged. He'll shy away from anything like a high-pressure spiel.

In the foregoing sample conversation, one bit of discreet selling was slipped in by the manager who mentioned that the vacancy was newly redecorated. Whenever a prospect reveals a need or desire, this may be another opening. For example, if you accept children and you learn that a prospect has a three-year-old son, you might say something like, "Your little boy will love it here. We have several children his age, a play area, and plenty of open space for them to romp in. And you probably know that the school in this district is one of the finest in the city."

Another example: if a prospect asks, "Is there a yard or garden where we can get some sunshine?" you'll certainly want to make a better response than merely, "Oh, yes. We have a very nice patio." Details should be at your fingertips so you can say something like, "There's a secluded patio on the south side that stays sunny until 3:00 o'clock, even during the short winter days. It's shielded by flowers and shrubs, and it's quite spacious — 90 feet long."

In fact, almost any question can be answered in a way that adds to the appeal of the apartment. If someone asks, "What kind of appliances do you have?" you can answer, "We have the . . . deluxe appliances." Both the "deluxe" phrase and the manufacturer's name are extra bits of salesmanship.

Even when someone merely asks, "Do you have an apartment for rent?" you can do far more than just say yes. Your answer can be something like, "Yes, we have a nice spacious five-room apartment with Danish modern furniture," or "We have several lovely apartments with spacious closets and modern kitchens." In other words, you should use every question as an opportunity to answer with several facts calculated to make your vacancies' attractive points stand out in the prospect's mind.

Sometimes, if you decide a prospect is particularly desirable, you can try a bit of persuasion, even though you don't have exactly what he wants:

"Oh, Mr. Hunter, we don't have a three-bedroom vacancy, but in the two-bedroom apartment there's a small sewing room which could be a lovely child's room. Do you have a younger child?" If he does, the sewing room might suffice.

THIRDLY, YOU TRY TO COMMIT THE PROSPECT TO A VISIT. Don't delay in attempting this. A long chat on the phone may do more harm than good. Telephone overkill has frightened off many callers; they won't go to a place where the manager seems likely to talk them to death.

As soon as you realize that a caller meets your requirements, and that your apartment is the kind he's seeking, you should shift smoothly into discussing an immediate appointment. In telephone selling as in any other kind, you'll only get action if you ask for it.

Instead of asking, "Would you like to come out and see the apartment?" it's far better to assume that he wants to see it. Do as trained salesmen do: ask "when," or "which," rather than "if," or "would you?" For example, you might say, "Is it convenient for you to stop by now, or will a little later in the day be better?"

An even smoother strategy is to inquire, "Are you calling locally?" If he answers yes, then you ask, "Where are you now?" When he tells you, maybe you can say, "That's only a few minutes' drive from here. You can reach our address very easily. Here's how to come . . . " and give him specific directions from wherever he is.

If the prospect can't come at once, your next move is to ask, "When would you like to come? It will be better if I set an appointment for you so as not to keep you waiting. I have an opening at 11:30 and at 2:00. Which is better for you?" Again, like any expert persuader, you avoid offering the prospect a chance to say no. As long as a generation ago, Real Silk knew this and trained its hosiery salesmen to ask, "How many pair do you want?" rather than "Would you like to buy some?"

YOU CAN GO STILL FURTHER in clinching the appointment. You can say, "May I have your phone number in case I need to call back?" Subtly this makes the prospect aware that he'll be getting calls from you if he doesn't show up; most people find it easier to keep an appointment than to face explaining why they didn't.

There's yet another strategy of salesmanship that you can and should use: if the prospect is married, try to make sure that both husband and wife visit the apartment together, so they can decide immediately when you show the apartment.

One way to do this, after the prospect has agreed to a time for the visit, is to say, "Thank you, I'll look forward to seeing you at 2:00, Mr. Hunter. Oh, by the way, will you be coming with your wife?"

He may answer, "No, she's at work at that time." If so, you say, "Probably you'd rather come when Mrs. Hunter is with you. We do have only one or two apartments that will be available, and you wouldn't want to delay your decision."

He'll probably say something like, "Oh, well then, I think I will wait until my wife can be with me."

Naturally, you're not letting him off the hook. You say, "Fine, will 7:00 this evening suit you? . . . Good, I'll see you at 7:00. Thanks so much for calling, Mr. Hunter."

If he won't make an appointment to see the property, offer to mail him a fact sheet or brochure. Then ask for his phone number as well as his address, so you can "check back in a few days to see whether you want more information."

SAY GOODBYE AT THE RIGHT TIME. Many a prospect has agreed to make a personal visit, and then has cooled off completely because the manager doesn't know enough to get off the line. In every phone conversation there is a psychological moment when it's time to stop. Here are some pointers to show you when.

A. When you feel the other person is losing interest, or
B. When you realize you're beginning to talk too much, or
C. When you've accomplished your purpose.

Recognizing the first two depends on your own instinct. But the third is a matter of fact. You know when you've obtained the information you need. You can tell whether the caller has all the information *he* wants, by merely pausing for a moment to see if he asks any further questions — and to give him the opportunity of ending the call.

It's customary for the one who makes the call to be the one who ends it. This isn't a point of great importance, but it is important to realize that a conversation seems to be rambling on and getting nowhere. That's the time to say goodbye, without small talk.

We've all been trapped on the telephone by a long-winded caller — a determined salesman, perhaps, or a talkative friend. Maybe your caller is one of the many people who aren't sure how to end a conversation. If so, he'll likely appreciate it if you take the initiative. Just say pleasantly, "Thanks very much. I'll look forward to seeing you. Goodbye," or any other friendly remark. But be sure to include the pleasant farewell. You don't want your prospect to be put off by the sudden click of a line going dead unexpectedly.

In the rare case where a caller keeps talking aimlessly, giving you no chance to say goodbye, when you're sure all questions have been answered, you can cut in at the first pause, "There's someone at my desk, so if we've covered everything, I'd better say goodbye," or "I have an appointment coming up now, so I'll say goodbye."

With this, you've done everything you can do to attain your goal, which is to persuade the prospective occupant to visit your place.

But don't bank on promises. Take all the calls that come in and encourage those who will qualify to come and see the apartment. Most prospects who agree to do so will make at least half-hearted plans to come. But they may keep answering other ads in the meantime. They may visit a whole series of apartments, and rent one before getting to yours.

You can only hope that you won't be eliminated sight unseen. When a prospect does come to your place, this is where you hit a home run or strike out. It's up to you to convert a "hunter" into a "renter." In Chapter 10 you'll see how to do so.

REMEMBER THESE BASIC POINTS:

* *Your telephone may be your most important tool. Make sure that people get a good impression of you when they phone.*

* *Make complete plans and preparations for your response to telephone inquiries about vacancies.*

* *Have a plan for screening callers to make sure that only the good prospects want to visit the property.*

* *Plan how to answer questions in a way that adds to the appeal of the apartment.*

* *Try to commit every good prospect to a visit. Ask "when" or "which." Try to get a married couple to come together.*

* *End the conversation with a pleasant farewell as soon as you're sure that its purpose has been accomplished.*

X Here Comes The Prospect

A resident Manager's or your main job is to maximize the value of the property. He does this by primarily keeping it filled with occupants who pay their rent and cause little damage or trouble. Therefore, he is a salesman — good or bad, like it or not.

As we saw in Chapters 3 and 4, it often takes salesmanship merely to retain desirable occupants; dissatisfaction can cause them to leave. But it takes more concentrated salesmanship to persuade desirable prospects to move in. This is where you, as manager, need certain tested selling techniques which we'll consider in this chapter.

HOW TO SET YOUR STAGE

Expert salesmen strive hard for eye appeal — just as expert showmen take pains with how a scene looks, background as well as foreground. The audience must be pleased.

FIRST IMPRESSIONS are even more crucial in selling than in showmanship; a theater audience seldom walks out in the first ten seconds, but a prospective customer may turn away or "turn off" in that time.

Let's assume that you've done as suggested in Chapter 7, and made your property as attractive looking as you can, so that drive-by and walk-in prospects are drawn to it as irresistibly as they are to a good display in a show window. Your entranceway, shrubbery, walks and corridors are immaculate and well-kept. Your office is well-marked and easy to find.

So far so good. As the prospects approach, they get a feeling that management is on the job and concerned. So they keep coming and knock on your door. When it opens, will their preliminary impression be enhanced or spoiled?

Of course, you answer the door promptly and greet prospects the way you'd like to be greeted. Maybe the door opens into your office, or your apartment, or a model apartment. Whichever it is, visitors must be favorably impressed, or you won't make sales. (At least you won't make the kind of sales you want. The prospect who doesn't care about appearances won't be a desirable occupant. A shoddy-looking place can rent only to shoddy tenants. In other words, good prospects don't rent just the apartment; they rent the resident manager, too.)

The prospect that you want is selective. He can afford to be. He probably can choose among many apartments. And, remember, this is important to him. He's considering contracting for a home, not buying a pack of chewing gum. So, he's looking for a place where he'll be proud to live, and will want to stay for years. If he doesn't think yours is well managed, he won't want it.

He judges by you and your office. Your office or apartment is an extension of yourself. It should be as presentable as you are. Is it neat and clean with no clutter? Is there plenty of comfortable seating for a whole family, in case one should arrive? Does everything look businesslike?

Some resident managers operate off kitchen tables in the middle of a seemingly continuous meal, against a backdrop of dirty laundry, strewn papers, and boards of apartment keys. You should operate very differently. Conceal the tools and debris of business and personal life as much as possible. Instead of them, try to embellish your stage setting with a few visual aids to selling.

Maybe you can decorate the wall opposite the door with management diplomas, membership plaques, inspection certificates for the swimming pool or elevators, autographed photos of other display items that will impress the eye of the beholder coming through the door. If you're managing a big complex, maybe you can put up a map or three-dimensional model of the complex, floor plans of standard apartments, samples of paint and wallpaper, cutaways of wall and floor construction, an attractive map of the community with your building's location highlighted.

Even if your kitchen is out of sight, if it is near a room where you receive unexpected drop-ins, be careful about cooking odors. The smell of sauerkraut or fish or onions is far more pungent to an outsider than to the cook. Keep the room as well ventilated as you can and use an air freshener spray.

YOUR APPEARANCE is even more important than the room where you work. A prospect automatically forms an opinion of you at first glance. If you're wearing a muu-muu or the jeans you normally paint in, and have overflowing ashtrays on the desk, with a blaring television in the background, the prospect may stay only long enough to rest his feet before looking at the apartment down the street.

Think of the resident manager's position as an outside job; at 9:00 o'clock pretend you're leaving home to go to work. It's hard to be presentable at all times, but this comes with organization. Jobs like vacuuming halls and cleaning apartments should be done first thing in the morning, before most prospective renters cruise the neighborhood.

Even when the dirty work is underway, it's possible to keep hair in bounds and work clothes changed regularly, so strangers won't see you at your worst. There's not much excuse for being unshaven, or having your hair in rollers, at an hour when it's conceivable that a prospect might walk in.

If you're repeatedly confronted by unexpected prospects, keep a record of the times when they call. Soon you'll see a pattern of calls, and a part of the day which is usually free from visitors. This is the time to schedule any work or recreation which may put your appearances awry. Allow yourself time to spruce up, and you shouldn't have to worry about being caught looking like something from a horror movie.

Another good idea in keeping ready for sudden visitors is to have all material handy that you may need when you rent a unit, or when you transact business with residents. This includes printed forms (such as rental agreements, leases, house rules), receipt book, carbon paper, file cards, keys, key tags, pens and pencils. This will save time later and spare you the embarrassment of rummaging through drawers and cupboards while visitors watch.

Your most important prospects, of course, are those who come by appointment rather than simply drifting off the street. You've already screened the former by telephone, as we saw in Chapter 9, and you know that they are qualified prospects. So, you should be thoroughly prepared at the time when they are due — appropriately dressed, shoes clean, notes of the telephone conversation handy.

Your clothes should be a blend of friendly informality and business. You need to dress close to the way your typical prospects dress, so that they'll feel comfortable with you. There was a time when the manager of any sizable building was expected to wear business attire — suit and necktie for a man, dress and high heels for a woman. Nowadays more casual wear is better. Suits are too formal for most rental offices; they remind the prospect of banks and law offices and put him on his guard.

Your problem of what to wear is further complicated by local peculiarities and your own taste. Just avoid extremes. Prospects would be nervous in the presence of a male manager who appeared to be dressed for Skid Row — or for an embassy tea party — and equally nervous near a lady manager in hot pants, heavy makeup and a splash of "You Ain't Gonna Be Able to Help Yourself" perfume.

HOW YOU TALK is also important. Here again, extremes are bad. Be mild in your choice of words. Remember that profanity would cheapen you in many prospects' eyes. Slang is risky, too — especially any slang term that refers to a racial or ethnic group or bodily functions. If you happen to have a bad habit of using such slang among close friends, you'd better break yourself of the habit. Familiar phrases pop from the lips at the wrong times.

With your first words you're starting to sell — in a subtle way. What should you say first? That's easy. You should introduce yourself and invite the prospect in. (No visitor feels welcome carrying on a conversation while standing at the door.) And, of course, you should use a friendly voice and smile. The first few lines of dialogue might go like this:

"Hello! I'm Ed Long. Come right in. Are you here to see an apartment?"

"Yes, we're Mr. and Mrs. Hunter. We phoned — I guess your wife?"

"She's on the phone right now. We're getting quite a few calls from people interested in the apartments. We're the managers. Won't you sit down?"

If the Hunters hadn't volunteered their name — or if you didn't know what it must be by their reference to the phone call — you should ask for it, as unobtrusively as possible. You might pull out a blank like the one shown on Page 116 and say, "I like to keep a little record of every rental inquiry. May I have your name?"

This blunt request is seldom necessary. Americans play a sort of Ping-Pong when talking business. If one offers his name, the other generally does, too. A cordial welcome evokes a cordial response.

Once you've got the prospect's name, remember it, and keep using it. People like to hear the sound of their name. Top salesmen always call a person by name, and it usually works; it helps develop a friendly personal relationship. If you must use the inquiry record gimmick to get a prospect's name, put it aside as soon as you've filled in the name, and complete it after he leaves. Asking a series of formal questions would be certain to put him on the defensive. How would you like it if a casual acquaintance pulled out a pad and began recording your address, occupation, number of children and so on? You may need a lot of information from a prospect, but you must get it gradually and tactfully, without letting him feel that you're cross-examining him.

Notice that in the brief dialogue cited above, the manager puts across the point that he's in touch with others who want to rent. Salesmen know that cool prospects may turn hot at a hint of competition. If the Hunters like what they see, the thought has been planted in their minds that they'd better take it quickly or lose it to someone else.

Always use this strategy if possible. Sometimes you can open with a remark like, "You're in luck, a fine two-bedroom apartment has just become available." Or you can mention casually, "Someone wants to come right out to see the apartment." Just be gentle. Don't bear down too emphatically.

Never, never indicate — verbally or visually — that you have many vacant apartments. People are suspicious of anything that isn't selling well. They want things that are in demand. The typical apartment-dweller likes to think of his apartment as a status symbol; he won't feel much prestige living in a place where no one else seems to want to live. So, your position should always be that your apartments are exclusive, and that being invited there is like being invited to join a club. Although it isn't easy to qualify, the present prospect seems to be the right sort of person and you want to do everything possible to help him.

A TAKE-IT-OR-LEAVE-IT ATTITUDE is suicidal. Unskilled managers may ask immediately, "Do you want a one-bedroom or two-bedroom apartment?" Some even ask this without rising out of their seat or moving from behind a cluttered desk. They're half hoping that the visitor will want an apartment size that isn't available, so they can quickly get rid of him and resume whatever they were doing. Worse yet, if they do have something the prospect might want, they say blithely, "It's a lovely apartment; the rent is $190 a month. Here are the keys; go take a look."

Such lazy managers ruin the financial prospects of whoever owns the property. Most of the time the visitor can't even find the apartment, much less appreciate it. He certainly won't rent it, unless he's an unusual undesirable. The owners have invested time and money to establish a marketable product. It's up to the manager or you to show pride in the product and sell it intelligently.

HOW TO SIZE UP PROSPECTS

You screen prospects by phone if they call ahead, in order to make sure that seeing the apartment is worth their time and yours. But when people drop in unannounced and ask about an apartment, you'll need to go through the "qualifying" process explained in Chapter 9.

This may seem to slow things down, but it's really a shortcut. If your unit has no garage, why show it to someone who insists on a locked garage for his new car? If your policy is to lease for a year, someone who's buying a house as soon as possible isn't a prospect for you. If you have no pet or no children rules, someone with pets or children isn't a prospect.

Still, you mustn't come across like an arrogant bureaucrat bullying an ignorant favor-seeker. Keep it uppermost in mind that your purpose is to help every visitor. In order to help, you must learn what he needs — in a pleasant chatty way. Is he new in town? How big is his family? Does he have pets? The minute you realize that you don't have what the visitor requires, say so, regretfully — and try to advise him where he's likely to find it. You never can tell when this prospect may be in the market for exactly what you have — or when he may recommend it to someone else.

How to qualify a caller should be fresh in your mind because it's essential that you do this screening now if you haven't previously done it by phone. The first interview is where your predetermined "tenant profile," mentioned several times previously, is vital. It is a checklist that shows whether a prospect is the kind you want.

Some owners and managers think that a resident's rent-paying ability is the sole standard they need to consider. You'll do much better by renting to residents who are desirable by other standards, too; they'll be compatible and stay longer. Put your standards in writing — just to clarify your own thinking, not to show to applicants — and you'll have little trouble deciding whether a prospect fits the profile.

Anybody can move strangers into empty apartments. But that isn't managing. The residents of your building are members of a team, in a way. More than anything else they determine the success or failure of the owner's investment. Like the manager of a ball club, your job is to select good team members. Since you have no staff of talent scouts to pick out the promising prospects, the job is up to you. How should you do this, beyond the qualifying process already discussed?

THE FIRST STEP IS OBSERVATION. It begins when you open the door, and continues through the first and subsequent conversations. It may be over within a few minutes if you see that a prospect wouldn't fit in with your residents and with your tenant profile. A slovenly appearance often warns of a messy resident. Someone who arrives in an old and dirty car isn't likely to take pride in his apartment. Little things like a careless hairdo, a spotted dress, or too much makeup can be tip-offs.

But don't be hasty. Some very good people wear beards and T-shirts nowadays. Use your ears as well as your eyes. You can tell a lot by the way a person talks. Even so, after a hectic day of hunting for apartments and sparring with incompetent managers, a normally pleasant person can be in a snarling mood. Your kindness and courtesy may bring him back to normal in a few minutes.

There are certain combinations of which you should be wary on sight. A young fellow with a flashy new sports car may want to party all night, and may be unable to afford the rent. A pair of girls who want to share an apartment are seldom stable residents; they may be unable to pay the rent. A florid face sometimes (but not always) indicates a drinking problem.

ASK OPEN-END QUESTIONS — the kind that can't be answered by a simple yes or no — to get more insight into someone. "How far from here do you work? . . . Where do you live now? . . . I gather you don't like it very well . . . Have you been looking long today? . . . What sort of apartment would you really like to find?"

Look out for prospects who seem full of grievances, or otherwise hint at a life full of friction. People who feel surrounded by enemies aren't friendly types. Never be tempted by a prospect who offers cash in advance, on condition you let him move in immediately. He usually claims he was very happy in his last residence — somewhere far away — but is forced to leave it by some business shift or family emergency. Because of this crisis, whatever it is, he "must get located right now, today." Although he sounds convincing, he may be a bad risk. All too often, such pressure means an occupant has just been evicted from somewhere for non-payment, and has sold his last possessions to raise cash with which to buy himself into another apartment. Managers almost always regret renting to someone who wants to get inside in a hurry. Usually, he turns out to be a clever deadbeat.

CAN YOUR APPLICANT PAY THE RENT? This is a delicate question. Approach it carefully. Never let yourself be convinced merely by good clothes, a good car, and a prosperous manner. You always must wait until the applicant fills out a rental application, and you check his references because only then can you feel confident that his financial position is solid. On the other hand, your first casual questions can sometimes uncover warning signals.

What kind of work does the applicant do? How long has he or she been there? Long employment at one place is a good sign. Job-hopping (like apartment-hopping) is a bad sign.

Someone on a payroll is usually a safer prospect than someone whose income is irregular, such as a salesman on commission, or an actor. Wages can be garnisheed, if need be, to collect rent. But it's hard to put legal pressure on someone who is self-employed. So the owner of a barber shop, filling station, small garage or restaurant may be prosperous and yet be a poor risk. This isn't to say that many people fail to pay their rent. It's just one of the possibilities you should think about in choosing the best available applicants for your apartments.

Well-meaning people may run up more bills than they can pay. A young couple with a child or two, buying a new car, can't live on the same salary as an older couple without children at home who've accumulated all the material goods they need.

If you have serious doubts about an applicant's financial responsibility, but are favorably impressed otherwise, you may want to take time to explore this subject gently with him before showing an apartment. You can mention that the Federal Housing Authority has made studies and worked out a rule of thumb; no more than one-fourth of monthly gross income (one week's wages, that is) should go for rent. Therefore, it's important for his own good that the applicant's income be at least four times the amount of rent he contracts to pay. Having explained this, you can ask in a friendly way whether the rent you're asking is higher than he ought to pay. Just be sure that when you talk money it's behind closed doors. A person's income is one of his most jealously guarded secrets.

IS YOUR UNIT REALLY RIGHT FOR THE APPLICANT? Someone anxious to find an apartment and enthused about moving into your building may overlook problems that you should point out. For instance, would you rent a third-floor apartment in a building with no elevator to an elderly person? Or, if a bachelor does no cooking, and eats all his meals out, would you rent to him without mentioning that the only restaurants nearby are worse than mediocre?

How about the distance from your building to the prospect's place of employment? Most people soon learn to hate long commutes, although they may not realize this is in advance. After bucking rush hour traffic awhile, your new resident may leave you for another apartment closer to his job.

PERSUASION IN THE OFFICE

DISCOURAGING UNSUITABLE APPLICANTS is easy sometimes. As mentioned earlier, if someone has special requirements that you can't meet, it's a simple matter to explain this and try to suggest some other solution to his housing problem. But it's not always this easy.

Maybe he's convinced that you have exactly what he wants. But he doesn't fit your tenant profile (wrong age, or whatever). You'll just have to tell him so: "I'm awfully sorry, but it's against the owner's policy to rent to college students . . . to people with motorcycles . . . " or whatever classification applies to his case.

Be careful to stay within the law in drawing up your tenant profile. It can't include anything about race, nationality, sex, religion or creed. Federal laws prohibit this, and they're sternly enforced. Don't try to get around them or to camouflage them in your tenant profile.

Of course, discrimination may be more apparent than real. The fact that you have no black or Chicano or Jewish residents doesn't necessarily mean that you refuse to rent to any. Maybe none have applied. Maybe those who did apply couldn't meet other standards set forth in your tenant profile. But you'd better be ready to prove what those standards are.

Some managers try to dodge the law through subterfuge. For example, instead of saying bluntly and illegally, "We don't rent to blacks," they tell blacks there are no vacancies. If there's a vacancy sign in the window at the moment, they claim the apartment "has just been rented," or "isn't ready to be shown." Sometimes they try to discourage a minority group by quoting a much higher rent than they normally ask.

Sometimes they resort to collusion with their friends. A friend fills out and signs a rental application, and the manager makes out a deposit receipt (undated) in advance. Then if a minority person asks to see the apartment, the manager can say, "I'm sorry, I just rented it." If the applicant demands proof of this, the manager ducks into another room to get the bogus papers, fills in the date and apartment number, and shows these.

But consider what may happen. Anyone who feels discriminated against (because of sex, religion, or ethnic background) in renting an apartment can sue in federal court or possibly in state court. If you're found guilty, you may be compelled to pay damages. Most apartment associations won't help an owner if they think he's guilty of discrimination. So you and the owner may have to fight the case on your own.

If either of you are hauled into court, your only chance to beat the rap may be by committing perjury — which is a felony punishable by fine and imprisonment. And a phony story may break down under questioning. On what date was the apartment shown to your friend? Will the friend confirm this? Is there proof that the friend ever saw the apartment in question? No friend is likely to give perjured testimony to help out an apartment manager.

Moreover, minority organizations know how to lay solid groundwork for a charge of discrimination. The rejected applicant sends two friends (one as a witness) who ask to see the same apartment that the applicant couldn't rent. These friends, of course, are chosen to be acceptable to the apartment manager. If the manager or you willingly show the apartment, or quote a lower rental rate, then the rejected applicant has grounds for a suit under the Federal Housing Act of 1968.

To be safe from false charges of discrimination, draw up a written statement about your rental policies, and keep it available. It should be specific about such requirements as income level, job stability, references, length of time in the area, appearance of the applicant, and whatever other standards you'll use in judging all applicants. It should contain a disclaimer: "No person or persons shall be denied the right to rent an apartment because of his or her race, color, religion, national origin or ancestry."

But now we come to the applicant you want to turn away even though he meets all your written standards. Sometimes you just realize, from his words and ways, that he'd be too hard to get along with. Or you have a creepy feeling that he's a Mafia hit man looking for a hideaway. You can't very well tell such a character, "You wouldn't fit in here, so I won't show you an apartment." And you dare not claim that there's no unit available, for fear he may be a member of some militant minority group looking for a chance to charge you with discrimination. So what can you do?

SALESMANSHIP IN REVERSE is your best chance. Let him see an apartment, the least desirable one. You can either toss him a key and tell him to go look, or you can take him personally to see it — via a route past the garbage cans and up the dirtiest stairs. Inside the unit you can mumble, "Thiz the parlor . . . thiz the bedroom . . . thiz the john," Your lifeless attitude can kill the sale.

If he still seems to want it, you can deepen the reverse salesmanship by bragging about aspects you're sure he won't like. If he's middle aged and grumpy looking, you can remark, "We got lotsa peppy young swingers here. Parties every night." Or you can bewail problems with "hippies, junkies, fruits and dikes." If he's young and lively, you can mutter, "Thiz a nice quiet place. Mostly old folks here. They insist on absolute quiet after 9:00 o'clock."

If he doesn't have a pet, you might launch into a long harangue about the stray dogs and tomcats that seem to hang around. Likewise for children. But if he has pets and children — and you permit these — you'd better talk sadly about animal haters and kid haters in the building and the neighborhood, about the lousy bus service, the hold-ups and burglaries nearby, the impossible parking conditons, and so on.

This should drive away almost any applicant, saving you the trouble of checking to make sure he is as undesirable as you suspect. (How to check, and how to reject an applicant after you've made the check, are covered in the first section of Chapter 11.)

However, it's worth emphasizing that this negative salesmanship is advisable only in extreme cases. Even when you must use it, try to maintain your role of helpful adviser, carefully considering the applicant's needs. You shouldn't ever be rude, even if he is. Rudeness might get your face bashed in, if by any chance an applicant really is a criminal or a psychopath.

TRUE SALESMANSHIP can and should begin the instant you're fairly sure that you've got what a desirable looking prospect needs. Don't stall while you try to sense whether this prospect is the best one you can find. (That can come later, after he has filled in the Application to Rent.) Start selling before you even rise from your chair to lead the way toward an apartment.

Turn the conversation toward whatever the prospect has shown an interest in, or has indicated is a problem. Examples:

"During our telephone conversation, Mrs. Angst, you mentioned that your husband often has to be away at night. Your apartment here would be right next to the assistant manager's apartment, so there'll be someone close by at night. And you'll be glad to know we have dead-bolt locks on apartment doors — the kind the police department recommends — and a peephole so you can see who's at the door before you open it even a crack. Come on and I'll show you the apartment."

"So you have young children? That's fine. There are good schools and buses and play areas, and baby sitters in the neighborhood . . . A really good environment for youngsters. We'll take a look at the play area on the way to see your apartment."

"I gather you folks want a nice quiet place. Along that line, let me tell you about one thing before you see the apartment, because there's no way to show it to you. That's the soundproofing. It gives you so much more privacy . . . "

Sales experts advise, "Don't talk about what you have; tell the prospects what they can have." That's basically what you should be doing as you chat with your prospect. Talk about the benefits, not just the facilities themselves; if a unit is close to the swimming pool, this means "The minute you get home from work, you're only a step away from a healthy refreshing swim, and from sunbathing and relaxation." If it is away from the pool, "You get more privacy, and yet you have easy access to a healthy refreshing swim . . . "

HOT BUTTONS, as salesmen call them — sales points that appeal most to a particular prospect — often come to light during the first chat on the phone or in your office. Your early questions can uncover them. When you ask, "What kind of apartment would you like best?" the answer may be, "One with more space than I have now," or "A nice quiet secure place," or "Well, we'd like a good view and plenty of light." Taking your cue from what the prospects say, you emphasize the advantages most likely to entice them.

Just by looking at a prospect, you may get other clues to hot buttons. An athletic looking person who might be a tennis enthusiast should be shown the unit closest to the tennis courts, if there are any in your complex or nearby. The mother of two children ought to see an apartment on the first floor with the shortest distance between the parking lot and the apartment. Someone with a deep suntan might be enthused about a unit near the swimming pool.

SHOW YOUR ENTHUSIASM about taking the prospect to see an apartment. If you've prepared well, then you know a lot about the property, and you should feel confident. Confidence makes you enthusiastic — which is a highly contagious frame of mind. If people sense that you enjoy showing the unit, they'll be more inclined to rent.

PERSUASION EN ROUTE

ON THE WAY TO THE APARTMENT, take a pre-planned tour that shows the buildings and grounds to their best advantage. Probably you should begin with the recreation facilities and the decorated model apartments, if any (assuming that they're reasonably close together). They can dramatize life style far better than you can describe it. If you wait until the end to show the recreation equipment, you may not get a chance to show it at all. Prospects might leave before seeing it — but they won't leave before seeing the apartment. (You can show some lesser facilities like the laundry room on the way back, or skip them altogether if you see there's no point in showing them.)

Even in smaller buildings, there may be several routes to the model apartment or the vacant unit itself, but there's only one best route. Maybe it's past the swimming pool, or through the game room, or past the bicycle rack and the carport area. Maybe it's in a motorized cart, maybe up the front stairs, maybe via the back elevator. Whatever it is, figure out the most pleasant and impressive tour.

Whether walking or riding (as in some of the larger garden complexes), be sure to call your prospect's attention to various features and benefits: the fine lawn, the private entrances and patios (privacy is a great sales feature), roomy play areas with shade for hot days and sunny open spaces for cooler weather, landscaping with large trees near windows to give added privacy, carports conveniently close to entrances.

More and more apartment buildings are installing a bicycle rack, with cycles for free use of residents. If you have something like this, novel enough to be unfamiliar to most prospects, be sure to tell them all about it — in terms of the benefits: "This is not only healthful exercise, but it saves you the time of walking, or the trouble of driving and finding parking places. It's a great car-saver. You can cycle to the Thriftee Mart and the drug store around the corner. And downtown is only three blocks away, with a wealth of shopping areas."

During the tour, ask plenty of questions that get the prospect nodding his head and saying yes. "Don't you think it's a good idea, the way these buildings are divided to give them individuality? . . . Don't you think these steel stair railings are more attractive than wood? They also provide more safety, you know, which is another reason we use them . . . Notice how quiet it is here? No children in this building . . . Do you think you can take advantage of this extra storage area set aside for each resident . . . Many of the wives relax at the swimming pool during the day, Mrs. Angst. This should make it easy to get acquainted, don't you think?"

GET THE PROSPECT SAYING "YES" as soon and as often as you can. Never ask a question that is likely to be answered by "no." Every time a prospect nods his head and says "yes," the closer he is to agreeing to rent. So keep phrasing remarks in such a way that listeners are almost sure to respond affirmatively.

Call attention to the "good maintenance" several times during the pre-planned tour. Point out how well maintained the grounds are, and the exteriors of the buildings. Some managers take this for granted, but prospects don't. If there are good trash collection and garbage collection services, be sure to mention it.

Encourage prospects to ask questions. Managers tend to be in too big a hurry. When a prospect begins asking questions, that's a sign he's warming up.

ONE WORD OF CAUTION. If you're thinking of emphasizing "security" to attract prospects, don't! Don't use the words "security" or "safety" or "protection" at all in conversation, or in your advertising or promotional literature. By doing so, you'd be implying a commitment for which a court might hold you liable if a resident met with violence on the premises. The truth is that you can't make the premises perfectly secure; only an army could do that.

Hotels generally are expert in providing security, but they never advertise it. Hotels know that proclaiming "security" is worrisome to guests, so they go at it quietly. You should follow this example: help your residents to be as safe as they can, but don't mention it.

Legally speaking, if you brag about security, you may well become responsible for it, when you otherwise wouldn't be. If something happens to an occupant, you could be sued because you didn't provide the security you "promised." No matter how good your security system is, someone can always claim you should have done more. You could have doubled or tripled the guards, put in TV monitors, provided watch dogs. It's better not to install any system that calls for control by anyone other than the resident.

The best you can do is provide residents with security devices that they can use personally. Dead-bolt locks are fine because the residents set them. Apartment-to-lobby intercom systems are fine because the residents use them. In short, anything that the resident controls is good; anything that involves another party is hazardous because of your legal liability for it.

THE ART OF SHOWING RENTALS

The most crucial part of your job as a salesman begins when you actually show a model apartment or an available vacancy to the prospect. Whether it's big or small, fancy or plain, your expertise in showing it will make all the difference. Everything that has gone before is useless if prospects lose their interest in renting when they see the apartment itself.

Plan this carefully. Rehearsals will help. Go over details and features until you know them perfectly. A good salesman learns all he can about what he's selling; then plans how to translate solid facts into memorable phrases and actions that give a prospect a mental picture of himself and his friends enjoying whatever is being pointed out. All rooms have benefits; it's up to you to highlight them.

Good salesmen keep the prospect in the foreground. So, when you open the door to a unit, step back. Always let the prospect go first, so he gets an unimpeded view of each room. And while he's stepping through the door, call attention to the room's spaciousness. Any room looks bigger from the doorway than from its center.

THE LIVING ROOM. Instead of saying, "This is the living room," as if the prospect were blind or stupid, say something like, "Notice how big this living room is. There's more wall space than you find in most apartments . . ." or "Isn't it light and airy? On a bright afternoon you can flood this room with sunshine . . ." or "How do you like the big picture window? Isn't that a nice view?" or "There's plenty of room for a sofa in three locations here. How do you think your mirror will look against that end wall?"

It's good salesmanship to get your prospects *doing* something instead of just listening, even if it's only making small decisions about where they might place a couch or mirror. A textile salesman carries a little magnifying glass and invites prospects to peer at fabric. Insurance salesmen hand a pen to a prospect and ask him, "Will you write these figures down as I give them to you?" It's a good way to hold someone's interest.

Call attention to the number of convenient electrical outlets — and how easy these make it to place lighting fixtures. If there's a built-in television antenna outlet, or if all units include cable TV (which gives interference-free reception on 20 channels), be sure to talk about it. Is there a new carpet, or one that's been freshly shampooed? Mention it.

People like a warm living room. Talk about the gas fireplace or the electric heater or the furnace. "This furnace really throws out the heat in a hurry when you want it. Notice it doesn't smoke or smell?" (Presumably, you turned on the heat in advance, as suggested in Chapter 6.) Emphasize how well-maintained it is. Mention that the rooms have individual temperature controls, if they do, or at least that every apartment does.

THE HALL. "You'll be glad to see those two large closets along the hall. Open them up and notice how big they are. Lots of space for your linens and towels." Again you get the prospect doing something. Touching and feeling are even better than seeing. Ask your prospect to feel the kitchen sink, or walk across the carpet, or touch the tile, or open the cabinets. Every time they do something like this, they subconsciously feel a bit more possessive toward the apartment.

THE BATHROOM. Explain that the color-keyed shower curtain is part of the rental price, as is the cleanliness of the sinks and bathtub. Talk about the built-in heat and sun lamp. Point out the decorative light, or top-quality shower head, or spacious towel racks — everything about the room that can conceivably be an asset.

Maybe you can say, "See this special tile floor? We use it because it's so easy to clean . . . " or "Have you noticed how small the shower areas are in most other apartments? Ours are extra large. Why don't you step right into it to get a better idea?"

BEDROOMS. "The master bedroom is easily big enough for twin beds. Or if you have a double bed, there'd be room for a desk and chair . . . You'll find you won't get street noise at night with your bedroom toward the back of the lot like this. Traffic noise is a nuisance at night, isn't it? . . . Just step out onto the balcony and see how pleasant it is. Only a sliding door to fresh air and sunshine. I'll bet you'll enjoy sitting out here with a tall cool glass of something-or-other . . . What do you think of this walk-in closet? Extra closet space is always useful, isn't it? . . . This second bedroom has a good closet, too . . . Notice that there are phone and TV outlets in each bedroom . . . Would you like to convert this bedroom into a den?"

KITCHEN. "Isn't this kitchen bright and cheerful? Notice that there's plenty of lighting from the window over the sink. Don't you feel it will make doing the dishes a little less boring? . . . The paint has just finished drying, so you don't have to worry about touching it . . . You see there are quite a few cabinets, which always come in handy. . . There's a double outlet behind the refrigerator. And here are outlets on each side of the sink for your toaster and blender and any other appliances . . . The double oven is the best of its kind you can buy today. Won't it be great for baking your cakes?"

The kitchen is the area where you should be thoroughly knowledgeable before showing it to women prospects. They'll ask questions and you'd better know the answers. If you don't, you can't sell the unit.

For example, someone may ask, "Do the drawers in the kitchen roll on ball bearings?" The way a drawer pulls out is something most women check when inspecting a kitchen. Suppose the drawers don't roll on bearings? Then give a frank answer and shift the discussion to another benefit: "No, they don't. But pull one out. See how easily it pulls? These drawers have been treated with a finish that repels stains and water. All you do is wipe them with a sponge — no mess! The cupboards have this same finish. Open one and feel it."

Again, something about the sense of touch makes everything real for people. If you say the oven door is light as a feather, it will mean much more to a prospect who opens and closes the door herself. If you say the garbage disposal is super-quiet, ask her to turn the switch on and off. The idea is to give her the feeling of possessing this kitchen and enjoying its conveniences.

Point out the garbage disposal, the dishwasher; don't assume someone realizes they are there. If appliances have well-known brand names, mention the brands. If the kitchen counters are coved, point out how this prevents spills on the floor. If the refrigerator has a large-sized freezing compartment, remind the prospect that this additional freezer space will enable her to store reserve food and take advantage of bargain prices. If the oven is big enough for a whole turkey, mention this.

SERVICE PORCH. "Notice how handy the service porch is to the kitchen. There's room out here for a washer and dryer. Do you have both? . . . You like to hang your washing in the sun? Then you'll find this sheltered landing convenient. Isn't this pulley clothes line handy?"

OBJECTIONS MUST BE OVERCOME

You can handle many prospects' objections by well-planned salesmanship. Figure out an answer to every criticism you think a prospect may raise. Even if the objections in themselves don't seem to constitute enough reason for refusing to take an apartment, they may become magnified by the prospect's mind if you let them pass. They create a negative atmosphere. Later the prospect may not remember what his objections were, but he'll remember there was "something" wrong with your unit.

YOU CAN TURN AN OBJECTION INTO A BENEFIT. Use the "yes but — " technique. If Mrs. Angst says the bedroom is small, admit this but show her that it's easier to keep clean. Cleanliness is a great selling feature. If a woman knows she isn't going to spend days cleaning her new apartment, she's practically sold.

In the bathroom, maybe Mrs. Angst says, "There sure isn't much linen space," you counter, "You're right. However, there's plenty of space in the hall closet. By taking less space for linens in the bathroom, we give you a longer bath and shower space." Then go on to the next room, giving her no time to brood about the linen closet.

If the kitchen is small, you can say, "A compact kitchen makes it easier to work in. You'd be surprised how many steps you save every day in a compact, functional kitchen. The smaller space in some rooms gives a larger living area where you spend your leisure time and entertain guests."

Suppose Mrs. Angst says, "I don't think we'd like that wall heater. I'd much rather have central heating. It makes everything warmer. We used to rent an apartment with an old fashioned furnace, and it never did give out enough heat." Your yes but: "I know what you mean. It probably didn't have enough heating capacity. But there's a difference in furnaces. Ours is a very efficient circulating type that circulates the heat all over the apartment. It has 75,000 BTU, more than you need to keep the whole place heated. Its big advantage is that it gives the most economical heat you can get. Your heat bills will be less with this — so you can save money and still be perfectly comfortable. Isn't it nice and warm now?"

If Mrs. Angst says the outside of the building looks shabby, you might say (if you can say it truthfully), "I'm glad you mentioned that because it certainly should be painted. But you can't do a good outside paint job in cold weather. The owner plans to paint outside as soon as the weather is warm enough. Won't the front look attractive with all new colors?"

If Mrs. Angst doesn't like the unit's location because "We'd be awakened at night every time somebody comes or goes," maybe your pre-planned reply is, "Of course, you don't want to be disturbed at all hours. But we have good steady residents who don't keep late hours. We haven't been bothered a bit by that." Alternatively, you might ask, "Will you take an apartment with a better location?" if you have one to offer.

YOU CAN ANSWER AN OBJECTION BY SWITCHING THE SUBJECT. This isn't as good as yes but. Still, it's better than ignoring a criticism. A prospect may say, "Just look at the horrible color on that house across the street." There's nothing you can do to change it or turn it into a benefit. Your best bet is a response like, "Oh, I'm usually so busy, I've never noticed it. Another thing you haven't looked at yet is the garage. Yours is only a few steps from your door. Won't that be handy when you're shopping?"

Suppose Mrs. Angst notices the hardwood flooring and says, "Oh, no, I hate having to polish floors." Perhaps you can change the subject slightly. "Wouldn't this floor look beautiful with an area rug?" and then try to convert the objection into a benefit: "Mrs. Angst, did you know that hardwood flooring is much warmer than tile? Just feel it. This is a great help in preventing colds in the family."

MAKING UP YOUR PROSPECT'S MIND

When a prospect begins making comments — even critical ones — that's a sign he's interested. If he definitely doesn't like it, he can easily say, "No, I don't want it," and leave. But if he's leaning in your direction, he uses questions and objections to escape having to decide. A decision to move is hard for some people to make. They need to be coaxed and reassured before they commit themselves. Subconsciously, they feel better about letting someone else carry some blame for "talking them into it." Such people need help in making decisions. They may never sign if you just stand back and wait for them to say, "I'll take it."

BE DIRECT. Even most of the ready renters wait to be asked. If it's obvious that they like an apartment, sometimes a manager tries to force the issue with a blunt question. "Will you take the apartment?" But this makes it too easy to say, "No, we haven't make up our minds." After saying no, prospects find it much harder to say yes later. So you should use better methods of helping them decide.

DON'T LET THE PROSPECT GO AWAY saying, "We'll think about it and let you know." This is the typical response from the many prospects who hate to get off the fence. They seldom come back. Usually, they look at other places, and meet a more persuasive renting agent. Countless rentals are lost by postponement. One way to counter this is to ask, "So you have questions in your mind? Probably I can clarify them. What is it you need to think about?"

Another way is a yes but, followed by persuasive reasons for deciding immediately: "Yes, many people prefer to look at several apartments. But this is the last apartment on the ground floor and it will probably go today. Some other people are coming in to see it this afternoon . . . Why don't we go back to my apartment for a cup of coffee and talk a little more?"

The let's-go-back proposal is for use primarily with a couple. They may need only to discuss the apartment privately before agreeing to rent. Women love to shop while men hate needless delays. During the stroll back to your apartment, you can tactfully fall behind – or even excuse yourself for a brief errand – so the prospects will have a chance to confer. Maybe there's some small budgeting problem that they want to discuss; if they work it out, they may decide to rent on the spot. (If you can't invite them anywhere for coffee or whatever, you can at least excuse yourself from the apartment they're looking at. "I'll just run a short errand while you look at the apartment a little further. Will you meet me out in front?"

ALWAYS WATCH FOR CHANCES TO CLOSE – to clinch the sale. Any expert salesman is constantly maneuvering for a possible close. He doesn't wait until the end of his presentation to give the prospect a chance to say "yes." He provides many chances – what salesmen call "trial closes" or "closing feelers."

He may pause and say, "Don't you agree?" or "Is this what you're looking for?" or "Which of these parking stalls would you prefer for your car?"

Early in the game, he unobtrusively pulls out the rental application or deposit receipt, and keeps it in plain sight. This avoids the awkward pause that would come if he stopped to search for the paper at the crucial moment. And it gets the prospect used to seeing it, so it won't scare him when the time comes to sign.

OFFER SMALL CONCESSIONS IF NECESSARY, when your trial closes haven't worked, and combine them with another trial close: "If I put in new wallpaper, would you be interested? . . . Shall I exchange the lamp shades for a lighter color? . . . Suppose I make this apartment an even better bargain by installing a top-grade shower head in the bathroom. Will you rent it?"

If the prospect asks, "Do you paint when needed?" Your answer should be, "Will you take the apartment if we do?" If he asks whether you'll clean the drapes, you can reply, "Do you want the drapes cleaned?" This tends to commit him.

Of course, no concessions need be offered if you're sure that many desirable prospects are coming to look at the apartment. In any case, don't offer the big concession – lowering the rent – even when someone says, "The rent is a little higher than we want to pay," unless you're desperate. Lowering your asking price lowers the value of the property. You should only do it as a last resort.

PRESS HOT BUTTONS AGAIN. If you're really selling, you've been watching your prospects' reactions to everything you show them. Whatever they particularly like is worth mentioning again when you're maneuvering for a close. If the husband has a new sports car, and you have a fully enclosed garage, he may sell her on the merits of a tiny kitchen if you remind him of the garage.

HURDLE THE BIG DECISION by asking a question which doesn't make the prospect say definitely that he'll rent the apartment, yet goes along with your implied assumption that he will. Here are samples of such questions:

"Do you want us to furnish a refrigerator, or will you have your own? . . . Would you rather pay your rent by check or cash? . . . Is the first of the month a convenient time for you to pay? . . . Do you prefer the single or split level? . . . You can probably put the bookcase you mentioned under that window, can't you? . . . Shall I include janitor service, or would you rather save the extra charge? . . . You have two cars, don't you? I can arrange parking for a second car if you like."

"When would you like to move in?" In the rare case of an extremely indecisive prospect, you can make this question a bit stronger. "When do you have to move?" Then you can respond by saying that the apartment will be ready at that particular date — and go on to arrange for the deposit.

ASK FOR A DEPOSIT. Decisions almost always become final when money changes hands. Without money, you risk the prospect changing his mind, even though he's said yes. He may see a better place on the way home. But with money paid down, the prospect stops looking around, because the decision has been made. Even an amount as small as $25 — or a post-dated check, for that matter — will signal a decision and turn the prospect's mind to his arrangements for moving.

Instead of forthrightly demanding, "If you'll get your checkbook out, we'll figure the amount of deposit needed," you can again ease into a close by asking *which*: "Would you rather pay the first month's rent now or just make a deposit so I can hold the apartment for you? Of course, the deposit will be applied to the first month's rent."

You can do this another way by starting to fill out the receipt for a deposit, and asking the prospect how to spell his name. If he spells it and sees you writing it on the deposit receipt, you've probably pulled him off the fence.

You can explain further that the deposit is a way of weeding out people who don't sincerely want the apartment. "So, it's a very practical preliminary to the rental application and lease agreement." Establish the date the prospect would like to move in, and explain the monthly rent, the utilities he'll be required to pay, and so on. Here is a sample holding receipt:

DEPOSIT RECEIPT

Application to rent Apt. No. _____ located at _____

_____ (city)_____ (state), subject to approval by the undersigned and to vacating by the present tenants.
Received the sum of _____Dollars ($_____)
as consideration for owner's promise to hold said premises for occupancy by _____adults and _____ children only, and no pets. Occupancy beginning on _____ 19____ , for_____ , who agrees to rent said premises at $_____ per month payable monthly in advance. In the event of such approval and vacating of premises, this deposit shall be applied on the first month's rent. If, after approval, full rent is not paid when due, all rights of applicant shall terminate and the deposit shall be retained by the owner.

Dated: _____ 19__ .

_____ _____
(Owner) (Manager for Owner) **(Occupant)**

In reading the receipt form, most people notice that it says, "subject to approval by the undersigned." But just in case they don't, you should always say casually, "As a matter of routine, the owner requires that all new residents fill out a rental application that gives character and credit references. I'm sure you've done this before. So, if you'll come up to the office and give me a little information, we'll get ready to move you in — and the rest of the first month's rent can be paid when you pick up your keys."

You realize, although you don't say so, that you must check up on this applicant, now that he's agreed to rent. (The details for doing this are explained in the next chapter.) The information on his application may warn you that he's a bad credit risk, or may be undesirable for some other reason — in which case, you'll refund his deposit. If he gets indignant and refuses to give character references or credit information, obviously he has something to hide and you don't want him.

SAY GOODBYE. With the deposit agreed on, stop talking! Many rentals are lost at the last minute because a manager says something that changes a prospect's mind. The lease arrangements and the house rules can be discussed later, after the rental application has been checked out.

IF YOU CAN'T SELL THE PROSPECT

No matter how good your sales technique, some desirable prospects are going to say no. Don't take it as an insult. Be pleasant, thank them, and remind them that maybe your building can serve their purpose at some future time.

IF HE WON'T SAY YES OR NO, apologize for rushing him, and suggest that he take as much time as he needs to decide. Give him an information booklet if you have one. Give him a floor plan of the unit, and a map of the complex, if they're available. Give him a rental application "just in case." And at the very least, give him your business card so he can call back.

This way, at the end of a hectic day of looking, the prospect will have a clear recollection of what you showed him, while other apartments may be blurred in his memory. There's a chance he'll come back.

IF A PROSPECT WANTS TO CONSULT SOMEONE ELSE — a wife, husband, roommate, rich aunt, or boss — you should agree wholeheartedly and ask, "When would be most convenient for you to come back, Thursday morning or Wednesday afternoon? . . . Is 2:00 o'clock a good time? . . . I want to make sure I'm free when you come." This subtly reinforces the idea that you're talking with others, too, and that the apartment may not be available more than a few days. Also, setting a specific time makes it more likely that the prospect will return because he feels that he has made an appointment.

If the wife has done the preliminary looking and has been pleased, she'll bring the husband and do the selling herself. She knows her husband better than you do and can probably be more persuasive. Just be ready to answer his questions, and point out any big selling points that she may overlook.

REMEMBER THESE BASIC POINTS:

* *Make sure that visitors are favorably impressed by the place where you receive them, and by your manner and appearance.*

* *At the beginning of the chat, screen visitors if you haven't previously done so by phone. Use your eyes as well as your ears.*

* *Discourage unsuitable applicants, but start low-pressure selling immediately if you think the applicant may be suitable. Stress whatever he shows interest in.*

* *Lead the prospect to the apartment by a pre-planned tour that shows the property to best advantage.*

* *In showing apartments, highlight the advantages of each room. Phrase remarks in such a way that you get the prospect saying yes.*

* *Be ready in advance with responses to any criticism you think a prospect may raise. Use the "yes but —" technique.*

* *Watch for chances to clinch the sale. Ask "when" and "which" instead of "will you?"*

* *Ask for a deposit.*

* *As soon as the deposit is agreed upon, stop talking.*

XI *Welcoming New Occupants*

So you've persauded an applicant to rent one of your apartments. He hands you a check as a deposit. You give him a receipt somewhat like the sample shown on Page 137. What now? Is it time to start preparations for moving him in? Almost.

You've worked hard to get him and he's eager for the apartment, and you can't make him wait very long before letting him take possession. But you should never, never approve an apartment-hunter on the spot. Always wait until he fills out a detailed rental application and you've used it to check on him.

TAKE TIME TO BE SURE

If you met a pleasant stranger on the street and he handed you a check for $25 or even $250, would you give him the keys to your car? Of course not — no matter how charming he seemed, how plausible his line of talk.

Yet, some owners and managers of apartments permit an unknown individual or family to move into their premises on the strength of a half-hour conversation. In effect, they're saying, "Here are the keys to my $15,000 investment. It's yours for awhile." This is just as rash as giving a stranger the use of your car.

DON'T TRUST YOUR INTUITION in renting. People are on their best behavior when they want an apartment. No matter how astute a manager may be as a hunch player, he can be disastrously wrong now and then. Many completely unreliable people give a convincing impression of reliability, while some odd-looking characters turn out to be solid citizens. Then, too, some applicants don't plan to bilk anyone, yet are so careless or moody that they make life miserable for a property manager. They, too, may have a charming side that beguiles managers into trusting them instead of checking up.

You'll be worse off than not renting if you rent to the wrong person. "I once took a new tenant without running any check on him," writes Richard F. Gabriel, a successful real estate investor. "He sub-rented one of his two bedrooms without my authority, and in the process brought more wear and tear to the apartment without any compensation to me. When *his* tenant left, *my* tenant could no longer pay. After a few months, I had to evict this tenant for non-payment, a lengthy process that cost me $250 in legal expenses alone, plus a similar amount in lost rent."

Ken Hansen, a Los Angeles newspaperman, wrote recently: "Four years ago I went into the apartment business. I sank most of my savings into two four-unit buildings. I operated them informally, on the basis of trust. I figured a tenant was like a friend sharing my building. I didn't figure right. At one time or another my tenants have ruined a hardwood floor; drilled a hole in the kitchen lineoleum; given me bum checks; lied to me about occupations and former residences; taken a Jeep apart, spreading oil and parts over an area where people like to sit in the sun; and set up a workshop, complete with noisy power tools, in a garage.

"In addition, I rented to a single individual only to have two more move in. The non-paying tenants brought another complete set of furniture. . . I've learned to protect myself. I demand security deposits. I demand detailed rental agreements and applications. I make more thorough background checks. I demand first and last months' rent and key deposits. I don't accept people at their word."

We say in Chapter 4, it takes time and trouble to oust an undesirable resident. Every day lost in such a predicament may be a day's rent lost, plus whatever damage the occupant does, plus your mental anguish.

Aside from these risks, there's another reason to be extremely careful — the potential for gain. If your residents are nice people. they're bound to attract others of the same quality. Good screening procedures can help fill your building with happy, long-term residents. Your check-up is cheap "income insurance."

ACCEPTING A DEPOSIT DOESN'T BIND YOU to rent, even though many applicants intend it this way. Make this clear — in writing, as well as in your conversations with applicants.

When you give the receipt, don't just use a blank form from a receipt book you may use for rent receipts. And don't scribble a simple note. Either of these might be legally binding on you as an implied contract, in case the applicant took you to court. Instead, be sure to use a special form, such as the one suggested in Chapter 10, or the alternative shown on Page 143.

Either of these forms avoids wrangles that can arise through "oral understanding." Whatever receipt you use should make clear that if the rental application is rejected by "the owner" or "the office" (not by you personally; let anonymous parties take the blame), the full deposit will be refunded — but that, contrariwise, if the prospect changes his mind and backs out, he loses the deposit. Avoid the word "forfeit" when you explain this. For some obscure reason, people can face the prospect of "losing" things but they hate to "forfeit" anything.

You'll notice that the sample Deposit Receipt which is shown on Page 143 specifies that the amount is applied partly to a security deposit and partly toward the first month's rent. This is a good policy because later, when the prospect signs a rental agreement, he gives you a legal right to collect rent, but you'll have nothing in writing to help you collect a security deposit which was agreed to but not paid.

Some managers go further. They get not only an advance security deposit, but a key deposit, and still another deposit against pet damage — perhaps paid before the rental agreement is even filled in. Of course, these deposits must be refunded if the management later turns down the applicant. And if the applicant moves in, they're still partially or wholly refundable (and collectible in court) if nothing has been damaged by the time the resident moves out.

WHAT IS A SECURITY DEPOSIT? It's often misunderstood and a bone of contention, especially when occupants move out. They often give their 30-day termination notice, and deduct the security deposit from the final month's rent. This is wrong. The manager may not know how much chargeable damage, if any, there is until the furniture is moved out.

It used to be standard to pay two months' rent (the first and last) in advance. This was done to weed out applicants who were short of cash, and to protect owners against those who skipped out.

But the Internal Revenue Service ruled that the final month's rent was prepaid

DEPOSIT RECEIPT

I/We deposit herewith the sum of $ _____ (cash___ check___ M.O.___) receipt of which is hereby acknowledged as a non-interest bearing deposit and not a rental payment on Apt. No. _____ located at _____ _____ Street, _____, California. The occupancy is to consist of _____ adults and _____ children only, beginning on _____, 19___ , at the rental of $ _____ per month payable in advance on the _____ of each month. _____

Of this deposit, $ _____ shall be acknowledged as received in consideration for execution of the Rental Agreement, if the Application is accepted by the Owner. The balance, if any, of this deposit will be applied toward a Security Deposit of $_____.

The Security Deposit, upon acceptance by the Owner, will be refunded within 14 days after vacating the premises provided they have been occupied for over _____ months and they are essentially in the same condition as received, normal wear and tear excepted.

If, through no fault of the Owner, the applicant does not occupy the premises on the agreed date of occupancy, the full amount of deposit will be retained by the Owner to recover loss of rental funds and application processing costs.

The Owner will refund the full deposit if the application is not approved or if possession of premises cannot be delivered to applicant on date specified above. The sum so deposited shall be returned to applicant and applicant shall not acquire any right in or to said premises, nor shall Owner be liable for any inability to deliver possession.

Dated _____, 19_____.   ACCEPTED AND AGREED TO:

_____
                    Owner / Agent

_____
                    Applicant

(Original to Owner – Copy to Applicant – Copy to Manager)

---

rent, part of owners' taxable income in the year they collected it. To get around this, owners called the payment a security of escrow deposit, to be held as a guarantee that a resident would live up to the lease.

This means that if a resident pays his rent and leaves his apartment clean after fulfilling his lease obligations, his security deposit must be returned. If there is damage beyond normal wear and tear, the manager deducts enough from the deposit to pay for repairs. Meanwhile, for the period of the resident's stay, the owner has the money to use or invest as he pleases in most states.

Some managers think they have a sacred right to a security deposit equivalent to a full month's rent. Without this, they say, they're not protected against an occupant who damages the apartment or violates some other clause of the lease. On the other hand, occupants hate giving the owner interest-free use of a month's rent money for as long as they remain.

Either from stories they hear or from actual experience, residents suspect they won't get back their security deposit without a struggle. So they secretly vow that when they leave they'll withhold the month's rent and tell the manager, "The security deposit covers it."

You can see where this leaves the manager and owner: holding the bag. Sure, the full-month security deposit can cover the final month's rent, but there's nothing left to pay for whatever damage is done. So they're still out of pocket if a resident breaches the lease or damages an apartment.

Their shortgage is worse if the rent goes up. If someone originally took an apartment for $250, and the manager later raises the rent to $275, the original security deposit of $250 will leave the manager $25 short on rent, besides whatever is needed to cover damage.

Theoretically, the manager can get tough and refuse to apply the security deposit to the final month's rent. But ultimately his only recourse is court action, which is expensive and takes time. The resident will be long gone before the case comes up. When it does, the court will usually order the deposit applied against any rent owed, so what's the use?

This is one reason why security deposits are falling into disfavor among owners. Another reason is that more and more states and cities are passing laws that force owners to pay interest on security deposits, and to give an accounting to residents if any of the deposit is withheld. Some states even make the owner put the money in a special account for eventual return. If he keeps it, and can't show that it was used to fix damage caused by the resident, in some locations he may be liable for punitive damages.

Laws vary from place to place concerning security deposits, but renters' feelings don't. A demand for a big security deposit provokes resentment, and a backlash hits owners later on. Worse yet, from the owner's position, security deposits may make the property harder to sell, especially when competing properties require smaller security deposits. A potential buyer, if he's sophisticated, realizes that those deposits will mean deficits — either as people move out leaving rent unpaid, or as they move out in good standing and collect the refunds.

Most prospects, when they sign up for a new suite, are already paying rent on their current one. So they face a heavy outlay if they are forced to pay two months' rent in advance — part of it disguised as security deposit — in order to make the move. Given a choice of two desirable suites with the same rent, they'll choose the one with the smaller security deposit.

For these reasons — residents' resentment, owners' losses and marketing disadvantages — the traditional security deposit of one month's rent is becoming obsolete. You'll be better off asking for a deposit significantly smaller than a month's rent.

CAN YOU CALL THE DEPOSIT A NON-REFUNDABLE CLEANING FEE? This used to be possible. "Since it is a fee rather than a deposit, the owner/manager may retain the full amount of the fee," various publications have stated. "A cleaning fee is collected in conjunction with the security deposit and is used in refurbishing the property for re-renting."

This still may be legal in some states, but not in California and at least a few others. There's no such thing as a non-refundable cleaning fee or security deposit under California's Civil Code Section 1950.5 — courts have made this clear in the 1970s. Any such deposit is held by the owner/manager for the resident. The manager may apply that deposit to rent, or he may apply it to cleaning. If there's any money left after rent has been paid and the apartment has been cleaned, this surplus must go to the ex-resident within two weeks after vacating. Any lease clause which says the entire deposit will be forfeited in case of default is illegal.

Even in states where you can collect a non-refundable fee, resentful residents may decamp without paying the final month's rent, figuring they've already paid it in the guise of "security deposit and cleaning fee," or "breakage deposit," or something similar. Recent experience all over the country teaches that managers are smarter to settle for a deposit of $25 to $200 — together with the first and last months' rent in advance.

Some managers try to collect cleaning charges when the occupant moves out. They don't have much luck. The vacating occupant can simply refuse to pay, and there's little the manager can do.

These facts leave the manager in a dilemma. How can he be sure of getting money rightfully due him to clean up a mess left by a departing resident? One possible way is by making clear in a "Resident's Handbook" (and in your chat with a prospective renter) that the rather nominal cleaning and security deposits are always refunded to residents who leave their apartments clean and ready for the next resident — and by building a reputation for paying these refunds. Word will get around. And people will be encouraged to pay their rent and keep their units clean.

Another way, fairly new, is by taking out insurance to cover damages that may be done by residents. In Northern California, at least, you can even get insurance against "lease default."

THE APARTMENT TENANT SECURITY DEPOSIT PLAN, introduced in 1975 by a company called Protech Insurance Services, Inc., is available to all insurance brokers and agents. Protech hopes to have nationwide offices eventually. Here's how the plan works:

A "master contract" is issued to the apartment owner covering all units in his building. Each new resident fills out a credit application. The insurance company runs a fast check on his credit rating. (The application and return report can both be made by phone, sometimes within a few minutes, for a nominal charge.) If the applicant's rating is okay, the company guarantees his credit for the full amount of the "normal security deposit," presumably whatever is considered normal in the locality. Then, if the resident breaks his lease or leaves the apartment in bad shape, he is theoretically obligated to pay for the damage — as he is anyway under common law. But if he doesn't pay, the apartment owner collects a minimum from Protech instead. Protech will try to make the ex-resident pay the full amount of the damage, at no additional cost to the apartment owner. Even if it fails, it reimburses the owner up to the amount of the "normal security deposit."

This seems to be an excellent arrangement. It prevents strife over security deposits. Managers can be sure of getting at least as much reimbursement for damage as if they'd collected the security deposit. Renters are money ahead, and happier, because they're not asked to pay the deposit.

Anyway, as you collect some kind of initial deposit from the prospective renter, be sure to tell him exactly what it is and how it works. Assure him that the deductions, if any, will be fairly applied, and that he can count on prompt refund if all goes well until the time (far distant, you hope) that he vacates. You may even go farther and pay the refund after a year of trouble-free occupancy. This works wonders for good will.

HOW TO USE THE RENTAL APPLICATION

Your next step: get the prospect to fill in an application to rent. You needn't hesitate or apologize. Good prospects won't object. Others may act insulted — which tells you all you need to know. If they don't want you to make the routine check on them, do you want them in your building?

Imagine how you'd fare if you went to a retail store and tried to walk away with merchandise on credit without filling in the complete credit information form. Yet, some managers accept new residents with little or no investigation "because it was Friday and they wanted to move in over the weekend."

IF A FAMILY IS IN A HURRY TO MOVE IN, because they're from out of town, and you're very favorably impressed by them, you can recommend that they spend the night at a motel while you do the necessary checking. Maybe you can even offer to deduct the cost of the room rental from the first month's rent. (Steer them to a moderate-priced motel, so they won't pick the most luxurious place within an hour's drive.) If they accept this offer and give you time for the necessary checking, they'll probably be good residents.

THE BEST WAY TO FILL IN THE APPLICATION is for you to do it and then have the prospect sign it. By asking him the questions and listening to his answers, you'll get a feel of what he's like.

Some owners and managers prefer to have the prospect take the rental application home, fill it out there, and mail it back. This does save time in the manager's office. And, of course, it's necessary if the application calls for information which the prospect doesn't have with him. Nevertheless, you can fill in at least part of the application as he answers your questions.

The document itself can take many forms. You'll find samples on the following pages. Draw one up to suit yourself — but remember that it should call for certain basic pieces of information which you'll need in sizing up the prospect.

YOU NEED FULL NAMES of the applicant, spouse, and all others who will live in the apartment. Your investigation might be stymied if you took only the last name and initials, because there may be other people with similar names. Ask to see identification such as a driver's license — and be sure the name on the license is the same as the name on the application.

More important, you need to pin down the exact number of adults and children who are to occupy the apartment. If you rent to a family with one child, but four children show up, can you *prove* the parents said "one" unless you have it in writing?

After a man and wife move in, can they later be joined by a sister or mother? Occasionally somebody tries. You can block them if the written application specifies just who the residents will be. Otherwise, you get into predicaments like that of a manager in Oakland who found his three-room apartment sheltering 16 people, comprising the families of three brothers; or of another manager whose tenant sublet a three-car garage to six adults and nine kids. In each case, there was nothing in writing that said or implied this couldn't be done.

Over-crowding is rough on the apartment and the building. It causes health and sanitation problems. Other residents may object because of noise, smells, and too much activity in the hallways. If a single person living in a studio apartment takes a roommate, nobody may grumble. But you can expect complaints — maybe complaints to the municipal authorities — if you let a family of six crowd into a two-bedroom unit.

Often several collegians or swingers plan to share an apartment and divide the rent and other expenses. This sounds groovy, but they don't realize that if one moves out, the others are still expected to pay the full rent. Are you sure they'll be compatible, so there'll be less chance of one leaving? Does one like to play records full blast while another wants to read in quiet? Who'll buy and cook the food, and do the cleaning? Are roommates' tastes similar? Are all these people sure of each other's

RENTAL APPLICATION & VERIFICATION

PERSONAL

Name _____ Date of Birth _____ S.S. No. _____

Name (spouse) _____ Date of Birth _____ S.S. No. _____

Name(s) of Children _____
Dates of Birth _____

Do you have any pets?   ( ) Yes   ( ) No   If yes, specify

Marital Status   ( ) Single   ( ) Married   ( ) Separated   ( ) Divorced
                       Anniversary Date____ Day_____ Month ____ Year ____

Present Address _____ Phone _____
Present Landlord _____ Address _____
         Phone_____ Term of Occupancy _____

Previous Landlord _____ Address _____
         Phone_____ Term of Occupancy _____

Driver's License No. _____ State _____ Spouse's _____ State _____

Automobile   Make _____ Model _____
             Year _____ License No. _____ State _____

Second Car   Make _____ Model _____
             Year _____ License No. _____ State_____

PERSONS TO NOTIFY IN CASE OF EMERGENCY

1. _____
2. _____

EMPLOYMENT

	Employer	Address	Phone	How Long

Present _____
Previous _____
Present (spouse) _____
Previous (spouse)_____
Present Occupation _____ Gross Mo. Income $ _____
  "   " (spouse)_____ Gross Mo. Income $ _____

Are you presently receiving   Welfare   ( ) Yes   ( ) No
                                     Unemployment ( )Yes( ) No

Have you, in the last two years received   Welfare   ( ) Yes   ( ) No
                                     Unemployment ( )Yes( ) No.

CREDIT/BANKING

Charge Accounts	Company	Address	Phone	OPEN?
1.				( ) Yes ( ) No
2.				( ) Yes ( ) No
3.				( ) Yes ( ) No

148

CREDIT CARDS

	Company	Card No.
1.	_____	_____
2.	_____	_____
3.	_____	_____

Have you had accounts with the following local utility companies?

Gas & Electric   ( ) Yes   ( ) No   Telephone   ( ) Yes   ( ) No

Water   ( ) Yes   ( ) No   Garbage   ( ) Yes   ( ) No

LOANS

	Lending Company	Address	Phone
1.	_____	_____	No. of Mo.
	Purpose	Approx. Balance	Payments
	_____	_____	_____
2.	_____	_____	No. of Mo.
	Purpose	Approx. Balance	Payments
	_____	_____	_____

BANK NAME _____   Address _____   Phone _____

     Checking Account No. _____   Approx. Balance $ _____

     Savings Account No. _____   Approx. Balance $ _____

MARKETING SURVEY

Reason for leaving present residence _____

_____

What first brought your attention to our vacancy?

     ( ) Newspaper   ( ) Vacancy Sign   ( ) Personal Referral

     ( ) Other (please explain)

What features do you particularly like here: _____

_____

ENDORSEMENT: Applicant hereby verifies that statements above are true and authorizes verification of all references given.

     DATE _____ SIGNATURE _____

     DATE _____ SIGNATURE _____

APPLICATION FOR RENTAL

(Each co-resident must submit separate application)

1. Applicant's Name _____ Age _____ Sex _____

2. Present street address (or apt. name)_____ How Long _____

3. Previous street address (or apt. name)_____ How Long _____

4. Marital status (check one)   Single __ Married __ Divorced __ Widowed __ Separated __

5. Social Security No. _____ Driver's Lic. No. _____ State _____

6. Employer _____ Address _____

7. Kind of Work _____ How Long _____

8. Phone at Work _____ Monthly Income _____

9. Spouse's maiden name _____ Age _____ Sex _____

10. Spouse's Social Security No. _____ Driver's Lic. No. _____ State _____

11. Spouse's employer _____ Address _____

12. Spouse's kind of Work _____ How Long _____

13. Spouse's Phone at Work _____ Spouse's Monthly Income _____

14. List name, age, relationship of all persons to be occupying the premises (including children, relatives, and other co-residents):

   Name _____ Age _____ Relationship_____

   Name _____ Age _____ Relationship_____

   Name _____ Age _____ Relationship_____

15. List all vehicles to be parked on the premises by applicant, spouse, or children (including cars, trucks, motorcycles, trailers, boats):

   Type vehicle _____ Year _____ Make_____ License No. _____ State __

   Type vehicle _____ Year _____ Make_____ License No. _____ State __

   Type vehicle _____ Year _____ Make_____ License No. _____ State __

16. Will you or the other occupants have a pet? _____ Kind, weight, breed, and age _____

17. Name of your bank _____ City _____ Acct. No. _____

18. Retail credit references _____ City _____ Acct. No. _____
    (active accounts or
    credit cards) _____ City _____ Acct. No. _____

19. Why are you leaving your present residence? _____

20. Have you or your spouse ever been evicted? _____ Have you or your spouse ever broken a rental agreement or lease contract? _____

21. Have you or your spouse ever been sued for non-payment of rent or damages to rental property? _____

22. Have you or your spouse ever been convicted of a felony? _____

23. How were you referred to us?   Just stopped by _____ Friend (name)_____

Locator agency (name) _____ Locator agent's name _____

Newspaper (name) _____ Other _____

24. In case of emergency, notify _____Phone _____

Street address _____ City/State _____ Relationship _____

CORRECT INFORMATION

Applicant represents that all of the above statements are true and complete, and hereby authorizes verification of above information, references, and credit records. Applicant acknowledges that false information herein may constitute a criminal offense under the laws of this state. Applicant agrees to the terms of the "Application Deposit Agreement" below.

APPLICATION DEPOSIT AGREEMENT

Applicant has deposited an "Application Deposit" (in the amount stated below) in consideration for owner's taking the dwelling unit off the market while considering approval of this application. If applicant is approved by owner and the contemplated lease is entered into, the application deposit shall be credited to the required security deposit. If applicant is approved but fails to enter into the contemplated lease within 3 days after notice of such approval, the application deposit shall be forfeited to owner. The application deposit will be refunded only if applicant is not approved. Keys will be furnished only after contemplated lease and other rental documents have been thoroughly executed by all parties and only after applicable rentals and security deposits have been paid. This application is preliminary only and does not oblige owner or owner's agent to execute a lease or deliver possession of the proposed premises.

CONTEMPLATED LEASE INFORMATION

Application deposit   Total security deposit   Total monthly rent
by applicant $_____   for apartment $ _____   for apartment $ _____

Apt. Street Address _____ City/State _____

Date of occupancy (move-in date)_____ Term of Lease_____

Apt. No. or Type_____ Furnished _____ or Unfurnished_____Total No. Occupants

Utilities Paid by Owner as Follows: _____

Monthly Parking Rent (if any) $ _____ Separate Pet Deposit (if any) $ _____

APPLICANT'S Signature _____ Date _____

SPOUSE'S Signature _____ Date _____

OWNER representative's signature _____ Date _____

sense of responsibility, or is there a chance that one will ask another to pay a month's rent and then renege on repaying? What arrangements are set up to pay in case one roommate loses a job, moves to another city, leaves to get married, or otherwise ceases to pay? Before approving two or more young people who want to rent jointly, you may be smart to explore some of these questions with them. And you should insist that each fill out separate rental applications.

AN APPLICANT'S AGE MAY BE IMPORTANT if there seems to be a chance that he or she is under age. You should get the age from the driver's license. Check your state law to find out how old a person must be to sign a valid contract. If your applicant is under age, get a parent or guardian to sign the lease before you let the applicant move in. A minor can break a contract, including a lease, and suffer no legal penalty; an adult can't. (However, sometimes a minor who is married, orphaned, or can show that housing is a necessity, can be exempted from the restriction against minors, and can sign a binding lease.)

YOU NEED THE SOCIAL SECURITY NUMBER — not because it's must help in tracking skips, but because it helps a credit bureau make sure it is investigating the right person. Credit bureaus file records of people under Social Security numbers. They also use the numbers to distinguish between people with the same name.

A PROSPECT'S PAST HOUSING HISTORY is vital. Someone whose record shows more than three addresses in the past two years isn't necessarily unstable — there may be good reasons for these housing changes — but you'd better investigate to make sure. Some people move incessantly from building to building in the same part of town. Some change jobs every few months and move to a different area every time. You don't want a new resident who'll flit away in a matter of months.

It's wise to ask past managers about the applicant's housekeeping. People who don't care about keeping a residence clean can cost you money. But don't bother phoning the manager of the place where the applicants live now. That manager may give a false recommendation to get rid of troublesome tenants — or, if they're good tenants, your call tips him off to a chance to talk them out of moving. Instead, check prior managers first. They'll give you the lowdown, since they have nothing to lose. Ask them about rent payment, behavior record, cleanliness, and length of stay.

How much rent did the applicants pay in their previous place? If they're making a big jump from what they pay now to what they say they'll pay you, there can be problems ahead. You'd better ask the applicant, in a friendly sympathetic way, how he or she can be sure this jump in rent levels won't be too steep.

ASK THE APPLICANT ABOUT HIS AUTOMOBILE: Make, model, year, color, and license number. This information will be helpful in controlling the parking in your garage or parking lot. It could also help in locating a resident who, despite your precautions, turns out to be dishonest, and leaves while owing rent.

THE EMPLOYMENT RECORD of the applicant is worth looking into. If he has been with the same company a long time, he's likely to stay with you for a long time. Of course, you delved into this tactfully during your early "qualifying" chat, but now it's time to make sure.

Someone may claim to have worked years at the same place, and yet turn out to be a new employee there, or no employee at all; some applicants gamble that references won't be checked. Others give the name and phone number of a fellow worker, and coax this friend into recommending them. Sometimes you can sense this by something strained or elaborately casual in the voice on the phone. If you're suspicious, you can make another call, this time to the company's personnel department. The department may tell you the name of the person's immediate boss; if so, call him and ask how he rates the applicant. You may also want to ask when payday is, in case you need to pick that day to camp on the doorstep and collect your rent.

Try to get the employment records of both husband and wife for the past five years. If either shows a history of job-hopping, ask about the reason. It could be legitimate. A highly skilled craftsman often has several employers in a year — but a semi-skilled worker who drifts from place to place may give you trouble collecting rent.

Also check with the employer about pay, to be sure it jibes with the statement on the application. And be sure to apply the "one-fourth monthly income for rent" rule of thumb. Consider only the regular pay in this test. Don't include overtime pay, even if it's consistent. And don't count income earned from a moonlighting job. If the applicant needs this extra money to qualify for your apartment, he's straining, and he'll be a collection problem sooner or later.

Count only half of the gross income of an applicant's working wife, especially if she is in her pregnancy years. Having a baby could end her job. Working people with pre-school children spend more money because of child care. But if the couple is past the age of parenthood, you can take the total of both incomes.

ABILITY TO PAY isn't the sole yardstick for judging applicants, but it's an essential one. Credit statistics shows that three-fourths of all household borrowers pay all or most of their debts on time. Another 15% are always slow in paying. And then there's the pesky 10% who don't pay at all. These latter types might be called professional con artists, although they're seldom as smooth as the big-money swindlers; they live from hand-to-mouth, usually just a jump ahead of skip tracers and bill collectors, sometimes changing names as often as they change locations. The rental application can screen them out.

One of the first items you check is the banking connection. People without bank accounts are bad risks. Most banks will cooperate if you talk to an officer, identifying yourself as manager of the apartment, and asking about the applicant's general credit. Of course, a bank won't tell you anyone's exact balance, but it will usually say something like, "he has a high three-figure balance," meaning his balance is usually $600 or more, or "he is a medium four-figure account," meaning he has $5,000 or so in his account.

A systematic deadbeat often has a bank account with the minimum balance to keep it active — typically, $5. He counts on careless apartment managers who go no farther than verifying that an account exists. You shouldn't ever accept an applicant whose bank balance is less than three figures (below $100, that is), unless someone cosigns the lease.

Ask about both checking and savings accounts — including account numbers. Remember that people use checking accounts to spend money, savings accounts to save. Someone with a savings account and no checking account is usually a better risk than with the opposite.

Also ask if the applicant has any bank loans outstanding. Beyond this, of course, you need to know if he owes money on charge accounts, or to a small loan company, or to anyone else on installment purchases. When the rent plus monthly payments on debts total more than 40% of an applicant's monthly gross income, beware. He's in trouble.

It's important in checking with loan firms and the like to identify yourself. Most of these companies will give data to business people like you, but not to unknowns. (Remember, this is confidential information, and if you pass it on to anyone including the applicant, you could find yourself in a lawsuit.)

Ask the applicant for three current references, as part of the rental application. For each, find out which branch, if it is a chain, and the account number if possible. Then make phone calls to these references. The companies will normally be glad to answer your questions; they like to know where their debtors live.

A CREDIT CHECK, done by a local credit firm, will give you basic information about your applicant: age, marital status, children, employer, current address. You can compare this with what the prospect tells you on his application. Beyond this, the credit bureau's speedy report may give you cross-reference material from several sources — stores, loan companies, banks, past and present employers, and so on. It's usually in a concise one-page standard form.

You don't get the report free, of course. You must pay for membership in the credit association. Or you may be able to arrange a reasonable fee per report — which is advisable if there isn't much turnover in your building. Another possibility: your local apartment association may be equipped to carry out credit checks for their members.

Whatever way you choose, be sure to have this checking done. It's cheap insurance against the loss of rent from a non-paying resident. However, be sure to mention to your prospective resident that you'll be getting a routine credit report on him. This is mandatory under the Federal Fair Credit Act.

A credit check isn't foolproof. You can't beat a seasoned con man. He'll rig up references so a credit bureau won't find anything wrong. The best way to check the application is by digging deeper yourself; a credit bureau can only tell you what it has on file from creditors. Besides, federal laws limit the information that credit bureaus can give out.

In whatever investigating you do personally, make notes to yourself on the application as you check it. Jot down the name of the person you talk with, telephone number, and answers to your questions. Never assume that you can carry any of this in your head. After several applicants, it will all be jumbled together. The notes can be filed as a permanent record, which you'll probably need occasionally in the future.

AFTER YOU'VE TAKEN THE APPLICATION

BE SURE TO HAVE THE APPLICANT SIGN IT. You can say, "Will you just check this over and make sure everything is in order, and then put your okay on the bottom? . . . Of course, every application is subject to the office's approval. We probably won't need more than a couple of days to verify yours." This makes plain that what the applicant says will be checked. And his signature implies that he is willing to have it checked.

The signature can be essential if you are ever sued for defamation of character, or for violating Fair Housing laws. You should keep all rental applications for at least two years. If you turn down an applicant, your reason for doing so should be noted on the application. One manager rejected a black for lying about his employment and his credit. The manager would have turned him down no matter what his color. But the black sued, charging discrimination. The manager routinely threw away rejected applications, so he lost the suit.

To be safe from false charges of discrimination, draw up a statement about your rental policies, along the lines of the sample shown on the next page. Keep printed copies handy, and give one to each applicant. It should briefly sketch the kind of residents you accept — perhaps mentioning income level, job stability, references, length of time in the area, appearance of the applicant, and other standards you use in judging all applicants. It should contain a disclaimer, "No person or persons shall be denied the right to rent one of our apartments because of race, color, sex, religion, national origin or ancestry."

STATEMENT OF TENANT SELECTION POLICY
(Date)

Dear Applicant:

_____
(Apartment Name)

provides apartment living exclusively for adults and young family members of fifteen (15) years of age or more. Occupancy is limited to one person in a studio, two in a one-bedroom, and three in a two-bedroom apartment. No animals are permitted on the premises at any time.

Tenants are further qualified as to a record of sound financial stability, tenant permanency and compatibility with neighbors.

_____(Apartment Name)_____ believes in the philosophy and operates on the policy of open and fair housing. No discrimination is ever given to race, color, or sex.

Building Name
Manager

To sum up, you'll probably be wise to reject any applicant who: (1) doesn't have a steady job, or (2) doesn't have a bank account, or (3) doesn't give satisfactory references, or (4) has stayed less than a year at several previous apartments, or (5) hasn't paid bills promptly, or (6) doesn't have a monthly income at least four times as big as the monthly rent, or (7) has been troublesome to managers of other apartments.

IF YOU MUST REFUSE TO RENT to an applicant, try not to give him the word by phone or in person. It's best to send a brief letter such as this:

Dear Mr. Doe:

I'm sorry to inform you that your application for residency in the _____ Apartments has not been accepted. Therefore, we are returning herewith your deposit which was made by check number _____, dated_____, in the amount of $_____ .

Thank you for your interest in the _____ Apartments.

Sincerely,
Manager

Holding a deposit check, rather than cashing it, saves trouble when you must make a refund. If you cash the check and then must send back the amount, you'd better wait to see if the applicant's check clears before issuing him one of yours.

You'll notice that the rejection letter gives no reason. The less you say, the better. An explanation could lead to a long argument, and maybe even legal action for libel or slander.

In situations where you must personally tell someone you're turning him down, be brief and vague. Try not to say any more than you would in the sample letter above. If someone demands to know why he wasn't accepted, you can say something like, "I'm awfully sorry, Mr. Doe, but it's against our policy to go into any details when we decline applications." You must always be careful to protect those who give you information, and to keep the information confidential.

Be just as cautious when someone asks about one of your past or present residents. Never say anything like, "He wrecked the place," or "He wouldn't pay the rent." Instead, just reply, "Our records indicate that he didn't fulfill the rental agreement," if you can't give a favorable report.

AS SOON AS YOU'RE SURE

It's full speed ahead when you've completed a satisfactory check-up. (The checking should be done fast, in no more than a couple of days. so that you don't lose a good applicant.) Telephone him the good news, and follow up with a confirming letter like the sample on the following page.

In the phone conversation as well as in the letter, be sure to make clear what amount of money you'll expect before turning over the keys. Certainly you'll want a full month's rent in advance. Managers have learned to their sorrow that anyone who moves in with a promise to pay the balance next week will probably never catch up. If a new resident can't pay for one month in advance, he's a poor risk for future monthly payments.

If you also require a key deposit, a security deposit, a cleaning charge, a deposit against pet damage, or anything else, be sure to explain this so your new resident can bring a check for the right amount when he comes to sign the lease or rental agreement. (When you receive the first check, make a note of the bank name, branch, and account number. This could be useful if you ever have collection problems.)

DON'T EXPECT PEOPLE TO READ the "House Rules" or even the lease. They almost never do, if left to themselves. Then they get furious when they collide with some important rule, regulation, or building policy after moving in. One common reason why relations go sour between a manager and a resident is the manager's failure to give each newcomer a thorough briefing on all policies and rules.

The briefing needn't — and shouldn't — sound like a military commander's orders or a high priest's decrees. It should be low-key, relaxed, friendly. The idea is to convince the new resident that he'll enjoy living in the building, and that it is a well-run operation with clearly defined procedures.

Residents get off to a good start when you make them aware of whatever obligations they're undertaking. In signing the rental agreement (to which Chapter 12 will be devoted), they commit themselves to live up to the house rules — so these rules should be discussed first.

EXPLAINING THE HOUSE RULES

The rules can be short and broad, or as long and pointed as you find necessary. They should cover potential problems such as guests, children, pets, parking, noise, care of appliances, disposal of garbage, responsibility for damages, and anything else concerning safety and good order. They should be gently worded for upper-middle class residents, but can be more forthright and even a bit harsh if your building is occupied by people who seem likely to be troublesome.

Some rental agreements include the house rules. As a legal matter, this is awkward — because nothing in the rental agreement can be changed during the tenancy without writing a new agreement. If you have problems with a resident, and want to proclaim a new rule to cover the situation, you won't want to ask him to agree in writing before you can enforce the rule.

So, you're better off merely to mention in the rental agreement that the resident agrees to abide by whatever house rules may go into effect from time to time. This leaves you free to change rules. But try to keep the rules posted where everyone will see them, such as on a bulletin board in the laundry room, and beside the mailboxes or apartment directory.

SAMPLE ACCEPTANCE LETTER
(Date)

Name
Address
City

Dear Mr. Jones:

We are happy to inform you that your application for rental of Apartment No. 24 at the above address has been approved.

The balance of the first month's rent, which amounts to $200, and the security deposit of $95.00 are payable prior to taking possession of the premises. Please make arrangements to stop by our office at your earliest convenience to review and complete the Rental Agreement.

Welcome to _____ (Apartment Name) _____ . We're sure you'll be happy living here, and don't forget, I'm here to help you.

Sincerely yours,
Manager

In your chat with new residents at the time they sign up, you ought to go over these rules item by item. This is especially important when you rent to young people such as college students. People in their late teens or early twenties lack experience. They avoid asking questions that would expose their ignorance. And they seldom notice the posted rules, because bulletin boards covered with trivial notices are part of everyday scenery at school.

Later, when they bring a pet ocelot or a basket of snakes into the apartment and are confronted with the "no pets" rule, they'll be upset because they never dreamed the rule existed — unless you brought it to their attention in the beginning.

So, your chat should touch on all rules likely to affect them: "Notice that the rules say you aren't allowed to keep a pet, or any kind of bird of animal . . . Remember if you should do any damage, I'll have to charge you for repairs . . . Your cleaning deposit is not the last month's rent . . . You'll be paying rent up to May 31, even though the school term ends on the 22nd."

NOISE IS A PROBLEM everywhere. You can cover it tactfully: "You know, the people here are very considerate of one another. They never play their stereos or TVs loudly after 10:00 o'clock — or they never play it loudly, period. Hardly anyone will ever disturb you here, and I'm sure you'll show them the same courtesy." Here are some of the matters that might come under house rules:

Guests (overnight, parties, etc.)	Recreation facilities	Parking
Pets	Children's behavior	Waterbeds
Laundry room	Storage	Deliveries
Keys and lock-outs	Damage and repairs	Emergencies
Disturbances	Complaints	Musical instruments, stereos, TVs

Decorating	Improvements by	Subletting
Rent payments	residents	Trash disposal

It's better to keep most rules broad, rather than trying to pinpoint details. Why? Here's an example: a county apartment owners' association drew up a set of rules which specified, "Do not keep dogs, cats, or parrots on premises." So residents brought in other kinds of birds that flew loose around the apartments, twittered all night, and left visible trails. The rule had to be rewritten to exclude all birds, not just parrots. Then a resident brought a six-foot pet alligator into his apartment. Again, the rules said nothing against alligators. The association would have been better off with a rule that simply said, "No birds, animals or other pets."

You'll probably want to keep control over musical instruments with a written rule that forbids them unless management gives specific approval. Some residents practice on saxophones and bassoons without disturbing anyone; others drive neighbors wild. So, you'll need to pass judgment on each case individually.

Whether children are accepted as residents or not, they may be in the building as guests. Either way, you probably need a rule to the effect that, "Children cannot be permitted to run or play in halls, entrances, stairways, or on the roof or porches." If there's a swimming pool, it calls for a whole set of rules posted at the pool. One sample set of rules is shown on the next page.

A RESIDENTS' HANDBOOK, if you have the budget for it, is a good way to set the tone of your property and let the residents know what is expected. Even a mimeographed booklet like the sample beginning on Page 160 can be helpful (although the style of this particular booklet seems a bit harsher than need be) and will save you money in the long run. Whether it is a guidebook or just a pamphlet or fact sheet, hand it to each newcomer personally — instead of mailing it or sliding it under the door — and then go through it with him.

This publication can set forth the house rules we've just been considering, along with other helpful information: what recreation equipment is available, how to dispose of garbage and trash, where the laundry room is and how to use it, do's and don'ts of the heating and cooling equipment, where cars should be parked.

The booklet is also a good way to explain rules in more detail than may be advisable on a bulletin board: your policies about notices to vacate, damage to furnishings, security deposits and refunds, rent payments, restrictions on drilling and cutting walls, what to do if a key is lost.

Often your new resident has just arrived in the area. Maybe the booklet should tell the location of the nearest supermarket, churches, garage, school, library, playground, post office, pharmacy and other facilities. Maybe it should tell how to get installations of telephone, gas, electricity, TV, and how to report maintenance problems with them.

Find a good writer to polish up your guidebook or fact sheet. If possible, illustrate it with cartoon drawings. Keep it lively and interesting so people will read it.

A REGULAR NEWSLETTER is another good idea, if your property has numerous residents. The bigger the property, the more useful your letters can be. You want residents to think of you as a person and a friend, not some faceless bureaucrat.

People like to know what's going on and why things are happening. Your newsletter can keep them informed of new arrivals and departures, of the future paint job or the problem with the swimming pool. You can make sure they know how taxes (or wage rates, or utility charges, or contractors' fees) affect the rent they pay and the service you provide. What better way is there of keeping residents aware of everything you do for them?

RULES AND REGULATIONS
POOL & POOL AREA

1. The Pool and Recreation Center are for the use and enjoyment of the Residents at this community only.

2. Guests are limited to **TWO PER APARTMENT**. Resident is responsible for the conduct of his guests. At no time are guests to use these facilities without the resident being present, or manager's approval.

3. No children under 14 allowed in Pool or Pool lounging area unless accompanied by parents.

4. Running, jumping, ball playing and/or any other noisy behavior, disturbing to other tenants, are forbidden in or around the Pool area.

5. Pushing or throwing persons in the Pool is not allowed.

6. No inner tubes, rafts, mattresses or other large objects are allowed in the Pool.

7. Radios, record players, guitars or other musical instruments may not be played loud enough to disturb others at the Pool.

8. No breakable glasses, bottles or plates are allowed in the Pool area.

9. Management is not responsible for articles lost, damaged or stolen in or around the Pool area. Personal articles must be removed when leaving.

10. No pets are permitted in the Pool area.

11. Protect Pool furniture from discoloration because of tanning oils and perspiration. Please place a towel over furniture while sunning.

12. Children ages 14 and under — Swimming hours are from 10:00 a.m. to 6:00 p.m. in the main Pool. Other Pool hours are posted at Pool.

!!!   NO LIFEGUARD ON DUTY   !!!

Your newsletter should come out on some regular schedule, but this isn't strictly necessary. What is necessary is that you rush out an immediate bulletin if there is news which residents should know quickly. In short, communicate! It's a vital part of making people feel welcome.

Your communications should be in plain language — and, especially, in tactful language. The idea is to explain, not to command. Avoid harsh phrases like, "It is strictly forbidden . . . you must . . . you cannot," and so on. Instead, gentle down the rules with words like "please . . . your cooperation will help keep everyone safe . . we ask that you avoid . . . state law requires that . . . you should always check with management before . . . " There's usually a good reason for every rule and policy. Explaining the reasons can avoid resentment.

As a sample of pleasant tone, here are the opening paragraphs from a booklet used by a big and successful apartment management company.

Welcome to _____ Apartments, your new residence. We hope you'll enjoy living here and that you'll find the following rules necessary and beneficial for all occupants.

Because of the close proximity, your activities will affect your neighbors more directly than in a separate dwelling. For this reason, the management asks that you exercise more care in conducting your activities than would be needed in an ordinary home. Your cooperation in abiding by the following policies will help to maintain desirable living conditions for all tenants and make your new home a quiet, respectable place to live.

TWO WORDS TO AVOID in your publication, bulletin board notices, and conversation — as well as in legal documents like the rental agreement — are "landlord" and "tenant." These are old, old words with unpleasant vibrations. They rub many people the wrong way, implying that someone can lord it over them. You can substitute words like lessor, owner, or management for "landlord" — and resident, occupant, or lessee for "tenant."

The wording of the lease or rental agreement is analyzed in the next chapter. For now, let's assume that you've gone over it clause by clause with the new residents and gotten their signatures. What next?

WHEN A NEW RESIDENT IS ABOUT TO MOVE IN

LITTLE EXTRAS CAN BE IMPORTANT. Make sure that every light fixture in the apartment has light bulbs. Put a bar of soap, in the original wrapper, at every water outlet. Put toilet tissue in each bathroom — still in the original wrapper. Put a roll of paper towels in its original wrapper at the sink, plus a few paper cups. You might even put fresh flowers, or a bowl of fresh fruit, in the apartment if you'd like to make a big hit.

A WELCOME CARD or letter can help. You might keep a supply of them printed up, ready to be signed personally by you and placed where the new resident will see it (but not on the floor) as he walks into the living room. Here's a sample:

WELCOME TO YOUR NEW HOME AT THE _____

We're happy to have you as a resident!

We genuinely appreciate your choosing this as your new home. We'll make every effort to maintain the friendly relationship so necessary for your continued confidence and good will.

You'll find all of us eager to do everything we can to make your residence a thoroughly comfortable and happy experience at all times.

Sincerely yours,

ESTABLISH A MOVE-IN PROCEDURE to make sure you handle every detail systematically. This can be especially important if several new residents move in on the same day. The better your checklist of details, the better impression you'll make on residents, and the fewer problems you'll have with them later.

Your checklist should include finding out from the new resident just when he plans to move in, so you can be on hand to welcome him. This scheduling may also be needed to coordinate the use of elevators, or to avoid crews of movers getting in each other's way.

If the apartment is already vacant, a newcomer may ask to move in a couple of days early. Technically, his rent payment doesn't cover those days. But what have you got to lose if the apartment is in total readiness? Earlier arrival may ease your scheduling problems, and bring you some good will at no cost.

Your checklist of things to be done before the move-in will probably include these items:

   — Are the new name strips on the mailbox and on the door?
   — If you've assigned a garage or parking stall, is it clean? Is there a name sign on it?
   — Is the temperature of the apartment at a comfortable level?
   — Is the refrigerator turned on?
   — Are the door keys and mailbox key ready? Do the locks work?

- Are all the lights working? How about the water taps?
- Are the windows clean? Do they open and close easily?
- Has the apartment had a fresh dusting? Is the carpet clean?
- Is the storage locker clean and secure?

YOUR PERSONAL WELCOME should include giving whatever assistance seems needed, answering questions, and showing the newcomers how all the equipment works. They should see where the fuse box or breaker box is, and how to turn off current in an emergency. They should be shown how to work all the thermostatic controls, the dials and switches in the kitchen, any special equipment in the bathroom or elsewhere. They should know about the garbage disposal unit, about the laundry equipment, about putting out trash.

DON'T FORGET THE INTRODUCTIONS. A newly-arrived family feels itself among strangers. How about making introductions to neighboring families that might be especially congenial? Are there maintenance people or other employees whom the family should know? What can you do to help the family get acquainted?

If you take trouble to get each new resident started right, it can save you much more trouble later. There'll be fewer questions at awkward moments, fewer complaints, a more cordial attitude toward you and the other people living there. A resident who's happy at the start will probably stay a long time. An apartment building full of satisfied, stable residents is about the best money machine ever invented.

LAKE MEADOW APARTMENTS

4730 Lake Drive

Brentwood, Illinois

COMMUNITY RULES

It is our intention and purpose to operate LAKE MEADOW Apartments as the outstanding residential development in this area. The management will strive to render prompt, efficient service and will maintain this property in a manner commensurate with the type of community you desire. Your cooperation in observing these rules will avoid confusion and possible embarrassment. Any expense incurred by the management as a result of violation of these rules will, insofar as feasible, be assessed against the resident responsible. Promptly notify the management of any needed repairs to equipment or fixtures.

NOTE: These Rules become part of your Lease Agreement in accordance with Paragraph No. 12 of the Lyndene lease; Paragraph 5, Article No. 1 of the Lake Meadow United Investors lease.

1. Emergency Telephone Numbers:

Fire   336-0924

Rescue Squad (ambulance)   336-3424

Police   366-9991

Resident Manager   336-1204

Washing Machine Servic 366-3689

If it should be necessary to call for Fire, Rescue or Police assistance, please (if possible) advise the Resident Manager immediately after this is done.

2. Rental Payments: All rents are due and payable each month. Monthly bills are not rendered. Please make checks payable to Lyndene Investments and mail to 1403 Fairview Drive, Brentwood, Illinois 34027. Please write your APARTMENT NUMBER and STREET ADDRESS on your check. Cash will be accepted by Manager only during regular office hours, 9:00 a.m. to 5:00 p.m. Monday through Friday.

3. Thirty (30) Day Written Notice: A 30-day written notice effective on the first day of the month, must be given the managing agent, Lyndene Investments, 1403 Fairview Drive, Brentwood, Illinois 34027, prior to tenant vacating. The notice is required if the tenant intends to vacate at the termination of the lease. The notice should state a definite moving date. Blank vacant notice forms are available at the Resident Manager's office.

4. Keys & Locks: Two apartment keys and one mailbox key are issued at the time of occupancy. Alterations or replacement of locks or installation of bolts, knockers, mirrors or other attachment to the interior or exterior of any door requires the prior consent of the management. The tenant is required to furnish Management a key for any lock similar to the chain bolt type.

5. Lockouts: In view of the increasing demands, and to reduce this problem to a minimum, authorized personnel will admit tenants who have been locked out at the following charge which may be levied at the management's option:

9:00 a.m. - 8:00 p.m. — $2.00

All other hours   — $5.00

6. Moving: Moving of furniture to and from the apartment must be scheduled between the hours of 8:00 a.m. and 5:00 p.m. on week-

days. No moving is permitted on Sundays or holidays. Please inform the Resident Manager of your moving plans and be sure to arrange with your moving company to dispose of all crates, barrels and packing boxes used in moving.

7. Maintenance: Please make request for repairs or maintenance by telephoning the Resident Manager whose phone number appears on Page 1, between 9:00 a.m. and 5:00 p.m. daily. Emergency calls will be handled immediately. No charge is made for repairs or adjustments unless necessitated by negligence or mistreatment by a tenant.

8. Light Bulbs: Each apartment will be equipped at time of occupancy with electric light bulbs. After move-in, tenant is expected to replace burned out bulbs. In the event tenant is physically unable to change bulbs, this service will be provided at a cost of $1.00.

9. Laundry Room: Coin-operated washers and dryers are located in each building. Please remove clothing from machines promptly. Do not use tints or dyes. Please report any malfunction of these machines to the Resident Manager, or call the laundry machine company whose number is listed on Page 1.

10. Trash Room: Please help keep the premises clean by using the trash room provided in each building. It is imperative that all trash be wrapped or put in bags and placed in the metal containers and the covers firmly affixed. Trash must not be left in the halls at any time.

11. Storage Rooms: Individual storage lockers have been provided for each apartment. Only one locker may be utilized by each tenant and it is the tenant's responsibility to padlock the locker assigned. While every effort is made to safeguard property, Management assumes no responsibility for loss of or damage to articles stored. Do not store gasoline, paint or other flammable materials in these lockers. Please identify your lockers with building number and apartment number on the 3x5 card provided.

12. Entrances and Hallways: In compliance with the Fire Code of Prince Georges County, children's toys, bicycles, wagons or carts are not to be left at the entrances or in the hallways at any time. Please do not place doormats or other obstructions in the public hallways at your entrance door. Signs of any type are not to be placed on apartment doors. Newspaper deliveries, etc., should be taken in promptly to minimize the possibility of accidents to others.

13. Disturbances, Noises, etc.: No tenant may make or permit any disturbing noises by himself, his family or friends. No tenant shall play or operate any musical instrument, radio or television set, or allow same to be played or operated between the hours of 12:00 midnight and 8:00 a.m. Loud playing of radio, television or other musical instrument is discouraged at any hour. Any boisterous conduct or other actions which will disturb the peace and quiet of the premises are absolutely prohibited.

14. Children: Children are not permitted to play in the halls, stairways, parking areas or anywhere in or around the buildings where they may endanger themselves or unnecessarily disturb residents. Organized games or sports are prohibited on the lawns, sidewalks, etc. Designated play areas must be used. Children of working parents must be adequately supervised by someone designated by the parents, and be provided with means of access to their apartment at all times. It is of the utmost importance that children be so supervised that they will not present a disciplinary problem for management.

15. Disposals: It is recommended that the cover be kept in the drain position when not in use to prevent foreign materails from accidentally dropping into the waste disposal unit. In using your disposal, be sure you have the COLD water turned on. It is important to maintain a sufficient flow of water to flush shredded waste such as potato peelings through the drains even after the disposal has been turned off. Do not put bottle caps, glass, pins, foil, crockery, rags, string or paper in the disposal. Any damage or costs for repairing the disposal because of negligence will be charged to the tenant. If the disposal should not operate, MAKE SURE SWITCH IS OFF; then using ratchet wrench provided, turn unit manually from the bottom position until mechanism turns freely. If unit does not then operate, call the management office for service.

16. Refrigerators: Your refrigerator requires defrosting regularly to prevent frost build-up on the freezing compartment. DO NOT USE any type of sharp instrument to pick or scrape off the ice. This action can very easily puncture the coil causing a loss of the refrigerant and requiring expensive replacement.

17. Air Conditioning & Heating: Your air conditioning and heat is provided from a central plant on the premises. You will be notified when each is turned on or off. It is not possible to change over by turning the control buttons. The unit located in the ceiling of the hallway closet is a circulating unit for your apartment, and not a supply unit. Our maintenance personnel are required to replace filters on a regular schedule and it is important that access to this filter is provided at all times. For most efficient results, the filter should be kept clean and free of lint.

18. Awnings: Awnings, sheds or other equipment on the exterior of the building will not be permitted.

19. Pets: Absolutely no live animals or birds of any description will be permitted under any circumstances without the express consent of the management. Management reserves the right to designate certain buildings as pet buildings and to charge nominal fees for the housing of pets. These charges will be paid as rent and continue during the term of occupancy or until tenant advises Management in writing that said pet has been permanently removed from the premises. Management reserves the right to request removal of any undesirable pet or request tenant to vacate premises.

20. Exterminators: Exterminating services, excluding moth control, are available on request or at the discretion of the management. For service, please telephone Resident Manager.

21. Floor Coverings: All residents are required to provide adequate floor covering for walking areas in consideration of neighbors who live below and in adjacent apartments.

22. Parking: Adequate parking space for private licensed passenger vehicles of tenants is provided. Vehicles must be headed into curb and parked within marked lines. "No Parking" areas must be observed. Trucks, trailers or busses may be parked only with the written permission of the management. Any unregis-

tered or illegally parked vehicle will be towed away at the owner's expense.

23. Solicitors: Door-to-door soliciting is not permitted without written consent of management, in which case the solicitor will carry a card of authorization signed by the management. Residents are requested to notify management when solicitors appear in the building.

24. Car Washing: Cars are not to be washed nor repair work done on cars while in the parking lot.

25. Lawn Areas: In line with a continuing program of beautification and landscaping of the property, cooperation in keeping lawn areas free of litter, parked bicycles and other equipment is requested.

26. Roofs: Only authorized personnel are allowed on the roof. Sun bathing or placing antennas or other equipment on the roof is expressly prohibited.

27. Damage to the Property: The Management reserves the right to charge a tenant for damage to the property as a result of negligence, carelessness or misuse.

LYNDENE INVESTMENTS
Managing Agents

REMEMBER THESE BASIC POINTS:

* *After giving the deposit receipt, ask an applicant to fill out a rental application. Take time to check it out before renting.*

* *Protect yourself against charges of discrimination by giving out copies of a statement about your rental policies, and by keeping all applications for two years.*

* *If you must reject an application, give no reason.*

* *Collect a full month's rent in advance before turning over the keys. If you require other deposits, be sure to explain these in advance.*

* *Go over the rental agreement and house rules with each new occupant.*

* *Consider putting out a residents' handbook.*

* *Establish a move-in procedure to help new residents get settled and to make them feel welcome.*

XII *The Rental Document*

Many owners rent their apartments with only an oral "understanding." They're afraid that written agreements would give residents more rights. But this is bad business. The owner himself has fewer legal rights if there's no written proof of any commitment by either party. And there are more misunderstandings and arguments when nothing is in writing.

Successful operators insist on a signed agreement for each rental unit. It gets new residents off on the right foot by giving them a clear understanding of their obligations — and, in case of trouble, it enables a manager to crack the whip over undesirables, even if he has only a month-to-month agreement.

MONTH-TO-MONTH OR YEAR'S LEASE? The agreement between an owner and occupant is known as a lease if it provides for a specific number of months. It is known as a rental agreement if it is on a month-to-month basis without specifying any length of time.

In your part of the country, it may be the custom to lease, usually for a year. Or leases may be rare in your area, with most residents on "month-to-month tenancies," which means that the agreement is understood to be renewed each month unless one of the parties gives written notice of intention to change it or end it.

In most cases, you'll find it more advantageous to rent month-to-month, because it puts you in a position to raise rents as you see fit (subject to any rent control regulations that may exist where you are). On the other hand, a lease does not give the owner more assurance of continuous occupancy, which may be important if tenants are scarce.

As a practical matter, if someone decides to break a lease by moving out, the only way you can collect is by going into small claims court month by month; the rent is due only as the month runs out. Talk it over with realtors and your apartment association to decide which arrangement is preferable in your particular situation.

READY-MADE RENTAL AGREEMENTS and leases are available in office supply stores. Or you can get a standard form at a real estate office — or from your apartment association. No two of these printed forms are alike. There are probably as many rental agreements as there are minds that have tackled the problem. But none may fit your situation perfectly. So, you may want to draft your own. It's not a hard job if you understand what terms you want — but be sure to have your attorney check every word afterward.

Remember that a written rental agreement is a legal document, just as binding as a contract to finance a car or borrow money. It needn't be notarized. The traps in some of the "standard" clauses may surprise you, unless you're a lawyer yourself.

For example, a lease must specify the rental amount for the total period of the lease — not just a monthly rent. If you fill in this blank with the amount of one month's rent, a court will probably interpret the document as a month-to-month agreement, despite the fact that it specifies a one-year term.

So you see, it's vital for you to understand every clause in the rental agreement — not only to protect the owner's rights, but also to enable you to explain the document to the new resident, thereby successfully completing the sales job you began with his first phone call or visit.

THE LEGAL BACKGROUND of leases is interesting. The age-old "common law" view of such agreements is short and (for owners) sweet. The idea was that an occupant promised to pay to the owner and to refrain from "waste," or damage to the premises. In return, the owner promised little except to leave the occupant alone and provide "quiet enjoyment" of the premises. This common law view, which some judges still follow (especially judges who own property) doesn't regard an owner as guaranteeing any services or any quality of living conditions.

In the bad old days, the "tenant" took the premises as they were. The "landlord" wasn't even responsible for injuries caused by a rotten floorboard or rats in the woodwork. Furthermore, the two parties' promises to each other were considered "independent;" that is, the tenant was bound by his promise to pay rent even if the owner broke the promise to provide quiet enjoyment.

Nowadays many judges and lawmakers are beginning to think of a rental agreement as more like a contract for services than like a grant from a feudal lord. Housing and sanitary codes often set minimum standards of upkeep; statutes protect residents against being evicted or locked out at the whim of an owner; some statutes even make it legal to withhold rent if the apartment isn't "fit for human occupancy." If something really bad goes wrong with an apartment and the owner doesn't fix it, the occupant may be able to move out regardless of a lease, and even collect triple damages from an owner who doesn't return his security deposit.

Some of this background may be worth mentioning to your new renter just before you produce the lease or rental agreement for him to sign. Go to great lengths to keep him at ease while he's looking at this document. Most people lack savvy with legal papers, and feel afraid when asked to sign one. Start by saying something like this, "Signing this is routine — but we all like to know what we're signing, don't we? Let's go over this paper together. I'll try to explain what each part of it means. Don't hesitate to ask questions as we go along."

The whole document can usually be typed onto one or two pages of legal-sized paper. Here is a set of sample clauses, in more or less standard form, together with explanations that may help you and the residents to understand them. The introduction to the lease is supposed to be a declaration of intent, and to establish the relationship between the owner and the occupants. It mentions the purpose for which the premises are to be used — because if it didn't the whole contract might be void. A contract is valid only if its purpose is legal.

Thus, if you and the renter planned to use the premises as a brothel, dance hall, gambling casino or anything else which would infringe on the rights of neighbors or damage the property's acceptability as a residential building, then the lease would be illegal. Farfetched? Of course. But it's just a safeguard that has grown up through decades of experience with all sorts of wild cases. So, here's what the introductory paragraph might say:

"This Agreement is entered into this _____ day of _____, 19___, by and between _____, hereinafter called Owner, and _____, hereinafter called Occupant.

Occupant hereby rents from Owner those premises known and described as Number_____ in the _____ Apartments, the street address of which is _____ , in the city of _____ , State of _____ .

The aforesaid premises shall be used exclusively for living quarters as a private residence."

While many apartments are known by name, on the lease you should also identify the premises being rented by apartment number, common postal address, city and state.

TERMS AND RENTAL: Set down the specific dates on which the lease, if you use one, begins and ends. The lease period can be any term acceptable to you and the occupant. Try to avoid leases that end in cold weather months, because fewer people are hunting apartments then. In hot country, the opposite might be best.

In a new building, set up your leases so they expire at staggered times instead of all at once, to save having to re-rent too many units at one time. If you're managing an existing complex where all the leases come up for renewal at once, you can begin staggering them gradually.

You should know about the legal trap of the "hold-over tenant." Suppose a lease expires and you don't renew it. The occupant pays another month's rent, which you accept. He might then be entitled to stay in his apartment at the same rent for another year! It all depends on the law in your location. To dodge this kind of trouble, you can have your leases run for a specific period "and month-to-month thereafter." This wording means that if someone stays after the term of his lease, he's a monthly tenant rather than a hold-over tenant, and you can give him a 30-day notice to leave whenever you choose.

The rent should start the day the occupant ties up the property, not the day his rent elsewhere may end. If the apartment is vacant, the rent would normally start the day the lease is signed and the premises are reserved. If the apartment is occupied, the rent would start the day after the present occupant moves out — unless there are repairs or cleaning to be done first. In that case, the rent should start the day the apartment is ready for occupancy.

The term of this rental agreement shall commence at 12:01 a.m. on the_____ day of _____ , 19____ , and shall continue from month to month at a rental rate of _____ dollars ($_____) per month, payable in advance on or before the_____ day of each month at the office of the Resident Manager. Checks shall be made payable to _____ .

Some owners collect all rents the first of the month. If someone moves in during the month, they collect a prorated payment for the balance of the month. This simplifies bookkeeping, but isn't necessarily the most profitable way to operate.

Vacating residents usually move on a rent termination date. So, if you happen to lose several occupants the same month, and they all move out on the same date, there's likely to be a costly delay before all your vacancies are rented. Then too, several moving vans in front of your building may make people wonder what's wrong with it. If you spread collections over the month, you also spread vacancies, making it easier to get the units cleaned and repaired and re-rented.

When you need to raise a resident's rent, it is much safer to have him sign a new rental agreement. You can legally write in a new rental amount and have all parties initial it, but residents tend to get suspicious when you do this. Another way is to attach a signed copy of the rent increase letter to the agreement.

Revenue can be increased by imposing a penalty for delinquent tenants. The penalty notice could read as shown in the first paragraph on Page 166.

LATE RENT PENALTY: Rent not paid by the fifth day after it becomes due is considered delinquent, and is subject to a late charge of five dollars ($5.00), plus an additional charge of one dollar ($1.00) for each day thereafter that it is unpaid.

Maybe the amounts in the above sample clause are too small. After all, they would total only $30 for a whole month's delinquency. Use your own judgment about this. The reason for late charges was explained back in Chapter 3.

In explaining it to new residents, you may want to point out that your apartment house, like other businesses, has payments to make each month, and stiff penalties to pay if you are late.

(When serving a three-day notice to pay rent or quit, you can't add late charges to amounts due — although you can collect them in small claims court.)

Some residents will overdraw their checking accounts to give you a check for the rent when due; after the check bounces, they'll claim that the bank made a mistake. If they know that the returned check clause is in the rental agreement and that it will be enforced, they won't try this stall. They know that banks seldom make errors in refusing to honor checks. A sample returned checks clause could read:

RETURNED CHECKS: A five dollar ($5.00) charge will be made for any check returned by a bank. In the event of bank error, there will be no such charge provided management receives the bank's written acknowledgment of such error.

Regarding Other Charges or Deposits, don't fill in any of the blank spaces until you actually receive the deposit or fee described. When you do fill in the blanks, fill them *all* in. If there is no entry for an item, mark N/A in the blank to show that that item is not applicable to this resident:

OTHER CHARGES OR DEPOSITS:

1. Refundable security/cleaning deposit of $_____, less any amount needed to place the premises, fixtures or furnishings in a good state of cleanliness and repair, reasonable wear and tear excepted.

2. Key deposit $_____.

3. Storage rent $_____.

4. Furniture rent $_____.

5. Cable TV $_____.

6. Occupant agrees to pay for all utilities and services furnished to the premises except_____.

INCLUDE THE NAMES OF ALL OCCUPANTS of the apartment in the lease, and insist that each adult occupant and employed minor sign, so that all are responsible for living up to it. The law usually refuses to recognize any such person as "Mrs. John Smith," so have the wife sign her given name — Alice Smith, or whatever it is.

If you rent an apartment to two or more people, but only one signs the agreement, and that person later leaves, you may have trouble collecting from the others. That's why you must get their signatures before you let them move in.

However, in such situations, it's a good idea to have at least an oral understanding about which individual is responsible for paying the total rent. If you try to collect parts of the rent from different people, obviously you're asking for trouble. The prospective occupants should decide just who is to be responsible for paying it all.

REGULAR OCCUPANTS shall be restricted to the following named persons only:

_____

If any additional persons occupy the said premises, or any part thereof, with Owner's prior written consent, Occupant shall pay as additional rent the sum of $_____ per month for each additional person.

This gives you a legal tool to use on someone who rents an apartment supposedly for himself alone, and then has several others move in with him. If a resident rents alone, and his girl friend follows later, this clause gives you the option of accepting or rejecting the newcomer or of raising the rent to compensate for her.

Make sure that if there are no additional "regular occupants" you write "none" on the blank line and have it initialed.

The owner probably isn't interested in charging extra for a guest for a few days. But he doesn't want to lose control of the apartment's occupancy. Few managers ever collect any money under the following clause, but it does prevent some potential problems:

GUESTS: Occupant will notify Owner or Manager of guests staying more than five days. No guest's stay shall exceed ten (10) days without written consent and authorization of Owner or his agent. Occupant agrees to pay $ _____ per day for each guest who stays more than five days.

You can explain to the applicant that this provision is in the agreement for his own protection. If the tenant next door has his ex-wife and three small children as guests and they keep everyone awake all night, you can use this provision to limit their stay to five days. But if his mother comes to visit for two weeks, you probably wouldn't charge him extra rent.

If your building accepts no pets, then you haven't much of a problem. But when you make exceptions, your problems begin. Before you give any permission, you'd better have the occupant bring the pet in for your inspection. This can prevent such surprises as hearing neighbors complain about a huge dog which the occupant's application described as a miniature show dog.

PETS: Occupant agrees that no animal, bird, or pet of any kind may be kept on said premises without written permission from the Owner or Manager.

It's common policy to charge an extra damages deposit of, say, $50 for a cat or dog because they're almost sure to do some damage.

The following is a sort of catch-all clause against trouble makers or lawbreakers. It keeps residents from opening offices or garages on the premises. Also, if someone runs his water all day or continually throws crates and boxes into the trash containers without crushing them, he is technically in violation of his rental agreement and you can "encourage" him to leave if you wish.

USE OF PREMISES: Occupant agrees not to violate any state law, statutes, or city ordinance, nor to commit, suffer or permit any waste or nuisance in, on, or about the same premises; or in any way to annoy, molest, or interfere with any other occupants of said building; nor to use in a wasteful or unreasonable manner any of the utilities furnished by management.

Just so it won't sound unduly threatening to the prospective resident, you can explain that this is another clause for everyone's protection, to keep their rights of quiet enjoyment and privacy undisturbed by obnoxious neighbors, if any.

The reason for a Subletting Clause is obvious. Unless you know and approve of the people living in your apartments, you're not in control. Under normal conditions, you will never sublet.

SUBLETTING: Occupant hereby agrees not to sign or sublet the whole or any part of his living unit or parking area to anyone for any purpose whatsoever, nor permit its use by anyone in the absence of occupant without prior written permission from the management.

You'd better emphasize the Renewal or Termination Clause. Trouble with terminating residents will probably be 9/10ths of your problems as manager. Make sure they understand these provisions at the beginning.

RENEWAL OR TERMINATION: This agreement is automatically renewed from month-to-month upon payment and receipt of rent, but may be terminated at any time by either party giving to the other in writing thirty (30) days' prior notice of intention to terminate.

During said 30-day period, Owner, or his agents, shall have the right to permit prospective occupants the opportunity of reasonable inspection.

Upon termination, Occupant shall return premises and contents clean and free from trash and in as good condition as when received, excepting for ordinary wear and damage by the elements, or shall pay the cost for repairing any damage done to premises.

If a prospective resident thinks a snooping manager will enter his apartment without good reason, he may not rent from you at all. So, you'll want to be ready for questions when you point out this clause:

RIGHT OF ENTRY: Management shall keep a pass key and have the right to enter the premises at any and all reasonable times, by himself or with others.

You can mention that you're much too busy for any snooping, and that this provision is another of those for the protection of residents and their apartments. If something like smoke or gas or leaking water is noticed during their absence, they'd want management to go in and investigate, wouldn't they? If a resident weren't seen around, and there was reason to suspect he might be injured or critically ill, wouldn't he want the apartment entered? Then too, there'll probably be times when utility and telephone repair people should be admitted, right? However, if you have work done in an apartment during the occupant's absence, always get his written permission in advance.

Even under emergency conditions, try to have a disinterested witness with you if you enter the apartment – just in case the resident decides to take you to court for trespassing or to recover some valuable he says is missing.

You need the right to show the apartment for re-rental, at reasonable hours, after an occupant has given notice that he is moving. But there are some occupants who don't want their apartment shown. (Perhaps it looks like a pigpen.) Usually, you can get around this by politely asking, several days in advance, for times when you can show the unit. If an occupant still refuses, you can pull out the rental agreement and remind him that he's committed to this.

REPAIR AND BREAKDOWNS. You need some protection against people who move into an apartment in good condition, cause damage, and then claim the damage was already done before their arrival. Your best protection is to inspect the apartment with the incoming residents, take inventory of the furnishings and fixtures, and make a written record of anything that is in poor condition (see Unit Acceptance Form). "The palest ink is better than the most retentive memory," according to a Chinese maxim. Don't trust anyone's memory about the condition of the unit at time of move-in.

Also, make a record of the unit's contents and their condition, preferably on a printed form something like the sample entitled Furnished Apartment Inventory on the second page following. This inventory should normally be part of the lease, appended at the end. Your lease can contain some clause like the following:

Occupant agrees that he has inspected the premises, furnishings and equipment, and that the same now are in good order and condition except as noted herein.

Occupant agrees to maintain and keep, at his sole expense, the premises and furnishings and equipment, and to pay Owner on demand for all loss, breakage and damage occurring during the Occupant's residence.

UNIT ACCEPTANCE FORM

Unit Address _____   Apt. No. _____   Unit Size _____

ITEMS	CONDITION	ITEMS	CONDITION

KITCHEN
Doors _____
Walls _____
Ceiling _____
Floor _____
Stove _____
Drainboard _____
Sink _____
Garbage Disposal _____
Refrigerator _____
Other _____

BATHROOM
Doors _____
Walls _____
Ceiling _____
Floor _____
Toilet _____
Basin _____
Tub _____
Shower _____
Other _____

LIVING ROOM
Doors _____
Walls _____
Ceiling _____
Floor _____
Other _____

BEDROOM NO. 1
Doors _____
Walls _____
Ceiling _____
Floor _____
Other _____

BEDROOM NO. 2
Doors _____
Walls _____
Ceiling _____
Floor _____
Other _____

BEDROOM NO. 3
Doors _____
Walls _____
Ceiling _____
Floor _____
Other _____

BEDROOM NO. 4
Doors _____
Walls _____
Ceiling _____
Floor _____
Other _____

WINDOWS _____
SCREENS _____
LOCKS _____
VENETIAN BLINDS _____
SHADES _____
DRAPES _____
PORCH & STAIRS _____
HOT WATER HEATER _____
KEYS _____

EXTERIOR CONDITION
BUILDING _____
FRONT YARD _____
REAR YARD _____
SIDE YARD _____
OTHER _____
_____
_____
_____

FURNACE OR OTHER
HEATING EQUIPMENT_____
_____
ELECTRICAL FIXTURES _____
_____
ELECTRICAL OUTLETS _____
_____
_____

COMMENTS _____
_____
_____
_____
_____

ACCEPTANCE:

TENANTS' SIGNATURES:

_____
                              Date

_____
                              Date

Owner   Manager   Agent

SIGNATURE_____

_____
              Date

FURNISHED APARTMENT INVENTORY

This inventory, when signed by lessor and lessee, is part of that certain rental agreement/lease dated the _____ day of _____ , 19___, pertaining to premises described as _____ number _____ located at _____ in _____ , California.

LIVING ROOM	LIVING ROOM	BEDROOM-BATH DRESSING ROOM
___ Beds, Day _____	___ Pillows _____	___ Beds _____
___ Beds, Wall _____	___ Rugs, Large _____	___ Mattress _____
___ Carpet _____	___ Rugs, Small _____	___ Pillows _____
___ Chairs, Desk _____	___ Rugs, Runners _____	___ Chiffonier _____
___ Chairs, Occasional _____	___ Shades _____	___ Chairs _____
___ Chairs, Overstuffed _____	___ Studio Couch _____	___ Curtains _____
___ Curtains _____	___ Tables, End _____	___ Draperies _____
___ Davenport _____	___ Tables, Coffee _____	___ Dresser _____
___ Desk _____	___ Mattress _____	___ Dressing Table _____
___ Draperies _____		___ Dressing Table Bench _____
___ Keys, Door _____	**DINING ROOM-DINETTE**	___ Lamps _____
___ Keys, Mailbox _____		___ Night Stand _____
___ Lamp Bulbs _____	___ Chairs _____	___ Pictures _____
___ Lamps, Floor _____	___ China Cabinet _____	___ Rugs, Large _____
___ Lamps, Table _____	___ Curtains _____	___ Rugs, Small _____
___ Mirror _____	___ Draperies _____	___ Soap Rack _____
	___ Dining Table _____	___ Towel Rack _____
	KITCHEN	
	___ Range _____	
	___ Refrigerator _____	
	___ Table _____	
	___ Chairs _____	

Lessee agrees that he has inspected the premises, furniture, furnishings and equipment and that the same now are in good order and condition; that the inventory above is true and correct, that he has received a copy of same and that he will on demand pay Lessor for all loss, breakage and damage.

IN WITNESS WHEREOF, the parties hereto have executed this agreement in duplicate on the day, month, and year first above written.

_____   _____
        LESSOR   LESSEE

BY _____   _____
        AGENT   LESSEE

It won't pay to be too tough in enforcing this. Sometimes it's better, for the sake of good will, to absorb repair costs yourself when there's damage to a long-time resident's apartment, especially if you're not sure whose fault it was.

In cases where you decide to have the resident pay, it's good practice to give him the numbers of several plumbers or repair services, and let him call to make the arrangements himself. This avoids confusion about who is to pay.

INSURANCE of the occupant's property is normally a matter for the occupant alone. An owner or manager hardly ever insures a resident's property. Nevertheless, many people think that the building insurance covers their possessions.

To avoid this problem, you ought to make sure residents know that they should carry their own insurance. You might suggest two or three reliable agencies which can write Transient Homeowners Insurance policies. You might also suggest keeping valuables in a safety deposit box or in a safe. But, whatever you do, make it clear in the beginning that your insurance doesn't cover the resident's belongings. Some owners spell this out in the rental agreement:

Neither Owner nor management shall be responsible for loss, injury, or damage to the personal property or person of Occupant or his guests or visitors, caused directly or indirectly by acts of God, fire, theft, burglary, malicious acts, riots, civil commotion, the elements, defects in the building, furnishings, equipment, walks or landscaping, or by the neglect of other residents or owners of contiguous property.

This may help to discourage most people from suing over minor damage. But in case of real damage, a lawsuit is almost inevitable. Any claims against the owner should be covered by the owner's liability insurance.

If you win a court case against an occupant, he'll probably be liable for court costs, and possibly for attorney's fees on both sides. But he doesn't know this, and it isn't a foregone conclusion anyway. You may end up paying your lawyer out of your own pocket — unless there's a clause in the rental agreement requiring the occupant to pay for collection. This clause might read as follows:

COST OF COLLECTION: In the event it becomes necessary for Owner to employ an attorney to enforce any of Owner's rights under this agreement or any law of this state, Occupant agrees to pay Owner the actual amount of all costs, expenses and attorney's fees incurred by Owner in connection therewith, whether or not suit is filed.

Furthermore, if you don't go to court this clause can force residents to pay your attorney's fees for taking any legal action, such as preparing legal papers, aimed at making residents pay what they owe you. Even if the attorney hires a collection agency, the legal fees will be the occupant's responsibility.

This encourages them to pay before you have to get legal help. Otherwise, they may say to each other, "Why worry about paying until there's a court judgment against us?" But, remember, this must be stated clearly in the rental agreement they sign, or you haven't a prayer of making them pay these fees.

HOUSE RULES (which we covered in Chapter 11, you'll recall) should become part of the rental agreement. The prospective resident should acknowledge in writing that he has read these rules, is familiar with them, and will comply with them.

Then if he breaks any of them, you have solid legal grounds for telling him to move immediately. This clause saves waiting until the end of a 30-day period in month-to-month renting, or until the end of a lease if you've given one.

Occupant acknowledges that he has read the attached Apartment Management Policies and Pool Rules, is familiar with them, and agrees they become incorporated with and made a part of this agreement, and that his compliance therewith is a condition of his occupancy.

This agreement or the attached Apartment Management Policies and Pool Rules may be amended or modified from time to time by management, giving Occupant thirty (30) days' notice in writing of said amendment or modification.

In order to stay within the law when you change any written policy, you should deliver a copy of the new rules to each resident personally. Normally, the changes don't take effect for 30 days, as provided in the above clause.

ABANDONMENT. Occasionally someone who owes rent will disappear without notice, leaving some belongings to make it look as if he still is around. Be careful what you do about this. Each municipality has its own definition of abandonment. If you violate it, you may be trespassing. Check your local law with an attorney; then word the clause in your lease accordingly. It might read something like this:

If Occupant leaves said premises unoccupied for seven (7) consecutive days at any time while rent is due and unpaid, this shall be deemed an abandonment of said premises, and Owner may, if he so desires, take immediate possession and exclude Occupant without further notice.

In such event, Owner may dispose of all of Occupant's property remaining on said premises, and may re-rent said premises.

You can explain to the new resident that this provision is included to avoid the delay and expense of legal proceedings in case of actual abandonment. If the rent is paid, you don't care whether he is in his apartment or not. Usually, the laws state that in case of abandonment, you must store property for a specified time before disposing of it. But, if an ex-resident comes back six months after the abandonment and demands his belongings in return for his back rent, and you've auctioned these belongings to cover his rent, this provision would block him from suing.

REMEDIES: In the event that Occupant breaches any of the terms and conditions of this agreement, and the agreement has been terminated pursuant to the provisions there, Occupant shall be liable as follows:

1. For all installments of rent and other charges while the premises remain vacant, for the remainder of the term of this agreement. Such installment and charges shall be payable as they become due.

2. For all expenses which may be incurred by management for reletting the premises.

3. For any deficiency in the rental installments on any lease or leases of the premises made by Owner for the Occupant during the term of this agreement.

Here's what this adds up to. If you put someone out for bad conduct, as defined in the rental agreement or house rules — or if he just decides to leave for reasons of his own — you can collect whatever rent is due, including rent for the remaining term of the lease if there is one. You can also dun him for the costs of putting the apartment in condition for renting, and for whatever money you spend advertising the vacancy.

In the following clause, the first sentence gives you the right to rescind the rental agreement if you find, after the resident is in the apartment, that any statement he made in his rental application was false. The second sentence protects you from any later claim that "the manager said he would do so and so, but he didn't, so he's violated the lease," if that isn't in the lease. Sometimes in conversation a manager may say something that is misunderstood or mis-remembered later.

REPRESENTATION. Any statement submitted by Occupant in the Application to Rent is to be considered a material inducement to execute this agreement, and the falsity of any part of such statement shall entitle Owner to terminate this agreement.

Owner and Occupant covenant that this agreement and its stipulated attachments constitute the whole understanding and supersede any preliminary negotiations or agreement and recites the entire consideration between parties.

For the vast majority of residents in a well-run apartment property, a lease or rental agreement is needed only to avoid misunderstandings, and to establish house rules and inventories. The penalty clauses of an iron-clad lease may never have to be enforced against any of your residents, especially if you've screened out problem people and selected good solid law-abiding residents. However, putting teeth into your lease, as suggested in this chapter, can protect the owner, and make the manager's job easier if a troublesome resident ever does slip in.

REMEMBER THESE BASIC POINTS:

* *If you use a lease, include the names of all occupants of the apartment, and get their signatures.*

* *Explain all the clauses of the lease to new residents.*

* *Make a written record of the contents and condition of the apartment at move-in, and get it signed by incoming residents.*

* *Make sure that residents know they should carry their own insurance.*

* *Put protective clauses in your lease or rental agreement.*

XIII *Record-Keeping Can Be Easy*

You possess something that's extremely valuable — probably because you can't buy any more. You can't even borrow any. You can't keep it in warehouses or vaults, or bury it in the backyard. All you can do with it is spend it. Or lose it.

This strange commodity is Time, of course. You have as much as anyone else. Do you use it profitably?

Truly successful investors and managers learn how to make time pay off — how to eliminate needless effort, get things done easily and smoothly, use each passing minute productively. They find time for everything. A big part of their secret is streamlining their paper work.

Some efficient property managers, if asked what they do all day, would prattle about bookkeeping they toil over, elaborate forms they fill out, filing they do. Some other managers have no records except shopping bags and cigar boxes stuffed with assorted papers, and maybe a rent receipt book. Both of these types of managers are time-wasters, of course.

A manager who spends hours compiling records isn't likely to be renting apartments, dealing with residents, or keeping the premises clean and painted and repaired. He's "too busy." Consequently, the owner loses money because the property is seldom fully rented.

And a manager whose records are hodgepodge or non-existent doesn't know whether rents cover expenses, how much money goes for utilities or advertising, whether the washer and dryer are profitable, or even when the final payment on the mortgage is to be made. They say they're "too busy" to sit down and figure out such things and, besides, they have an accountant who does the taxes. So, the owner can't tell whether his investment is making money or drifting toward bankruptcy. The latter is likelier, of course. Cash is probably leaking away in all directions.

RECORDS AREN'T THE MOST IMPORTANT JOB of a manager, but they're essential. They enable you to keep track of your position and to keep on the right side of the law. They also can help prevent waste or theft, and point your way toward maximum return on investment.

Just don't confuse property management, which is the game, with record-keeping, which is posting the score. The less time a manager spends, the more he has for the property. Therefore, you should simplify the record-keeping as much as possible.

Ask yourself, "Why make this notation? . . . Why keep this piece of paper? . . . Will it help in my work? . . . What will it add? . . . What would I lose if I didn't keep it? . . . Am I doing this just because 'we've always done it this way?' . . . Am I doing it 'just in case?'"

If you're piling up great collections of data, files, and scraps of paper for no apparent reason except that "it's our policy," you'd better re-examine the policy.

Get rid of records that nobody can show you a reason for compiling or keeping.

If you're keeping them "just in case," think about statistical chances that they'll be needed — and think about the costs in time as compared to the remotely possible value of the record. Cancelled checks? Sure. You'll need them for six years back or farther, if the Internal Revenue Service should make an audit. The same is true of bills and receipts. But minutes of the Apartment Association meeting? Contractors' estimates on jobs never done? A log of telephone calls from the year before last? How much chance is there that you'll be in dire need of such records?

Many a file cabinet and desk drawer is like the attic loaded with relics of yesteryear which we keep for sentimental reasons or because they once were needed. We never get around to throwing them out. In fact, we keep adding more of the same. This causes a general clutter that makes it harder to find what we really need.

So get tough. Don't let excess paper pile up on your desk or in your closet or your files. Throw out what you don't need. And if there's no real reason for writing down certain numbers, stop. Needless record-keeping means lost time. Do only what's necessary. Use the fewest and simplest possible forms, and the minimum time. We'll see how this can be done in the following pages.

Let's start with a key question: what records are necessary or even helpful? We can work toward an answer by considering the manager's responsibilities. His or her obligations include:

Keeping the property as fully rented as possible — collecting rents — paying bills — paying taxes — keeping up the insurance — keeping the premises in good condition — making sure that the owner's funds are spent productively and prudently — informing the owner about property shortcomings and defects — preserving vital documents such as leases, insurance policies, title papers, original paid invoices, records of tax payments and mortgage payments, reports of termite inspections, and the like.

HOW RECORDS CAN HELP YOU

A manager's records should enable an owner to see that these nine responsibilities are being carried out. Most of the nine require some record-keeping even if the owner isn't interested in checking up. For example, a manager obviously needs a record of all bills and their payments. He needs a record that shows what taxes will be coming due, and when.

Likewise, there has to be a record of rent payments. But most managers keep the wrong kind of rent record. They post payments on resident ledger cards. The trouble with resident ledger card systems, and with many other systems as well, is that they are designed to show the residents' payments, but not the status of rental units within the property.

When you keep tab only on the tenant, you're keeping a record of the variable. What you really need is a system that helps you watch and control the fixed asset; namely, the apartment units. The airlines don't keep track of passengers; they keep track of seats. The auto factories are more interested in knowing how many cars they produce and sell than they are in knowing who buys them.

Scientific apartment management should take the same viewpoint. The rental unit, not the resident, is the asset to be watched most carefully. The bottom-line question is, "How many units are bringing in how much money?"

What are the benefits that a good set of records can bring? Here are some:
—   They can spot expenses that are getting out of line;
—   they can minimize the risk that cash will end up in the wrong hands;
—   they can spot disappearances and possible thefts of materials or money;
—   they can show — or forecast — when replacements and improvements should be made;
—   they can show reasons for vacancies;
—   they can show how long it takes to fill vacancies;
—   they can indicate how well rental ads are pulling;
—   they can indicate how successful a manager's telephone tactics are in converting a telephone inquiry into a personal visit;
—   they can indicate how successful a manager's on-the-spot sales techniques are in converting visitors into renters;
—   they can show whether all occupants are paying the scheduled rents;
—   they can help an owner determine whether rents are too high, too low or about right;
—   they can show whether management is responding well to complaints.

Without an adequate set of records, the manager and owner are like doctors trying to treat a patient without knowing what ails him. Good records not only spotlight what is wrong, but show how well the attempted remedies are working. Information makes good management possible.

Some records that will be suggested in this chapter are designed primarily for reporting. They give an owner a means of checking on the manager and staff. If the owner does all his own managing, of course, he won't need such reports. You, as reader, can be guided in choosing among the following suggestions depending on whether you're an absentee owner or an owner-manager.

So much for background. Now let's consider just what records are needed, and what forms should be used. Basically, you need to keep track of money that comes in and money that goes out. It's that simple. Control over income and outgo is the name of the game. So, let's take up these two purposes in turn.

KEEPING TABS ON INCOME

RENT MONEY is obviously the big source of regular income. Control of it starts with a rental schedule — which is a sort of price list.

All you need for a rental schedule is a sheet of paper, ruled into columns as shown on the following page. List all the apartments and other rental spaces in their numerical order, whether they are rented or not.

This sheet must be the manager's bible, so to speak, in renting apartments. It's up to the owner, not the manager, to make final decisions in setting rents. Of course, the owner will consult the manager — but will keep in mind that the average resident manager doesn't want to ask as high a rent as the building will realistically support. The lower the rent, the easier the manager's job in keeping the building full. This is why managers must be held strictly accountable for sticking to the rent schedule.

On the other hand, no owner or manager can consider the rent schedule as graven in stone. It should be reviewed, and maybe revised, from time to time — particularly when vacancies seem harder to fill (which may mean rents are too high), or when it looks as if residents could reasonably pay more than you're charging. We'll go into the whole question of the rent scale in Chapter 18. Right now, the point is that a written

RENT SCHEDULE

Managers _____
Phone _____
Apt. No. _____

Unit No.	TYPE				Other	Rent Schedule	Cleaning or Security deposits	Comments *
	F *	U *	Bedrooms	Bath				

* Note amenities such as private balcony or patio, view, carpet condition, etc.

F = Furnished
U = Unfurnished

rent schedule prevents any misunderstanding between manager and owner about how much rent is to be charged and collected for each unit.

The owner can make sure that the rent schedule is being followed by arranging to receive a duplicate copy of each lease or rental agreement. And, of course, he can check the schedule against the monthly summary of income, which we'll get to in a few pages.

RECEIPT FOR ALL RENT moneys are a must. They enable you to keep close watch over the property's income. In addition, a receipt gives the rent-payer a record and a proof that he's paid; it tells the manager and owner who has paid how much for what; like a cash register tape, it gives the owner some assurance that incoming cash is being recorded.

DATE *June 1*, 19*77* NO. **3550**

RECEIVED OF *Clarence Ferguson*

ADDRESS *1121 Mountain Drive, Wichita, Kan.*

Ninety-five and —— no/100 $ *95.00*

FOR *Rent of Apt. 71 from 6/1-6/30/77.*

HOW PAID	BALANCE DUE	*Stone Canyon Apartments*
Cash	$ *30.00*	BY *Frank Robinson, Mgr.*

8K820   Rediform

RECEIPT   Date *May 1*, 19*77*   **4224**

Received From *Lucius T. Bondomerty*

Address *Apt. 207, Viewcrest Apartments*

Two hundred twelve and no/100 Dollars $ *212.00*

For *Rent of apartment 207 from 5/1/77 through 5/31/77*

ACCOUNT		HOW PAID		*Viewcrest Apartments*
AMT. OF ACCOUNT	*212 00*	CASH		
AMT. PAID	*212 00*	CHECK	*212 00*	By *Kathleen Mills, Mgr.*
BALANCE DUE	— —	MONEY ORDER		

8K800   Rediform

To meet all these purposes, you'll want receipts made out in triplicate, on consecutively numbered blanks. You can buy books of the 8K800 Rediforms, or the 8K20 Rediforms at almost any stationery store.

Why triplicate? So the original can be given to the resident, one copy to the owner, and the third can be kept in the manager's receipt book as a semi-permanent record.

Why numbered? Because otherwise someone in the office might be pocketing cash and destroying the office copies of the receipt. Every receipt must be accounted for. If a mistake is made in writing a receipt, the receipt should be marked "VOID" and sent in — all three copies stapled together — along with all the other receipts in numerical order.

This system makes it easy to keep track of all regular rent collections. But unscheduled income is a trickier problem.

More cash in this category is "lost" or stolen than you might imagine. It comes from residents to pay for damages, or for use of the hospitality or recreation rooms; from concessionaires; from lease settlements or cancellation fees or unrefunded deposits; from payments of back rent on accounts that were written off; from building-owned laundry equipment. You never know when it's coming in. It can add up to thousands of dollars in the course of a year. It's a temptation to any employee with sticky fingers.

No system can guarantee that employees will be honest in handling money. But your system should minimize the risk of petty embezzlement. One way to do this is to establish an iron-clad rule, widely known to residents as well as to employees, that a receipt must be made out immediately whenever any money is received. No employee must ever say, "I'll write a receipt later when I have a minute to spare," or scribble a "temporary receipt" on a scrap of blank paper. Even when promises are made in good faith, and the regular receipts are actually written later, errors are bound to creep in — writing the wrong amount or the wrong payer or the wrong transaction.

Other safeguards are possible, too, through rules that can be established in the manager's office. Good rules include:

1. All checks for rent, deposits, or any other purpose are to be made payable to the apartment complex, if it uses a name, or to the owner — never to the resident manager.

2. All checks are to be stamped with the bank deposit stamp as soon as received. (This makes them non-negotiable except for deposit into the designated bank account.)

3. All moneys received, without exception, are to be banked. (The manager should be provided with an entirely separate petty cash fund for incidental expenditures such as postage stamps, small shipping charges, gas for lawn mowers, and minor office expenses. A revolving fund of $50 should be enough for most properties. Don't ever use the petty cash fund to pay vendors. If you do, you'll soon need a large supply of cash on hand to satisfy all the vendors demanding cash.)

4. Make deposits at least weekly, so that money doesn't pile up in the office. Checks can be deposited daily by mail. In any case, be sure to make a deposit on the last business day of each month. This is important because a month is the normal accounting period. Your banking records, like all your other records, should reflect what actually happened during that period. Otherwise, your accountant or auditor will need extra time to unravel the books.

5. If a resident pays money for more than one purpose, issue separate receipts, even when he pays with one check. If he isn't there to take the receipts write them up anyway — don't wait until later — and get them to him as soon as possible. (If you receive a check for both rent and a deposit, leaving a balance owing, credit should go first to the deposit, because you can issue a notice to quit or pay when rent is overdue, but not when a deposit is owing.)

6. Never mingle rent moneys — which belong to the owner — with the funds on which the manager draws. There can be no dipping into rent receipts to pay building expenses, make refunds, cash personal checks, or lay out money for other purposes. All money collected for the owner should go promptly into a bank account separate

Monthly Rental Report (Income Or Cash Receipts Journal)

PROPERTY _____ REPORT from _____ 19__ to _____ 19 ____

Date	NAME	Apt No.	Prev. Bal.	Rental Rate	Rental Period		Cash Received			Rec. No.	TOTAL	Bal. Fwd.
					From	To & Incl.	Rent	Deposit	Misc.			
			$	$			$	$	$		$	$
	TOTAL		$	$			$	$	$		$	$

COMMENTS _____

_____

EXPENDITURES (Itemize)		MONTHLY VACANCY REPORT			
		VACANCIES - BEGINNING OF MONTH			
	$	Apt. No.	No. of Rooms	Furn. or Unfurn.	Rental Rate
					$
TOTAL EXPENDITURES	$				
BALANCE ON HAND	$	TOTAL (1)		$	
PETTY CASH REPORT		**MOVE-INS THIS MONTH**			
		Apt. No.	Date Moved in	Date Rent Starts	Rent Collected
CASH ON HAND	$				$
CASH FROM OWNER	$				
TOTAL	$				
CASH DEPOSITED FROM RENT		TOTAL (2)		$	
		MOVE-OUTS THIS MONTH			
DATE	RECEIPT NUMBERS		Apt. No.	Rental Rate	Rent Paid This Mo.	Net Loss on Move-outs
	to	$			$
	to	$			
	to	$			
	to	$			
TOTAL DEPOSITS	$	-TOTAL (3)		$	
Must equal total cash received		Net Loss From Vacancy (1-1+3)		$	

from the manager's account. The laws of most states, as well as the ethical codes of management associations, require a separate custodial account for the owner.

BANK DEPOSIT SLIPS should likewise be made out in triplicate: one each for the bank, the owner, and the manager. If you're dealing with a bank that has branches, the local branch where the manager makes the deposit can automatically route it to the owner's account in his own branch.

To make it easier for the owner (or some third party like a tax auditor) to verify that all the property's income is being banked, each deposit slip should total to the penny the amounts represented by a specific sequence of receipt slips. These receipts should be attached to it when it is sent to the owner.

RENT COLLECTION RECORDS are obviously necessary to keep track of the amounts due from each apartment You can keep them on cards — either by the resident's name (as shown on Page 183) or by the apartment number (as shown on Page 184).

As mentioned earlier, there are advantages to having a card for each apartment (with lines to record name changes) instead of for each resident. It gives you a continuing record of the unit's occupancy and income over an extended period of time. This can be enlightening. Certain units may have more turnover, or may be vacant longer, than others. There's always a reason. And you'll want to investigate the reason so you can remedy it if possible. This is why apartment cards are valuable clues. On the back of each card, you can keep a continuous record of maintenance and repair and improvements in the apartment.

On the other hand, there are advantages to having the cards alphabetized by residents' names. You can look up residents' phone numbers more easily — nowadays so many people have unlisted phones — and can see the date when their rent is due. Keeping these numbers and dates at your fingertips can save you some fumbling and wasted trips.

Even though the first two sample cards don't have specific spaces for them, you should jot down each resident's current checking and savings account numbers on whichever kind of card you use — so you'll know what to attach if you ever have to collect a court judgment. The savings account number should be on the rental application. The checking account number will be written in those funny looking magnetic numbers at the bottom of the resident's rent check.

An even simpler form of record, entirely adequate for a property with a dozen units or fewer, is shown on Page 185. When a resident moves out, cross him off this sheet with a yellow or pink highlighter felt pen. It does a neat job and still leaves the information easily readable. New residents can just be added to the list. They won't be in order according to apartment numbers, but what's the difference if everyone is on the same sheet?

Because you'll refer often to this Resident Record sheet, yet may not need to replace it for several years, you may want to keep it clean with a transparent sheet protector that slips on and off easily.

In a large apartment complex where rent collection is a big part of management's job, rent cards can be set up in a box divided into front and rear sections marked "unpaid" and "paid," respectively. As soon as a payment is received and the receipt written, it is posted on the card, and then the card is placed in the "paid" section until the beginning of the next rental period.

THE MONTHLY RENT SUMMARY is another simple yet vital record. Without it, your only records of rental income would be scattered through many separate receipt forms and individual cards. The summary is, in effect, your income journal.

RESIDENT'S LEDGER

NAME _____ PHONE _____ APT. NO. _____

_____

IN CASE OF
OF EMERGENCY NOTIFY: _____ PHONE _____

_____

EMPLOYED BY _____ PHONE _____

_____

LEASE FROM _____ TO _____ RATE PER MO. _____

Date	Name	Apt. No.	Mo. Rent Chg.	From Thru / Period Cov.	App Fee	Security Deposit	Other Dep.	Misc.	Receipt No.	Total Amt. Rec'd.	Bal. Due	Previous Balance
				Payment Credited To								

184

APT. NO. _____ DUE DATE _____

RENT FURNISHED _____ STYLE _____
UNFURNISHED _____ DEPOSIT _____

NOTIFY IN CASE OF EMERGENCY

TENANT'S NAME	PHONE	EMPLOYER'S NAME	PHONE	NAME	ADDRESS	PHONE	DATE IN	DATE OUT

Receipt No.	APARTMENT DATA			NAME	F OR U	CASH RECEIVED					BALANCE	PAID TO	REC'D. BY	MISC. DEDC.
	Mo	Day	Apt	Type		Rent	Deposit	Code	Misc.	Total Pd				

RESIDENT RECORD

Location _____

	Unit	Tenant	Phone	Moved In	Moved Out	Rent Date	Deposit/ Rent	Bank/Chg. Acct. Nos.
1								
2								
3								
4								
5								
6								
7								
8								
9								
10								
11								
12								
13								
14								
15								
16								
17								
18								
19								
20								
21								
22								
23								
24								
25								
26								
27								
28								
29								
30								
31								
32								
33								
34								
35								

You will find two useful forms of such a report on Pages 187 and 188. You could set either one up in triplicate, using NCR carbonless type paper (or some similar product) so that your entries are simultaneously recorded on all three. At the end of each month, one copy could go to your accountant and one to the owner, keeping the original with the resident manager's other records.

The first form, as you'll see, enables the owner to tell at a glance how much additional income, aside from the regular rents, was collected. There are separate columns for rental furniture, security deposits, pet deposits, and miscellaneous income such as key deposits, storage fees, late charges, cable TV payments, and so on. The form helps an accountant or auditor check deposit slips against income. It also helps an owner or manager to see at a glance whether on investment in laundry machines or the like is paying off. The instructions for balancing the sheet are written in on the bottom lines.

The second of these forms doesn't call for such a detailed breakdown of types of income. It's probably preferable in a well-run propety with low turnover, where there aren't any miscellaneous collections from residents. The one sheet gives an overall view of the financial position for the month — income, outgo, vacancies and move-ins. Many owners prefer a one-sheet summary which they can read quickly and understand easily.

The part of this sheet set aside for the vacancy report is intended not only for the owner's information but also — and more importantly — to focus the manager's attention on the amount of rent lost through vacancies. Merely by having to add up vacancy losses each month (and also, perhaps, by having to explain them to the owner) the manager is forced to give more thought to the vanished income than he might otherwise.

For balancing the columns on such sheets, an adding machine with tape is essential. Sometimes just one incorrect entry causes the error, and you can find it without laboriously adding each column again, if you simply compare the tape of the columns you're cross-checking.

DEPOSITS CAN DECEIVE YOU in judging your financial position. Receipts for security deposits, pet deposits, key deposits, and the like, must be given just as for rent payments. But these deposits aren't true income, since they eventually have to be refunded. They really represent a potential asset to the occupant, liability to the owner.

State or local law may require that such money be kept in a separate escrow account, held in trust for occupants until they forfeit all or part of a deposit. You may be required to compute and pay interest on the money being held. You'd better find out. Regardless of the law in your area, you may want to keep a separate accounting of these receipts anyway, so you won't count them as income.

REFUNDS of these deposits should never be made from petty cash, rent receipts, or any other loose money the manager may keep lying around. Sometimes it's best for a manager to explain to residents that all refunds of security deposits are made by the owner as a matter of policy. This cuts down the chance of collusion between manager and resident, and gives the owner a chance to check the premises himself before parting with the money. But if an owner lives far away, or just doesn't want to bother, the refunds still should be issued from a special checking account, or from the owner's income account. In any case, it's nice to have a written record such as that entitled "Security Deposit Refund Request" shown on Page 189.

DEPOSITS BY APPLICANTS who want to rent apartments must also be receipted, of course, and must be returned if the manager rejects the application. Other-

RECORD OF CASH & RENT RECEIVED FOR MONTH OF _____

Date	Name	Apt. No.	Monthly Rental Charge	Period Covered From	Period Covered Thru	Payment Credited To Furn.	Payment Credited To Security Deposit	Payment Credited To Pet	Payment Credited To Misc.	Re-ceipt No.	Total Amt. Rec'd.	Balance Due	Previous Balance		Rent Prior Month	Rent Current Month	Rent Future Month	Comment	Misc. Chgs.
			(1)			(2)	(3)	(4)	(5)		(6)	(7)	(8)	1					
														2					
														3					
														4					
														5					
														6					
														7					
														8					
														9					
														10					
														11					
														12					
														13					
														14					
														15					
														16					
														17					
														18					
														19					
														20					
														21					
														22					
														23					
														24					
														25					
														26					
														27					
														28					
														29					
														30					
														31					
														32					
														33					
														34					
														35					
														36	(9)	(10)	(11)		

SUMMARY

Amt.	Recpt. No.	Rent Paid	Total Rec'd.
(12)		(13)	(14)

TO BALANCE LEFT-HAND SIDE OF JOURNAL:

Total Columns 1, 2, 3, 4, 5 & 8　　Columns 5 & 12 should total the same

Total Columns 6 & 7　　Columns 13 & 14 should be same total as Column 6

Columns 9, 10 & 11 should equal Column 1　　which should be your total bank deposit

Manager's Statement _____John Doe_____   **APARTMENTS**   **Date** _Aug. 10, 1976_
                 (Name)

Signed _____

Apt.	Date Paid	TENANT	UTILITIES Paid To	Amt(1)	RENT PAID From	To	Amt (2)	Misc (3)	
1	8/1	Arthur Jackson			8/1	8/31	110 00		
2	8/3	Carol Lamebull			8/1	8/31	80 00		
3	8/7	James Obbanya			8/1	8/31	90 00	5 00	
4	8/1	Lawrence Swain			7/28	8/28	110 00		
5	8/1	Don Brouse			8/1	8/31	90 00		
6	8/4	Ortha Mondy			7/20	8/5	55 00		
7	8/1	F. Taylor			8/1	8/31	110 00		
8	8/3	Phil Campbell			8/1	9/15	165 00		
9	8/2	Mrs. Burman			7/20	8/31	130 00		
10	8/1	Lee Schriber			8/1	8/31	95 00		
11	8/2	Paul Jones			8/1	8/31	100 00		

OTHER RENTALS & INCOME (Enter amts. Col. 3)

Late charge - Apt. 3

						TOTALS (1)	(2) 1,135 00	(3) 5 00	

Date Pd.	Disbursements Paid To	For What	Amt(4)		
				Total Col. 1	
7/21	Honny's	Lock Repair	6 50	Total Col. 2	1,135 00
7/20	Jack's Plumbing	Toilet Seat	14 50	Total Col. 3	
				Tot.Gross Inc.	1,140 00
				Ded.Disbrs(4)	21 00
				Net Receipts(5)	1,119 00
				Deposit Dates	Amount
				1 8/3/76	1,119 00
				2	
				3	
				4	
				Total Dep.(6)	1,119 00

INSTRUCTIONS
Enclose with statement:
(a) Duplicate rent receipts
(b) Vouchers for cash disbursements
(c) Dupl. bank dep. slips
(d) Net receipts (5) must balance with total dep.(6)

	Total Disbursements (4)	21 00

SECURITY DEPOSIT REFUND REQUEST

DATE_____ PROPERTY_____

RESIDENT_____ ADDRESS_____

LEASE INFORMATION

LEASE DATED _____ TO _____

DATE VACATED _____

DEPOSIT INFORMATION	On Deposit	Deductions	Balance Due Resident	Balance Forfeited
KEY DEPOSIT	$	$	$	$
PET DEPOSIT	$	$	$	$
SECURITY DEPOSIT	$	$	$	$
TOTAL	$	$	$	$

EXPLANATION OF DEDUCTIONS

KEY _____

PET _____

SECURITY _____

_____

For Office Use Only

Approved By _____ Date _____

Check Issued By _____ Date _____ Check No. _____

Forwarding Address _____

_____

wise the money is applied to the first month's rent — or, if forfeited by an applicant who doesn't move in, can be kept as liquidated damages.

KEEPING CONTROL OF OUTGO

As we've seen, a manager probably should be provided with a small supply of petty cash, replenished regularly, for the little incidental expenses that come up in the course of the day's work. But an active owner will want to pay all major bills personally. It's a way of keeping his finger on the pulse of the money machine — to mix a metaphor — and also helps him spot chances for cost-cutting that he might otherwise overlook.

This doesn't necessarily mean that the owner should do much of the purchasing, or should insist on the manager getting permission for each routine purchase. Usually, it saves time all around, and makes for smoother operations, if you set up open accounts with certain contractors and suppliers who've proven themselves reliable and economical. Then the manager can draw on these accounts as necessary, within reasonable limits.

These regular accounts, billed to the owner every month, are a safeguard against any scheme for bill-padding or kickbacks that a dishonest manager might want to arrange. Of course, the bills should be approved by the on-site manager before an absentee owner pays them because suppliers have been known to submit bills for fictitious services and supplies.

It's dangerous to send the checks to the manager and have him pass them along to the payees (or let him withhold them if he's not satisfied with performance.) The danger is that it gives the manager a chance to angle for kickbacks from vendors, even if it's only free lunches. Just by phoning the tradesman and saying, "I've got your check here," the manager may be applying subtle pressure. It makes for bad vendor relations, which in turn can cost an owner money. If a manager thinks a payment should be held up, the time to say so is when the bill goes to him for approval.

THE MONTHLY SUMMARY OF DISBURSEMENTS, produced by the manager or bookkeeper, is simply a running history of cash outlays. It can be a simple, almost primitive report — or it can be highly elaborate, if the owner wants it that way. Regardless of form, there surely ought to be a summary, rather than just a file folder full of receipts which is all some managers keep.

The simplest form would be a listing of all checks issued by number, date, and amount. But most managers go beyond this and set up columns to classify items of expense. For example, you might have one column for supplies, another for repairs and maintenance, a third for utilities, a fourth for insurance, and so on. Then you can simply add the amounts in any one column to see the total expenditures in that category for a given period of time. It helps with budgeting and accounting.

However, such a statement is on a cash basis. It doesn't reflect any unpaid bills. So it might give an owner a deceptively rosy picture of the operating costs. One way to avoid this is to include at the bottom a total of expenses incurred but not yet billed or paid for. (A file of written purchase orders will help the manager compile this total.)

How much detail — how many column headings, in other words — you'll find useful will depend mainly on the size of the property. A big building with big operating costs ought to show more information than mentioned above. For example, it won't be enough to show that utilities cost $600 in May of this year, but only $400 in May of last year. You'd want to know which specific utility costs went up — electricity, water, fuel, gas, telephones, or trash collection. Knowing this, you'll be able to seek ways to economize. Always keep in mind the relationship of vacancy to utility costs.

In fact, even if total utility costs are staying about the same, it could be useful to know that your phone bill or electric bill is creeping up. Maybe you carry some of these figures in your head, but there's nothing like a month-by-month written record to bring them painfully to your attention.

Repair costs are another example. Segregating them by type is rather pointless if they add up to only a few hundred dollars per year. But if the year's repair bill is in the thousands, there must be some waste you can squeeze out by analyzing it.

In a really big complex, you may want to keep separate running totals of costs for —

Air conditioning repairs	Painting & decorating of interiors
Carpentry repairs	Painting & decorating of exteriors
Electrical repairs	Plumbing repairs
Elevator repairs	Refrigerator & stove repairs
Furniture repairs	Roof repairs
Heating system repairs	Miscellaneous repairs
Masonry repairs	

This same principle of categorizing can apply to everything for which the property spends money. Wherever you suspect that additional details will point the way to worthwhile economies, you simply break down the costs into smaller subtotals. Conversely, you can combine two or more categories where the costs are consistently too small to justify itemizing.

MORTGAGE PAYMENTS don't ordinarily call for much record-keeping. They're usually the same amount each month (although the proportion allotted to principal and interest keeps changing). You hardly need a separate column in your monthly disbursement sheet for this item. The lender will be keeping a separate record (with a copy for you, ordinarily) of the amounts applied against principal and interest each month, so there's not much point in duplicating this detail in your disbursement journal.

Simply enter the gross amount of the payment in a column headed, "general ledger," best located at the extreme right, usually, and code it or otherwise label it to show what it is. You may want to use this same catch-all column for refunds of deposits and miscellaneous expenditures that don't seem to fit in any other column, yet are too rare or too small to deserve columns of their own.

PURCHASE ORDERS were mentioned a few pages back. They're essential if you are to keep track of what you ordered, what orders are outstanding, and whether the bills agree with the quoted price.

Use serially numbered forms. Two simple forms are shown on the following page. Use carbon paper so each form will be made out in triplicate: one each for vendor, owner, and manager. If any part of the work or materials went into repairs or improvement of a specific apartment, this can be posted on the back of the apartment record card. You may need the data in deciding what the apartment rent should be, or in billing residents for work made necessary by them.

Drop a copy of each order in a file folder. Then if the building is sold, you can quickly cancel orders not yet filled. Otherwise, the vendor may fill the order and bill either the new or previous owner, which can lead to disputes. If both refuse to pay, the vendor may put a lien on the building. All such headaches can be avoided if you cancel unfilled orders — which is much easier to do if you have a purchase order file.

192

Original   **PURCHASE ORDER**

Date: _____   Order No. _____

To: _____

Please furnish and deliver the following materials and/or service to:

QUANTITY	MATERIAL	PRICE

It is expressly understood that the vendor or vendor's agent accepting this order does so with the understanding that no liability shall be incurred or attached to the under-signed, Lyndene Management, who issues this order as agent only. This order is subject to further instructions as shown on the reverse side.

Lyndene Management

By _____

The above order number must appear on all invoices

Invoices must be submitted in duplicate

PURCHASE ORDER   This Number Must Appear On
All Invoices, Packages, Etc.

TO _____   **NO.** _____

Address _____   Date _____

Ship To _____   For _____

Please Notify Us Immediately If You Are Unable to Ship Complete Order By Date Specified

	Quantity	Please Supply Items Listed Below		Price
1				
2				
3				
4				
5				
6				
7				

Date Required	How Ship	Please Send	Copies of Your Invoice

TERMS: **PURCHASING AGENT**

YOUR CHECK RECORD is routine. Nobody tries to maintain a checking account without recording each check as he writes it. Just be sure to enter enough information so you'll know, a few years hence, what each check was for. If specific invoices or statements are being paid, include their numbers and dates on your check record. This is easier if you use one of the big checkbooks, with checks printed in sheets of three, and lined pages in the back for recording the checks. The stubs in a small-size checkbook are too cumbersome.

IF YOU WRITE PAYROLL CHECKS, the law says you must give the employee a statement of the gross pay, deductions or withholdings, and net amount. Therefore, you may want special checks for payroll, with attachments on which to tabulate this information. You'll also need your own record of the same information, in order to distribute the withheld amounts to the right accounts and to compile the W-2 forms for the Internal Revenue Service at the end of the year.

The best way to keep these payroll records is to make up a separate payroll journal, or a special set of pages in your disbursement journal. You'll need enough columns to show amounts withheld for various purposes — and, of course, the usual information concerning payee, check number, date, and amount.

But this isn't enough. You'll need a separate ledger card for each employee. It will help you avoid withholding too much where tax ceilings exist, and will simplify compiling W-2 forms and other tax reports. You'll find suggested formats for your payroll journal records and individual ledger cards later in this chapter, as part of the streamlined system suggested for handling all your key income and expenditure records.

Because of complicated laws affecting wages, hours, taxes, and reporting, many property owners turn the payroll job over to a qualified accountant or a computer firm. If you're willing to take on the task yourself, make sure you do it correctly, because there can be stiff penalties for failing to file reports or pay taxes on time. To help you avoid mistakes, Uncle Sam offers you at least four good handbooks, all free. They are:

Publication 15 — Employer Tax Guide
Publication 334 — Tax Guide for Small Business
Publication 505 — Tax Withholding & Declaration of Estimated Tax
Publication 535 — Tax Information on Business Expenses

As for state and local payroll tax laws, you can usually get whatever information you need by calling the appropriate government bureaus. Or your Apartment Association may have it all neatly packaged for you.

WATCH THE VACANCY FIGURES

Rent payments are the lifeblood of an apartment enterprise. Vacancies mean that the bloodstream isn't pumping at full volume. Any owner with an ounce of business sense wants to get vacancies filled as fast as possible, so they'll be producing income. Therefore, he needs to know how many vacancies exist, and how long. If those numbers get too high, he may need to find a better manager soon.

If the property is large, the monthly summary of vacancies isn't enough. The owner and manager need more detail, more often. They need a weekly vacancy report like the one shown on Page 194.

During the week, the manager should keep this sheet on his desk and enter events as they occur — not the next day, or at the end of the week. Just the effort of keeping

WEEKLY VACANCY REPORT

from _____ 19 ___ to _____ 19 ___

_____ Location _____

NOTICES RECEIVED THIS WEEK

Apt. No.	Name	Rent	Date Notice Given	Date Vacating	Reason For Vacating

APARTMENTS VACATED THIS WEEK

Apt. No.	Name	Rent	Date Vacated	Paid To	Balance Due	Forwarding Address

RENTAL MARKET ACTIVITY — Inquiries Received (I)   Apartments Shown (S)

Mon		Tue		Wed		Thurs		Fri		Sat		Sun		Total	
I	S	I	S	I	S	I	S	I	S	I	S	I	S	I	S

APARTMENTS RENTED THIS WEEK

Apt. No.	Name	Rent	Deposit Received Date	Amount	Starting Date

TOTAL VACANCIES, END OF WEEK

Apt. No.	Furn./Unfurn.	Rent	Vacant Since	Condition

IMPROVEMENT WORK COMPLETED THIS WEEK

Apt. No.	Work Completed	Date Completed

IMPROVEMENT WORK NEEDED

Apt. No.	Work Needed	Date Scheduled For

SUGGESTIONS: _____

_____

_____

this report up-to-the-minute will sharpen the manager's alertness toward the most important events happening in the building; namely, rentals and vacancies. At the end of each week a copy should go to the owner.

You'll notice that there is a section for "Rental Market Activity." This is a testing entry, a barometer of market conditions. "I" stands for inquiries, either phone calls or personal visits by prospects. If an ad is running and pulls only two or three inquiries a day, the owner or manager should know that advertising money is being wasted. It's a signal to try a differently worded ad.

If there are numerous inquiries, but few apartments shown, again the owner or manager must try to find out what is wrong. Did the ad omit mention of price so that the calls were to ask the price? Or does the manager lack the ability to keep people interested over the phone? If so, it may be time to take the phone number out of the ad. On the other hand, if the building is in a borderline area, and the resident manager is good with telephone technique, the phone number may be more important in the ad than the property address. This section of the vacancy report helps measure the sales power of both the ad and the manager.

Likewise, if many apartments are shown but few rented, either the condition of the apartment turns away interested prospects, or the manager is weak in selling. Either way, it's causing the property to lose money, and the owner must correct whatever is wrong or he'll keep on losing money. A day of rent lost can never be recovered.

If the report shows the property is full with no residents having given notice of plans to vacate, and several inquiries daily although no ad is running and no vacancy sign is out, the report still tells the owner and manager something. It indicates that demand is strong and the rental rate maybe under the market.

If the weekly reports show an upsurge of "notices received" and "apartments vacated," this is a danger signal. Why are people moving out? Maybe the rents are too high by comparison with properties nearby that may be newer or lower-priced. Maybe some newly-arrived residents aren't compatible with those of longer standing. Maybe the premises are getting seedy looking. Whatever the reason, an unusual number of move-outs calls for investigation by the owner. It may mean that the manager should be replaced.

"Improvement Work Completed This Week" is another important part of the card. If "Total Vacancies" shows that a unit has been vacant for several weeks, while improvement work on it is still unfinished, there's something wrong with the manager's priorities.

"Improvement Work Needed" gives the manager and owner a chance to shop for the best buys, and to schedule the work. Painters or rug cleaners usually can't come on short notice, but if you give them two or three weeks' leeway, you'll get improvement work done fairly promptly.

ARE YOU ON TARGET?

Your money machine, the apartment building, is humming along night and day — pulling in money, churning it out. The income and outgo fluctuate continuously. Only a financial genius could tell from any given day's figures whether the machine is as profitable as it seemed likely to be when the owner bought it. Some telltale numbers show up in the weekly vacancy report, as we've just seen. They indicate the money machine's state of health that week, but not its profitability. How do you judge whether it is making an adequate profit?

THE MONTHLY OPERATING STATEMENT can be the test. One fairly simple sheet of paper should show you whether the machine's basic product, cash flow, is being pumped forth as plentifully as expected. And if the cash isn't coming, the sheet should tell you why. Read in combination, the weekly vacancy reports and the monthly operating statement enable an owner to monitor the money machine, spot any parts that aren't working right, and keep score on the manager's performance.

The statement can consist mainly of a summary of all cash receipts and all disbursements during the month, arranged in some logical way, and broken down in as much detail as the owner wants. Usually, there's no need to go to the trouble of working out allowances for depreciation on the statement, since these don't affect the cash flow.

On the next pages you'll find three different kinds of format for the monthly summary. Using these for ideas, you should easily be able to design one that suits your own taste.

No matter what format you use, you'll probably find it worthwhile to set up enough columns so that you can easily record monthly amounts for a given item side by side for an entire year. Then, by running your eye along the line, you can see whether that item of income or expense is staying on target.

Some owners want the statement to show money being set aside for certain big expenses to be met later: maybe a monthly payment into the owner's real estate tax fund, with an indication of the balance; deposits for future capital outlays; or a regular monthly accounting of an established reserve for replacements. If the insurance premiums are paid yearly or twice yearly, they can still be divided into monthly portions on paper and can be shown for each monthly operating statement. By subtracting all these allotments from the month's cash income (or from the month's net profit, or by adding them to the month's expenses), you can get a picture of how the property is doing for the year as a whole. Otherwise, the "net profit (or loss) from operations" may fluctuate violently from month-to-month as the big expenditures come due.

If you do show sums being set aside in reserve accounts, transfer them into the operating account when they are actually spent. In this way, the bottom line for "net profit or loss" is likely to stay on a more even keel throughout the year.

HOW TO STAY SIMPLE

In this chapter we've looked at the essential parts of any good system for recording and controlling a rental property's income and outgo. We've seen how the management office writes receipts that can make possible all income accounting — because the data on them can be transferred onto bank deposit slips, onto the individual cards for apartments or residents, onto the monthly rent report, and finally onto the monthly operating statement.

Likewise, we've seen how the checks that the management office writes can be the raw material for all records of expenditures. The office uses the names and numbers on them in keeping the cash disbursements journal, in tabulating payroll information, and finally in compiling the cash expenditures part of the monthly operating summary.

This may sound like a mountainous job of record-keeping — of copying from one record to another, with limitless potential for errors. But it needn't be as complex and burdensome as it sounds.

Since we're working with just two basic bits of paper — receipts and checks —

MONTHLY OPERATING STATEMENT

PROPERTY _____   PERIOD _____

INCOME
    Rental Income $ _____
    Cleaning Deposits
    Laundry
        TOTAL INCOME $ _____

EXPENSES
    Resident Manager's Expenses
        Resident Manager's Salary $ _____
        Resident Manager's Utilities
        Resident Manager's Telephone $ _____

    Bookkeeping $ _____
    Advertising
    Pool Maintenance
    Repairs and Supplies
    Gardening
    Pest Control
    Property Insurance
    Property Taxes
    Miscellaneous $ _____

    Utilities
        Electricity $ _____
        Gas
        Water
        Rubbish $ _____

    Cleaning
        Apartments
        Carpets
        Drapes
        Tenant Refunds $ _____

        Total Operating Expense $ _____
        Net Operating Income $ _____

    Capital Improvements
        Carpet Replacement $ _____
        Drape Replacement
        Furniture Replacement
        Exterior Painting
        Roofing
        Water Heater Replacement
        Pool Filter or Heater Replacement $ _____

    Investment Expense
        Professional Property Management $ _____
        Accounting
        Legal $ _____

        Total Investment Expense $ _____

DEBT SERVICE
    First Trust Deed $ _____
    Second Trust Deed
    Third Trust Deed $ _____

        Cash Flow $ _____

PREVIOUS CASH BALANCE $ _____
LOANS $ _____

        Cash Available $ _____

OPERATING STATEMENT

	JANUARY	FEBRUARY	MARCH	APRIL
GROSS INCOME				
Mortgage Payable				
1st Principal				
Interest				
2nd Principal				
Interest				
3rd Principal				
Interest				
Depreciation (Apportionment)				
Taxes (Apportion Accordingly)				
Insurance (Apportion Accordingly)				
Incidental Repairs				
Carpentry				
Decorating & Painting				
Electrical				
Plumbing				
OTHER EXPENSES				
Advertising				
Auto (15 cents per mile or actual)				
Cleaning & Hauling				
Commissions to Secure Rentals				
Garbage				
Gardening				
Janitorial				
Legal & Accounting				
License & Permits				
Office Rent				
Outside Services				
Salaries, Management, etc.				
Telephone				
Travel				
Utilities				
Miscellaneous				
TOTAL EXPENSES				
NET PROFIT OR (LOSS)				

MONTHLY OPERATING STATEMENT

OWNER _____   FROM _____ TO _____

LOCATION _____

	Total Annual Operations	Jan	Feb	Mar	Apr	May	June	July	Aug	Sept	Oct	Nov	Dec
Rentals													
Other Income													
TOTAL INCOME													
OPERATING EXPENSES													
Payroll													
Utilities: Electricity													
Water													
Gas													
Telephone													
Misc. Disbursements													
Laundry & Cleaning													
Management Fee													
Maintenance Contracts													
Elevator													
Refrig.													
Pest Control													
Rubbish													
Gardener/Janitor													
Supplies													
Repairs													
Furniture													
Building													
Maintenance													
Painting													
Plastering													
Plumbing													
Electrical													
Miscellaneous													
Replacements													
Furnishings													
Carpet													
Linens													
Equipment/Miscellaneous													
TOTAL OPERATING EXPENSES													
NET PROFIT FROM OPERATIONS													
Capital Exp.													
Insurance													
First Mortgage - Princ.													
Interest													
Second Mortgage - Princ.													
Interest													
S.S. Taxes													
Reserve Account													
TOTAL CAPITAL EXPENSES													
NET INCOME													

what we really need is a system by which the information written on these will automatically appear on all other pertinent records. It's just a matter of duplication, which has already been worked out by several manufacturers of business forms. You can have a mass produced system or a custom-built system, using basic forms and procedures available from almost any big supplier of business forms.

These systems are known by various terms, such as Hodley, One-Write, and Pegboard, but they're all based on the same principle. They use a board with pegs in it to hold various forms. The forms are on smudgeless NCR copy paper, so that when you write something once it appears in the right places on all the right copies. This magical elimination of manual copying is accomplished because holes in the paper line up with pegs on the board.

A SIMPLE CASH RECEIPT SYSTEM (accounting for income) is an example. You'll see how it works as you look at the next page, headed "Property Management System." You can get the sheets and the systems from any National Business Systems dealer.

First, you place a monthly rent report (journal) form on the board — probably in duplicate, so both the manager and the owner can have one. Over this, using the pegs on the left, you lay a pageful of shingled, numbered control slips to be used as receipts. Also, using the pegs on the right, you lay a deposit record form over part of this same monthly rent report. Now you're almost set. The columns on the control slip and deposit record correspond with those on the underlying rent report journal.

Here's what happens when a resident makes a payment. To record it, the card for his apartment (also designed to be compatible with the journal) is pulled from its file box. It is placed under the shingled control slips but over the journal pages so that the right lines and columns correspond. Then his payment is entered once. Because of the copying material on the backs of the forms, this entry is made simultaneously on the top control slip, the deposit record, and the underlying ledger and journal forms. Then the control slip goes to the resident as his receipt, and the apartment card goes back in the file. That's all. We're ready for the next entry.

We continue making entries this way until we reach the end of the page, or until we make a bank deposit. If we make a deposit first, we take off the deposit record and send it to the bank, along with the money and the regular magnetically-coded bank deposit slip showing only the date and total. Then we put a new deposit record form on the board and continue the entries. (Of course, there can be extra copies of the deposit record and the deposit slips, if you want them for the files.)

When the sheet is completed, we can easily verify that all entries are correct. We cross-foot the totals on the page and look to make sure that the totals from the deposit slips part of the journal equal the total amounts reported as received. After this is done, the manager sends one copy of the completed page to the owner — who, of course, can compare the deposit totals as shown on these pages with the corresponding totals on the deposit slips and bank statements. Consider some of the advantages of such systems:

1.   By making one entry, you create records with all the essential information for owner, manager, and residents.

2.   You save more than two-thirds the time needed to prepare all these records separately.

3.   You never have to copy from one record to another. So, there's no chance of errors in copying, or errors caused by not copying.

4.   The system virtually audits itself. All records automatically reflect the receipts for cash taken in.

PROPERTY MANAGEMENT SYSTEM.

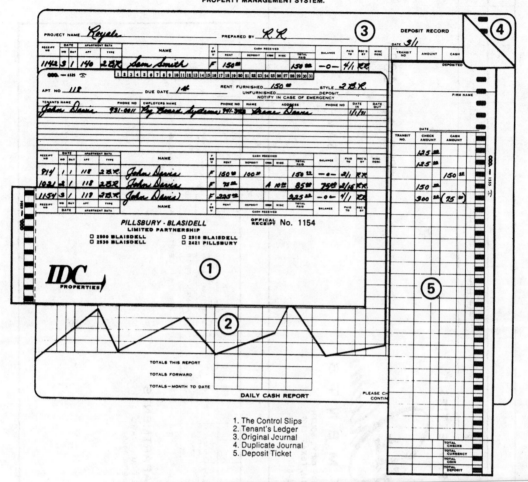

1. The Control Slips
2. Tenant's Ledger
3. Original Journal
4. Duplicate Journal
5. Deposit Ticket

MAINTENANCE RECORD

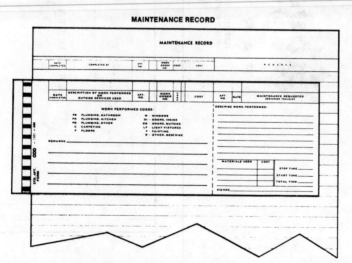

202

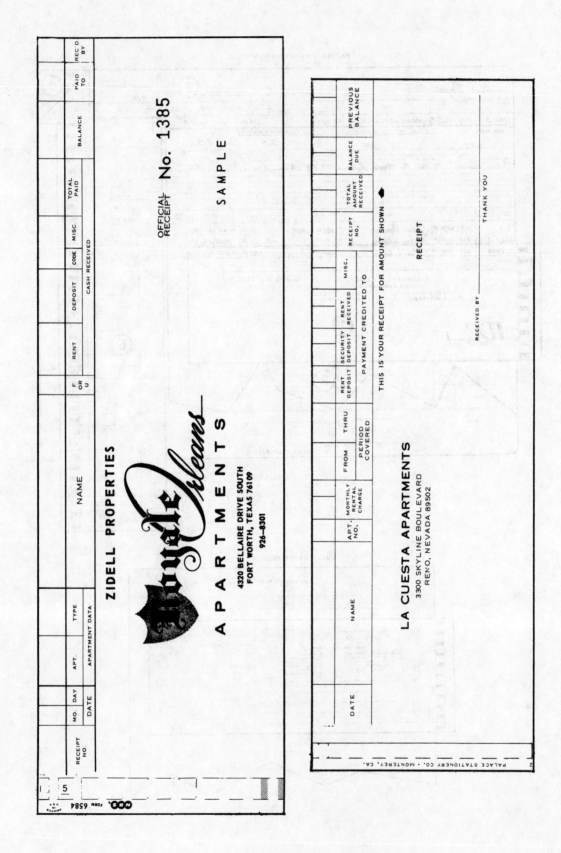

5. Chances for employee dishonesty are almost eliminated.

6. Almost anyone can master the whole system in a few minutes.

7. Inexpensive standard forms are used (although you can order specially designed forms if you wish).

APARTMENT MAINTENANCE RECORDS are available as parts of these same stack-of-pancakes systems. We keep the maintenance record on the back of the Apartment Ledger Card (see following pages). Other cards can be used for general maintenance work that isn't confined to specific apartments.

The basic idea is the same. We place a stack of shingled, numbered work order forms on a pegboard. When a maintenance job is to be done, we pull the appropriate ledger card and slide it under the work order (which can consist of more than one copy). We write in the necessary information; then tear off the right-hand part and give it to the service company or maintenance man. We leave the left-hand part on the board, but fold it over to the left. This keeps management aware that a work order is unfinished.

After the job is finished, we again slide the ledger card under the remaining part of the work order form. We write down what was done, who did it, the charges, the invoice number, the completion date, and anything else that should be recorded. The resident manager signs the form, to indicate his approval, and sends it to the owner along with the invoice for payment. (If the order is in duplicate, the manager can keep the extra copy and file it away by number for his records.)

COMBINING THE PAYROLL AND CASH DISBURSEMENT SYSTEMS is easy if we use the same concept of writing once on a pegboard. Pages 206 and 207 show the necessary forms, as produced by National Business Systems.

We start by putting a combination cash disbursement and payroll journal in place on the board, as the bottom sheet. On its left is a page for listing all checks and for entering payroll information. On its right is a page with blank column headings. You can fill in the headings with whatever categories you want to use for keeping track of various types of expenditures. Over this sheet we place a special check, with stubs for both payroll and other disbursement information. We lock it in place with the pegs on the left.

If it is a payroll check, the employee's payroll record card (Form 7519 in the illustration) is inserted under it. We write the check and fill in the appropriate information on the stubs; then give the employee the check with both stubs.

If the check is for some other purpose, we use the inner stub to record the number of the invoice being paid and other appropriate data. We discard the outer stub since its spaces are only for payroll information.

Maybe you want a duplicate register of checks. If so, there's a variation of the illustrated forms available to meet this requirement.

OTHER CARDS CAN BE ADDED to set up a complete accounts payable system if you want one: vendors' ledger cards, a purchase journal, and expense distribution ledger cards — all available from NBS. But these aren't likely to be worth the extra record-keeping unless a very large number of apartments is involved. The same is true of the available accounts receivable pegboard systems.

Once you know your needs, the simpler your system for meeting them, the better off you'll be. With a one-entry system like those described, you have no posting, no catch-up accounting, no complicated procedures to learn. Your records are easy to audit. Your quarterly and yearly tax reports are easy to compile.

Even a big company running many apartment complexes can have a simple system by using standard journals designed for electronic data processing. And whether you're

204

APARTMENT LEDGER CARD

DUE DATE →	1	2	3	4	5	6	7	8	9	10	11	12	13	14	15	16	17	18	19	20	21	22	23	24	25	26	27	28	29	30	31

NAME   **PHONE**   **APT. NO.**

IN CASE OF EMERGENCY NOTIFY: **PHONE**

EMPLOYED BY   **PHONE**

LEASE FROM   **TO**   **RATE PER MO.**

DATE	NAME	APT. NO.	MONTHLY RENTAL CHARGE	FROM	THRU	RENT DEPOSIT	SECURITY DEPOSIT	RENT RECEIVED	MISC.	RECEIPT NO.	TOTAL AMOUNT RECEIVED	BAL. DUE	PREVIOUS BALANCE
				PERIOD COVERED		PAYMENT CREDITED TO							

COO FORM NO. R.L. NCR   **TENANT'S LEDGER**

(Alternative Standard Pegboard System Format)

	1	2	3	4	5	6	7	8	9	10	11	12	13	14	15	16	17	18	19	20	21	22	23	24	25	26	27	28	29	30	31

LEASE DEPOSIT _____ NAME _____ APT. NO. _____

CLEANING DEPOSIT _____ ADDRESS _____ DUE DATE _____

MONTHLY RENT _____

FURN. ☐ _____

UNFURN. ☐

DATE	RENTAL PERIOD		CHARGES				TOTAL RECEIVED		CHANGE GIVEN	RECEIPT NUMBER	BALANCE DUE
	FROM	THRU	RENT	DEPOSITS		MISC.	CASH	CHECK			
				LEASE	CLEANING						

FORM 8025
PEGBOARD SYSTEMS, INC.
SAN FRANCISCO, CA 647-0686

(Alternative Standard Pegboard System Format)

206

Combination System for Payroll and Disbursements

ANOTHER **NBS.** CARBONLESS PEGBOARD SYSTEM

EQUIPMENT

Databord

Posting Ring Binder

Journal Storage Binder

Posting Tray Size 8½x11
For Earnings Records

This system is also
available in a compact
folding Databord

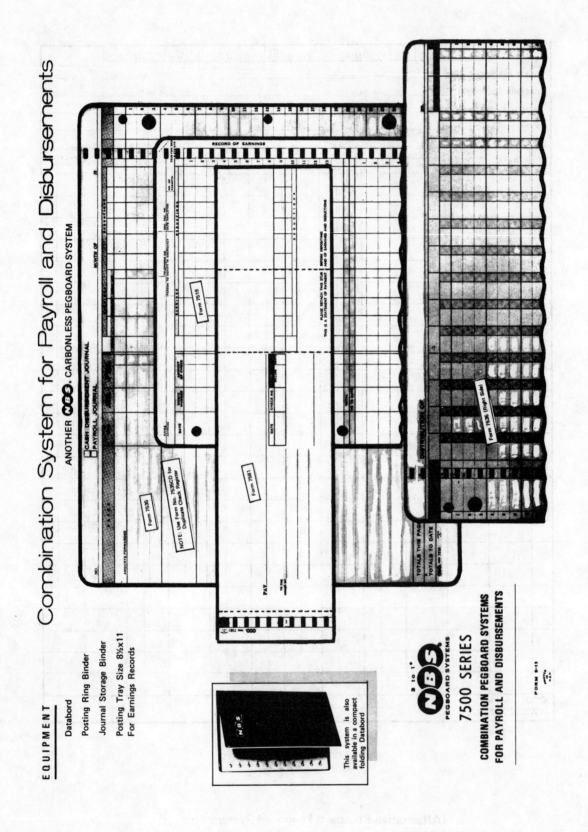

NBS.
PEGBOARD SYSTEMS

7500 SERIES

COMBINATION PEGBOARD SYSTEMS
FOR PAYROLL AND DISBURSEMENTS

FORM 5-13

ACCOUNTS PAYABLE CARD

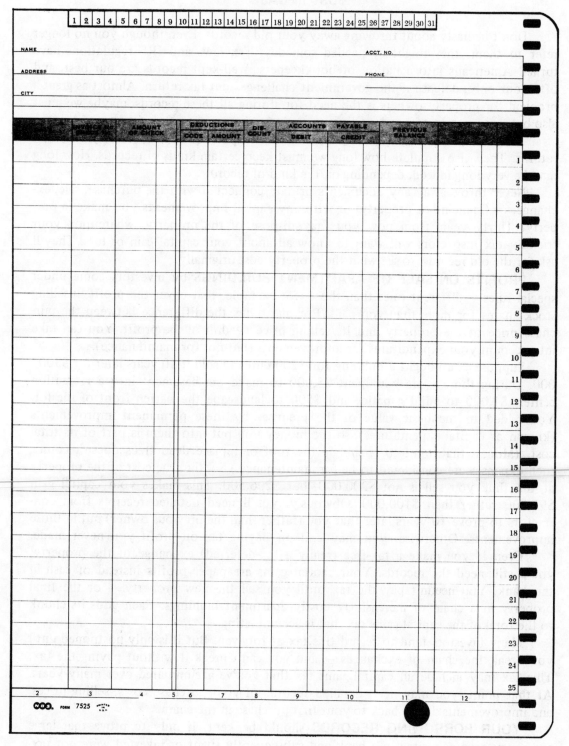

| | 1 | 2 | 3 | 4 | 5 | 6 | 7 | 8 | 9 | 10 | 11 | 12 | 13 | 14 | 15 | 16 | 17 | 18 | 19 | 20 | 21 | 22 | 23 | 24 | 25 | 26 | 27 | 28 | 29 | 30 | 31 |

NAME   **ACCT. NO.**

ADDRESS   **PHONE**

CITY

	PURCHASE	AMOUNT OF CHECK	DEDUCTIONS		DIS-COUNT	ACCOUNTS PAYABLE		PREVIOUS BALANCE		
			CODE	AMOUNT		DEBIT	CREDIT			

COO. FORM 7525

| 2 | 3 | 4 | 5 | 6 | 7 | 8 | 9 | 10 | 11 | 12 |

large or small, if there are no ready-made forms that fit your peculiar needs, you can have special forms made up for you. NBS and similar companies are glad to do this.

JUST IN CASE

Don't be hasty about throwing away your old records. Even though you no longer refer to them, they might be needed someday. Tax laws and IRS regulations have turned Americans into a nation of bookkeepers. Well-kept records are our best, and often our only, defense if the government challenges our tax return. Almost as great a problem for property owners is the need for storing all these records; maybe we must also become a nation of warehousemen.

The laws provide for penalties if we don't keep adequate records to justify our returns. They also stipulate how long we must keep certain kinds of records. How long may be very long indeed, depending on the kind of record.

Never throw away any documents or data connected with the purchase, sale, exchange, or financing of property, or with any capital improvements you make in property. Thirty years from now you may dispose of the property, whereupon your friendly tax inspectors will want to know all about your capital gain or loss. They'll ask for the old records, to see what the property cost originally.

PROFITS ON SALE OF APARTMENT BUILDINGS by investors come under special rules — different rules than those, for example, that cover the profit in selling stock shares for more than you paid. For one thing, the difference between the purchase price of the property and its selling price needn't all be profit. You can take into account your expenditures for improvements (but not for maintenance).

Suppose you bought a building for $200,000 and sold it 10 years later for $300,-000. During those years you spent $5,000 to make the basement into a recreation center, $1,000 to build a patio, and $500 to landscape the barren front of the lot. You added to the basic value of the premises by these permanent improvements (known as capital expenditures), so the money you put into them is part of its total cost. (Money that went to re-shingle the roof or replace dead trees doesn't count; such expenses are considered to be for maintenance.) So, the true cost of the property at the time you sell is not $200,000, but $206,500. This makes your capital gain $93,500 rather than $100,000. Obviously, you'll need detailed receipts from contractors to prove 10 years later that you (rather than the previous owner) put in those improvements. Otherwise, you may end up paying tax on profit you never made.

Even if you make a tax-free (really a tax-deferred) exchange of the property, you'll still need the records. Your capital gains are paper profits instead of cash in the bank. You needn't pay the tax until you sell the new property — or the final property in a chain of increasingly costly apartment buildings. Each adds its chunk to the total of the capital gains tax that is accumulating.

Many investors tend to regard this tax as forgiven. But it is only postponed until you break the chain of exchanges — and you can't break it without paying the tax. This tax may include all capital gains tax that you've accumulated over many years. At that point, you may need detailed records of your purchase costs, selling prices, and improvements dating back to your first purchase in the chain.

YOUR BORROWING RECORDS should be kept, if only to prove that large sums you have deposited in a bank and subsequently spent or invested were not taxable income. Money you obtain by borrowing isn't taxable. But you'd better be able to prove you borrowed it. Otherwise, you might be charged with fraud for not reporting it as income. Another reason for keeping these financing records is that you may find, when you try to sell the property, that some loan you've long since paid off is still shown as a lien against the title.

OTHER KINDS OF RECORDS should generally be kept for at least six years. This includes paid invoices, receipts, cancelled checks, journal records, bank statements and the like.

Basically, the IRS has three years from April 15 filing deadline for any given year to examine your records and assess additional taxes for that year. But if the IRS has reason to suspect you may have understated your income by more than 25%, it has six years to catch up with you and adjust your tax. There is no limit at all if fraud is involved; civil penalties and fines can be imposed at any time. However, criminal prosecution on tax-evasion charges is barred by a statute of limitations after six years from the filing date.

RENTAL APPLICATIONS AND JOB APPLICATIONS from people who drifted away without renting an apartment or taking a job can safely be discarded after one year in most states. Keep them at least that long in case a rejected applicant charges you with discrimination. And check your state law to see what time limit is set for such charges.

The records of residents and employees should be kept indefinitely. Many years later, some questions conceivably could arise about social security or an injury claim or some other unusual matter.

OTHER RECORDS TO KEEP INDEFINITELY include a running history of each apartment unit, who occupied it, for how long, what damages if any were done, what appliances were installed or repaired, dates of painting and decorating, rent increases, and so on. Everything about a specific apartment should be filed together for easy reference. However, there's seldom any need for the rental applications of departed residents, or their leases or rental agreements, after they've been gone a few years.

A DEAD FILE — some sort of storage space that needn't be readily accessible, since it's only for data kept "just in case" — is almost essential for old, unused records. Don't let them take up valuable space in the office.

READY FOR THE TAX MAN?

Real estate and personal property are called ad valorem taxes. Ad valorem means "according to value" or "to worth (of the property)," as opposed to income tax, which is "according to income." Computing ad valorem taxes can be almost as complicated, as fraught with technical traps, as figuring income taxes. Unless you're an expert accountant, you'll be money ahead by getting expert assistance in recording the amounts used in computing the "tax basis" of the property and its depreciation allowances. These first entries in the records can have a big effect on an owner's income tax liability for many years.

You may also want to consult a good accountant about the rental income schedules to be submitted with income tax returns. He can do the whole job if you wish. However, if you expect to own several properties in the future, you'll generally find it worth the effort (as well as thrifty) to try to work up these schedules yourself and then ask your accountant to go over them. This way, in a few years you'll develop a keen awareness of the tax consequences of your realty transactions.

In any case, it's up to an owner or manager to keep a file of tax information about the property. This file should contain:

1.   The legal description of the property;

2. the permanent identification number;
3. data about the valuation of the land and building;
4. timetables and procedures for reassessment;
5. history of the tax rate up to date;
6. name(s), address(es), and phone number(s) of the owner's tax attorney(s);
7. copies of paid tax bills;
8. special assessments and other taxes, and
9. correspondence about protests, appeals, and complaints.

It's the manager's responsibility to see that real estate taxes are paid whether or not a bill comes in. If no bill is received, the manager must find out why. When he does get the tax bill, he should check it closely to see that it applies to the right property.

If personal property taxes are collected in your area, you'll need to set up a similar file for these. Some municipalities collect sales taxes on rents; if this is true where you own property, you'll need a record of payments made and returns filed.

HOW TO SURVIVE A TAX AUDIT

Some taxpayers discover the importance of full and well-kept records at the worst time — when they are challenged in an audit. The IRS has strict rules about what kinds of proof it will accept at the auditing stage. For example, don't be shocked if the tax agent refuses to accept a cancelled check as evidence of an expenditure. He may want to see work orders and vendors' bills, too.

Nobody looks forward to a tax audit. But you needn't fear one if you kept the kinds of records suggested in this chapter, and prepare your tax returns accordingly. Usually, about 7% of all taxpayers who are audited turn out to have overpaid. And around 40% of the audits produce no change in the amount of tax owed. If your income is above $25,000, or if you show unusual deductions and offbeat transactions, your return may be flagged for audit even if it is as innocent as a Walt Disney movie.

IF YOU GET A NOTICE BY MAIL, you're probably in for something less than a full audit. The odds are with you. One or two items in your return may be questioned — the notice will most likely tell you what they are. In fact, the audit may be carried on entirely by mail. The letter may ask you to send in further information about specific items, or evidence supporting certain figures in your return. If your explanations don't satisfy the IRS agent, you'll get another letter telling you that the claim in question has been disallowed, your tax recomputed, and your bill for additional tax is enclosed.

If you think you can explain better across a desk than by letter, you're entitled to an interview. And if questions raised by your return aren't simple enough to be handled by mail, the IRS itself will summon you to its local office. Probably it will ask you to bring records and other papers supporting certain items in the return. Such relatively simple audits, including those conducted by mail, account for about four-fifths of the returns audited.

An unlucky few first learn they are being audited when an IRS man phones, or rings the doorbell, and says he would like to "sit down with you and ask some questions." When bulky records will be involved, his audit will normally take place on the taxpayer's premises, for convenience. But if an agent appears on the doorstep of your home, it is bad news.

YOUR FIRST STEP when an IRS agent confronts you is to take a close look at his or her identification. If the agent is a revenue agent, the audit is probably routine.

But if you see that you're facing a special agent, you'd better terminate the interview politely, answer no questions, and phone your attorney. Special agents investigate possible criminal tax fraud; revenue agents are concerned with ordinary civil tax questions.

Although a special agent is supposed to read you a summary of your rights, he sometimes tries to keep a low profile by quickly flashing his identification or by working as a team with a revenue agent. So you should make sure which type you're dealing with. Always be courteous and pleasant, in either case. An agent who takes a dislike to you has many ways of causing trouble for you.

YOUR SECOND STEP is to ask the agent to outline the scope of the audit and what records he would like. Usually, an agent seeks supporting evidence for certain claims you've made. When you know exactly what he wants, you and your accountant can prepare the necessary documentation and quickly complete the audit.

NEVER LET AN AGENT BROWSE casually through your papers and records. It will lead to more questions, and may expand the scope of your audit. Answer all questions but don't volunteer information or give overly detailed answers. You need to find the narrow middle path between being evasive, which stimulates suspicion and prolongs the audit, and being so helpful that the agent may stumble onto something in your return that he wasn't originally looking for.

Taxpayers who have gone through office audits usually report that the proceedings were courteous and businesslike. The IRS is trying to erase the tough-guy image it acquired in past years. However, its people are professionals. They've inspected countless returns like yours, so they don't miss many chances to pick up extra tax dollars. They have wide discretion, and use it in handling cases. Much depends on their attitude, so good rapport may be important.

You can serve your interests best with a cooperative attitude. Answer questions openly, not grudgingly. Provide any records that are requested, if you have them. But don't get talkative and, above all, don't volunteer information.

AN AUDIT ISN'T A JUDICIAL PROCEEDING. The normal rule of law, that you're innocent until proven guilty, doesn't apply. You have made certain statements on your return, like "My maintenance expenses were $2,783 last year," and the IRS is now asking you to substantiate this figure. The burden of proof is on you. Uncle Sam isn't assuming your guilt; he is just following the normal procedure followed when you make any factual assertion. If you claim, "This is my car," a policeman is entitled to ask, "How do I know that?" So you show him your registration.

IF AN EXAMINER DISCONTINUES AN AUDIT suddenly, don't celebrate too soon. It may not mean that he feels further digging is a waste of time, or that you'll be forgotten. According to Section 10.19 of the IRS Audit Technique Handbook, "The Manual requires that a revenue agent immediately suspend his investigation, without disclosing to the taxpayer or his representative the reason for his action, when he discovers what he believes to be an indication of fraud."

So, the departed examiner may be turning over his suspicions, and his work papers, to the Intelligence Division. You'd better discuss the matter with an experienced attorney.

WHOEVER PREPARES YOUR TAX RETURN SHOULD BE PRESENT during an audit. Sometimes your CPA can handle the whole audit without your being on hand. There have been many cases where a taxpayer tried to be his own accountant or lawyer, and turned over papers that the revenuer wasn't entitled to see, or gave incorrect explanations of transactions through fallible memory, with disastrous consequences. Often two explanations of a transaction are possible — one of which results in a big tax; the other in no tax, or a small tax. Your memory in all honesty can be quite wrong when you are asked why you bought a certain piece of property 20 years ago. More often than not, the worst explanation is the one that is volunteered. It's much better to have an accountant or attorney review the situation and check your records before any explanation is given. A professional tax adviser's fees are tax deductible and may be a big bargain for you in terms of money, time, and peace of mind.

Be particularly prepared to account for all income received. An IRS auditor will be likely to check the deposits shown on your bank statements as a means of verifying your income. So you may need to identify the source of every deposit listed. The IRS will assume that all deposits represent income unless you can prove this isn't the case. Rent receipts, apartment ledger cards, and monthly rent reports may also be checked to see whether all income was reported. Other audit procedures will probably include a check of vacancies during the year.

IF YOU DON'T LIKE THE DECISION announced by the tax agent, you needn't settle immediately, although he hopes you will.

He'll suggest that you sign a waiver form and make payment on the spot to avoid paying future interest that is charged on deficiencies, or that you can pay later when the IRS sends you a bill. But if the sum involved is important to you, you can ask for an extension of time to review the matter. This gives you a chance to look for supporting evidence, or to consult an attorney or accountant if you don't have one with you at the time.

Sometimes you can work a compromise with an agent, conceding one grey area in return for his concession in another. But if you choose to fight his decision, there is a step-by-step escalation you can follow through administrative hearings and the court system. However, bear in mind that tax experts generally agree that a case should be settled as early as possible — preferably at the audit stage.

If the issue is simple and you think you received unjust treatment merely because of the agent's personality, an informal first step may be open to you. Ask for a review of his decision by his group supervisor. In some of the smaller, more neighborly IRS offices, the request may be granted, although the rules don't provide for it, and the IRS doesn't encourage it.

There are various steps you can take beyond this — each involving more time, and probably more fees to a professional. You can even go over the head of the IRS, into the federal courts; and there is a new speeded-up Tax Court procedure for disputes involving $1,000 or less.

As an alternative, you can pay the tax, file a claim for refund, and ultimately sue for the refund in the Court of Claims or the District Court if your claim is denied. You can appeal all the way up to the Supreme Court if you choose. But the disadvantages of a protracted fight with the government are obvious. Most taxpayers prefer to close the case early unless the amount at stake is crucial to them.

REMEMBER THESE BASIC POINTS:

* *Keep a written rent schedule. Make triplicate receipts for all rent moneys. Number the receipts.*

* *Bank all moneys at least weekly, using triplicate deposit slips.*

* *Keep a monthly rent summary with space for a vacancy report.*

* *Bills should be paid by the owner, after approval by the manager. All disbursements should be summarized monthly, with space for an additional total of expenses incurred but not yet paid.*

* *Use written purchase orders, in triplicate, for all materials and services.*

* *In large properties, a detailed weekly vacancy report is essential.*

* *A monthly operating statement should summarize receipts and disbursements, with columns to record monthly amounts for a given item side by side for a year.*

* *Consider using one of the mass-produced record systems sold by makers of business forms.*

* *Keep complete files of all tax data about the property.*

* *Don't let an IRS agent browse casually through papers or records. Answer all questions, but not in unnecessary detail. Don't volunteer information. Whoever prepared your tax return should be present during an audit.*

XIV *Be Your Own Controller*

Probably you think the top executives of big businesses are fiercely devoted to profits. This is one of the great myths of American capitalism. Almost any management consultant can tell you that a company's top executives are likely to put a lot of things ahead of profits — and what's more, their pursuit of these other aims may seriously crimp their company's earning power.

This same surprising fault is often characteristic of the owners, and even the owner-managers, of apartment property. Many of them are obsessed with other goals than profit-making. There are at least four distinct non-profit motives in the apartment business, and these might be described as "empire building," "fort building," "perfectionism," and "sentimentalism."

FOUR WAYS OF FORSAKING PROFITS

EMPIRE BUILDERS want to be the biggest in their neighborhood or their city, or even the world. The famous William Zeckendorf was one of these. He actually did put together the world's biggest real estate empire. Almost inevitably, his dreams outran his resources. He got himself financially over-extended (another way of saying under-capitalized) and his creditors foreclosed on him.

The smaller, more typical empire builder can be found in every community. He buys too many properties, or too big a property, and can't pay enough attention to management. Mismanaged properties soon lose money. But the empire builders don't notice because they're concentrating on getting bigger.

Another type of empire builder is the property owner who wants to be worshipped as the richest man in town. He spends his capital gains — and even his cash flow — on flashy cars and boats, a mansion like a maharaja's palace, costly parties and trips, and other highly visible luxuries. To get more and more spendable cash, he borrows too heavily, or invests too little in the upkeep of his properties (or both) and gets caught in a liquidity squeeze.

FORT BUILDERS, on the other hand, pass up profits through fear of taking risks. They hoard cash in readiness for a "rainy day," or "the depression that's surely coming," or some other catastrophe. They watch each dollar as if it had a life of its own, like a daughter or son. They won't expand or improve their property. They have a horror of going into debt. They won't die broke like Zeckendorf, but they won't make much profit either.

PERFECTIONISTS go around their buildings turning off lights and picking up cigarette butts. They fix their eyes on a goal of efficiency like "keep turnover to 5%," even if this keeps deadbeats in the building, or "net profit must be 20% per year," even if this pushes rent higher than prospective renters will pay.

Other perfectionists are mad for gadgets. They want the newest electric pencil sharpener and photocopier and paper-shredder. They buy high-speed chain saws for lopping off occasional palm fronds and damn the expense. Obviously, profits don't come first with perfectionists.

SENTIMENTALISTS keep a building unchanged because "Daddy owned it and Daddy was never wrong" — or sometimes they keep improving it because of their own pride of ownership. They may put marble statues on the front steps, or install camphorwood closets in every apartment, even if the building is on Skid Row. Or they may let old friends stay on for years without paying rent.

Empire builders, fort builders, perfectionists, and sentimentalists all need a controller. A controller sees profits as the big objective.

WHAT CONTROLLERS DO

In a corporation the controller is the person who is expected to gear the company's operations toward planned goals of profitability, eliminating overspending and waste along the way. As business life becomes more complex, industrial controllers have become more important. They are expanding their work to include analysis of external business conditions as well as internal operations. In fact, controllers are rising so fast that scores of them have reached company presidencies. Countless others have moved into the executive suite next to the president's office.

A generation ago the controller, or comptroller, was just somebody with a green eyeshade and a sharp pencil, poring over invoices and expense accounts, and challenging everything he thought was too high. (The word comptroller comes from the French *compte*, meaning account — so perhaps it is a more legitimate word for the job than controller, which comes from counterroll, a Middle English word for the duplicate record kept on one officer's accounts by another. A modern controller must be, first of all, an accountant, and is seldom involved in double-checking anyone's books. But the word "comptroller" sounds clumsy and archaic, as if it means someone trying to keep things under "comptrol." So it is dying out. Look up "comptroller" in most new dictionaries, and you'll find only the curt reference "see controller.")

The control structures of modern business enterprises are getting bigger and bigger. U.S. Steel employs more people (18,000 by recent count) in its accounting and statistical departments than in its sales force, besides which each of its units has its own controller. Evidently, these people are extremely useful. Could you use one of them in your apartment building?

Probably you could. Controllership can be defined as "the branch of management charged with controlling an organization's income and expenses and with enhancing its overall financial health." Somebody has to do this for every money machine, whether it's an apartment building or factory or bank. The chances are that you, as owner and/ or manager, have the responsibilities of a controller without the title.

YOU CAN BE YOUR OWN CONTROLLER. Luckily, the skills of controllership can be rather easily mastered when the enterprise to be controlled is residential income property. And you ought to master them, even if you delegate them to someone else. Since the controller is supposed to nourish and enhance an enterprise's earning power, his work is vital to owners and managers who should be able to judge how well he's doing it. You need to be sure that your controller has the insistent drive for profits that he should have, and sometimes a hired hand lacks this.

If your controller — whether it's you or someone else — is an easy-going, carefree, trusting type, you're in trouble. A controller needs to be skeptical, even suspicious. As one controller expressed it, speaking metaphorically, "I'm always looking for dirt swept under the carpet."

Do you question the facts and figures that cross your desk? Do these figures add to the total shown? Are all receipts accounted for? Did the bank deposit really include all the money you took in? Are you paying too much for maintenance? Are the bids for that repainting job realistic? Why are there more move-outs this year than last? Are the property tax assessments too high? Why are the water bills up? Is there enough cash flow to pay the bills, and will there be enough two months from now?

YOU DON'T NEED PAGES OF CLOSE-PACKED FIGURES to be a good controller of a comparatively small enterprise such as an apartment building, even if it contains several hundred units. Most of the figures you need are easy to get. Precision isn't important. You're looking for trends and signals, not for stray dimes. The idea is to make sure that your building's financial resources are put where they bring good results. Obviously, this includes knowing what its financial needs will be, and trying to make sure that needs won't outgrow resources. Okay? Now let's consider exactly how this can be done in your business. Give your brain some exercise.

TO MAXIMIZE INCOME, ANALYZE IT

THE VACANCY REPORT, as we saw in Chapter 13, is a sort of barometer. If vacancies are rising, you're in for trouble. Chapter 13 stressed the importance of keeping income flowing in by keeping apartments rented — in other words, minimizing turnover and vacancies. But we didn't consider how a controller would analyze vacancy reports.

He would want to know why each vacancy occurred. Was it because of a resident's personal problems, over which the apartment manager had no control? If so, okay. But it's not okay if a resident moved because of dissatisfaction with the apartment, or with the building as a whole, or with other residents. It means that others may move, too.

Nor is it okay if the resident moved simply because the rent was too high. Maybe the units are over-priced now because the area is over-built and competing buildings have lowered rents in order to get tenants. Residents will ordinarily have a very good idea of what the rent should be; the controller ought to know as much as they do.

Assuming that you're acting as your own controller, you could ask the resident manager to find out the reasons for every move-out. But the manager's version may not be fully truthful if the whole truth would put him in a bad light. A much better way is to print up a blank form, "Notice of Resident's Intention to Vacate," with space included for the resident to state the reasons. Then ask the manager to send these completed forms along to you or to hold them for your inspection.

The form should include some polite questions about the resident's opinion of the apartment, the building, and its management — with boxes labeled Excellent, Very Good, Good, Fair, and Poor. Just knowing that you'll see these comments will help to keep the manager alert.

COMPARE VACANCY RATES over a period of time. Comparison is one of a controller's tools for digging into business figures. How does the current vacancy rate compare with those of one year and two years ago?

If vacancies have declined sharply and are now almost nil, the resident manager probably should receive a pat on the back and something extra in the pay envelope. But both of you should also consider whether the building's rental rates are lower than they should be. To answer this question, you need to make another comparison: are your building's rents higher or lower than those of comparable buildings?

If vacancies have increased, you should know why. Have they also increased in comparable buildings? If so, the rental market is slack, and maybe you'll have to cut rents to avoid losses. But if yours is one of only a few similar properties that are losing residents, probably something is wrong with the apartments or the management. Again, maybe it's your rent scale that is out of line; a tip-off to this would be a jump in vacancies soon after you last raised rents.

Are units re-rented promptly? Or do they sit vacant for weeks? If vacancies aren't filled as fast as possible, investigate; go back and review Chapter 13's section headed, "Watch the Vacancy Figures" for suggestions about the various possible causes and remedies.

And what about *where* your vacancies occur? Are some units empty oftener than others? If one-fifth of your units are causing four-fifths of the vacancies, this could tell you something. Check back on the comments by departing residents of these units. Maybe the locations are noisier than most, or hotter or colder. Maybe they're too dark. Can you keep them rented with better lighting, or brighter color schemes, attractive new fixtures? If the locations are less than desirable for reasons you can't cure, such as the noise or an ugly view from the windows, could you keep them filled by charging less rent for them?

HIGH TURNOVER can persist without high vacancy losses, and may lull an owner into a false feeling of prosperity. "The building always seems to be full, so it must be making money," he may think.

But the manager's speed in re-renting vacant units may mean only that the manager is a sharp salesman — and that people keep moving out as they realize they've been conned. Turnover can mean a constant outflow of money to advertise vacancies. It can mean too much time spent by the manager talking to prospects, when he should be doing other things. And, of course, it means expenses for cleaning, repainting, and repairing to make units ready for re-rental.

If existing records don't give you a clear picture of turnover, take a look at advertising costs. And if you're keeping a maintenance cost record on the back of each unit ledger card (as suggested in Chapter 13), thumb through the cards. You may find the maintenance figures startling.

If there's high turnover, you can increase total net income by finding ways to cut it.

KEEP LOOKING AROUND at rental and vacancy rates for similar apartments in the area — especially if population is changing rapidly or some big employer is hiring or firing a lot of people. An influx of people usually means a tight rental market and rising rents. An outflow means the opposite. If you're not keeping in touch, your rents may be out of line.

COMPARE INCOME WITH GROSS SCHEDULED RENT. Much of what a controller sees in figures is due to the way he arranges and compares them. Often a figure may have important relationships with other figures that aren't normally its close neighbors on the report sheets. This is often true in the case of net operating income, as a percentage of gross scheduled rent; the percentage is the most important single indicator of how the property is doing.

Let's suppose you, as owner/controller of Hudson Manor, notice that its net revenue in April is 106% of gross scheduled rent! Miraculous! How did it happen? Analyzing, you find that $700 of the income was in security deposits — which eventually may have to be returned, at least in part, to residents when they leave.

Even so, you muse, the manager must be doing a great job of keeping Hudson Manor full and the credit losses small because vacancy and credit losses together were only 1.25% of schedule rent in April, and 2.41% for the past four months.

But there's another way of thinking about these figures.

Could it be that the manager has made life too easy for himself by charging too little rent? When the new swimming pool went in, should rents have gone up? Maybe not across the board, because the best time to raise rents is between tenants. But there've been plenty of in-between times, because the $700 of deposits show that turnover must have been higher than usual. Is it significant that the apartments have been re-rented quickly, without any advertising and very little refurbishing? Check the market to see whether Hudson Manor apartments are a ridiculous bargain.

Now imagine another property, Georgia Pines. The controller there finds that net revenue averaged 64% of scheduled rent for the first four months of the year, but was down to only 56% in April. Sudden variations make a controller's nose twitch. What pushed the percentage down in April?

He looks at vacancy and credit losses. They were almost 10% in April — somewhat higher than the average for the year to date. He also finds that the manager had to refund $315 in deposits in April. That means there were move-outs. What's the situation now, in mid-May? Three more residents have given notice, he learns. Why? Is it because the manager raised their rents in April? Or is there some other reason.

The only way the controller can find out is to go to the premises, quiz the manager, and maybe chat with residents who are leaving. Probably something can be done to re-rent vacant apartments faster. How does the manager respond to telephone inquiries and to drop-ins? How well does he clean the units before trying to re-rent them? Would it help to spend more money advertising vacancies?

Then the controller of Georgia Pines glances over some other figures, wondering if they'll show him any way to improve cash flow. He notices something about the monthly payments he is making on the mortgage: they used to be mostly for interest, only a little on the principal. The amount is the same each month, of course, but less of that goes for interest now than is apportioned to paying off the principal.

Now that the principal payments exceed the interest, equity in Georgia Pines is building up fairly fast. The mortgage will be paid off in another 10 years or so, whereupon the property will be owned free and clear. That's a pleasant thought, but can it be useful right now in increasing cash flow? Yes, indeed. It means that the existing short-term mortgage can be refinanced. He can take out a longer mortgage that calls for smaller monthly payments (providing he gets the new loan at an interest rate not much higher than he is paying now). His monthly mortgage payments are a painful drain on the cash income. But a new mortgage will let him spread his payments over a period of maybe 20 years instead of 10 years. Smaller payments will mean bigger monthly net income.

TO MINIMIZE EXPENSES, ADD THEM UP

THE LIMITATIONS OF A MULTI-COLUMN WORKSHEET (the kind suggested in the previous chapter) for comparing monthly operating statements will become obvious to you when you begin pulling them apart as a controller should.

Too many items on the statement fluctuate from month to month. You can see the variations as you run your eye along the line of the worksheet, but it doesn't tell you much. An item may be higher or lower because of the season of the year, the date when the bill arrived, when the roof leaked, or when last year's supply of paint finally ran out.

Furthermore, the size of a given item in a given month may depend on when you and your resident manager decide to get started on some of the refurbishing you've talked about. And if you spent $600 in legal fees in October, but nothing in September or November, this may mean merely that October was when a lawsuit finally came to trial.

These "random factors," as analysts call them, cloud the picture so badly that it's hard to see whether differences are significant. But a good controller can clear away most of the clouds. Here's how.

KEEP A "MOVING TOTAL" WORKSHEET. Set up the same multi-column layout recommended in Chapter 13, so that monthly amounts for a particular item can be recorded side by side over a long period of time. But on this worksheet you don't enter the monthly amount of any item. Instead, you enter its total for the past 12 months. That is, in one column you might enter the total costs for advertising from January through December. Next month, in the column beside it, you would enter advertising costs from last February through this January, and so on.

You needn't go through the chore of adding up the latest 12-month figures each time a new month comes along. Simply add the latest month's figure, and subtract the one for the month you are dropping.

These moving totals pretty well smooth out the seasonal and random month-to-month ups and downs. They show trends. Of course, there is some good or bad luck in every total, but you'll be able to see strong and weak points of your money machine.

For example, you might notice a steep uptrend in your latest yearly totals of fuel oil expenditures. Probably you knew that fuel oil prices had risen since the latest Arab-Israel trouble, but the seasonal dips might have obscured the tremendous impact this was having on your fuel budget. Only by computing the annual costs monthly (or the average monthly cost over the past 12 months, which requires more adding and dividing) would you get a quick signal that your budget is in trouble. Perhaps it warns that you'd better reconsider that storm window and insulation job you vetoed a few months ago. Maybe it wasn't worth its costs then but will be now.

What about the other running totals? How are they changing in terms of a percentage of total expenses or total revenue? If costs for certain kinds of maintenance are eating up a bigger percentage of total costs, maybe some things are wearing out and should be replaced. Or maybe your manager neglected them, and is now catching up on overdue maintenance. On the other hand, maybe your upkeep problems aren't really any worse than last year, but your service firm has boosted its charges sharply. A changing total gives clues to the questions that need asking, but you may have to probe for answers.

WHAT'S PAR FOR THE COURSE? Suppose your moving-total worksheet gives you a soothing picture of annual costs: they are level or even declining. Does that mean a good controller would ask nothing further about them?

On the contrary. They could be too low because the manager has been spending too little all along. Or they could be high because some suppliers have been padding bills all along.

For a sharp job of cost control, you need to know how your costs compare with those of other similar apartment complexes in the area. If your costs for janitorial supplies or roof maintenance or whatever are holding steady, but are running percentage-wise twice as high (or twice as low) as those of your competitors, hadn't you better find out why?

Once again, the controller's responsibility is to make comparisons. As a rule of thumb, in most older multiple dwellings, the total annual expenses are roughly 45% of the gross annual rent roll. In newer properties, they may be only 35% or less. So, if your expense total falls outside these broad guidelines, you know there's something unusual about your money machine — and you'll want to compare your expenses item by item with those of comparable properties.

You can get valuable cost data from your local apartment association, and from the nationwide Building Owners' and Managers' Association, known as BOMA. You can write to BOMA International, 224 S. Michigan Avenue, Chicago 60604.

The smaller your building, the wider the range of costs. You'll need to keep track of what you spend during a year or more in order to find "par" for your own property. Meanwhile, here are some rough ratios. If your own costs fall in these areas, you are probably close to the national par.

Apartment cleaning, including labor and materials, should run $20 to $120 per apartment. Carpet shampooing is about $25 to $45 per apartment. Drapes can be cleaned for $12 to $25.

Utilities — gas, electric, fuel, water, trash collection and sometimes sewer tax — should average between 7% and 10% of the total rent roll.

Repairs shouldn't cost more than $110-$175 per year per apartment. This figure doesn't include painting, capital improvements, or the cost of replacing such equipment as carpets, refrigerators or heaters.

Painting of interiors (or "redecorating" as it is often called in the eastern U.S.) should cost between $35 and $70 for each apartment with one or two bedrooms, plus $25 to $30 more for paint. If you hire painting contractors, this will double the cost.

Plumbing costs can soar sky-high if you use a master plumber instead of a handyman for minor work. A plumber charges $25 to install a 10-cent faucet washer. Replacing a toilet bowl seat is about an hour's job which may cost $5 for a handyman or $18 for a plumber.

The percentage of gross scheduled rent which is actually collected averages 94% for the country as a whole. The total expenses of apartment buildings average 45% of the scheduled rent, leaving 49% as total net operating income. In the western U.S. these latter two percentages are slightly different on the average; total expenses run 43%, so that the total net operating income is 51%. Taxes (included in expenses) vary more than most items; they average as low as 12% for the U.S. as a whole, but are almost 16% in Los Angeles; even higher in New York City.

PAR CAN FOOL YOU SOMETIMES because of differences in the size of buildings, or in rent levels. For example, a 50-unit building and a 250-unit building may each have a 24-hour doorman service, or may each have the same size swimming pool. If you look at the cost of doorman service or of pool maintenance as a percentage of revenue, they'll seem strangely different in the two properties; yet, both buildings may be very efficiently managed. It's because you're computing percentages of dissimilar numbers.

Even the national percentages cited a couple of paragraphs ago — the percentages of rent roll actually collected — aren't always good yardsticks. The reason is that some major expenses such as taxes and insurance are the same whether the building is full or almost empty, and the percentages at different occupancy levels will vary widely.

Another reason is that the water bill may be 5% of gross possible income in one property and only 1% in another, when families in the two buildings pay the same amount for water. Here it's the rent scale that distorts par. Suppose a family lives in an $80 apartment and pays $4 for water, or 5%. Another family lives in a $400 apartment with the same water bill of $4, which is 1%.

SHARPEN YOUR NUMBERS SENSE. People in corporations often notice that a controller can immediately see that an extra $51,800 of earnings spread over the 2,611,000 outstanding shares would be roughly two cents a share. They marvel at his mental speed. No doubt he has greater inborn ability with figures than most people, but he isn't necessarily a wizard at mental math. Most business number experts use a bag of tricks enabling them to think more easily about numbers. You can pick up some of their tricks with very little trouble.

ROUND NUMBERS ARE EASIER to think about. This is one of the tricks that controllers know. For example, thinking about the figures mentioned in the previous paragraph, the controller merely noticed that 26 (rounding off the 2,611,000 shares) goes into 52 (rounding off $51,800) two times, or .02, adjusting for decimal places. Whenever he looks at figures, he automatically thinks in terms of approximations instead of precise amounts.

This trick may seem like such ordinary common sense that it isn't worth mentioning. But it's rather uncommon in business, and especially uncommon in the apartment business. The ordinary report handed to a property owner looks something like this:

Operating Expenses For Four Months Ended April 30, 1977

	April	Year to Date
Property Taxes	2,614.89	10,459.49
Insurance	700.08	1,672.65
Accounting	101.48	220.56
Water	190.92	681.39
Fuel	246.05	2,589.91
Electricity	419.06	1,631.68
Salaries & Wages	1,394.71	4,563.02

etc., etc.

But suppose a controller told the office to prepare those same figures like this:

Operating Expenses For Four Months Ended April 30, 1977
(Rounded to nearest hundred)

	April	Year to Date
Property taxes	26	105
Insurance	7	17
Accounting	1	2
Water	2	7
Fuel	2	26
Electricity	4	16
Salaries & Wages	14	46

Now, doesn't your eye scan the columns more easily? Don't you see inconsistencies sooner? You're more likely to notice, for example, that the payroll must have grown in April because salaries and wages for that month are more than one-fourth of the year to date total. The sharp drop-off in fuel bills during April stands out — although you notice that water bills are up, and probably remind yourself that both these changes are typical of springtime.

Psychologists say that the mind can't grasp the meaning of more than two or three digits at a time. Fortunately, the Arabic numeral system minimizes the error involved in looking only at the first few digits, because they count for the most. That's why they set a price like $199.95 instead of $200.00 — customers react primarily to the "1," so the first amount looks delightfully smaller than the second. A controller would automatically round it to $200.00.

Business enterprises seldom use rounded figures because they need exact bookkeeping. They couldn't make the proper checks and reconcilations unless they kept track of sums down to the penny. Nor could they comply with laws. (Imagine the reaction of the IRS to a tax return that showed income to the nearest ten thousand dollars.) Because exactitude gets to be a habit, accountants never think of serving up rounded numbers unless an executive requests it.

LOOK FOR INCONSISTENCIES. Unfortunately, they don't jump out from a thicket of figures. You only see them when you know what to look for. In the columns of figures just shown, as soon as you noticed that they were for one month and four months, you should be asking yourself, "Is the first column about one-fourth of the second column?" That's how you would spot the slight inconsistencies in the items for salaries, fuel and water. Or, suppose your electrician sends you a bill for installing nine new wall outlets. If you check back and find his bill is bigger than his previous one for 16 outlets last winter, you may want to ask some questions.

LOOK AT PROPORTIONS. The fact that 30% of your apartments account for 30% of your repair bills isn't interesting. But what if 80% of your repair bills turn out to be caused by 10% of your residents? Wow!

Similarly, if you advertise vacancies in three different newspapers, one of which produces 55% of your inquiries, you think, "Maybe we can fill our vacancies by advertising in that one paper alone."

In every field of business there's a kind of cluster effect whereby a small group of inputs accounts for a much larger proportion of outputs, and vice versa. Disproportions are clues for investigation or action.

Another way to use proportions is to figure your costs and profits in terms of square feet of space, number of units or rooms, number of bathrooms, categories of tenants (married-single, younger-older, etc.) or any other ratio that might be significant.

At the very least you'll want to think about costs per apartment. A two-bedroom apartment might be worth much more to you, under certain market conditions, if you converted it into two or three studio apartments.

Also look at proportions of your own time spent on various chores, in relation to productivity. Do you spend hours adding up totals on stacks of invoices for amounts less than $100 each? If so, how much money have you saved by catching errors on these invoices? If you save about $4 for each four hours used this way, isn't your time worth more than a dollar an hour? Maybe you should concentrate your watchdog work in areas where there are bigger prospective savings.

YOUR TAX BRACKET (or the owner's, if you're not the owner) is one of the most important proportions of all. Yet, strangely, many investors don't take it into account. They know that expenses are tax deductible, so they fall into the trap of thinking they're better off because their high expenses will bring them high deductions.

Of course, this is a fallacy. No matter what tax bracket you're in, you deduct from your tax dollars only part of every dollar you spend on deductible expenses. You can never be better off by running up expenses.

To make sure you understand this, consider an example. Suppose you are in the

50% tax bracket. When you spend $100 on tax deductible expenses, you reduce your taxable income by $100 — but you reduce your deduction by only $50. It's nice that Uncle Sam is paying half your expenses, but don't forget who pays the other half. If it makes you happy, you can say that the last painting bill really cost you only $120 instead of the $240 you paid. But you had to collect $240 in income to pay the painter. Furthermore, most people aren't in the 50% bracket; they're lower. In the 40% bracket, Uncle Sam pays only 40 cents of every dollar of your expenses, while you pay the other 60 cents.

PROFITS THROUGH PLANNING

As a controller, you are supposed to forecast gross revenues, and plan how to use them wisely and profitably. Unfortunately, however, there are no facts about the future. One of its few known characteristics is that those who forecast it are often wrong. The question is, how wrong will you be and how often?

The closer you are to the period to be forecast, the more you can rely on your estimates. So your planning should be updated continually — every month, say — as expectations change in the light of new information. A budget for a year ahead, set up by estimating annual collections and subtracting estimated operating expenses, is only a vague guide. At the end of the year you'll know how well you did, but by then the damage is done. If your forecast was wrong, there's no way to adjust.

Nevertheless, you'll want to work on a 12-month budget, keeping it flexible and adjusting it monthly. The one-year period is necessary because it gives you a better view of certain variables such as supplies, maintenance, repairs, advertising, and payroll. And you can plan for peak spending needs, such as taxes, capital expenses, and large seasonal bills. Even in months when those costs are low, you should be setting aside money for them.

WHAT IS A BUDGET? Basically, it is a set of estimates: how much money will be coming in, and how much should be spent, broken down by category of expenditure. No doubt you have a rather exact estimate of your property's earnings potential. And if you're lucky — or if you've been associated with the property for some time — you have plenty of data about the property's past performance. So you begin with this basic information. You add whatever you know or guess about market conditions, inflation, climate, and other external factors. Then — perhaps after communing with occult informants — you spin a web of interpretation and prediction that becomes a budget.

Next, you set up controls to try to make sure that your budget, or spending plan, will be followed. One way of doing this is by showing month-by-month estimates, so that you'll immediately spot any variation from the plan. When the actual operating figures don't jibe with budget projections, either things are getting out of hand or the budget was unrealistic — or both.

If you're a controller but not the owner, the budget you give the owner should be much broader than the one you keep as your own guide. The fewer categories there are in the owner's budget, the less chance that minor fluctuations will make you look bad. That is, if gas and electricity and water are listed as separate categories, gas will be up in one month and down in another. Electricity will be the opposite. But total expenditures for all utilities stay level. The owner will notice the changes in electricity and gas. But if you combine all three under a utility category, without a specific breakdown, there'll be less difference between your budget and your performance. For your own purposes, however, the more categories you have, the easier it is to spot problems.

You need at least the following categories:

Advertising and promotion	Repairs and maintenance
Insurance	Services (trash collection, window
Legal and audit	washing, exterminator, etc.)
Management and administration	Supplies
Payroll and related costs	Utilities
Real estate taxes	Miscellaneous

MANAGERS DISLIKE BUDGETS, especially those laid on them by someone else. They see a budget as just a textbook exercise, with no relevance to the unpredictable everyday business of managing apartments.

Department heads dislike budgets even more. Almost everybody resents the idea of being "controlled," and a budget implies controls. But even worse than being controlled is being judged, and budgets seem to be taken as personal score cards.

If your property is big enough to include several departments or operating groups, you'll find that your budget is resented for, among other things, "putting pressure on employees . . . emphasizing only past performance . . . failing to show why cost targets were overrun . . . implying that people must be needled into doing a better job." On the other hand, you and other money people may tend to feel that a budget is useful only when it isn't met — by showing up someone who overspends.

Operational people think of a controller as a pencil pusher, a pinchpenny who reduces to numbers a job he knows little about. These differing views are the big obstacles to success in budgeting and controlling. While bridging the communications gap, you may find that it is you, not the manager or department heads, who changes most.

In fact, where budgeting is more successful, the financial people work directly with the operational people, learning the daily problems in order to find out the real meaning of costs and profits. The best controllers aren't just figure specialists; they are expert consultants who understand the whole business in detail.

START BY SITTING DOWN WITH THE MANAGER (unless you're both manager and controller, as is often the case) and going over the operating statements for the past several years. Examine each category of expense and income. After adjusting for inflation and other changes, do the figures seem typical of what you can expect next year?

Were the repair and maintenance costs in line with normal needs? Or were they higher than normal because you were catching up on postponed maintenance work? Or too low because you are *still* postponing?

How about costs for supplies? Did you restock a depleted inventory? How long should the current inventory last?

Were some past expenses too high or too low because a former resident manager was doing a poor job?

To budget operating expenses, make allowances for everything that you expect to be different next year — the fact that a garden has been replaced by a tennis court; that plumbers have just raised their rates; that the tax on your property will jump; that your new roof should eliminate bills for roof repairs. Obviously, the manager and other employees can call your attention to factors like these.

USE ROUND NUMBERS when you finally set your targets. Exact dollars as estimates will merely make you look silly. The more exact your figures, the narrower the limits implied. For example, if you budget $2,110 for something, you seem to be saying, "Don't miss that target by more than $10. If you're above $2,120 or below $2,100, the difference will stand out and be questioned." But if you set the amount at $2,100, you're allowing for a variance between $2,000 and $2,200.

Of course, your numbers can't be *too* round. Or at least your limits can't be too loose. Budgeting $2,000 for a category doesn't mean that anything between $1,000 and $3,000 is okay. But with amounts of $9,000 or more, a thousand dollar difference might be acceptable. After all, budgets are only estimates, and a 5% or 10% margin for error is reasonable.

One exception to this round number suggestion: where the items are out of your control, and are known in advance — such as taxes, insurance, and debt service — use the exact amounts minus the pennies.

For income, use the current month's figures as a base. Then calculate month-by-month the changes to expect if you plan to raise rents or pick up other income. Be realistic, though. If you've budgeted for an increase in rents on August 1 to be justified by improvements you're planning, but you find that the improvements won't be completed by August, lower your income projection.

CAPITAL EXPENDITURES can be budgeted too, but in a separate section under a separate subtotal. Major long-term improvements or additions are called "capitalizable" because they will be investments of capital for a betterment that didn't exist before. They increase the value of the property. (Notice that repairs and replacements aren't considered capital investments.)

Such expenditures are outside the normal cash flow. Maybe they can be paid from operating income, if the property is netting a healthy surplus. Or maybe there'll be new financing to pay for them. Either way, it's best not to blur your projection of operating income by making these special plans with it. Keep your operating and capital budgeting apart.

If you won't have enough surplus to install that new laundry room in March, but can afford it in August, this doesn't necessarily prevent you from putting it in before August. Can you get a loan to pay for it? If so, what would this financing cost? And how much income would the laundry room produce in the meantime? Maybe the room would pay for itself in a year or two, meanwhile permanently upping the value of the property.

Here is where your profit targets come in. It's well known that you must spend money to make money. If you budget a kitchen remodeling job, you also should budget the increased rental income it can be expected to bring. Some owners and managers look only at the costs of capital improvements, and decide not to spend because they don't figure on the profits they would make through such investment. By plowing back some current profits — or sometimes by using borrowed money they can surely repay from profits — they could assure themselves of much greater wealth in the future.

PROFIT PLANNING, as contrasted with budget control, is more a matter of setting policy. You try to decide what basic changes and improvements in the building (or sometimes in operating methods) will bring the biggest return on investment. Then, through budget control, you try to adjust day-to-day operations so that the various items of income and expense will fit your plan for making an improvement and paying for it.

PROFIT PLANNING BEGINS WITH A MARKET SURVEY. You analyze the community and the neighborhood to estimate the future demand for rental housing, and the range of rents that prospective residents will pay. Talk to other owners or managers in the area. Ask about their rent scales. Look at their buildings. Try to estimate their vacancies; often you can tell by simply counting how many mailboxes have no names.

What do the properties with low vacancy rates seem to have in common? What kinds of facilities seem to command higher rents? Could you install such facilities? What rental policies seem to attract the most profitable tenants? Could you do better by catering to a different type of prospect than you do now?

There's still much truth in an old real estate joke: "Question — What are the three most important features to look at in residential property? Answer — Location, location, location." Think carefully about your property's location when you consider its potential for future profits. Maybe you'll realize that it should be sold instead of improved, and the proceeds reinvested in other property elsewhere.

For future profitability, your property should be located where values are rising or at least stable. You may want to get long-range forecasts from the chamber of commerce, or the research department of your bank, or a regional development commission in the area. They can tell you about population and employment trends, income levels, the direction of business and population growth. Is the region on the upgrade or downgrade? Is it in the path of expansion? When will that new regional park be completed? Will that new medical center mean that higher income people will want to live nearby?

Look for easy access to mass transit. This will grow more and more important if the energy shortage worsens. Some neighborhoods well served by bus lines or commuter trains are already filling up; they have vacancy rates of only 3% to 4%, while some far-out suburban districts have rates two or three times as high. The transit factor alone might have a big impact on the future profits of your property.

In the light of trends you see developing, maybe your long-range profit plan should include a thorough renovation of your building and its apartments. If there's a new research park, for example, that will bring flocks of well-paid professional people into the area, could you appeal to them by putting a new front on your building, some elegant new landscaping, a fountain, good outdoor lighting? Is this the time to consider replacing those aging stoves and refrigerators?

Maybe your building is really a dump in a seedy neighborhood, and no improvements would add much to its profits. In that case, you may want to make some cosmetic improvements and try to sell it. Or your best plan may be simply to keep things as neat and clean and well-repaired as the circumstances will permit, and try to widen your profit margin.

OPERATING POLICY can be an important part of your profit plan. Would an electric floor waxer and polisher pay off? Could you cut costs of heating and air conditioning through better insulation? Could your employees' time be more productive with a one-write pegboard system like those mentioned in Chapter 13?

How about the crime rate in your area? If you put a security guard on duty, would residents be willing to pay enough more rent to pay for him?

Are there working mothers in your building? What would happen if you put in a baby sitting service or a supervised nursery? Would it pay off in fees, or in reduced turnover, or by filling vacancies faster?

Would your residents put more quarters in your own laundry machines and fewer in the laundromat around the corner, if your laundry room were brighter and better-heated?

Of course, you can't get the answers to such questions by sitting in your office and pondering them. You need to look into the cost of any possible improvement, and then chat with residents to see if they would be enthusiastic about it.

THE PAYBACK PERIOD is what controllers look at in judging any improvement that costs money. So, when you know what an improvement will cost (getting bids, if necessary), your next step is to judge how soon you should reasonably be able to recover its cost in the form of higher rent, other new revenues, or savings in labor, material, and other expenses.

For example, you'd be crazy to make improvements that won't produce much more revenue until three years from now when the new factory or community redevelopment project is scheduled to be completed. You need improvements that start repaying their cost almost immediately.

They should fully pay for themselves within three years. Anything longer is questionable. And be sure you make liberal allowances for errors in estimating both costs and benefits. Lean to the high side in cost estimates, to the low side in forecasting payoff.

Other considerations being equal, give priority to improvements that will pay for themselves fastest. They will help provide money for other improvements with longer payback periods. Remember, if you change your schedule of improvements, this will also change your expense forecast and your prospective revenue. And if you plan to borrow, don't forget to budget the payments you'll have to make each month.

After all these estimates and calculations, you're ready to draft a tentative budget — both the cash-flow budget and capital budget. At the same time, you should prepare a less detailed budget for the years while you'll still be amortizing capital improvements.

As you study this budget, you should see answers to some questions: will your cash flow be adequate to finance your improvements as scheduled? If not, can you borrow enough to make the difference? Or can you dip into other resources available to you? Maybe the budget will show that your cash flow should enable you to speed up your improvement schedule. Or maybe you'll see that you'd better back off from some capital expenditures because your budget will be too delicately balanced.

After a second draft, you should have your profit plan completed. You'll know where you are going and why. You'll have a sound plan for getting there — a road map and timetable.

CHOOSING AND USING YOUR BANKS

Does it really make a difference which bank gets your checking account? Aside from the convenience of having a branch near you, isn't one bank as good as the next?

On the surface it would seem so. Each bank sits quietly in its spacious splendor, waiting for customers to seek it out. People come in and make deposits; others come in and ask to borrow money. Competition among banks may be vigorous in the great money centers, but elsewhere relations have been cozy for decades. Every banker who is anybody knows all the other bankers, and a banker gets a particular piece of business merely because he knows one of the right people a little better than his rivals do.

However, this has changed somewhat in the 1970s. Bank stocks are now busily bought and sold on national exchanges. Even middle-size banks send teams of executives to speak at meetings of stock analysts. Banks' published profit figures have become important. Apparent trends in profit can boost or depress the price of bank's stock — and the stock price has become the name of the game. This is because banks have been fighting to diversify by acquiring control of finance companies and leasing companies and computer service bureaus — and even control of other banks, when the government would allow it. Banks have become holding companies and then financial conglomerates, reaching across the U.S. and the world. Like any conglomerate, an expanding "bank holding company" tries to take over other enterprises not by cash purchase but by an exchange of stock. The higher the market price of the bank's stock, the smaller the number of shares needed to pay for an acquisition. So, if you're interested in rating various banks near you, look at their stock prices and their price-earnings ratios.

A decade of super-growth has led to super-problems. One retired banker chuckles about "all these young MBAs from Harvard who were wizards in making loans. They're turning out to be not quite so good at collecting them." Three giant banks failed and there may be further casualties. Bankers all over the country realize that they have reached too far, taken too many risks, and must retrench. So now banks aren't lending money as eagerly as they were in 1974.

Of course, the small independent bank has always been more conservative than the big statewide outfits. On the other hand, with policy being made on the local level, it can give you a quicker and more knowledgeable decision. It's the bank to ask about rentals or general business conditions in the neighborhood.

Many small banks are still run by old-time fatherly types who are concerned with their community, who put service to customers above other considerations — and who don't worry much about internal efficiency since the help don't get paid overtime. If there's such a bank near you, probably you should keep some savings there and open a checking account. Get acquainted.

But you also ought to be a customer of a big faceless metropolitan bank because it offers a much greater range and depth of service. Major banks have tremendous research departments. Of course, big rich banks prefer big, rich customers. But you can establish a relationship with someone on "the platform," the central open area where the loan officers sit. Take out a small loan simply to establish credit, and pay it back before it is due, which you can easily do if you hold onto the proceeds of the loan. Stay friendly with your friend on the platform; say hello now and then. He'll come in handy when you have a problem.

He can get you in-depth advice from a specialist in whatever business matter you're likely to get into. There probably won't be any such specialist in your independent neighborhood bank. And if you need a bigger mortgage loan than the local banker is willing to give, your man on the platform may okay it. Believe it or not, if a loan officer likes you, he can be a lot nicer than if he doesn't know you.

But choose your faceless bank carefully. They're not all alike. Some go in heavily for trust accounts, some for international finance or retail business or manufacturers. Some are very big in consumer finance; others have no faith in it. Luckily for owners of residential income property, some are interested in real estate and know plenty about it. Obviously, they're the banks for you:

Sooner or later, you'll need to deal with three different banks if you're going to be active in buying and managing and selling apartments. One bank should be where your property is. If you work and bank in Chicago, but want to buy an apartment building in Skokie, Illinois, get acquainted with the savings bank in Skokie rather than your commercial bank's branch in Skokie. Yet, you should also have an account with the latter, simply for the convenience of transferring your money between Skokie and Chicago — and perhaps between Skokie and a branch in Winnetka, if that's where you live.

The third bank, of course, would be the really big one that can give expert advice on real estate market conditions, regional population trends and the like. This might be the same Chicago-Skokie-Winnetka giant that you use for inter-branch convenience. Even so, if you're well known at three different banks, you're improving the odds of getting a loan or other services when you need to shop around.

TO BE WELL KNOWN AT A BANK, get acquainted with one or more of its senior officers. When you open your account, don't just go to a clerk. Step over to the manager's desk and introduce yourself. His desk is probably out in the open, rather than in a private office. Tell him something about the property you've bought, and your plans. You'll find him glad to chat for a few minutes, since you are obviously a person of substance and thus a potential borrower who might be a good credit risk.

Don't overdraw your checking accounts because this makes you seem sloppy in the eyes of the bank. But don't leave large sums piled up in those accounts either; a banker won't respect your judgment if he sees you leaving too much money where it doesn't draw interest.

File a financial statement with each of your banks and bring it up to date every six months or so. It will help when you need a loan; in fact, a moderate loan can be yours for the asking at an hour's notice if a solid financial statement is already on file.

Keep in touch with bank officers you know by asking their advice occasionally on some investment problem – even if you think you already know the answer. Like most human beings, bankers are pleased to be asked for advice. Besides, you might learn something you didn't know.

When you need a sizeable loan, do your homework first. If you need it to finance improvements, work up a detailed list of the improvements and their estimated cost, including an allowance for contingencies. Get bids to support your estimates. Then take photocopies of your last few monthly operating statements. Attach a projection of what you think your income and expense will be after the improvements are completed.

The idea is to show your banker that you've planned this outlay carefully, and that the loan is easily repayable out of your profits. (And if these improvements don't pay off for any reason, your financial statement should have convinced him that you can repay out of your other assets.)

When all this is neatly typed up, phone for an appointment. This is no time to drift in as if by impulse. You want the atmosphere to be thoroughly businesslike. And you want to be sure your banker buddy has set aside enough time to discuss your proposition adequately.

Dress quietly. Mod clothes make bankers uneasy. An open shirt and work pants may be okay in the Southwest, where the wealthiest men dress that way, if your financial statement has established you as wealthy. Otherwise, suit and necktie are safer.

When you arrive, get right down to business. This reinforces your image as a no-nonsense type. And, of course, you shouldn't seem hesitant, apologetic or needy. Never talk to a banker in terms of need. Never say, "If I can borrow X dollars, then I'll be able to do so-and-so." If he thinks you're afraid you may not get the loan, he'll be inclined to say no. As the old joke goes, bankers lend only to people who don't need money.

So you exude calm confidence. This should be easy if you've figured out your profit plan carefully. You can say, "Here's how I'm going to generate more profits in my property." You assume that the question isn't whether you get the loan, but how much, for how long, and at what interest rate.

Don't wait for the loan officer to ask, "How much do you want?" Early in the conversation, mention a figure larger than you're after, for a slightly longer time and lower interest than you really expect. Just keep these within reason, so they won't sound crazy. Let the loan officer be a hero to his superiors by cutting you down while you still get approximately what you're after.

Once you've struck an agreement, shake hands and leave. Some loans are lost because a borrower keeps talking and says something that makes the loan officer change his mind. However, if he hands you a carefully prepared note for signature, study it before you sign it. What he calls the "standard terms" may contain some trick clauses. Be ready to question them.

YOUR BUDGET AND PROFIT PLAN CAN IMPRESS A BANKER. Maybe your projections indicate that you'll be running $4,000 in the red in August, but that the deficit will narrow steadily and you'll be showing comfortable profits by February. If the facts and figures support you, he won't be appalled at the prospect of the temporary shortage. He understands payback periods and how revenues are generated by expenditures, and he likes to see it all worked out in a month-by-month budget.

But don't wait until August because then there'll be no indication you foresaw going in the hole. Tell him in May that you'll want to borrow in August, and he'll probably say that he's pretty sure he can make the money available when the time comes. When that time does come, he'll check your latest operating statement against your budget, and if they're in line with the plans you explained earlier, he'll have no qualms about advancing the $4,000 or whatever it is you need.

IF A BANK DOES TURN YOU DOWN, the best thing you can do, surprisingly, is broadcast the fact all over town. People will assume the turndown was unjustified or you wouldn't be talking about it.

Publicizing the refusal puts pressure on the bank. Other investors may feel the bank is cold to investors and look elsewhere for their banking. Banks need customers. They don't want to lose those personal savings and checking accounts, those non-interest-bearing Christmas Club accounts, those service charges which all contribute to their essential cash flow. So they don't like their image to be marred by rumors that they won't serve small businessmen or small investors.

Later on, when you make it big, don't forget which bank refused to help you. Too often people run back to the same source, giving bankers the impression they can turn anyone down with impunity. It will be good for all investors if you remind everyone that Ultraconservative National refused you a loan. Your success proves they were wrong.

But for now, when you're on the way up, don't hesitate to ask another bank for the loan you failed to get from the first one. Banks have their own grapevine, and if they hear that you're complaining all over town about the treatment you got from Ultraconservative National, they'll think twice about treating you likewise. Tell the new bank you were turned down and the vague reasons given you. (Banks' reasons for rejecting loans are almost always vague.) The second banker will be impressed by your frankness. And if your budget and profit plan are really sound, he'll want to advance you the money.

PAY AS AGREED. Slow payments not only bother a banker, and set him thinking of foreclosure, but can also impose penalty charges on you. Your doctor or department stores may let bills go unpaid for months, but a bank will be calling you right away.

If anything happens that may prevent you from making a loan payment in full on the due date, get in touch with your loan officer as far ahead of time as you can. Explain your problem. Usually, he'll help you work out a plan for repayment on easier terms, enabling you to keep your credit record more or less unblemished.

When the principal comes due, if you've been making payments on time, you'll probably find it's easy to get a renewal or another few thousand on the loan. Just call up and ask for it, explaining that you had a few unpredictable vacancies or whatever. You've already passed the credit check hurdle, the interview, the bank's private and confidential evaluation of you as a customer. And, of course, you've been paying. A loan renewal is almost automatic under those circumstances.

KEEP SURPLUS DOLLARS AT WORK

In a small business such as apartment management, it's even more important than in big business to deploy your resources where they bring results. If your capital is gathering dust in a checking account or low-interest savings account, you're not doing your job because part of a controller's job is to keep capital working productively. Cash in the bank may be alright for widows, but not for a businessman. The only time you park any operating funds in a savings account is when you know you'll soon need it for budgeted items. Most banks pay daily interest now.

MAYBE YOU'VE BEEN POSTPONING BADLY NEEDED REDECORATING of various apartments. Fresh paint, new drapes and carpeting, new tile on their bathroom floors would make these apartments more inviting — and worth more rent. What better use for unneeded cash than to generate more rental income?

MAYBE THERE'S A DEMAND FOR FURNISHED APARTMENTS in your area, but your units are unfurnished. In that case, maybe you should furnish your next vacancy before you re-rent it. Of course, this would mean a change in tenant profile — probably less stability and more turnover, higher costs for cleaning and repairs — but it still might pay because of the higher rent. It's worth a thought.

SOMETIMES YOU SAVE BY SPENDING. Consider stocking up on any out-of-season items you'll need later. Buying garden and pool supplies in fall instead of spring can mean a double savings: you'll get them at lower prices and you'll get a tax deduction for the expense a year earlier. Similarly, buying larger quantities of some items may get you a discount.

Prepaying various expenses near the end of the year can also mean reducing your income tax for that year. How about that property tax bill that isn't due until April? And that state income tax installment that comes due in January? And don't forget the interest on your mortgage. Of course, the mortgagor must be willing to accept the prepayment, but most institutional lenders will. Just check with your accountant or attorney to make sure this is a good move for you.

YOU CAN GET A 36% YIELD WITH NO RISK by taking advantage of discounts for prompt payment. When a bill reads, "2% 10 days, net 30," this means you can pay within 10 days, but are obligated to pay within 30 days anyway.

So pay on the 10th day if you possibly can. Delaying another 20 days means foregoing a profit equivalent to an annual return of 36% of the money. (There are 18 of those 20-day periods in a year, so your 2% gain in one period becomes 36% if you do this year 'round.) Where else can you be so much money ahead with absolute safety?

You might be tempted to breach the terms and stretch out the payment period to 60 days, thus in effect borrowing money from your creditor for a month interest-free. But that's less profitable than taking the discount. The difference in profit is 14.6% per year. And you'll certainly have much happier relations with your supplier if you pay him within 10 days. The time may come when you'll need emergency service from him, and he certainly won't give his best service to slow paying customers.

KEEP ENOUGH CASH IN RESERVE. Never risk being trapped in the position of having borrowed recently, only to find that you're running out of cash again. Presumably you can project your cash position accurately most of the time, but things

FH-1
Rev. 3/76

Form Approved
OMB No. 63R-0037

DEPARTMENT OF HOUSING AND URBAN DEVELOPMENT
FEDERAL HOUSING ADMINISTRATION

CREDIT APPLICATION FOR PROPERTY IMPROVEMENT LOAN

This application is submitted to obtain credit under the provisions of Title I of the National Housing Act

(PLEASE ANSWER ALL QUESTIONS)

TO: Lending Institution which will provide the funds: | Date

1. Do you have any past due obligations owed to or insured by any agency of the Federal Government? *(If the answer is "Yes", you are not eligible to apply for an FHA Title I Loan until the existing debt has been brought current.)* ☐ Yes ☐ No

2. Have you any other application for an FHA Title I Improvement Loan pending at This time? ☐ Yes ☐ No *(If yes, with whom-name and address.)*

3. I hereby apply for a loan of $ _____ (Net)

to be repaid in _____ Months.

4. APPLICANT

Name | Age | No. of Dependents

Address *(Street, City, State and ZIP Code)* | How long | Name- Co-Applicant | Age | Home Phone

| | | Name and Address of nearest relative not living with you | Relationship

Previous address *(Street, City, State and ZIP Code)* | How long

(Check One)

1. ☐ White *(Non-Minority)*   3. ☐ American Indian   5. ☐ Spanish American
2. ☐ Negro/Black   4. ☐ Oriental   6 ☐ Other Minority

The Information concerning Minority Group Categories is requested for Statistical Purposes so the Department may determine the degree to which its Programs are utilized by Minority Families.

5. EMPLOYMENT AND SALARIES: *(If applicant self-employed, submit current financial statement.)*

Employment-Name and Business Address	Type of work or Position	No. of Years	Business Phone	Salary *(Week/Month)*
				$ Per

Previous Employer-Name and Business Address

Co-Applicant's Employer-Name and Business Address	Type of work or Position	No. of Years	Business Phone	Salary *(Week/Month)*
				$ Per

Other Income- Source *(Note: Income from alimony, child support, or maintenance income need not be shown here unless you will rely upon it as a basis for undertaking or repaying this loan.)* | Amount *(Week/Month)* $ Per

6. BANK ACCOUNT:

☐ Yes ☐ No   ☐ Checking ☐ Savings | Name and Address-Bank or Branch

7. CREDIT ACCOUNTS: *(Give name and address of finance companies or stores which have extended credit and which you have paid in full.)*

a. | b.

c. | d.

8. DEBTS: List all fixed obligations, installment accounts, FHA loans, and debts to banks, finance companies, and Government agencies. *(If more space needed, list all additional debts on attached sheet.)*

FHA Ins. Yes	No	To Whom Indebted *(Name)*	City and State	Date Incurred	Original Amount	Present Balance	Monthly Payments	Amount Past Due
		Mortgage/Contract			$	$	$	$
					$	$	$	$
					$	$	$	$
					$	$	$	$
					$	$	$	$
A U T O	Lien Holder		Year and Make		$	$	$	
	Lien Holder		Year and Make		$	$	$	

FH-1 Rev. 3/76

234

9. PROPERTY TO BE IMPROVED: —

If this is a residential structure, has it been completed and occupied for 90 days or longer? ☐ Yes ☐ No

Address *(Number, Street, City, County, State and ZIP Code)*		Type-Home, Apt. Store, Farm, etc., *(If Apt., No. of Units)*	Date Purchased

FILL IN ONE	Is Owned by;	Name of Title Holder	Date of Mortgage	Price Paid $
	Is being bought on Installment Contract By;	Name of Purchaser	Name and Address of Title Holder	Price Paid $
	Is Leased to:	Name of Lessee		Date Lease Expires
	Name of Landlord		Address	Rent Per Month $

10. PROCEEDS OF THIS LOAN WILL BE USED TO IMPROVE THE DESCRIBED PEOPERTY AS FOLLOWS:

Describe each improvement planned	Name and address contractor/dealer	Estimate Cost
		$
		$
		$

WARNING

Any person who knowingly makes a false statement or a misrepresentation in this application or causes such a false statement or misrepresentation to be made shall be subject to a fine of not more than $5000 or by imprisonment for not more than 2 years, or both, under provisions of the United States Criminal Code.

IMPORTANT-APPLICANT READ BEFORE SIGNING

The selection of a Contractor or Dealer, acceptance of materials used, and work performed is your responsibility. Neither the FHA nor the Financial Institution guarantees the material or workmanship or inspects the work performed.
I (We) certify that the above statements are true, accurate, and complete to the best of my (our) knowledge and belief. This application shall remain the property of the Lending Institution to which submitted for the purpose of obtaining a loan.
I (We) hereby consent to and authorize the Lending Institution or the FHA, after the giving of reasonable notice, to enter the improved property for the purpose of determining that the improvements specified in this application have been completed.

Name_____ (LS)   Name_____ (LS)
(Applicant)   *(Applicant)*

NOTE TO SALESMEN: If proceeds will be disbursed to the Contractor/Dealer, the person(s) selling the above described improvements must sign the following certification.

I (We) certify that: 1 - I (We) am (are) the person(s) who sold the job. 2- The Contract contains the whole agreement with the borrower. 3- The borrower has n-t been given or promised a cash payment or rebate nor has it been represented to the borrower that he will receive a cash bonus or commission on future sales as an inducement for the consummation of this transaction; that the improvements have not been misrepresented; no promises impossible of attainment; no encouragement of trial purchase; no promise that the improvements will be used as a model for advertising or other demonstration purposes; and no offer of debt consolidation.

(LS) Name _____
(My true name and signature are as shown above)

If application is prepared by one other than the applicant, the person preparing the application must sign below.
I (We) certify that the statements made herein are based upon information given to me (us) by the borrower(s) and are accurate to the best of my (our) knowledge and belief.

Prepared by: _____   Address _____
(Signature of preparer other than borrower)

Representing: _____
(Name of Dealer/Contractor)

(Reserve for use of Lending Institution.)

Term *(In Months)*	_____
No. of payments	_____
Amt. of mo. payts.	$ _____
Amount of note	$ _____
Discount	$ _____
Net proceeds	$ _____

FH-1 Rev. 3/76

✿ US GOVERNMENT PRINTING OFFICE: 1976-690-033/584

can happen to throw a forecast badly out of line. Your boiler may spring a leak. Fungus may kill all your shrubbery. An unexpected layoff by a big employer in your area may leave many of your residents unable to pay their rent.

How much reserve is enough? As a rule of thumb, one-and-a-half times your gross scheduled rent is generally safe. That is, if you're prepared to ride out a six-week period when your rental income is totally used up by expenses, you can sleep soundly. So, when you take out a loan, try to get one big enough for this margin of safety.

You can line up additional temporary protection by opening an "overdraft protection" or "guaranteed reserve" account at one of your banks. This is a checking account which you can overdraw up to a specified amount without the checks bouncing. It's another way of borrowing — an expensive way. The interest on your overdrafts will probably be 1½% a month (18% per year), but you've got a source of ready cash in a dire emergency, without even asking for it. Just be sure to keep this privilege intact until the emergency arises. Don't overdraw for anything other than a real crisis.

REMEMBER THESE BASIC POINTS:

* *Analyze all income from the property and compare it over a period of time. Dig into reasons for variations, using a "moving total" worksheet.*

* *Know how your costs compare with those of similar properties.*

* *In complex tabulations of figures, get them prepared so only the first two or three digits of each item are shown. Look for inconsistencies. Look at proportions.*

* *Work on a 12-month budget, but update it monthly.*

* *Have a long-range profit plan. Give priority to improvements that will pay for themselves fastest.*

* *Deal with three different banks, choosing them for different purposes. Get acquainted with some of the senior officers.*

* *If you'll need a sizable loan, work out a detailed prospectus to show the bankers. Ask for a figure slightly larger than you're after.*

* *If a bank turns you down, broadcast the fact all over town, and ask another bank for the loan.*

* *Keep your surplus dollars at work. Look for chances to save by spending. But keep an adequate cash reserve, usually 1.5 times your gross scheduled rent.*

XV *Coping with Costs*

"Beginning owners often discover that investing profitably in residential property is harder than it looks. In some ways it's harder than ever." *Money* magazine noted in a 1976 article. "Profits have been squeezed thinner than a landlord's smile by increased costs of fuel, taxes, financing and maintenance."

Keeping costs down is important in every business nowadays. Because of high prices of materials, soaring wages, expense of new equipment and burdensome tax rates, many firms are broadening their markets or raising their prices, only to see profits shrinking anyhow. In such a predicament some of them get panicky and decree across-the-board budget cuts — which sometimes turn out to be like reducing weight by cutting off a hand and a foot.

Expenses, like extra pounds around the midriff, are easy to put on, but hard to take off. The best bet is to keep working to hold them down, and gradually reduce them, rather than make big slashes in a hurry. Tackle the problem methodically and continuously. Make it part of every day's work.

DON'T THINK COST CUTTING. THINK PROFIT IMPROVEMENT. The difference is more than semantic. What you're really after is to make every dollar work harder. To do things better for less. To get your money's worth. Obviously, you can't just stop spending, because this would cost you residents and ruin the property's resale value. The trick is to spend wisely and productively.

Let's look at various types of expenditures in turn. Maybe you'll see ways to buy more for less or to eliminate waste.

First we'll take the unavoidable, recurring expenses: insurance, taxes and utilities. Is there any hope of economizing on these?

INSURANCE

Being over-insured is wasteful since all insurance is totally unproductive. But being under-insured could be ruinous. So your problem is to buy maximum protection at minimum prices.

It's no accident that some insurance company headquarters are as splendid as Buckingham Palace, and that some of America's tallest buildings are named for insurance companies. Insurance is a billion dollar business. You can contribute to its profits.

One reason big insurors are so rich is that they sometimes take advantage of small businesses and individuals. No matter how hard you try, you'll continue to help underwriters get richer. But there are ways that you can buy enough protection for your own buildings while paying only for the fluorescent lights in the insurance offices, rather than contributing to the crystal chandeliers in their lobbies.

The lowest rates for insurance normally go to major organizations, just as a merchant gives better prices to big customers than to smaller ones. Since you are comparatively small, you won't be handed any favors. You'll have to extract them.

Therefore, buy insurance the same way you buy groceries or an automobile — by comparative shopping. There are hundreds of insurance plans, dozens of ways of insuring for a specific need, a throng of companies in the field, regiments of "agents" ready to sell insurance. Let the insurance agents compete for your business; put your insurance out for bids. Then study the bids.

Many insurance problems are our own fault because we accept our insurance policies almost blindly. We think that all companies sell the same coverage, that an "old-line company" gives better service, or that we can't go wrong in buying from a friend. We forget that it is hard to get the right insurance coverage.

The cost of insurance, and the coverage, vary from company to company. Rates are set to suit the companies. Insurance bargains do exist. But it's also true that bargain hunting may leave you without protection — either because the company goes broke, or because of hidden loopholes in the policy, or because the company's lawyer out-maneuvers you when you try to collect a claim. So how can you find a true bargain? We'll see.

SEEK PROTECTION FIRST in buying insurance. All other considerations are secondary. A policy with a smaller face value but fewer exclusions is better than the other way around. To know what is and isn't covered by a policy, you must do a little research. Insurance companies seldom tell you all you should know. They befuddle buyers with complex language. Sometimes their paragraphs of fine print are so obscure that their own agents can't fully explain them.

You won't even get to see the fine print — unless you ask — until after you've agreed to buy the policy. Your policy arrives with your bill.

Of course, you weren't high-pressured. Most insurance men aren't salesmen; they're order-takers. Chances are, your friendly insurance agent didn't sell you enough insurance. He told you about a coverage plan and you ordered it. He delivered or mailed the policies — and you both forgot about them. He never checked to see whether your insurance needs were changing because you were improving the property or adding new facilities or doing something that heightened your risks.

"Too often an agent is more interested in the sale of a policy than in the protection it may provide," says a bulletin of the Institute of Real Estate Management. "In many instances the addition of one or more clauses may be the difference in protection and non-protection. It behooves each property manager to determine the extent to which he or the owner is covered."

WHAT HAPPENS WHEN YOU HAVE A LOSS? Then your insurance man is Johnny-on-the-spot. He is there to get an immediate look at the loss so his company won't pay a dime more than necessary. He collects any evidence that may help the company lawyers argue that the loss was really your fault and not covered by the policy.

You get the policy out of the files and try to understand it. Your insurance man tries to explain, "I didn't know that you converted those rooms," he may say, or "You didn't tell me about this," or "If I had known that this was what you wanted . ." or "You could have had that coverage if you had asked for it."

THE BEST WAY TO BUY, and to ferret out good protection at reasonable rates, is to find at least one good independent insurance agent. This is a broker, one who can place business wherever he wants, as opposed to a company agent who represents a single company or group and sells only its policies. (Many insurance companies belong to groups or boards that fix prices; non-members of such groups are far more competitive.)

Naturally, a broker is more likely to work for this customers' benefit than a company agent is. A broker is familiar with a wide range of insurance plans, so he should be able to find good coverage at a low price. He usually represents many companies and has authority to bind them to the coverage he specifies. He can even settle losses on his own.

He collects premiums, renews policies, and adds broader coverage onto policies through endorsements. His commissions on "old" accounts are as valuable as they are on new ones — unlike those in life insurance and health insurance accounts, where the commission is mainly earned during the first year. Therefore, a broker who writes property insurance will nurse and coddle his accounts.

If he is good, his drawback is that he is a busy man with many clients. Your phone calls and letters may go unanswered for some time. Unless you represent a big risk with a hefty premium, you may be slighted for better clients. Don't feel frustrated; he's worth waiting for, like a good doctor or lawyer.

GET BIDS FROM SEVERAL BROKERS if you possibly can. Your apartment association will know several who are experts in apartment insurance. But instead of turning each loose to shop the market, ask each broker which company he feels he has the most clout with. Then assign him to approach that underwriter for a bid on coverage of your property. (The types of protection you will need will be described in a moment.)

There are several reasons for this strategy. Companies want to keep all their brokers happy. If a company were approached by more than one broker on your behalf, it would want to avoid the deal, for fear of a squabble between them. Not knowing which broker to talk to, it probably wouldn't figure out a bid for either.

Every company has its favored brokers. However, once a company makes a bid, it won't go lower for a favored broker even if it wants to; this just isn't done in the insurance business. That's why each company should be first approached by one of its favorites.

And yet, a very sophisticated broker can go back to an underwriter and get a lower quote. He does this by slightly changing the terms of the policy. It should not have any significant effect on your coverage, but it will give the company an excuse if any other broker complains, "The premium is lower because the coverage is different." So, when you're convinced that one particular broker is best for you, but think that his bid is too high, you can ask him to try for a lower rate on a slightly different policy.

PROTECT YOURSELF AGAINST LOWBALLING, which is a bid much lower than the others. Inexperienced or unethical brokers occasionally come in with a lowball in order to get the business for a mediocre insurance company. Take a long hard look at the coverage offered; probably you should have your attorney read the fine print. Occasionally, you can grab a real bargain this way, but in most cases the below-cost bidder won't be able to deliver the future service specified in the policy. This brings up the tricky question of cancellation clauses.

Except for life insurance and some medical plans, every insurance policy has a cancellation clause. The insurance company can cancel without giving a reason; some clauses allow a company to stop the policy after only five days' notice. Always negotiate this clause when buying property insurance, especially if the bid seems strangely low. Demand as much as 90 days' notice of cancellation, but be willing to accept 30 days if the company agrees to guarantee the first 90 days of the contract. Lowballers won't want to stay in that long.

Two ways to protect yourself: (1) Get a letter from the broker telling you what risks are covered by your policy and what risks aren't. But, remember, if the broker makes a mistake, the insurance company isn't bound by what he says. So: (2) Insist that the broker provide you with a certificate of insurance — a type of "malpractice insurance" for brokers. Make your coverage through him contingent on such a certificate. This means that if the broker makes some error that affects your coverage — such as omitting a critical detail in reporting to the underwriter, or perhaps not following through on a "binder," you can collect via the broker's own coverage.

Get a binder on anything which needs coverage as soon as you acquire it. All this takes is a phone call. Of course, this doesn't give you any legal record of having ordered the coverage, so you're at the mercy of your agent, but the system is such a convenience to the insurance agents that there are few cases of abuse. If you're skeptical, you can always have a few people witness the call.

CONSIDER CHANGING AGENTS periodically, even if your agent is your pal. Taking bids from his competitors will keep him on his toes. Get written presentations from another broker or two, and let your agent also put in his own bid if he has served you well. You can feel safe in sticking with him when no one offers wider coverage at lower rates, or can guarantee better service. But remember that insurance laws and companies are always changing, and that your property and its value may be changing, too, so never stop getting bids every few years. In most states there is great room for savings, especially in liability insurance.

When you let one agent handle both property and liability insurance, you can expect less service. The agent will argue, "Buying everything from me will make you a big enough customer to get more of my time." In practice this is seldom true. Two agents give you twice the service — and you get better advice too, because two agents' ideas are better than one.

Other ways to save on insurance: (1) Buy coverage with deductibles whenever available. You need insurance to take care of catastrophes, not the small emergencies of everyday operation. The higher the deductible, the lower the cost of your insurance. (2) Have your property insurance written for the maximum length available. This is now three years in most states. A three-year policy will save you 10% or 15% a year, even if you pay your premium only one year at a time. You save even more if you can prepay for the whole period. If you borrow for this purpose, the financing may cost less than the savings on your premium.

WHAT COVERAGE YOU NEED: (1) Physical damage to buildings and contents. This would include fire. The policies are sometimes called Fire and EC (extended coverage) or Fire and Allied Coverage. The coverage can include wind, hail, lightning, collapse, explosion, riot, smoke and flood. If you're in a part of the country which is never badly damaged by hail, lightning or flood, don't buy a package that covers them. On the other hand, if you're in an earthquake zone or on a slope where a landslide could ruin your building, you should try to get coverage for these, although few underwriters provide it. Insurance against flood is also hard to find. You may think you're getting it when you insure against "water damage," but you're not. Water damage covers only "accidental leakage of discharge." It excludes damage by floods, high water or backed-up sewers. And how about crime coverage? If vandals lay waste an empty apartment or tear your laundry machines apart for the coins, can you afford the loss? If you can't, add crime coverage to your EC policy.

(2) Rent loss insurance. Damage to a building can snuff out your rental income during the time the apartments can't be occupied. Some investors who have ample resources prefer to take the business risk of not carrying rent insurance. But to an owner whose major income depends on one building, the loss of its rents might be disastrous.

(3) Liability insurance. This protects the owner and manager from claims, most commonly for accidents on the premises. A liability judgment that wipes out assets is a terrifying thought. You're a sitting duck for a big damage suit if you have substantial assets. You can become liable if you fail to warn a resident or guest of any dangers you should know about — from a broken stair to broken glass by the swimming pool. But you can buy protection. Liability limits of $300,000 are considered modest, and limits of $1,000,000 aren't unusual. Protection can also include liability for property damage as well as bodily injury.

You may not feel enthused about buying all the above policies. Probably they can be combined into one "multi-peril package policy" that costs less than the same protection bought separately. Most property and casualty (to distinguish them from life) insurance companies offer a package policy for apartment buildings. There is a choice of perils to be covered. A package deal is a good way to economize on insurance — but make sure you really need everything in the package.

ALL-RISK INSURANCE IS A MYTH. There are loopholes in even the best plans. (As one obvious example, you can't insure yourself against the consequences of your own criminal actions, such as arson.) Certain coverages are prohibitive. Your "all risk" package will cover only a smattering of sharply-defined risks. You can only hope for partial coverage at best, as you pick and choose. You'll have to compromise, not only on the type of coverage, but also on the amount.

Specialized insurance protection is available, either as part of a package policy or bought separately, depending on the insurance company. Such protection can include:

(4) Contents insurance for damage to things inside the building, such as lobby furniture, equipment in the manager's office, lockers, tools, mop truck, waxing machines, vacuum cleaners, uniforms, etc.

(5) Fine arts insurance, covering paintings and tapestries and statuary in the building or on the premises.

(6) Boiler insurance, covering explosion, breaks, and related losses. In transferring this risk to the insurance company, you also buy the services of the company's boiler inspector who will give you expert advice on operation and upkeep. The same is true of elevator insurance.

(7) Landscaping, shrubbery, fences, driveways, walks and outer trimmings can be covered by an endorsement on your Extended Coverage policy.

(8) Plate glass insurance.

(9) Sprinkler leakage insurance.

(10) Auto insurance, to protect the property from claims against its employees driving their own cars on the owner's business.

(11) Dram shop or host insurance, to cover liquor-related injuries or damage.

(12) Fidelity insurance, to protect against losses caused by crooks on your payroll. You can buy a broad form "3-D policy" (disappearance, destruction, or dishonesty) which can include burglary and fraud losses, raising and altering of checks, forgery, loss from a safe deposit box, and other mysterious or criminal happenings.

According to one insurance company, employee dishonesty causes about 30% of all business failures. One common mistake by businessmen is to forgive and forget when they catch a sticky-fingered employee. If they keep the employee on the payroll, they probably invalidate their fidelity insurance. Another mistake is to fire the employee without pressing charges. This means that they can't take a tax deduction for the amount of the loss; any loss due to crime must be reported to the police in order to be deductible.

Here's another quirk in fidelity insurance. If someone is managing property on a contract basis, the owner's insurance won't cover losses caused by dishonesty of a manager or a management firm. The fidelity insurance covers only dishonesty by employees; the manager and staff are classed as "private contractors." The owner can protect himself by having the manager furnish him with a "contract bond."

WORKMEN'S COMPENSATION INSURANCE isn't included in your liability policy, nor in any package policy. It is always separate. It is a must for residential income property owners, even if they don't have any employees, because they surely will hire part-time painters or carpenters or plumbers occasionally. The law requires every employer to carry this insurance. Each state has its own plan, and the coverage varies, but in general, anyone who does any work for you is probably entitled to get compensation (sometimes for life) for any illness or injury connected with the work.

Suppose an occupant offers to paint his apartment if you buy the paint. You say, "Go ahead. Buy the paint yourself, and I'll deduct the cost from your next rent payment." From that time on, he's in your employ. If he gets hurt while painting, his medical bills are on you, unless you took out workmen's compensation insurance, in which case the state will pay.

Maybe you have relatives who occasionally help you without pay. You'd better pay them at least nominal wages so that if they're hurt while working, they can collect liability payments.

If you don't carry this insurance, even if you're blameless of neglect, the law can make you pay medical bills for someone hurt on the job, and may make you support them if they can't return to work. One owner-manager had a tenant who answered his phone for him when he was out. She tripped on the phone cord, broke her hip, and became an invalid. Because she wasn't covered by workmen's compensation insurance, she became a crushing financial burden to him.

THE CO-INSURANCE CLAUSE in property insurance is another complication you should understand. Sometimes it is called the "average clause" or the "reduced rate contribution clause." By whatever name, it is the least understood clause in the whole field of insurance. Its purpose is to discourage under-insurance, or so the insurance companies say.

Because most fires are small and don't damage much of the building, many owners used to insure for much smaller amounts than the value of the building. They considered they were self-insuring themselves for the difference between the face value of the policy and the value of the building — which was another way of saying that they were gambling there'd be no major fire. If they could afford a total loss, they really were self-insured; if they didn't have the resources for this, they weren't self-insured at all.

To sell more coverage, insurance companies began offering lower rates to owners who could insure their property for a specified percentage of its actual cash value. (Cash value means replacement value less certain depreciation factors.) The higher the co-insurance percentage, the lower the insurance rate.

The clause, as usually worded, "limits the liability of the company to a proportion of any loss which is the proportion that the amount insured by the company bears to a stipulated percentage of actual cash value of the insured's property at the time the loss happens." Is that clear?

Let's try to unravel it, because it is an important clause, and it conceals a penalty that could cost you a sack of money.

When the standard 80% co-insurance clause is in effect, you won't be fully reimbursed for any partial damage or loss unless you've insured your property for at least

80% of its "actual cash value." In other words, if you insure for less than 80% of the value and you suffer a partial loss, then you must bear a proportionate amount of the loss. You yourself, in the jargon of insurance men, "co-insure" or are responsible for the difference between the amount of insurance you carry and 80% of the value of the property. (The co-insurance clause doesn't apply if you suffer a loss of 80% or more. Then you collect the full amount of the loss, up to the face value of your policy.)

Why don't the companies say you should insure 100% of the value of the property? Why are they satisfied with 80%? Because they admit that 20% of the value of a building survives virtually any disaster. Foundations, water and sewer lines, heavy boilers and the like, probably won't suffer.

Now, suppose your policy carries this 80% clause, and your building would cost $100,000 to rebuild, but you carry only $60,000 insurance because you don't think a disaster is likely to do more than $60,000 worth of damage. You are considered to be under-insuring by one-fourth, or $20,000 of the $80,000 you should carry to be fully covered.

The formula used by the companies is:

$$\text{Percentage of loss to be paid by the company (up to the limits of the policy)} = \frac{\text{Amount of insurance carried}}{\text{Amount of insurance which should be carried}}$$

Using the numbers we used above, here's how the formula works out:

You carried 3/4 of the $80,000 insurance the underwriters figured you ought to carry. If you suffer a $2,000 loss, the insurer will pay only $1,500.

"Fair enough," you may think. "It's like a $500 deductible." But it isn't. It's a 25% deductible, which can really hurt if there's a major loss.

In one actual case, an investor built a new apartment house which would be valued at $360,000. To save on insurance, he told his broker that the completed value of the building would be $300,000. This saved him $113 in premiums. There was a fire, and the loss was appraised at $184,000. He thought, "I'm glad I insured for $300,000. Now I'll get the whole $184,000 back." Not so. He lost $27,000 because the insurance company applied the co-insurance penalty and paid only $157,000.

Some states take a dim view of this clause, and prohibit its use with certain types of property. However, on certain other types the clause is mandatory under the laws of most states. There's no use arguing about whether it's fair or unfair. It's the way insurance companies work.

YOU WILL SOON BE UNDER-INSURED unless you keep increasing your coverage as construction costs go up, and as you add to the resale value of the property by improvements. The cost of rebuilding keeps rising with inflation. When your coverage falls below the 80% that you committed to maintain, you become a co-insurer and must pay for part of any loss. It's up to you to see that your insurance broker checks your coverage. (Likewise, you'll probably want to raise your rental income insurance whenever you raise rents.)

However, if you have an over-age and obsolete property that would never be rebuilt if it burned, and you feel that insuring to 80% is a burden, you can request a 50% or 60% co-insurance clause. The rate will be higher, but the total premium will probably be less.

DEPRECIATION CAN SLASH YOUR INSURANCE PROTECTION. Most insurance policies stipulate that they will pay only the cost of new construction minus depreciation. Those last two words can cost you thousands. If you rebuild a damaged part of an old building, you'll have to build it new at today's prices. But there's a way to protect yourself. For a small extra charge, you can have your policies written so that they'll pay for actual replacement cost, without any deduction for depreciation. Or you can ask for "special form" insurance which also excludes a depreciation clause. Or a "depreciation endorsement" enables you to insure the amount of value which the building has depreciated. Ask your broker which form of protection will cost you least. There are many ways to reduce hazards that could cost you money — all are commendable, but some are expensive. A good broker's advice is essential.

ALWAYS INSIST ON AN INSPECTION of the premises before agreeing to any insurance program. Insurance inspectors will point out the hazards and tell you how to correct them. Thus, you will benefit right away from the lower rates you can get because of your corrective steps. You'll also eliminate the danger of later cancellation for the hazard you did not correct.

WHO IS INSURED? Unless stated otherwise, the insured must be the sole owner. If husband and wife own property jointly and only the husband is named on the policy, the company will pay only half the loss. It considers that the husband owns only half the property.

The manager (if he isn't also the owner) should be named as an additional insured on policies covering workmen's compensation, liability, non-owner auto, and dram shop or host insurance. In this way, both owner and manager are protected if there should be a damage suit.

Lending institutions must be listed as still another insured party, to the extent of the mortgage on policies covering fire, extended coverage, vandalism, and malicious mischief, rent loss, or anything else that may harm their collateral, the mortgaged property.

Fairly complete insurance coverage on your properties can be surprisingly cheap, if your brokers shop around. Make sure that one of them gets a bid from State Farm; its Apartment Owner's Policy is said by some owners to be the best and most complete buy they've found. "The cost runs less than the cost of garbage service alone," writes Leigh Robinson in his *Landlording* manual.

PROPERTY TAXES

THE LARGEST SINGLE COST in operating the average apartment house is the property tax bill. And it is spiralling. In 1961, $18 billion in local property taxes were paid throughout the U.S. Ten years later, that sum had soared to $40 billion. By 1976, it was more than $58 billion. It's a rare community where property taxes haven't doubled during the past decade, and in some cities, they've tripled and quadrupled. Millions of Americans now pay a bigger tax on their property than on their incomes.

The property tax is assessed according to the estimated "current market value" of your property, including all improvements. Since improvements are included in assessed value, many urban owners are discouraged from fixing up their property, and occupants suffer. Also, high property taxes frighten away industry and homeowners, which means that the local tax base keeps shrinking.

So, there are good arguments for clamping down on this fast-rising tax. Some two thousand organized citizens' groups are vigorously bringing these arguments to the attention of the authorities. Faced with voter resistance on one hand and swiftly rising expenses on the other, some local governments are on the verge of financial collapse.

Special commissions at almost every level of government are trying hard to find better ways of balancing municipal budgets. Property tax relief may be on the way.

But don't wait for it to arrive. If you do, you may wind up paying more than your share of your community's costs for years to come. There is a saying, "You can't fight City Hall," but you certainly can fight, and win, when it comes to the assessment of your property.

Exorbitant and unjust assessments are widespread. Commercial and industrial property owners are now challenging property tax assessments as a matter of routine, and are winning repeatedly in the courts. That shifts more of the local tax load onto owners of homes and apartments, unless they too challenge their assessments.

UPSETTING ASSESSMENTS begins with finding out when and where you can see the assessment roll, and what the cutoff day is. After the day, the assessment is frozen for the current tax year, so you'll want to make preparations as far ahead of it as you can.

You prepare by checking a few comparable properties. Get addresses of several apartment houses in your community that are as much like yours as possible. Check with the owners or managers about taxes. They'll probably tell you (indignantly or sadly) what their assessments are. If yours are higher than theirs, you're on the right track. Look up additional buildings like yours. You'll want to show that your property is rated higher than typical apartment buildings in your taxing area.

Even if you find that your assessment is lower than comparable ones, go to the assessor's office. The average assessor is a part-time, poorly paid official with no training for his job, and little time to acquire training once he's in office. He may be so busy that instead of trying to inspect property, he'll just drive past and make "windshield assessments." Some don't even do this much; they simply copy onto the new tax roll the property value as listed on the old roll. But don't assume that they're your enemies. Be polite and friendly.

IN THE ASSESSOR'S OFFICE, start by checking the property record card on your own building for errors. Descriptions, measurements, or arithmetic may be off. Compare the measurements with your deed, abstract, or engineer's survey. You can do it in minutes. You have a legal right to whatever information was used in arriving at your assessment, and you shouldn't have any trouble getting it.

Next, ask to see the records on the other buildings you've chosen. This may be harder. Some communities try to limit access to these cards. But by insisting or by going to higher authority, you should be able to get a look.

Make sheets comparing your property with others like it. Note such data as the grade assigned each building, square foot cost, depreciation allowed, and land valuation per front foot.

If you don't like what you find, the first step in filing for a reassessment is simply talking to the assessor. He may change the assessment, especially if you've uncovered a glaring blunder. He may not want higher authorities to hear about the mistake.

IF YOU GET NOWHERE WITH THE ASSESSOR, the next step is appealing to the local assessment review board. Usually, this just means filling out a form; the assessor will explain the procedure. You can get expert help from lawyers or firms that specialize in appealing property assessments, but you might do quite well on your own. Something like four of every five appeals to a board of review result in reduced property taxes. Be thorough but brief, stay calm, and know what the proper assessment should be. It's good strategy to use charts and maps in making your case.

IF THE REVIEW BOARD SAYS NO, your state may have a tax appeals division to which you can carry the fight. You can ask in writing for a review of your case;

application forms will be available at the assessor's office, and his staff will help you fill it out.

AS A LAST RESORT, you can pay your taxes under protest, and take your local government to court. At this point, you'll need help from an experienced attorney.

Two excellent recent books on this subject are *You Can Get Your Real Estate Taxes Reduced,* by Ronald E. Gettel (McGraw-Hill), and *Lower Your Real Estate Taxes,* by Robert G. Jonson (Walker).

HOW TO MINIMIZE UTILITY COSTS

Gas, electric, fuel, water, rubbish, and occasionally sewer tax, are classified as utility expenses. They average about 8% to 10% of the total scheduled rents, but can be kept lower in your property if the manager watches them carefully.

Some utility expenses are fixed (garbage collection and sewer tax, for example), while others are variable. Obviously, you're better off to pay the fixed expenses, if you have a choice, and have your occupants pay the variable ones, so they'll be careful about holding them down. You may be bound by law or local custom, but try to avoid renting on a "utilities included" basis.

If you're paying any utilities for occupants, make sure the billing doesn't start any earlier than an occupant's lease date or move-in date. Have the new resident sign the utility application and turn-on card when he signs the lease. Otherwise, you may be billed for an unoccupied unit.

Your bill will probably be for a smaller "net" amount if paid in 10 days, or a larger "gross" if payment is any later. This is the way utility companies bill apartment houses in most parts of the country. Obviously, you should pay promptly enough to take the discount. But you may be able to persuade a company to extend your net period to 15 or even 30 days, if you're a big enough utility customer.

Garbage and trash collection is done by municipal services in some areas, and the property owner is legally obliged to pay for it. If not, you're probably better off paying anyhow because this means that the garbage will be picked up and the property will be kept clean. You control the garbage area if you pay. Otherwise, there'll be disputes about the invasion of one resident's garbage can by someone else's. The first resident may dump it out, and then begins the great garbage war.

PUT ALL RESIDENTS ON SEPARATE METERS if you possibly can, especially for the heating bills. With one boiler for the whole building, its meter dial may spin faster than a moon rocket's altimeter if just one apartment isn't getting adequate heat; you'll have to turn the controlling thermostat up to 80 degrees to keep that one family from freezing, whereupon other units will keep the windows open night and day to avoid being heated like a crematorium.

Maybe each unit has its own separate gas meter for stove and water heater. If so, you can install new direct-vent heaters in every apartment, and connect them to the individual meters. The heaters will pay for themselves in utility bill savings.

ELECTRICITY is the most expensive form of energy. Obviously, you can make some savings by reducing the amount of lighting in the corridors and outdoor areas of your property. Lighting specialists often recommend levels of illumination that are wastefully high.

The wattage of a bulb doesn't measure how much light it gives, but how much energy is needed to light it. Light is measured in lumens, which are marked on the bulb package. Read these packages carefully to buy the most light for the same wattage.

You'll be surprised to learn, for example, that a 100-watt bulb gives much more light than four 25-watt bulbs. Replacing two 60-watters with one 100-watt lamp will provide the same illumination for 12% less energy.

You'll also learn that fluorescent lighting is less expensive, watt-for-watt or lumen-for-lumen, than incandescent bulbs. Fluorescent lamps give five times the light and last up to 30 times as long as ordinary bulbs. They're cooler, too. One big property owner saved 63% in kilowatt usage by converting the basement garage to fluorescent lighting.

If you have parallel rows of fluorescent tubing, taking out one of every four lamps can give you a small saving. If corridor lighting fixtures are spaced too close together, maybe you should disconnnect some.

YOU CAN SAVE ON OUTDOOR LIGHTING by using the newest types of sodium vapor lamps which give 180 lumens per watt — as compared to incandescent bulbs which give 20 lumens or less per watt, and fluorescent tubes which put out about 60 lumens per watt.

Another simple way to save is by using the common photoelectric cell. This low-cost device turns off the outdoor lights at dawn, instead of waiting for someone to get around to it later.

ELECTRIC HEATING AND COOLING are your greatest users of energy. And this is where you can make your biggest savings. Your maintenance people probably know just what should be done. They know where the trouble spots are, where heat is leaking out, where drafts come in. If you ask them to report all chances for savings, they'll be glad to make valuable suggestions.

If you have heating units in the lobbies and public halls, consider cutting down their output. Maybe you don't need to keep these areas as warm as they are, especially between midnight and morning. If you use building exhaust fans for ventilation, they can be turned off during the night, preferably by an automatic clock that will restart them at the appointed hour.

Don't put thermostats where the temperature fluctuates, such as near an entrance to the building. Don't put them near a window where sunlight warms the air, or where cold drafts could trigger them. Don't put a large piece of furniture immediately in front of a thermostat, nor a TV set anywhere near it.

To start the heating system, set the thermostat at the temperature you want to maintain; Edison recommends 68 degrees. During the late night hours, the thermostat can be set at five or ten degrees lower and nobody will notice.

Unless you live in a mild climate, heating will be your second largest expense, surpassed only by taxes. In most buildings, a bundle of money goes up in smoke needlessly, because a heating system can lose one-fifth of its efficiency merely through poor adjustment.

For example, forced air systems usually include filters that get clogged, thereby reducing the amount of heat that somes through. Some manager aren't even aware that their heating plants have filters, so residents turn the heat too high and still don't feel warm enough. If you're not sure about your own system, take a look. Somewhere in the equipment, usually near the base, you'll see a wide slot. It contains a slide filled with fiberglass or metal mesh. If you can't see through it while holding it up to a bright light, it needs changing.

You should check this filter monthly and clean or replace it as needed. Otherwise, the furnace will work longer and harder trying to satisfy the thermostat. A draft gauge, either fixed or portable, is a good investment, because it tells your maintenance man when to change a filter.

248

If you burn gas as a fuel, make sure the control is correctly set. The burner's efficiency depends on air and fuel being mixed in correct proportion. The setting can be quickly adjusted by a furnace repairman or by the utility company service man who may do it without charge.

Oil burners are more complicated. Not only must air and fuel be mixed properly, but valves and screens must be kept clean. Periodic cleaning and adjusting by a professional are needed to keep them working economically.

If you have electric furnaces, the dirty filter problem is worse. As the filters collect dirt, they cut down the air flow — which causes the electric coils to overheat and burn out quickly. Solid state thermostats are available for modulating the output of these heaters, but they may cost more than they're worth in savings. A better bet may be an outdoor thermostat which cuts off the combustion when outside temperature rises above 60 degrees.

YOUR BOILER ROOM, if you have one, is a place where you can make quick and substantial savings. If you are getting the usual 65% combustion efficiency, and it is boosted to 78%, you increase efficiency one-fourth, and you'll use 16% less fuel per season.

To get the efficiency up, have a competent service man check and adjust the combustion equipment. This must be done with instruments. If he says he can do it by eye, show him the door and call the company. They'll send someone to do the job right.

Many apartment buildings have a much bigger heating unit than they need, with the firing rate set at maximum. If you've been getting through cold spells with no complaints about chilly rooms or insufficient hot water, you may have more capacity than you need. Ask the service man to reduce the firing rate 10% or 15% as a brief experiment. If there still are no complaints, you can keep the setting. Of course, you do have to be careful not to short-change the apartments' hot water because people notice this immediately.

DOMESTIC HOT WATER temperature is usually set at 140 degrees — but that's too hot for use at the faucet. Unless you lose a lot of heat from long runs of uninsulated water piping, you'll do better to have the water available at 120. Just adjust the mixing valve.

The laundry rooms may not need hot water. Some owners are notifying residents that the washing machines will use only cold water and that cold water detergents are available.

Do you have a large storage tank for domestic hot water? Is it insulated? If not, you're wasting scads of heat.

Hot water pipes are more costly if they're exposed to cold air because they lose heat. Insulating these pipes will save money in the long run.

IF WATER CONSERVATION IS IMPORTANT in your area (as it has been lately in most of the country), here are some possibilities to consider:

— Install pressure-reducing valves in showers. Install water-saving devices in toilet tanks.

— Act immediately on all reports of leaky plumbing. A small drip can waste 50 gallons a day, but an inexpensive washer can usually stop it.

— Ask residents not to run the hose while washing their cars. A car can be soaped down from a pail of soapy water and the hose is needed only to rinse it.

— Don't let children play with the hose and sprinklers.

— Turn off or remove faucet handles from outside taps.

— Select efficient laundry appliances that save on water.

— Place sprinklers so that water lands only on the lawn or garden, not in areas where it does no good.

— Use a broom instead of a hose to clean driveways, walks, and steps.

— Prune the landscaping so less watering will be needed. Put a layer of mulch around trees and plants to slow the evaporation of moisture. Make sure that new plantings are drought-resistant trees and shrubs that thrive without irrigation.

A GUIDE TO INSULATION

Even when your heating systems are in perfect order, apartments still may be chilly — and running up high heating bills — if there are cracks that let the air leak through. You may need insulation, weatherstripping, and/or storm sashes.

No doubt you know that insulation is a hot subject, now that the energy shortage makes it important to conserve power used in heating or cooling. In 1977 Congress passed tax deductions for the cost of adding insulation to older buildings that give a 15% credit to homeowners and renters.

YOU CAN'T HAVE TOO MUCH insulation in apartment houses with electric heating systems or with air conditioning. Many experts now say to put in as much as you can, no matter what the climate.

Of the heat lost from apartments in winter, or gained in summer, roughly one-third passes through the ceiling and about 70% through walls, glass areas, floors, cracks around doors and windows, and through ventilation. Insulation can seal in nearly all heat escaping through the ceiling, and almost two-thirds of the loss through walls.

AREAS THAT SHOULD BE INSULATED are ceilings, if there are cold spaces above, and walls between an apartment and an unheated garage or storage space.

Residential buildings constructed before 1950 aren't likely to be well insulated. You can test by feeling for drafts around windows and doors; weatherstripping can keep out those drafts. This caulking can more than repay its cost if heating bills have been high in your building.

You may be able to see for yourself whether there is insulation in the floor over an unheated basement. As for walls, you can test them in very cold weather when the heat is on by feeling the inside of an outer wall; then immediately feeling an interior wall. One shouldn't feel much colder than the other. Another test is to hang two thermometers in an apartment, one in the center of a room and the other on a wall adjoining the outside. After four hours, the temperature difference should be no more than five degrees.

Large windows are where the greatest heat loss occurs; the icy glass even sucks body heat away from people in the room. Drapes can add some insulation to the window surface. You can suggest that residents keep draperies closed at night and on cold overcast days. On sunny days, take advantage of solar heat by leaving the draperies open when the sun shines directly on the window.

YOU'LL BENEFIT from adequate insulation and weatherstripping in at least four ways:

— Fuel bills will be lower. In fact, you'll probably cut heating costs between 35% and 45%. Your heating and cooling equipment should last longer because they won't have to work as hard. When it comes time to replace them, you can install smaller and more economical equipment in a properly insulated building.

— Everyone in the building will be more comfortable all year round. Insulation keeps heat in or out, depending on the season. It also eliminates winter drafts created by cooler air creeping down the walls as heated air rises in the rooms.

— The building will get certain side benefits. Warm walls attract less dust and dirt then cold surfaces. Insulation helps with soundproofing, and may be a barrier to fire.

— You'll be helping conserve energy resources — electricity, fuel, oil, natural gas, coal — that are becoming scarce. Cutting down on fuel consumption also lessens air pollution.

ADDING INSULATION to accessible areas like ceilings, floors, and bare basement walls is fairly easy, and so is weatherstripping and installing storm windows and doors.

However, adding insulation to existing walls is difficult because they are probably webbed with electric cable and perhaps pipes. The job can be done by blowing loose-fill insulation into the walls through holes drilled from the outside of the building.

A good insulation job depends as much on good workmanship as on good materials. So don't try to do it yourself unless you understand what you're doing. If you do tackle the job, be sure to follow the manufacturer's instructions carefully. If you bring in an insulation contractor, choose him with care.

The costs will depend on the job. Insulation material may cost from $5 to $10 per hundred square feet of space to be covered, or $14 to $28 for plastic foam. The cost will be doubled if a contractor installs it. Loose-fill blown into existing walls costs about $16 to $28 per hundred square feet installed.

AIR CONDITIONING

If your building uses air conditioning, you'll save even more by insulation and weatherstripping. But the cooling equipment itself may be a bigger factor.

WINDOW AIR CONDITIONERS of the smaller sizes sometimes do a better job than the larger models — which aren't necessarily the best just because they're bigger.

The effectiveness depends mostly on dehumidifying the air, not just cooling it. A good window conditioner will suck from two to nine pints of water out of the air every hour. But if it's too big for the room, it pulls the temperature down quickly and must be shut off before it dries out much of the humidity. The result: a damp, and uncomfortable room. The occupants usually overwork the air conditioner, trying to get "cool."

"HEAT GAIN" IS THE KEY to figuring the best size of conditioner for the area you're cooling; the equipment should be big enough to remove this much heat. A good appliance dealer will calculate the heat gain for you. But a slipshod dealer will just recommend the biggest (and most expensive) conditioner he thinks he can sell you. If you prefer to do your own figuring, get a form for calculating heat gain by sending a stamped, self-addressed envelope to the Association of Home Appliance Manufacturers, 20 North Wacker Drive, Chicago 60606.

In the case of larger air conditioning systems, the operating costs may be more important than the purchase price. In an era of energy shortages, a conditioner that is a glutton for electricity is no bargain at any price. Several states and cities now require energy labels on air conditioners.

HOW TO GET GOOD SERVICE FROM CONTRACTORS

Once you graduate from the do-it-yourself role as all-around handyman for your building, you'll use contractors more and more. The larger the building, the more often you need reliable contractors on call for major hurry-up jobs of plumbing, painting, carpentry, roofing and the like. You'll also need specialized contractors for occasional problems with the swimming pool, elevators, landscaping, electrical wiring, and whatever other facilities are part of the property.

The main point is that arrangements for emergency services must be made before you need them. Line up the specialists and keep their phone numbers handy. Their rates must be known in advance — at least approximately — so that their bills will be promptly approved and paid. If contractors get the idea you're slow pay, they'll be slow to help you.

Electricians and plumbers usually charge extra for parts. Go out and price these parts at your local supply house or hardware store to see that your supplier isn't overcharging for these items.

CHECK UP ON ANY CONTRACTOR before you arrange for him to be on call for emergency service, as well as before engaging him for major work. This business has more than its share of mediocrity and unreliability. Ask to see other work a contractor has done, and ask the owners if they were satisfied. Ask for a bank reference. Ask the contractors' association and the local apartment association. Ask the real estate board.

Does the prospective contractor have a license or permit if one is customary? When you see it, you can feel easier because he must guarantee most of his work for at least a year in order to keep his license.

Is he bonded, so that a bonding company will have another contractor complete his job if necessary? If he can readily furnish a bond, you probably don't need one. If he can't get a bond, better not use him.

KEEP TWO OR THREE ALTERNATIVE CONTRACTORS on call for small rush jobs, so that if one can't come immediately you can call others. Watch for ads in the classified section of the newspaper, placed by people who solicit work you may need. For fairly small jobs, there are often "moonlighters" who, because of limited overhead, are willing to charge less for their work. But some may be unwilling to stand behind a job, so you'd better get references from previous customers.

AVOIDING OVERCHARGES on contract jobs is a matter of putting them out for competitive bids. Include blueprints or a sketch if possible, and make the specifications as precise as you can so that the contractors will be bidding on the same work. Contractors like to know answers to questions like, "How many coats of paint and what brand? . . . For how long do you want the work guaranteed?. . . How close do you want the studs, 16″ or 24″?"

Maybe you don't know enough to be that specific. If not, begin by asking one contractor to look over the premises and make his own suggestions about spacing the studs, or whatever. Using his ideas on how the job can best be handled, he can give you a written estimate.

Then you can make photostatic copies of his estimate and mail them to other firms who specialize in the same kind of work, asking for their bids on the same job. Every bid you get back will be lower than the original one, unless some contractors recommend doing the job in a distinctly different way. Their differing advice will help educate you.

You can educate yourself further by telling the unsuccessful bidders that a certain contractor has underbid them. "Do you know anything about his work?" you can ask them. Sometimes they may shrug and say, "He's a good man. I don't understand how he could bid so low." Other times, some may say, "Naturally he could bid low because he always thins his paint," or "He skins his roofs." This may be just sour grapes. But if someone can tell you locations where the alleged shoddy work was done, you can check up.

If a low-bidding contractor is from another town, and nobody knows much about him, beware. He could be a fly-by-night swindler who will take your money and run. Checking his references is essential.

On the other hand, a good contractor may underbid the others simply because he has a slack period and wants to keep his crew working. Or he may be a young man just getting started and doing much of the labor himself. Or he may use efficient labor-saving techniques that are banned by union workmen or other contractors: spray painting, for example. Some unions insist on laboriously installing flooring or wallboard in small segments, even when it is manufactured in eight foot panels.

AFTER YOU CHOOSE A CONTRACTOR, put all details of your agreement with him in writing. Maybe he will come prepared with a paper for you to sign. Whether it is printed or typed, whether it is headed ORDER BLANK or STANDARD AGREEMENT, or is scribbled on wrapping paper, be sure to read each word. And be sure you understand it before you sign. It just might contain a little trap — responsibility for damage done to the property, for example, or responsibility for paying debts incurred by the contractor — which could cost you dearly.

Instead of signing his paper, you're almost always safer to use a printed form of your own — such as the purchase order shown on the following page, with limiting clauses as shown on the bottom half of the next page. The clauses about insurance protection are particularly important. For your own protection, always make sure that your contractors are properly insured.

TERMS OF PAYMENT should be specified in writing. Some artisans want part payment in advance. No sane manager puts out money until he knows the quality of the work. If a contractor insists, "I need cash in advance to buy materials for this," it tells you something about him. If he can't fund himself sufficiently to buy materials, is he solid enough to undertake your contract?

Payments should be scheduled so that there is always more work completed than you are paying for — say, 40% of the price when the job is half done. Otherwise, some contractors will leave you dangling with a not-quite-finished job while they concentrate on easier or more profitable work.

The agreement should include a work schedule, showing when the job is to be started and finished, with stated penalties for late completion. Such clauses don't mean that you're afraid the contractor won't perform as promised. They simply impress on him the importance of living up to his commitments, and give him incentives to do so. Some contractors, being human, aren't good at managing their time, and tend to be too optimistic about how fast they'll work. A strict contract is a good taskmaster.

Don't sign "cost plus" contracts; they can be a shortcut to bankruptcy. The agreement should hold the contractor to his bid, but provide for cost adjustments if he uses lower-price substitute materials — which he shouldn't be allowed to do without written consent.

YOU MUST CHECK ON WORK AS IT PROGRESSES, despite the written timetable and specifications. Contractors can make mistakes. Every big property

PURCHASE ORDER

NO.   Req. No. _____ Date _____ , 19 ___

TO _____

ADDRESS _____

SHIP TO _____

ADDRESS _____

For		Date Required	How Ship		Terms	
	Quantity	Please Supply Items Listed Below		Price		Unit
1						
2						
3						
4						
5						
6						

IMPORTANT — Our order number must appear on all invoices, packages, etc. Please notify us immediately if you are unable to ship complete order by date specified.

Please Send _____ Copies of Your Invoice

_____ Purchasing Agent

Original

Clauses — Reverse Side of Purchase Order

1. All materials furnished or used under this order shall be new and of the best quality except where otherwise specified.

2. All work under this order shall be done in a workmanlike and substantial manner.

3. That the person, firm or corporation doing work under this order shall furnish skilled workmen and provide all materials, labor, tools, equipment, power, light and heat, together with permits from public authorities and other things necessary for said work.

4. That the said person, firm or corporation shall not be relieved of any responsibility for faulty materials or workmanship by acceptance or, nor by payment for, the work or materials; but he shall remedy any and all defects and pay for any damage to the work resulting from such defects, or the removal or replacement, appearing within one year from the completion of said work, unless separate guarantee shall exceed such period of time.

5. That the same person, firm or corporation shall maintain such insurance as will protect him, the Owner and Agent herein for claims for damage to the property or for personal injury, including death, and including workmen's compensation claims that may arise from operations under this order, whether by himself or any subcontractor or any other person directly or indirectly employed by either of them; and that said person, firm or corporation shall furnish a certificate signed by the issuing company, of the issuance of each policy and date, giving the policy number, the name and address of the party protected, description of work covered, limit of policy and date of expiration, with a further pledge from said insurance company not to change, cancel or terminate such policy without fifteen (15) days' written notice to the Owner or Agent.

Issue all bills in triplicate
Make no changes in price, terms, quantity, quality or delivery without our written consent.

manager has had painful surprises: workmen have installed furnaces in the wrong building, or painted the wrong apartment. But such experiences aren't costly for a good manager because his agreement with any contractor states exactly where the work is to be done. Thus, an erring contractor gets no money until he corrects his errors. Sometimes this means that a manager gets an extra furnace or paint job free.

Even when the job is complete, your agreement should enable you to hold back 10% or 20% of the money while you see whether additional service turns out to be necessary. The contractor will come back faster if you still owe him money. The agreement should require him to remove all debris and leave the premises "broom clean" when his work is done.

There is also a risk that your contractor may not have paid his own suppliers or subcontractors. They can file a lien on your property if he owes them, even though you paid him the full amount of his bill. A lien enables the holder to start foreclosure proceedings on your property if you don't settle his claim.

To keep yourself lien-proof, never pay the contractor's full amount until required inspections have been made, and until the statutory lien period has expired (unless your man is thoroughly reputable). This period ranges from 30 to 90 days in various states.

EVEN IF YOU'RE FLUSH WITH CASH, TRY TO GET A CONSTRUCTION LOAN from a bank or some other lending agency to cover building or remodeling work. By paying the financing cost, you get a lot of benefits. Most lenders do the checking up that you'd otherwise have to handle. They will verify the contractor's reliability, approve the plans, inspect work as it progresses, hold back payment until the work is satisfactorily completed, and make sure that subcontractors and suppliers have been paid before making final payments.

YOU CAN BE A THRIFTY BUYER

PURCHASING AGENTS are part of any major apartment complex because buying can be encyclopedic in its ramifications. It's a full-time job to find suppliers who will give good value (not necessarily the lowest price), service as fast as you need it, and an honest bill.

But you need to be alert against possibilities that your purchasing agent himself may take bribes or kickbacks. Here's what to watch for.

SIGNALS OF POSSIBLE DISHONESTY in a purchasing agent:

— The buyer takes no vacation. He may fear that a pinch-hitter would discover what he is up to.

— The list of suppliers and vendors never changes. Most firms change one-fifth to one-quarter of their suppliers every year.

— The life-style of a buyer is better than you'd expect from his salary.

— He makes buying decisions with little or no assistance from superiors or from technical staff people.

— Major purchases are split into small and misleading elements, such as add-ons and changes, instead of being bought with one order.

— Salesmen complain to management that they can't get an appointment with the buyer.

IF YOU DO YOUR OWN PURCHASING, try to pick suppliers who specialize in serving apartment buildings. Ordinary retailers aren't aware of your problems, and work on larger mark-ups. This is true of service organizations, too; the casual repairman charges more and gives poorer service than apartment specialists.

TIMELY BUYING can save money. If any of your apartments will need furniture, linens, carpets, drapes, refrigerators or whatever, you should find out where and when to buy. Prices vary widely between one supplier and another, or from one month to another. Retailers' traditional off-season sales will enable you to make savings by planning your buys. The trick is to know when to expect a sale on each kind of item.

For example, if you buy towels, sheets, or table linens, you'll pay more in any month except January or August, when these items are marked down in the traditional "white sales."

Conversely, if you foresee a need for new tableware, you'll do best by buying in early fall. Stores offer discounts on this merchandise in September or October.

Merchants follow a fairly standard schedule for their "promotions," some of which are sales. Here is a list of various apartment needs, together with the months in which they are likely to be sold at bargain prices:

Air conditioners	July
Appliances	January
Bedding and blankets	February and November
China and glassware	February or March
Cleaning supplies (waxes, mops, scrapers and the like)	April or May
Furniture	February, June or July
Garden Supplies	July or August
Housewares	March and September
Lawn mowers	August
Lumber	June
Mattresses	February
Paints	April
Refrigerators	June
Rug cleaning	June
Sprinklers	August
Storm windows	June
Table linens	January or August
Yard tools	August

CARPETING PURCHASES must be shopped for more carefully than most any other items in your building. Genuine sales are rather rare because styles don't change much and there's no special buying season. Quality department and furniture stores do advertise sales, but these are usually to get rid of odd lengths or ugly colors. You'll see carpet sales advertised every few weeks by stores that specialize in carpeting, but you should be skeptical of the supposedly rock-bottom bargains they proclaim. Rug dealers are shrewd.

Sometimes you find really good buys at places that specialize in cleaning (not selling) carpets. For some strange reason, many people who send rugs out for cleaning never get around to claiming them. Big cleaning establishments may advertise lists of unclaimed items from time to time, but you needn't wait for their ads. Just phone and ask what they have for sale.

FURNITURE can often be bought at big savings. Reputable furniture and department stores generally carry quality furniture, and they have seasonal clearance sales. By watching for the best stores' genuine sales, you can save 15% to 30%. In fact, you may be able to bargain your way to still better prices, even on quality items. If you've shopped the market and can honestly say, "I can buy this same furniture for $50 less from Thrifty Furnishings if I wait six weeks for delivery," you'll be surprised how often a haughty salesman will cut prices to meet competition.

Even better buys can be found in used furniture. The better auction houses dispose of high-grade furniture for a fraction of the original price. The classified pages of newspapers list householders' sales of good furniture at very low prices. However, you should know prices and quality before buying. Some people make a living by filling their houses or apartments with shoddy furniture during the week and unloading it via Sunday want ads, pretending that they must move to another city.

Be careful, too, when you step into a store that advertises a "distress sale." Some merchandisers buy schlock furniture from a factory that can churn it out during slack periods. They call it a "special purchase" or "fire sale;" then advertise so powerfully that they jam the store with people fighting to buy junk at top prices. On the other hand, the merchandise may be truly distressed — a bankruptcy liquidation, perhaps. You need to know furniture values to tell the difference.

A whole class of furniture dealers passes out "discount cards" to sucker lists. Card-holders think they can sneak in the back door, figuratively speaking, and buy at near-wholesale prices. It's usually a con game.

So are most "going out of business" sales. Once in a blue moon, you'll find big bargains at such a sale. More often, the furniture will later prove flimsy. If it does, the store may have closed its doors by the time you go back — or may simply tell you, "All sales are final. No returns permitted. That was stated in our advertising." A sly merchant, knowing months ahead that he's quitting business, may build up his inventory with cheap stuff for that final rip-off.

There is still another class of furniture dealers — good dealers who never never advertise, and who display hardly anything in their showrooms. They sell in quantity to purchasing agents of hotel chains and other large companies. Because of their low overhead, they sell at prices significantly lower than retail. If some friendly purchasing agent will give you a telephone introduction to such a dealer, you may have found the best way to buy.

BUYING AT GOOD DISCOUNTS may also be possible through your local apartment house association, or a regional association. Most of the big ones publish monthly magazines or newsletters, carrying ads by major manufacturers and wholesalers who give discounts to apartment owners. If there is no such publication in your area, check with the association anyway. Manufacturers like General Electric, Westinghouse, Frigidaire, Wedgwood, and others give substantial discounts to accredited Lowry/Nickerson association members. (For information on real estate seminars and creative financing, contact: Education Advancement Institute, 50 Washington Street, Reno, Nevada 89503, or call ((toll free)) 800-648-5955.)

REMEMBER THESE BASIC POINTS:

* *Buy insurance by comparative shopping. Look for policies with the fewest exclusions. Deal through an independent insurance agent if you can.*

* *Make sure you understand the co-insurance penalty. Have your broker keep checking to make sure you're not under-insured as costs rise.*

* *Have your policies written so they'll pay for actual replacement cost, without deduction for depreciation. Insist on inspection of the premises by insurance inspectors.*

* *If your property tax seems too high, ask for a review.*

* *Put all residents on separate utility meters if you can.*

* *Have your maintenance people look for ways to save on electricity.*

* *Adjust mixing valves so hot water runs at 120 degrees, not higher.*

* *Put in as much insulation as you can.*

* *Check the operating cost of an air conditioner; this is more important than the purchase price.*

* *Line up contractors in advance for emergency services.*

* *Get competitive bids on contract jobs. Put all details in writing. Check on the work as it progresses.*

* *If you use a purchasing agent, be alert for signs of kickbacks.*

* *Find out the best times and places to buy various furnishings and accessories.*

XVI   *Keeping Down Upkeep*

"After an apartment is rented, I spend as little on it as possible until it's vacant again," an owner said. "I hold maintenance expenses down to small change. This gives me a supply of reserve cash for prettying up an apartment when I need to re-rent it."

Is he smart? Not if he wants to be making money in six months or a year. He's taking a slow cruise into red ink.

By ignoring small upkeep jobs until they become big emergencies, he is condemning himself to spend much more money within a year, when he'll have to patch up the havoc and put apartments back into rentable condition.

Long before then, he'll feel the residents' resentment. Neglected maintenance makes people mad. They slam things around in the building, grumble to neighbors, and soon move out — vengefully taking every light bulb and loose fixture they can carry, and leaving their apartments as messy as you wouldn't believe. So the owner is plagued by vacancies, by bills for cleaning and repairs and replacements. Also, he takes in less rent because he has to reduce his rates in order to get the apartments rented. As rougher-type people move in, they abuse his apartments even more. It becomes a vicious circle.

Worst of all, this stupid owner will take a terrible loss when he finally has to sell the building. It's lower rental income is cutting down its re-sale value, and so is its delapidation. Any prospective buyer will take note of the costs of fixing it up, and subtract these from his offering price.

All this is an old story. Blind owners and lazy managers are found everywhere, and they bleed properties bankrupt. One banker wrote, "Recently I had a buyer who reduced his offer on an apartment building from $550,000 to $475,000 due to lack of attention by the janitor and minor deferred maintenance in the rear hallways. What a price to pay for negligence."

FOR WANT OF A WASHER, A RESIDENT MAY BE LOST. Studies show that "unsatisfactory maintenance" is the most common reason given by residents who move out. According to one survey of 2,000 properties, the owners of poorly-maintained buildings averaged 9% loss of rental income through vacancies.

You wouldn't be reading this book if you weren't a serious student of the apartment business. (For additional information on real estate investment, see *How You Can Become Financially Independent By Investing In Real Estate*, by Albert J. Lowry, Ph.D., published by Simon & Schuster.) As such, you probably don't need statistics to convince you that proper upkeep is essential. Your knowledge of human nature should be enough. How long would *you* live in an apartment where a broken window wasn't replaced? Or where the oven wouldn't work properly because a temperature dial was missing? Or nothing was done about a leaky shower stall?

Occupants who expect reasonable comfort and convenience soon forsake any owner or manager who is penny wise and pound foolish, or who neglects upkeep for other reasons. A badly managed building ends up with tenants who don't mind living in a dump.

Early in this book, throughout Chapters 2 and 3, you saw the importance of responding quickly to requests and complaints from residents in order to keep them happy. There's no need to review the principle further, but we might add that you can do a little more than respond quickly. You can actually *encourage* occupants to ask for maintenance work as soon as they see the need. Some long-term residents hesitate to ask for service. One way to encourage them is to provide a handy supply of Maintenance Request blanks like the following, to be slipped under the manager's door at any time:

MAINTENANCE REQUEST
Bon-Ami Apartments
1116 Quagmire Street
LaBonza, California 91745

Apt. No. _____ Date _____

MAINTENANCE REQUIRED

_____
_____
_____

_____
Resident's Signature

This is good business as well as good psychology. It will actually save you money in the long run. We'll see why in the next few paragraphs.

DOING REPAIRS BEFORE YOU MUST will give you time to shop for the best materials, the best tradesmen, and the best prices. As an example, suppose a resident says a water heater isn't working well. This gives you an idea. You check all your water heaters, and you notice that three are damp underneath or show other symptoms of wearing out. You ask an expert to look at them, and he predicts that the three will have to be replaced within a few months.

You're in a good position. Buying three heaters at once, you can bargain for a better price than if you bought them singly. If you had let the heaters stay until one of them burst some night, forcing you to drag a plumber over to replace the heater under emergency conditions, you'd have had no choice but to pay whatever was demanded.

But wait! Look back at the records and see when the rest of the heaters were installed. Do you find that all 24 in the building were put in at the same time? Doesn't this tell you something? Heaters have a predictable lifespan. If three begin to go bad in one month, you can expect that others of the same age will shortly develop trouble. There's no need to buy 24 heaters immediately, but you'd better budget money for them (or make preliminary arrangements for a loan), and you'd better make inspections monthly to watch for signs of impending trouble. Probably you can make a package deal for all 24 heaters, to be installed and paid for as needed. Or maybe you can extend their life by installing a water treatment facility; ask a specialist.

In making any plumbing changes, you'll be wise to tackle them before serious trouble develops, so that you can pick a time that's best for you and the occupants.

It's better to shut down your whole building for one day, while you replace all the worn plumbing parts before they fail, than to shut down several times in emergencies, with no warning.

REPAIRS NEVER GET CHEAPER IF YOU WAIT. The longer the delay, the higher the risk of bigger costs and worse damage if something breaks down altogether. In fact, delay makes higher costs inevitable in some cases. For instance, if you re-coat a tar and gravel roof in its sixth or seventh year, the roof will last another seven years. But if you wait until the ninth year, the felt fibers will have rotted so badly that you'll be forced to get an entirely new roof.

Likewise, if a door lock is repaired soon after it begins to stick, the cost is minimal. If you do nothing, it can jam completely, whereupon a locksmith may have to pull it out (possibly at midnight, for a resident trapped on the wrong side) and install a new one.

GET READY IN ADVANCE

YOU CAN SIMPLIFY AND SYSTEMIZE repair operations by making preparations ahead of time. As soon as you take charge, go through the property and take note of all the appliances — built-in ovens, ranges, shower heads, air conditioners, even the plumbing fixtures. Write down the manufacturer's name and model number for each of them — not just the big appliances. The equipment you're seeking includes fans, motors, pumps, door checks, fire extinguishers, ventilators, and everything else that moves and needs maintenance. Someday you'll need to know whether the faucet is Repcal or Sterling, whether the toilet bowl is Standard, Western, or Olson. Identify each by name, its maker, and the model number. Generally, you'll find this information stamped or engraved right on the equipment.

Your next problem is to locate suppliers of parts for each appliance. This isn't easy. But it's easier if done at your leisure than if you have to solve the problem under pressure from impatient occupants.

Start by looking up the factory branch in the yellow pages of the phone book. Call and ask who in your area has the parts for the appliance.

Expect to be told that you can't get parts; the hardware stores don't carry them; the "authorized distributor" insists that the entire unit must be replaced. Or maybe the distributor has moved or gone out of business. Even for appliances only five or ten years old, many distributors say parts no longer exist because the model number is no longer manufactured. Every model more than ten years old is called obsolete.

Don't believe any of this. When you write or phone the factory, you'll learn otherwise. (Phoning is best and may not cost you anything. First, make up a list of all companies you need to call. Then dial 800-555-1212 to find out which companies have toll-free numbers. You'll find that nearly all do.)

Most manufacturers can give you the names of distributors who keep the parts in stock. If not, the manufacturers will supply the parts direct. In a company as huge as General Electric, a parts branch may claim that certain parts are no longer available, but if you go over the branch manager's head to his superior, you'll get those parts.

Joseph Schwartz, a do-it-yourself apartment owner who wrote an entertaining book about his experiences in managing property, told of writing to the Minneapolis Honeywell factory in search of a plastic cover for one of their thermostats:

"I was told locally by their factory distributors that I had to purchase the entire thermostat. I did not take that for an answer.

"I addressed my letter to the president of Minneapolis Honeywell. Not only did I receive two letters of apology and a long distance phone call, but I also received two plastic covers free of charge.

"Another similar instance: It was impossible to get a motor for a bathroom ventilating fan manufactured by one of the major companies. I went to the factory authorized distributor and was told I had to buy the complete unit for $26 for they did not sell motors separately. I had about twenty of these fans in the building, all of which would one day require new motors. Two of them had already burnt out, and the others would soon follow.

"I scoured the city's electric motor companies, even the rebuilt motor suppliers, but it was impossible. So I contacted the factory and was immediately handed a motor for $5.

"Because I knew that I would need more in the near future, I put in a supply of one dozen motors at the cost of approximately two complete units."

At the time you're in touch with manufacturers, ask about instruction booklets and maintenance information. Probably booklets came with the equipment but were lost long ago. Most companies will gladly send you more; they want their products to work well. Some manufacturers will even offer to train your employees in proper maintenance procedures.

Many breakdowns happen because equipment isn't maintained according to the manufacturer's instructions. Pumps may need periodic disassembly and cleaning. Fans and motors may require regular oiling. You can save trouble and money by setting up a permanent file that tells you all these things.

Millions of dollars are paid to repairmen, plumbers and electricians for service calls which aren't really necessary. If your furnace goes out, check the fuse box, circuit breakers, cut-off switches. Don't try to overhaul equipment you don't understand, but do everything short of that to diagnose the problem before you call a service specialist. He might be able to tell you over the telephone what you should do.

EMERGENCY PHONE NUMBERS should be where you can find them in a hurry. Duplicate lists in various handy places are best. Your list of numbers for major emergencies should include the gas company for gas leaks; the electric utility company for power line breaks; the police, fire department for fires and general rescue squad requirements, including a stalled elevator; an ambulance service; and the nearest hospital for medical emergencies.

Be sure your staff understands that these numbers are to be called in case of serious danger. Not every maintenance problem is a disaster. A service problem with a gas stove is more likely to be a job for an appliance repair shop than for the gas company's emergency crew.

For ordinary maintenance problems you might need to call:
- a company that can repair your elevators
- a swimming pool maintenance service
- a company that can repair your heating plant
- a company that can repair your air conditioners
- a plumbing contractor, able to handle anything up to cleaning a sewer
- an electrical contractor
- an appliance service company
- a locksmith
- a tree surgeon
- a sprinkler maintenance service

But it isn't enough just to have a list of numbers to call. When you need hurry-up help from any of the contractors and maintenance firms, you may not have much luck unless you've made advance arrangements with them, so there'll be no need for purchase orders, credit references or other paper work. A company seldom gives priority to a service request from a stranger. Get acquainted before you need to.

YOUR FIRST INSPECTION, if the building is more than five years old, will probably reveal that one air conditioner's grill is damaged, a kitchen has a burned Formica counter, an oven handle is missing, some lights are burnt out, a lamp post is leaning, and so on.

You may decide to ignore these faults as long as you can, in order to conserve cash. But deferred maintenance is always most costly. That leaning post can be straightened now for less cost than you'll pay later when it topples altogether. The other small items will keep irritating people — and maybe cause them to move — if you do nothing. But if you put them in condition immediately, you'll be a hero to the residents.

Sometimes a quick fix seems impossible. Maybe you'll be faced with such a ridiculous alternative as buying a new $200 oven because it lacks a temperature-calibrated knob worth $1.50. If the oven can't cook without that knob, the ridiculous alternative may be inescapable — unless you've prepared in advance by finding out that you can get the knob by going all the way to the factory in Alabama.

KEEP A SUPPLY OF SPARES (unless you know an inexpensive supplier near you) including at least these items:

ice cube tray	toilet seat
crisper	tank ball and rod
reflector pan for stove	ball cock
broiler pan	motor for ventilating fan
oven rack	garbage disposal
thermocouples	faucets
electric light bulbs	filters for heating and air
shower head	conditioning units

FAUCETS ARE THE MOST COMMON PROBLEM. Their washers and stem valves constantly need to be replaced. Lay in a supply of washers of the right sizes — especially the simple little rings (which are very thin washers, costing only pennies). Finding the source of these parts may take hours, but it will save you headaches later because you'll use the parts often to solve many plumbing problems.

Whenever you have to pull out an entire faucet because an irreplaceable part is missing, or because the whole faucet won't work, keep it. Later you may need its handle, stem escutcheon, spout or body for an identical faucet.

For the same reason, hold onto garbage disposals as they break down. When another comes in with a different broken part, combine parts and put together a reconstituted machine. When this is impossible, you're better off to buy a new garbage disposal than to try to repair an old one. The repairs often cost more than buying a new one.

DON'T GO IN FOR CANNIBALIZING as a widespread habit, however. That is, don't take parts from one apartment to repair another. When you do this, you double the work; you must take out both a working part and the defective part. Sooner or later, you'll have to replace the working part you took out. Then, too, a resident feels ill-treated when he sees used parts being installed. There's no need for cannibalization if you keep a stock of parts on hand or know where to get them quickly.

Any building as large as six units should have a supply of electric light bulbs, washers, o-rings, a new garbage disposal, and other items such as those listed a few paragraphs back. Not having the right parts and supplies means you'll be scrambling whenever something is broken or burned-out. And if you run out of 100-watt bulbs and start using 150-watt replacements, you'll make the place look spotty, and also need to snatch bulbs faster because of the heat build-up.

Try to balance your inventory so that you can take advantage of quantity discounts, yet won't be overstocked. A big supply always tempts petty thievery.

Figure what you'll need for the next few months and group your orders so a truck can deliver them, instead of wasting an employee's time on frequent jaunts to hardware stores and paint shops. Only the manager should authorize purchases. This will lessen the chances of employees buying too much, buying personal items, or getting kickbacks from suppliers.

Buy in bulk. This is another way of discouraging theft. Paint especially disappears fast, if you store it in one-gallon cans. Buy 15- or 30-gallon drums. Then you can pump or pour it off as needed into open pails — which thieves aren't likely to put into their car trunks. Some chemicals also can be bought in bulk and dispensed from smaller containers. But make sure they're not substances that will spoil before you use them.

Avoid chemicals in aerosol spray form. They're expensive and easy to steal. You can buy equally effective fluids in less costly dispensers. One widely-advertised household cleaner costs $59 if you buy enough to do as much cleaning as an industrial cleaner can do for $4.95.

MAKE A SCHEDULE

Just as you need regular check-ups by your doctor and dentist, just as your car needs an overhaul every five thousand miles, so does your apartment property need regularly scheduled inspection and upkeep. If you plan this systematically, most of your maintenance will be routine. You can do it faster —with fewer people, for less money — than if you "conserve cash" for emergencies. You'll avoid unpleasant surprises. And you'll lengthen the life of many components of the property.

In planning your maintenance schedule, use the file of manufacturers' instruction booklets mentioned earlier. This file should also tell you what items are protected by warranties. You can usually find the information in the companies' manuals — as well as on separate certificates, and perhaps on invoices. Apartment appliances, heating and air conditioning equipment, pumps, and the roof are generally guaranteed for definite lengths of time.

There are two reasons why you need these warranties, guarantees, insurance policies, service contracts and similar documents. One, if an item needs repair or replacement, and the supplier is committed to take care of this, you'd be wasteful to pay for it yourself. Two, some warranties provide that the company must do the servicing; if you fiddle with the equipment yourself, or let an unqualified serviceman do it, you may void the protection.

You've already gone through the premises and listed all mechanical equipment. Now, use this list to make up a year-long calendar showing just when each piece of equipment should be checked and overhauled. The instruction manuals will tell you what should be done and how often.

On this same calendar, indicate whether an item is still covered by a guarantee, because this is obviously crucial if you find something wrong during the overhaul. And, of course, if the guarantee stipulates that the manufacturer's people must perform the service — or if free servicing is available, as it is from many utility companies

— this should appear on the maintenance schedule. "Who" does the overhauling is as important as "what."

"When" can be important, too — not just the "how often" but what time of year. For example, all air conditioning units should be inspected and put into shape shortly before warm weather; you don't want a dozen breakdowns on the first hot day, when you won't be able to find a serviceman. Likewise, heating units should be checked in ample time for the first cold snap.

Many non-mechanical parts of the property belong on your maintenance calendar, too. Structural components go bad so gradually that you may not notice them until a crisis comes. At least twice a year, your calendar should call for inspection of these facilities.

THE ROOF, the most important part of the building. A neglected roof can cause trouble all the way down to the foundation. A leak may weaken an inside ceiling and wall, corrode plumbing, ruin a drape or carpet, wreak dangerous havoc in electrical systems, and maybe even cause shifting of the building structure.

When you inspect the roof, walk carefully so you won't scuff holes. Begin with a look at rooftop antennae to see if there are rusted or corroded turnbuckles, stays, or pole base plates. Sometimes you'll find a whole installation corroded or tearing loose.

Next, take a regular house broom and just sweep dirt away from suspected spots. If dirt has collected in places, they probably become puddles during a rainstorm. Other danger signals to look for are blisters, cracking, peeling, lifting, damaged or missing tiles, and evaporation rings that mark where a puddle dried.

Leaks are likely to develop wherever the roof surface joins something else: chimneys, skylights, air vents, fire walls, parapets, flashings. Over the years, heat and cold cause parts of a roof to expand and contract, which eventually brings wrinkling and splitting. If areas have been sealed with mastic, the mastic will pull away from walls and pipes, leaving cracks that water can run into. Most of these problems can be solved for another year or two by resealing with mastic.

The better a roof drains, the less likely it is to leak. Therefore, the downspouts, outlets and gutters should be cleaned twice a year. And if there are any broken brackets or rusted-through sections, these should be fixed before they become an emergency repair. Check the concrete splash blocks at the bottom, too; often they get dislocated, letting pools of water collect around the foundation.

If you see any roof surface that seems to need more than a small patch, your best bet is to call a roofing contractor. Most roofers give free estimates, and are glad of a chance to talk with you just so you'll know who they are. A good roofer will seldom try to sell you anything you don't need because he gets most of his jobs through customers' recommendations, and must guard his reputation. Then too, he knows that you'll probably get several estimates, and he would be in a peculiar position if he turned out to be the only one insisting you need a new roof instead of repairs.

PAINT should last for years if it is good. Any unexpected signs of deterioration should be taken up with the contractor. South and west walls get the most exposure and turn shabby soonest. Many managers find they can paint the north and east sides only half as often as the others.

WINDOWS need to be well caulked to prevent rainwater from leaking in. The lintels shouldn't have any mildew, cracks or water stains.

BALCONIES, SLABS, AND OUTDOOR STAIRWAYS can shift position and work loose as a building settles. Slabs can crack or can pull away from foundation walls. Take a particularly close look at slabs beneath air conditioners. If these slabs aren't level, the bearings in the machinery will wear unevenly and break down. Make sure that stairway railings are secure, and that there are no loose or cracked steps. Check the balconies for poor drainage; water collecting there may seep inside, and water is the greatest cause of apartment damage.

WALLS, SIDING, AND BRICKWORK. Look for loose or missing mortar, which you can usually repair by spot-tuckpointing or caulking. If you ignore the problem, the cracks will get bigger and moisture may work its way through the whole material.

THE BASEMENT AREA is almost as important as the roof. Electrical connections leading to central heating, water and air conditioning units are potential trouble spots. Discolored pipes in the basement may signal corrosion long before the pipe upstairs begins to leak. Signs of dampness anywhere mean that moisture is getting in — maybe by the sponge-like action of capillarity, maybe by condensation, maybe by direct leaks.

This moisture can damage anything stored in the basement — including whatever heating, air conditioning, or laundry facilities are located there. You can treat some forms of dampness by ventilating or heating the basement; others by dehumidifying; others by improving the masonry or waterproofing. Many new products are also designed to correct various aspects of the problem. You may need an expert to help you find the best remedy.

Dampness under the building can also cause two other serious problems: dry rot and insect colonies. Rot can destroy wood foundations. Cockroaches, termites, and other vermin will thrive where they find dark and damp areas. If you see any signs of invasion by insects, or dry rot, call in someone qualified to deal with them. And don't limit the exterminator to the basement or some other area. Have him do the whole building. Otherwise, you'll simply drive the pests from one area to another.

PAVED SURFACES — including walks, driveways, and parking areas — can crumble so badly in just five years that they'll have to be entirely replaced at heavy expense. Any overloaded truck may break down the surface in spots. But if you protect paved areas by making minor repairs as needed, they may last for 50 years.

Paving contractors can patch holes and seal the breaks. If a surface is black-top, you may be able to do the job yourself with an inexpensive liquid sealant. Anyhow, don't let any chuck hole develop, nor any crack big enough for a small child to catch a foot in; otherwise, you may find yourself the target of a lawsuit for personal injuries.

If you plan to have a driveway re-sealed with a film of liquid coating, be sure to alert the residents and arrange for cars to be moved so the coating truck can get in and out. You'd better try to keep pedestrians away too, because people will pick up the coating on their shoes.

Of course, any paved area where automobiles drive or park will need maintenance far oftener than every six months, to clean up grease and oil. Otherwise, some of the grime may get tracked indoors, causing extra maintenance work on floors and carpets. Don't try to remove ground-in dirt or even surface oil with a solvent; this will just spread the problem. Use one of the highly concentrated industrial cleaners, following directions that come with it.

LANDSCAPING is usually the last item to be budgeted, and the first to be skimped on if the owner's money runs short. But it's one of the most important items in keeping a property fully rented — because if you can't get prospects past the landscaping, you won't get them inside the apartments at all.

Whatever you do, keep up the bushes and lawn and gardens, or whatever greenery you have, well enough so that they always look attractive. (This means almost daily maintenance, which is another subject. But there are certain long-range maintenance factors which we can consider here.)

Try to lay lawns, trees, shrubbery and flower beds so they can be easily maintained by machines instead of costly hand labor. Narrow strips of grass along buildings and walls usually have to be hand-trimmed; consult a landscaper for ideas about better ground covers for such strips.

Think a long time before installing sprinklers. Of course, they make watering easier (if you're not in a drought area), but they often develop leaks, and can be damaged by frost.

Most major lawn care should be done in the fall, surprising as this sounds. The lawn is sending its roots down deepest in preparation for winter, and feeding now will pay off later. A pound of fertilizer in the fall is worth 10 pounds in the spring or summer.

KEEP A RESERVE FUND for maintenance surprises. About one-fourth of the year's annual rental income should be in a savings account where you can draw on it readily for contingencies such as a major roof repair, or replacement of any of your big heating, plumbing, or electrical installations.

How much should you allocate for scheduled maintenance? Anywhere from 5% to 20% of the property's gross annual income; studies indicate that the average among successful operators is about 10%. This doesn't include any management costs, but does include all run-of-the-place maintenance and repairs requested by residents, with something left for unexpected emergencies.

MAINTAIN EACH APARTMENT, TOO

Your system of preventive maintenance should include inspecting apartment interiors every three or four months. Sometimes residents cause minor damage which can grow worse if it isn't repaired soon, and sometimes things get out of kilter through no fault of a resident.

INSPECT WHILE RESIDENTS ARE ABSENT, if you can. Be sure to leave a notice that you entered the apartment for "the regular routine check of appliances and installations," or something to that effect.

In the case of a resident who seldom goes out, you can get permission to make an inspection by offering a pretext like, "One of the other apartments is probably going to be carpeted, and I'd like to check the workmanship of the people who installed this apartment's carpet. Do you mind if I come in and look it over?"

CARPETING should last approximately five years, depending on the quality of the carpet and the care given to it. Because a resident stays year after year is no reason to ignore the investment in the carpeting. To preserve this investment, a regular shampooing every 12 to 18 months will prolong carpet life and please the resident. But check first with a carpet expert. Sometimes proper spotting and vacuuming will be enough.

If a carpet is badly stained but not worn, you can have it dyed for one-third the cost of replacing it. The dyeing should be done in the apartment; if you take carpet out to be dyed, it will shrink during the process.

When you do install new carpeting, be sure to save all extra pieces for later patchwork in case of damage from cigarette burns and the like.

DRAPERIES should be cleaned every two years or oftener. Dust and chemicals in the air may cause drapes to fall apart when they are cleaned; this isn't the cleaner's fault, but is the result of the dirt's friction with the fabric when agitated during the cleaning. Not every dry cleaner has the equipment and know-how to work with today's drapery fabrics, so when your calendar shows that it's time for drapes to be cleaned, send them to a drapery specialist.

Clean drapes give a very good impression of the apartment. Between cleanings, residents who vacuum their draperies every couple of months will lengthen the fabric's life as well as improve its looks. If apartments have interchangeable draperies, you might try to rotate them so that all get equal sun exposure.

By tumbling draperies at low heat in a dryer, and then spraying lightly with a deodorizer, you can give them a fresh look. But you'd better get accurate information about the care and maintenance of whatever fabric is in your draperies, and keep this on file because some synthetics react badly in a washing machine; there have been cases of whole families getting skin rashes from the residue.

PLUMBING FIXTURES in all apartments should be eyeballed. If they drip, they're wasting significant amounts of water.

VENTILATOR FANS in the kitchen and bathroom may need oiling, unless they are the type that are permanently lubricated.

FILTERS in heaters or air ducts should be changed because, when they get dirty, they cause the furnace and air conditioning to work harder (see Chapter 15).

CAULKING or grout between bathroom tiles and the tub or shower will gradually work loose as the building settles. When you find cracks, replace the caulking or grout; otherwise, water will eventually seep into the cracks and damage walls.

WHO DOES THE MAINTENANCE?

After you've made the inspection and drawn up the schedule, there's the question of who is going to carry out your plan. If you follow the preceding suggestions for programmed upkeep, you should be able to keep the costs and man hours down. One person doing the job systematically — preventing trouble rather than waiting until it erupts — can accomplish more than a whole crew called in for rush jobs.

As a rule of thumb, you'll need one full-time maintenance worker for each 60 apartment units. Any building with 20 units or more will need someone always on call — either a superintendent who gets a free apartment, or one of the owners. Apartment cleaning is often done on contract by an outside firm which specializes in heavy-duty cleaning — probably with professional equipment, trained workers, and fairly steep prices.

While you'll save money by personally doing as much routine maintenance as you can, beware of a maintenance program whereby the property could wind up owning you. Unless the property is very small, and you really enjoy being a jack-of-all-trades, you probably should hire a local handyman to take care of minor plumbing, electrical and carpentry repairs. You shouldn't have to call a plumber every time a faucet leaks or a drain clogs.

A resident caretaker is preferable to part-time employees. Otherwise, the owner and/or manager will be getting calls from residents at all hours. An accessible resident handyman can be played up as an advantage in your rental ads. Ladies and the elderly are attracted by the assurance that a caretaker is at hand to help them out in times of need. Then too, a resident handyman will probably take more pride in the property and its appearance than any off-premises maintenance people would.

Sometimes you can offer a resident caretaker a partial rent reduction in lieu of salary. How much? It varies with local custom. Find out through your broker what other apartment owners pay.

For larger properties, where several people are needed, you face the choice of using your own employees or outside organizations. Owners disagree widely on which system is best, and so do managers.

HIRING OUTSIDE HELP has advantages and disadvantages. You can get specialized skills you don't have yourself. You can bring in extra people whenever needed, without adding to your permanent payroll. Sometimes you can trim costs by settling for less-experienced help or fewer mechanical gadgets; college students can be hired for $4 to $6 an hour. And you may avoid union pressures if the maintenance people aren't on your own payroll.

THE DISADVANTAGES are that you lose control. You can't give orders to a crew of outsiders, but must work through their supervisor. Their reaction time is slower. Most contracts specify just what the crew will do, with no provision for anything else. And, of course, the outside crew will cost more than your own employees.

OUTSIDE SERVICE FOR SPECIALIZED JOBS is almost always advisable. If you have central air conditioning, you need an expert to start up the system at the beginning of the season and shut it down correctly at the end. If this isn't done right, you'll find yourself paying for costly repairs during the season. However, your own crew can probably take care of individual apartment air conditioners.

Elevators should always be adjusted or repaired by a certified service organization. Never try to fix an elevator yourself and never let any casual laborer try; there's too much danger. You'll have to pay stiff hourly charges for repairs to a balky elevator — but this may never become necessary if you have it inspected and overhauled yearly (most localities require this anyhow).

Routine swimming pool maintenance can be done by anyone with a book of instructions, a suction cleaner, and a set of chemicals for testing. But you'll probably need an expert to prepare your pool at the start of the season and close it down at the end. And you may find that the rates for weekly cleaning and checking are so reasonable that you'd rather have the experts handle it.

Window washing is another job that your own employees can do, unless your building is a tall one or your windows are in places that can only be reached by special rigs.

Television antenna systems need almost no maintenance if they're the newer solid state kind. If you have the old type, you'll probably need an antenna service.

Pest control may be left to your own employees if you have nothing worse than ants and flies. However, some state laws prohibit the sale of exterminating chemicals to anyone except a licensed exterminator. In any case, a serious problem with rodents, roaches, bedbugs or termites should never be a do-it-yourself job; call a professional.

Fire extinguishers probably should be checked and refilled by a professional service. This is another situation where local laws may require that the job be done by a specialist. (Incidentally, are you sure your extinguishers work? One sizable building had an extinguisher hanging in a hallway for five years before anyone discovered that the thing was empty.)

Many residents will want to hire someone to do their personal housekeeping or cleaning. Each one will have different needs and preferences. You should know where residents can hire this service on any basis from daily to monthly. Or you can provide it at an added charge to residents.

SHOULD YOU SIGN CONTRACTS FOR OUTSIDE SERVICES, or order them when you need them? There is no all-purpose answer; it depends on the contract and on what you need. The more the contract covers, the more it will cost. Maybe you want just regular routine check-ups, with the unlikely emergency jobs to be billed separately. Some contracts cover parts and labor; others don't. Some are like insurance policies, with a deductible amount to be paid by you. You may need advice before deciding whether to sign contracts for the various kinds of maintenance service.

You'll also have to decide whether you should deal with an independent contractor or with the company that sold you the installation. The company will charge more. But it knows the equipment better and has faster access to parts.

YOUR OWN MAINTENANCE PEOPLE will need careful supervision by you or your resident manager while they're learning the job. You can't just turn them loose and say, "Keep everything in good condition." Their daily and weekly duties should be written out as specifically as possible; leave nothing to guesswork or imagination.

A GENERAL LIST OF DUTIES, with details to be filled in according to the needs of your own property, might look something like this:

— Clean all public areas of the premises first thing every morning and last thing every afternoon — picking up trash, mopping up messes, sweeping or vacuuming if necessary.

— Clean the apartment office before visitors' hours every morning — empty waste baskets, clean the ash trays, dust the furniture.

— Clean the glass panes in the entrance door and vestibule door daily; polish the brass or bronze fittings; check the lock mechanism.

— Scoop off bugs and leaves from swimming pool surface daily or more often, as needed.

— Hose down pool and patio area (or sweep if water is scarce) as needed.

— Sweep or hose walkways, stairwells, porches and balconies weekly, or as needed.

— Clean laundry rooms thoroughly once a week. Inspection and pick-up daily.

— Check all landscaped areas for trash daily. Water and trim as needed.

— Sweep or hose garage, driveway and trashcan areas weekly. (Many big buildings have a monthly sweeping service for carports and driveways, but the manager must make sure these areas are reasonably clean between times.)

— Keep all lighting fixtures clean and bulbed with correct lumens, in uniform sizes.

— Check all vacant apartments daily (see Chapter 6).

— Straighten up mailbox area daily.

— Check basement for dampness and debris twice weekly, or as needed.

To repeat — the foregoing are just generalities. You must fill in the details. Does "clean" include a full scrubbing of walls and ceiling or just removal of spots? When your maintenance man tackles stained grouting, he should be told that scrubbing isn't enough; he must use a brass brush and hydrochloric acid. When equipment is to be cleaned, tell how: "The grille must be removed, the filter taken out and washed in hot suds and then replaced, and the grille put back — once every two weeks."

CARPETING in hallways, stairs and lobbies gets heavy wear and should be maintained carefully. Daily attention is essential. You see the carpeting every day and may not notice that it's getting dirty, worn or shabby. But any prospective renters will notice instantly.

You may be able to economize by moving carpet from less-traveled areas — say the top floor — down to the entrance lobby, instead of always putting brand new carpeting wherever it's needed.

ELEVATORS can become the worst looking part of the property overnight because of their concentrated use. So, daily cleaning is a must. People tend to stick chewing gum or candy wrappers or cigarette stubs in openings in the walls and ceilings.

Some people like to write on the walls or even carve in them. Because of the updraft in an elevator shaft, dust will collect on the frames on each floor and on the edges of elevator doors. The carpets in the cab wear out quickly, and the numeral on the first floor button gradually gets worn away. Train a maintenance man to look for all these defects and correct them immediately.

JUST FOR APPEARANCES' SAKE is the reason for most of the upkeep chores mentioned in the past few pages. Are they worth the hours of paid work, the cleaning materials, the vacuum cleaners and other paraphernalia?

You'll find they are. They pay off indirectly by making a good impression on visitors and occupants, so that you'll always be able to rent vacant apartments faster, taking your choice of high-quality prospects.

People probably won't mention it, but they're at least subconsciously pleased by gleaming varnish, fresh paint, neat gardening, nice clean smells, shampooed carpets, spotless walls, unsmudged glass and all the other details that spell good maintenance and good management. Even your employees will do better jobs if their surroundings are immaculate. And so will you. Everyone feels better in a well-kept place.

REMEMBER THESE BASIC POINTS:

* *Get upkeep work done as soon as the need is known.*

* *Watch for signs of deterioration so you can plan major repairs or replacements in advance.*

* *Write down the manufacturers' names and the model numbers of everything that moves and needs maintenance. Locate suppliers in advance.*

* *Keep emergency phone numbers where you can find them quickly.*

* *Keep a supply of spare parts needed most often.*

* *Figure what you'll need for the next few months, and buy in quantity.*

* *Make a year-long calendar showing when all maintenance work should be done.*

* *Inspect apartment interiors every few months.*

* *Make up detailed lists of duties for maintenance people.*

XVII   *So You Want to Raise Rents*

Paradoxical as it sounds, you can lose money either by setting rents too high or too low. A good return doesn't necessarily come with maximum occupancy. You may get a better return with vacancies.

TWO WAYS TO LOSE

When you raise rents, naturally you expect a bigger gross per month. Probably you'll get it. But you may not if too many residents move out and you don't fill the vacancies. Your gross may also shrink because of the refurbishing costs in vacant units that were occupied until you boosted the rents.

On the other hand, if you scale down rents in order to fill up vacancies, your scale may be lower than the going rate. In that case, your quickly filled building will pay less than it easily could. And you'll probably discover that you're operating in the red.

A BUILDING WITH NO VACANCY LOSS for a long period is almost certainly charging unrealistically low rents. Sure vacancies are bad, and a full building is good — but not if its profits are dwindling to the vanishing point. Property managers say, "Show me a building that's always fully rented, and I'll show you a poorly managed building." Suppose you boost rents by 10%, whereupon move-outs cut your gross by 4%. In that case, you still collect 6% more money than you did before. You'll be even farther ahead as you fill the vacancies. (We saw how to do this in Chapters 5 and 10.)

It all goes back to the old law of supply and demand. Apartments, like shoes or cabbages or Cadillacs, go up or down in price according to the size of the supply and the number of people who are willing to buy at the asking price.

When people prosper, they usually "trade up" — switch to more costly things. If these people are numerous and the supply of something they want is small, then they'll bid more for it.

An owner of high-quality apartments who doesn't raise rents when the market is large and eager, won't make as much money as he could. But if he raises them when prospective renters are few and there's an over-supply of such apartments, he may turn away potential occupants and even lose some of those he has. In other words, he may price himself out of the market.

The markets for different quality apartments may be quite different, just as in the case of Cadillacs and Volkswagens. But sometimes the prices of all cars go up more or less simultaneously, due to underlying market factors — as we've seen in the 1960s and 1970s. Likewise, the markets for many kinds of apartments have pushed rentals up — but not as far as you might think.

THEORETICALLY, RENTS SHOULD RISE in an expanding economy like ours, because housing is a necessity and is in short supply. Nevertheless, rents haven't risen as fast as the costs of building and maintaining any kind of rental property. There are several reasons for this.

For one thing, apartment owners can't adjust rents every few weeks to keep pace with a changing market. The price of groceries may change daily in response to changing economic conditions. But rents in some buildings may stay the same for a period of months or years, especially when they're tied to leases or to governmental rent controls.

For another thing, managers usually prefer not to raise rents, and won't do it unless prodded by owners. We'll go into this problem later in the chapter.

A third reason is this: in many rental properties, the rent schedule is specified in the mortgage application. This application may have been filed months or even years earlier when costs were much different. But the property manager uses this old schedule without any adjustment for the changed market.

The rental market and costs of operating rental properties change much faster than rent schedules. Rents stay steady (with scattered exceptions, of course) through minor dips and rises in the economy. Even when industrial layoffs hit a city hard, the city's average rents are slow to drop. And they are slow to rise when inflation is ballooning the prices of almost everything else.

In the late 1970s, the rate of inflation has averaged about 7% per year. Utility bills have jumped anywhere from 15% to 50% in various areas within a single year. Property taxes have climbed so high that property owners have organized for militant protests in several cities. Yet, in these same years, rents have been rising on the average only 3% to 5% per year. This means, in many cases, that owners of apartment properties are actually losing money. They are charging less rent than they need to keep abreast of their own rising costs.

YET, SOME RENTS MAY BE TOO HIGH right now. In these past few years, as vacancies increased in lower-rent buildings, some managers or owners chose to let units stay empty rather than scale down their rents. Consequently, their vacancy losses mounted because the demand for their kinds of apartments happened to be slack. Dilapidated, poorly managed apartments are often over-priced.

When the economy is doing well — as it is in most places at this writing — studio and efficiency apartments tend to rent slowly. And older apartments may go begging because their former occupants can afford bigger or more luxurious residences. Impoverished people must make do with smaller units than they really need, but in prosperous times there aren't as many impoverished apartment dwellers. So, the real market for these apartments becomes even poorer than before. If the rent scale keeps some apartments out of the reach of poor people, those apartments may stay empty.

DIFFERENT KINDS OF RENTERS WANT DIFFERENT KINDS OF APART-MENTS, so the changes in local or national business conditions have different effects in various price ranges. Hard times increase the demand for small apartments with comparatively low rents, because people who previously occupied a bigger place find they can no longer afford it. Yet, recessions don't dampen the demand for larger three-bedroom units (especially those in moderate-rent districts) partly because there's always a shortage of such units, partly because people with sizable families are moving into apartments after failing to find houses they could afford to buy.

Conversely, in boom times there's a strong demand for better accommodations. The newer, more spacious — or more showy — apartments rent well, while older buildings suddenly have more trouble filling vacancies. And the big three-bedroom and four-bedroom suites, especially those in newer complexes, are vacated as their former occupants buy homes.

STUDY THE DEMAND

Just by studying the local demand for various size apartment units, anyone can get an idea of business conditions in the area. You should be aware of the shifts in demand. You and the manager need to know the prevailing rent rates in your own community and in similar communities nearby, so you won't lose money by pricing your apartments too high or too low.

In most metropolitan areas, people with approximately the same incomes and the same housing needs can choose between several areas that are much the same in living conditions. These areas may not be side by side geographically, but they'll look equally acceptable to a prospective renter scanning ads in his Sunday newspaper. So, you should know what's happening in neighborhoods that compete with yours.

Getting good data on your market may take several days, but is vital in setting the right rents. Don't go by what brokers say. Pose as a prospective tenant and go comparison shopping. Go to apartment association meetings, and ask members what they charge for comparable units in similar locations. Check the classified ads.

Notice what is being offered by way of conveniences and facilities, and what rent is being asked for it. Notice the locations. When you find that you can look at units — or even hear about them or read about them — and predict their rent rather accurately before it is mentioned, you'll know that you have a feel for your market. You're ready to set rents for your own units.

HOW TO SET RENTS

A RULE OF THUMB in property management is that an apartment building's total monthly rents should equal about 1.19% of the building's sale price. How did experts arrive at such an odd figure? By reversing the common yardstick that a building's value is about seven times its annual gross rents, or 10 times its annual net. (Net is the figure you arrive at by subtracting all expenses except debt service from the gross rents.)

However, this is just a crude guide and not an iron law. Beware of setting rents by formula alone. Your building is unique. There is no other building exactly like it within miles. And most of your units probably differ slightly from each other, even when they're the same size.

Some high rise complexes foolishly use a printed rent list with all apartments jumping in price as you go up each floor. Occasionally, the higher view is worth higher rent, but when it isn't the market for the higher-up units will be sluggish.

Property managers in Chicago used to think that apartments with a view of Lake Michigan were far more desirable than those with any other view, and should command the highest rents. They couldn't understand why so many lake view apartments stayed vacant. One by one they found out. Residents had learned that the night view of a body of water as large as Lake Michigan offered only black with an occasional light. Views of the city, on the other sides of the apartment towers, were what the public preferred.

And it's generally true that in high rise buildings almost anywhere, as you get above the midpoint of the building, the improvement in the view from floor to floor is imperceptible. People resist paying more for an 18th floor apartment when they know they can get the same view for less money in an identical apartment on the 14th floor.

276

Another foolish formula is often applied in a garden development where one set of uniform rents is charged on the ground level, with another one-price rule for the second level. There are advantages and disadvantages to both levels. Maybe an upper is brighter, airier, and quieter than a lower — but maybe a prospective renter is elderly (or young, with small children) and therefore doesn't like stairs. Other renters may consider that a lower unit is cooler in the summer and more convenient when lugging in groceries. Contrariwise, people afraid of prowlers don't like ground floor windows through which someone might get in. Or a second floor unit with a view of a trash-filled alley may be worth less than one on the ground floor with windows opening onto a nice patio.

If you set rents strictly by formula, you'll find that your residents discover some units are worth more than others. They'll ask to move to the better unit if the rent is the same, or to an equally good unit if it rents for less. You need to study each apartment before pricing it.

Inexpert managers don't do this. Ask a manager what units are in greatest demand and you may get a quick answer, "The one bedroom corner apartments are always rented," or "Units overlooking the park are never vacant more than a day or two." Such a manager doesn't realize that the units he mentions are snapped up because they are better than people can get elsewhere at that price. He hasn't matched price to demand.

Your underpriced apartments will go fast, leaving you with the most difficult to rent. So, if you see that certain apartments are renting much faster than others, raise the rents of the best sellers. This automatically makes the slow movers more desirable by comparison, because of their lower price tag.

Maybe you're thinking, "Won't it be confusing if we charge many different rates for the same type of apartments?" Sure it will. But you'll still make more money. The way to overcome the confusion is to keep types of mimeographed rent schedules showing the rent for each available unit. You can show this to prospects, and to rental agents if you use any. The schedules will reassure everyone that your rents are firmly established, not set by guess and by haggling.

LOOK AT EACH APARTMENT IN THE PROPERTY when you're working out the rent schedule. Look at all apartments of a certain type together — all the studio apartments, say, or all the one-bedroom units — and look for the very best apartments of that one size or type. Decide which has the best combination of qualities. Here are some of the qualities on which you might rate each apartment:

— The view from the windows.

— Light and air. Corner apartments have more, obviously. Narrow apartments have less. Cross-ventilation usually makes a place more desirable. Dark apartments are worth less per square foot. Too much sun on windows, balconies and patios may make an apartment worth less because it's hotter — unless the sun is softened by good drapes, venetian blinds, air conditioning and other factors. Then the sunniness may well make it worth more than the others, especially if it's in a part of the country where winters are cold.

— The floor plan and the square footage. Usable space brings more rent per square foot. An awkward layout brings less.

— Access. If people must climb stairs or walk through long corridors to reach a unit, it isn't as desirable. But if there's an elevator, the higher floors usually command higher rent. Closeness to parking is a plus factor. Closeness to a noisy elevator, a boiler room, or anything noisy is a minus.

— Facilities such as bathroom, kitchen, refrigerator, drapes, carpeting, shelf space, closet space. They may be better or newer in some of your units than in others.

    –   First level versus second level, and higher floors versus those a bit lower. These are variables you'll have to decide according to the local geography and the needs of your particular market, as mentioned a few pages back. If you rent primarily to young couples with children, your first floor will be your best rent producer. If most of your prospects want quiet, and dislike any noise from an apartment overhead, your top floor apartments can be scheduled for top rent.

Find the apartment with the best combination of qualities. Then ask yourself, "What is the highest possible rent I can get for this particular apartment?" Now that you've developed a feel for the market, you should have a clear idea of how this apartment compares with the competitive ones, and what it can rent for. Set the rent at that figure, regardless of how many apartments you must rent, or what the total rent projection calls for.

Now pick out your second best apartment of the same type. Schedule it for slightly less rent than your very best one – unless the differences are so small that you decide not to discount it at all. Continue this process down to your very worst unit of the same size and type. Then move on to another group of units – all your two bedrooms, perhaps – and go through the same best-to-worst process for setting their rents.

Doing this, you're doing just what your prospective renters will do. They'll look for an apartment with the best combination of access, airiness, spaciousness, facilities and so on. And they'll compare its value to the price asked for it. Your pricing should equalize desirability. What renters don't get in better location and extra features they should get in lower rent.

This best-of-type pricing is different from the usual system, which is to establish a "base rate" for an average apartment and then set prices both up and down from the base. If you start from the best and work down, you'll find that your total rent schedule is about 5% higher than if you work both ways from a base rate. That extra 5% is entirely within your reach.

Some owners and managers, when taking charge of a new development, are anxious to fill up the property quickly so it will start producing income. They set rents low just for the sake of immediate move-ins, figuring they can make boosts later, as vacancies occur or as leases are renewed. This is a mistake which may cost them dearly. If they set rents below what the market will pay, they simply forego income. Later, when they try to raise rents at lease-renewal times, they may have a surge of move-outs all at once, making people wonder what's wrong with the property. In the meantime, operating costs probably are soaring, and the property may actually have a net deficit by the end of the year. To recover his losses, a panicky owner may do something drastic like doubling all the rents, causing greater losses from move-outs.

YOU'LL MAKE MISTAKES in your first rent schedule, no matter how carefully you evaluate each apartment. You'll under-price some apartments, over-price others. But these needn't be costly mistakes if you keep reviewing your schedule and fine-tuning it.

When one type of apartment is taken much faster than other types, you've priced it too low. Evidently the renting public gave more credit than you did for newer kitchens, larger closets, or some other feature. Try to react immediately by setting higher rents for all vacant units of that same type.

If you react too slowly, you won't be able to raise the faster-renting apartments in time; they'll all be taken. On the other hand, you mustn't overreact by boosting the price too much. If you're not sure why the corner units are renting faster, or the second floor units, or whatever, make your raises small — just two or three dollars at a time. Gradually, you'll find the point where value balances price, so that all your units are renting at about the same speed.

New occupants will usually tell you frankly, if you ask, why they chose that particular type. Once you know what features they valued, you can raise the rent in all similar apartments containing those same features. The raise will make them slightly less desirable. And the slower-renting units will become comparatively more desirable because of the wider gap in rent. Then you'll have a more even flow of rentals, which tells you that your prices are right.

Maybe the whole property is renting much faster than the competition. This means that your location, or decor, or some other factor has given you an edge. You can raise all your rents to the point where vacancies become more numerous or longer lasting. Don't worry if a few residents move out after a raise. A turnover rate of 2% to 8% is acceptable; anything lower means your rents are probably sub-par. Trial and error will show you what the market will support.

If you find that your rents are higher than your prospects will pay, you needn't necessarily — and shouldn't — rush to knock down the rates. Instead, you can make adjustments in other forms. Find a way to improve apartments so they're worth what you're asking. This is much better than lowering the rent; when new occupants pay less than the older ones are paying, the word spreads, and dissatisfaction grows.

Rental property is an investment. As such, its value is usually judged by its rental income. Smart investors look for at least a 10% annual return on the price they pay for a building. For every dollar you reduce monthly rent, you reduce the value of the building by $120. (A dollar monthly reduction = $12 yearly income, which is 10% of $120.) This is why a hasty cut in rents can cause a serious decline in value. If there's any chance that the property will be up for sale in the next few years, try to keep the rent schedule high, even if it calls for costly improvements.

STATUS IS A FACTOR to take into account when figuring how much rent you should ask. People are proud of living in good-looking, well-located apartments. It's one of the ways they gain prestige. Other ways, in the past, were wearing good clothes, and driving a good car — but now, for various reasons, clothes and cars aren't such status symbols. This has left housing as the chief way of displaying personal achievement.

Consequently, city dwellers are willing to pay higher rents for impressive entrances and lobbies, and for amenities such as doormen. Garden complexes in the suburbs meet the same need for prestige with their pools, tennis courts, recreation rooms and the like.

Many of the residents who gladly pay extra for these highly visible attractions aren't so much interested in swimming or tennis or recreation rooms. What attracts them is the thought that they can invite friends over. The friends will be impressed. If this need for prestige weren't common, apartment buildings would be drab functional honeycomb-like places, about as homey as the Pentagon Building. Keep status in mind when you set your rent schedule, and when you consider improvements that can make your property look more luxurious.

For example, if you beautify one wing of the building, or its top floor, in the common corridor alone, you'll find that you can charge and collect as much as $20 more per unit. Put in carpeting and wall coverings that are noticeably richer than in the rest of the building. Add a few impressive ashtray urns. Put fine panelling around the elevator doors, or expensive-looking lighting in the corridor, or distinctive door knockers on the doors. Instead of the usual apartment doors, use wood grained doors —

maybe teakwood or rosewood — with superior knobs and nameplates or door numbers. Even though the apartments themselves are the same in size and equipment as others elsewhere in the building, they'll command higher rents. They give a resident a quick way to show that he is superior to residents in the less-impressive sections. Visitors will understand that this bit of extravagance costs money. They'll also think that the resident must be more successful since he has more money and spends some just to get this nicer location.

This same psychology crops up in another way just before a major holiday: occupants make many more service requests than usual. Why? Because their relatives and friends will be dropping in during the holiday season. Anything that looks shabby or broken-down will detract from a resident's prestige in the eyes of visitors. When you cater to the psychological hunger for prestige and status, you can make people willing to pay you more.

Conversely, if you set your rents to be "competitive;" that is, slightly cheaper than comparable buildings, if yours is fairly new and attractive, it will lose status appeal as well as the extra revenue. There's a widespread belief that if something costs more, it's better. The belief is part of the subconscious mental process by which prospective renters choose their apartments.

WHEN IT'S TIME FOR RAISES

Most of the points we've just considered are useful primarily when you're setting a rent schedule as you take charge of a new property. More commonly, an owner or manager of an older building will find himself stuck with a schedule below the going rates, and must face the need to raise practically all rents. What's the best way to handle this?

MANAGERS HATE TO RAISE RENTS. They know that raises can cause move-outs, and they're afraid of a stampede followed by a lower occupancy rate. Managers think their performance is judged by the occupancy rate, so they resist anything that will lower this rate.

Moreover, managers know that almost all residents gripe about a rent increase. Facing angry residents is no fun. Nor is it fun to undertake the extra work of refurbishing, advertising and showing apartments, interviewing prospective renters, and so on, whenever vacancies occur. It's far more fun to manage a building full of contented people. No wonder managers want to keep rents unchanged.

All too often, when the manager warns of a mass exodus, an owner will back down on his instructions to raise rents. If the owner resists, the manager may be sullen in putting the raise into effect. Residents are likely to sense that he doesn't think it is really needed, and there'll be bad feelings all around.

OWNERS NEED TO EDUCATE MANAGERS about why raises are needed. Managers seldom understand the property's financial position. They may be fully familiar with its operating costs — repairs, maintenance, supplies, payroll, advertising and so on — but they don't see the bigger checks the owner must write for real estate taxes, debt service, insurance, maybe utilities, and certainly for his own living expenses.

A manager may imagine that the owner is getting rich from the property and doesn't need more income. But when mortgage payments and taxes and other costs are figured in, owners of multi-family rental housing may wind up with a spendable return of something like 2% or 3% of their invested dollars. If you're an owner, educate your manager, even if there's no need for rent raises right now. The need will arise soon enough, if inflation continues at merely its average rate of the past 50 years.

Part of your educational job is to show the manager that, despite some vacancy losses because of a rent increase, the property will be in better financial shape. Even though occupancy is less, total income will be bigger. Full occupancy isn't really the name of the game; greater return is.

Maybe you should set up an incentive bonus plan that will motivate your manager to produce the best return. You might do this by paying him on the basis of the property's dollar rental income rather than on number of apartments rented.

You might also pay a special bonus — say $25 — for each unit rented and occupied within three days after it is ready for occupancy. The bonus could go down on a sliding scale, perhaps to $10 per unit for those rented no later than 30 days after they are ready. (If your manager tends to be slow in getting units ready for re-renting, you may want to figure your bonuses according to the number of days between move-outs and the subsequent move-ins.)

THE SIZE OF A RENT INCREASE SELDOM MATTERS MUCH, if there's been an adequate interval since the last one. A manager may think that a raise of $12 or $25 per month will cause worse problems than a $5 or $8 raise. He is usually mistaken about this. He'll face unhappy occupants either way, and he'll probably get about the same number of vacancies either way.

Experienced operators say that one substantial raise is better and easier to put across than three smaller raises at intervals of a few months. Some owners think they'll lose fewer residents by a series of $5 or $10 "nuisance" raises because occupants will feel it's more expensive to move than pay the increase. But when these small increases come often, they generate a smoldering wrath throughout the building ("What?" "Again?"), and eventually trigger an even greater exodus just from spite. Try not to hit anyone for a raise oftener than once in nine months.

If you were to follow up on people who move out, they say, because of a rent increase, you'd find that almost all these people move into a similar apartment at a higher rent than they were paying even with the rent raise. Someone who screams bloody murder because his one bedroom apartment rent is boosted to $185 from $165 will often go out and rent a similar apartment for $195. He can afford it because average earnings of Americans have risen faster than consumer prices — and far faster than average rents.

Every year, people say they don't see how they can pay for the steep climb in grocery bills, insurance rates, automobile prices, and everything else. They've been saying this since the 1950s. But people have managed to keep on paying — because incomes have risen, too. No one likes paying more, but they do. The average resident is earning enough to pay more rent. You must train your property manager to keep this in mind when thinking about the rent increases you need (of course, if you have a building full of old folks on small fixed incomes, the problem is different. A raise might force them out willy-nilly).

RAISING RENTS ON VACANT APARTMENTS is no problem. Charge a higher rental than the last similar rental, and you'll almost always get it — because apartments newer than yours are priced to keep up with inflation, while yours are lagging.

Therefore, a manager who is told to raise rents will often propose a compromise. "We'll raise rents the amount you need," he may say to the owner, "but let's put the raises into effect only as apartments fall vacant. Then we won't get squawks or move-outs."

This compromise will never bring you as much income as you expect. Maybe you've had a 40% turnover rate, which would seem to imply that you'll have all new tenants in two-and-a-half years. But you won't. Most of your turnover will keep happening in the same 30% or 40% of your units. The remaining 60% or 70% of your residents will stay on for years, and will soon be paying far less than the going rate for newcomers. So you won't get 100% of the raises you expect, if you count on turnover to accomplish it.

Still, a good long-term resident is worth holding as long as you can. Such people are hard to find and they cost you far less in many ways than short-termers do. Your old-timer may be replaced by someone who'll stay only a matter of months. If someone has been with you for five or ten years, and is likely to stay permanently unless you anger him by boosting his rent too high, figure the long-run benefits. Losing him will mean losing rent for a month or two; then perhaps spending $500 or $800 redecorating the apartment to suit the new occupants when you finally do acquire them. How long will it take you to recoup these losses from the higher rent?

YOU NEEDN'T RAISE EVERYONE at the same time, nor by the same amount or percentage. (Imagine the anger of a resident who is hit by an across-the-board raise a month after he moves in.) You can use the same technique you did when you originally worked out your rent schedule. Make selective raises. If some apartments are in greater demand than others, capitalize on the demand by raising their rents more than you raise the hard-to-rent units.

A GOOD TIME FOR AN INCREASE is when you're making improvements — putting in new carpets or drapes, or painting, or fixing up the grounds. People are less resentful of a raise when they see a tangible increase in value. They feel that the owner or manager is making the place more desirable, so they're more inclined to reciprocate by paying more. The average person expects to pay higher rent for better living conditions.

Another good time is early fall. Residents have sent children back to school and are settling down for the winter. They don't want to go out and start apartment-hunting. If you expect an influx of seasonal or student renters, obviously this is the time for a general raise.

Surprisingly, January 1 is also a good time for raises. Psychologically, a new year means a fresh start in many kinds of endeavors, rent and budgets included. Some of your residents may have collected Christmas bonuses, and will be feeling good now that they're past the turmoil of the holidays.

If you're pretty sure that you'll get numerous vacancies because of a general increase, early spring is a good time for the increase in many parts of the country. It allows you the whole spring and summer — traditionally an apartment-hunting season — to recover from any vacancies that develop.

For the same reasons, you may want to avoid announcing raises in midsummer or late summer. It's the easiest and most logical time for people to move. If you suddenly get a lot of vacancies, they may not be filled before prospective renters have put their children in school and made up their minds to stay where they are.

Another unfavorable time is just before Christmas, when holiday expenses are on everyone's mind. News of a rent boost then may make them throw up their hands and cry, "We simply can't afford it!"

If you use leases, the time when a lease expires is obviously the time to raise the rent. Maybe you can negotiate a new lease with a provision for an automatic increase as expenses increase. Office buildings have used such escalator clauses for years. Escalator clauses are also a part of Social Security benefit payments, and of most wage contracts.

You could write a lease provision tying your rents to the Consumer Price Index —

a well known, impartial government tabulation which is published monthly by the Department of Labor, and is usually front-paged in newspapers. It shows changes in the cost of living not only nationwide but pinpointed for most major cities.

If you decide to use an escalator clause, make sure that your renters know about it. You can't assume that just because someone signs a lease containing the clause, he has read and understood it. Courts no longer assume that tenants understand the leases they sign. So, it's your responsibility to call renters' attention to an escalator clause.

You might do this by putting a sticker on each lease, "This lease contains a rent escalator clause tied to the Government's Consumer Price Index. Please read carefully." It also helps to discuss this personally with new residents when they sign.

BREAKING THE NEWS

When you want to raise the rent, you can't just tell a resident, "I've raised your rent effective immediately." Always give notice in writing, and allow ample time for the change to take effect. A 60-day notice is better psychology than 3 days; the news doesn't seem so painful. Even if recipients say to themselves, "We'd better look for another apartment," they don't feel as much urgency if the increase is two months away, and they may not get around to looking.

SHOW YOUR RESIDENTS WHY an increase is needed. If you or your manager know your expenses, know your residents, and know your competition, you'll be able to justify the increases. Be specific. A vague statement about "increased costs makes this necessary," isn't convincing, even though people do know that their own costs of everything are increasing. They may think you're a fat cat getting fatter at their expense, or a bloodsucker bent on squeezing every possible dollar out of them. Remind them that their incomes are increasing, while yours isn't unless you get more rent.

Let people know what is included in their rent bill and how much it costs. You can clip and reproduce local news articles about boosts in property taxes, insurance rates. You can provide figures on operating costs and finance charges as compared to previous years. You can chart these, and chart their rent rate underneath to show visually how rents have lagged behind other costs. All such exhibits make good enclosures to be sent along with your announcement of an increase.

AVOID USING A COLD PRINTED "NOTICE OF INCREASE." Most operational manuals for property managers provide documents starting out, "You and each of you will please take notice that the terms of the agreement under which you hold possession of the premises known as . . . " or "NOTICE TO CHANGE TERMS. You are hereby notified that on the . . . day of . . . the rental of the premises you now occupy under tenancy from month-to-month . . . " These may be delightful to lawyers but they sound hateful to renters. They make you sound unpleasant and ice cold.

A far better way is a personal letter from you to the resident. Let him see you're sorry you have to raise his rent. He is your customer and ought to be your friend. He pays you a lot of money and you want to keep him. Tell him so. You might word a letter something like this:

As you know, we're in a period of runaway inflation. I'm doing my best to keep costs down — and rental rates down. But there's no way I can cut the expenses for this building back to what they were last year. Maybe the enclosures with this letter will help you to understand my problem.

I have absorbed the increases as long as I could, but now I am forced to raise your rent by $_____ . This is only ____% from $ ____per month to $ _____per month. Don't you agree that this increase is fair under the present circumstances?

This notice is to comply with the legal requirements of a 30-day written notice, although I'm giving you 60 days' notice instead of only a month. All other terms of our Rental Agreement will stay in effect as heretofore.

Cordially yours,

Owner

If you or the manager can hand the letter personally to the resident, so much the better.

There's no reason you should subsidize low-rent housing all by yourself. Public agencies do this. You've put your money into a building to make a profit. Why else would you accept the risks, the worries, the time and expense?

If some of your residents can't afford higher rent, this doesn't mean that you're unfairly depriving them of a home. They simply have to shop for something within their budget. Many a person would like to own a new car, but they expect to pay more for it — and if they can't afford it, they settle for something less expensive. They'll do the same in renting an apartment. So don't let residents run your business for you. Run it yourself.

REMEMBER THESE BASIC POINTS:

* *Keep aware of shifting demand, in order to set your rents near the going rate for similar units.*

* *Don't set rents by a rigid formula. Fix them according to the advantages and disadvantages of each individual unit. Use best-of-type pricing.*

* *If there's a chance the property will be up for sale in the next few years, try to keep rents high, even if this necessitates improvements.*

* *The owner must make sure the manager understands why raises are needed.*

* *Certain times are better than others for raising rents. Choose your times carefully. Try to give 60-day notices.*

XVIII *Tenant Power*

It would be easy to manage apartments if nobody lived in them. We'd only have to be caretakers — making sure that broken windows got repaired, leaky roofs got mended, the grass got cut, and the plumbing stayed okay.

But people do live in our apartments. Most of our problems are people problems, as pointed out in the early chapters of this book. And the people in our apartments may pose harder problems in the years ahead.

That's mainly because of what happened long ago. A lot of people in our business used to be greedy, or inefficient, or insensitive, or unethical. In various parts of the world, including America, fortunes were made by buying real estate cheap (or simply grabbing it free) and charging high for the use of it. The very word "landlord" conjured up such evil images that we now prefer to call ourselves "managers" or "owners," although we're still called landlords by those who think we're profiteering at the expense of the downtrodden "tenants."

WHY LANDLORDS GOT A BAD NAME

Centuries ago, in feudal societies, a landlord really was a lord. He held his lands by royal decree. People who lived there were his serfs or vassals. They paid whatever tribute he demanded and did whatever he commanded, in the humble hope that he would let them continue to live there.

Not many decades ago in our own country, countless landlords owned city tenements where swarms of tenants lived in poverty and discomfort. If any tenants angered their landlord, he could (and sometimes did) cut off their heat or light, or put them in the street for any or no reason. There were always plenty more to fill the vacancies.

And in some rural areas, huge landholders kept "tenant farmers" or "transient crop pickers" in bondage by charging high enough rents so that these luckless people were always in debt to them. Such people had no better place to go. And they had no rights, as far as they knew. So they were meek.

THE BALANCE IS TILTING in the other direction now. Tenants in badly run buildings are getting together. They are discovering what labor and civil rights workers learned long ago: there is power in group action. A shrewd militant organization of residents can tie up an owner in the courts for months unless he makes costly concessions.

Until recently, anyone who lived in a rented apartment was afraid of his landlord, and of the resident manager (often a surly character who simply acted as janitor and was seldom in a hurry to respond to requests for service). Tenants signed leases full of tricky fine print, paid the rent, took the premises "as is," and if they didn't like what they got, either moved out or were forced to move by the owner or manager.

Consumerism is changing all that. Some people (even convicted criminals) are now pushing what they consider their "rights" to the utmost legal limits. Purchasers want greater protection when they buy — safety in automobiles, understandable interest rates on credit purchases, purity in foods. Legislators are waking up to the votes they can win by siding with millions of consumers against a relative handful of businessmen who seem to hate any restrictions on freedom to make money. Consequently, laws are being changed. "Let the buyer beware" is no longer a cornerstone of common law.

Nowadays people who live in rented apartments are less quick to sign whatever a manager puts before them. Some of them read their leases and rental agreements and perhaps demand changes. If a manager won't oblige, they may go to a lawyer for help. Judges are reversing ancient doctrine by deciding that renters have new rights and landlords have new responsibilities. Sometimes owners are forced to put security deposits into escrow and pay interest on them, and to guarantee that each unit they rent is fit to live in.

Occasionally, instead of going to law, tenants take more vigorous action. They may call a rent strike, a sit-in, a noisy demonstration in the streets. They may picket a property. They may join with tenants of other buildings in a "Tenants' Rights Day" rally to demand city-wide rent control or at least a housing court, a landlord-tenant commission, a repair-and-deduct statute, or other measures to limit the powers of landlords.

WHY DO TENANTS ORGANIZE? Some still live in dread that the rent will be boosted sky-high, or that the owner will evict them if they annoy him by joining a protest group. There are managers who still threaten vengefully, "I'll throw you out in the street." This isn't legally possible now, unless there's been a clear violation of the lease or rental agreement, but the news hasn't yet spread widely. So a silent majority stays silent for fear of a manager's vengeance.

Silent or not, many also fear that management will neglect heating and plumbing, or shirk repairs. And sometimes they fear, conversely, that management will make some improvement they don't want or need, and will charge them for it. All this arises from a lack of open communication between residents and landlords. The worse the communication, the more possibility that tenants will organize.

THREE PATTERNS OF COLLECTIVE ACTION are emerging. In the most common pattern, tenants organize just to make the owner treat them fairly and honor his responsibilities. Such groups have no particular ideology. They tend to be nonpolitical, although sometimes they work for legislation to give residents more protection.

And they come from all economic classes; militance isn't confined to the poor or the blacks these days. Middle income renters and even the wealthy sometimes form tenant organizations if they feel that maintenance is shoddy, or that they're not adequately protected from violence. If a couple of muggings or rapes, or maybe a murder, is reported in or near your building, your supposedly conservative residents may take up picket signs and make your life miserable even if they inhabit luxury apartments. They may also form a united front if you suddenly double their rent. In 1970 there were seven different rent strikes among luxury tenants in Washington, D. C. Today in Washington, if residents have a fixed income, you can't raise their rent.

A second less common pattern of collective action is ideological, aimed at taking profit out of housing. Emily Atchenberg, a leader in bringing rent control to Massachusetts, bluntly proclaimed, "Our goal is to change the ownership of property in America." In Berkeley and Palo Alto, California, where rent control measures have been on the ballot several times, the college communities are liberal and intellectually oriented, and a prevailing sentiment is concern for the needs of low-income people and the downtrodden. Their political action manual is a handbook entitled, "The Cities' Wealth: Programs for Community Economic Control in Berkeley." It says:

"Rent . . . may actually reduce the present value of a property. This is essentially community expropriation in favor of tenants . . . The city could purchase the property at below market prices or aid tenants in converting the property to co-operative ownership."

Such groups sincerely feel that profit is anti-social, and that all multiple housing should be quasi-public utilities, managed by the democratic vote of tenants as part of a fundamental change in our governmental system.

A third pattern of group action (and an even more rare pattern) is fiercely interested in stirring up disorder, with housing as only one of several targets. Its small groups are conspiratorial, hoping to harass owners into abandonment or bankruptcy. Some of these groups also believe in bombing and other terrorist tactics. Their aim seems to be to cause chaos, out of which can arise a revolutionary dictatorship.

Obviously, there's little an owner or manager can do to make peace with the second and third types. But he can do much to head them off. They only flourish where tenants hate their landlords — and smart management never makes itself hateful.

HOW TO HEAD OFF TENANT UPRISINGS

ALERT MANAGERS CAN MINIMIZE MILITANCY among normal tenants. We need to be sensitive to people. We need to let them know what to expect, when to expect it, and who to go to about their problems. We must follow up fast to take care of their legitimate grievances.

If you, as manager or owner, respond to a complaint by calling a repairman who says he can't come that week, it isn't enough to shrug and say, "Okay, come next week," and forget about the tenant who asked for the repairs. Maybe you've done all you can to keep your word, but no news and no action will give occupants a real grievance. Tell them immediately if you run into delays.

The fewer causes for complaint, the less chance of mass action. Never try to stall your way through a crisis, because stalling is itself a cause for complaint. "Good management is in the eyes of the managed," as Sanford R. Goodkin points out. He is a research consultant to the real estate industry.

Chapter 17 suggested raising rents when the demand would clearly support a raise. But it also pointed out that people on small fixed incomes might be exceptions to this policy. The point is worth elaborating here.

HOW BIG A RAISE IS ETHICAL? The "right" raise isn't necessarily the biggest raise that the traffic will bear. Some owners, soon after buying a building, double or even triple the rent. They are trying to milk the property, then unload it on some unwary purchaser. These are the owners most likely to run into a rent strike and other costly trouble from tenants.

The best way to increase cash flow from a property is through renovation and good maintenance, which makes residents willing to pay higher rent if they can afford it. If you rent to people who can't afford a raise and can't easily move elsewhere, probably you'd better hold down your operating costs and postpone most of your profit, raising rents only on turnover. You can use two different rent schedules: a lower one on good tenants of long standing, and a higher one for incoming new tenants. This isn't inconsistent; many businesses give better rates to existing customers than to new ones.

WHAT IS A REASONABLE RENT? Enough to pay normal operating expenses and losses through deterioration and whatever is needed for debt service, plus a return on the owner's cash investment. This still leaves the question, how much return should the owner get?

If he put his money in a savings institution where he could draw it out any day, and where he needn't spend a minute watching his investment, he could get 5% or 6%. There are stocks and bonds that would pay him 7% with no trouble. So it takes about 9% return to give him the incentive to buy rental property, with all the risks and difficulties involved. Smart investors look for 9% or 10%, and this is a bargain for the average occupant.

Naturally, an owner hopes to do better than this, but he knows that his chance of a big payoff will come when he sells the property. He'll be wise to go slow in raising rents if he sees a likelihood that it will trigger mass action by tenants. In such situations, he can steer clear of trouble by keeping raises to 6% or 8% at yearly intervals. And he should make sure his residents fully understand his need for a raise — as we saw in Chapter 17.

GOOD MAINTENANCE IS A GOOD BUFFER against militants. To put this another way, unsatisfactory maintenance is the grievance which most commonly leads to the rise of tenant unions. Obviously, it's better to make repairs without being asked; an ounce of prevention is worth a pound of cure.

Nothing makes residents see red more quickly than unsafe and unsanitary conditions in and around the place they call home. If the grounds are weedy or trash-strewn, this may not be unsafe or unsanitary, but it certainly makes residents ashamed of where they live. The same is true of anything unsightly on the stairs or in the corridors. And if there are broken locks or buzzers, or burnt-out lights in halls and entryways, the complaint will not only be poor maintenance, but lack of security, too. These faults are simple and inexpensive for any manager to correct. He owes this much to the residents who pay his salary.

Badly managed buildings would all have emptied long ago if there were plenty of surplus housing. But the U.S. is a country where a housing shortage is a fact of life. People who live in standard dwellings don't always have the easy option of moving elsewhere. Legislators and courts and government bureaus know this. They figure that apartment owners know it, too, and have taken advantage of the shortage by jacking up rents and skimping on maintenance. So, whenever there's a dispute between an owner and tenants, the authorities will cast a skeptical eye on the owner. He'd better be prepared to prove that he's treating his tenants fairly.

GOOD COMMUNICATIONS ARE THE NEXT BEST buffer. Not only must tenants be treated fairly, they must realize that they're being treated fairly. Tell them what you're doing to solve any problem that concerns them — including your problem of inflated operating costs. Let them know about every cost-cutting step you take. Explain your reasons for any policy that might irritate residents.

For example, suppose it's a hot day, and a resident makes a glass of lemonade, then sips it beside the pool. She'll be infuriated if a building employee points to the printed rule, "No glasses on the pool terrace." But if an employee explains that a glass can drop and break, and that broken glass is dangerous to bare feet on a pool deck, she'll understand. As a matter of fact, this explanation should appear in the printed rules. Every rule that might annoy people should be accompanied by an explanation of the reason for it.

Incidentally, management newsletters aren't a good channel for important communications. They're fine for upbeat news about residents, useful information about shopping and transit and recreation — but they may be tossed aside to read later (or never). Don't you often do this with your own second class mail?

When you must announce a rent increase, or a problem with maintenance, or some new management policy, you'd better do so in a personal letter to each resident, or, better yet, by phone or face-to-face. You might also post the notice near the mailboxes — but do this after, not before, notifying residents personally. Either a posted notice or a newsletter seems too impersonal for anything that's really important.

DON'T HELP FORM ANY ORGANIZATION OF TENANTS, even if it's just a group planning a barbecue. A bridge club or tenant-edited newsletter can suddenly turn into a forum at which complaints are aired and plans for anti-management action are laid. You may think you're being nice by encouraging your residents to arrange for a social evening, but you'd better not if there's the least chance that it would lead to demands for "a voice in the policies of the building." Of course, you can't openly oppose ideas for resident gatherings, but you can avoid making it easy.

WHAT TO DO WHEN TENANTS ORGANIZE

IF A GROUP DOES FORM, don't answer letters or calls from it, and don't attend any meeting it calls. If it complains to you about anything specific, be sure to respond to the complaints — but to each tenant individually, not to the group. Remind everyone that you intend to treat them as individuals.

In other words, try to ignore the group. Avoid quarreling with it. It will probably go away if tenants have no real grievances. Its organizers are probably people who love the excitement of group action; taking charge of any enterprise is an ego trip for them. But if a group needs an objective, such as winning a battle with a quarrelsome owner, if you give it no target, then its reason for being — and its ego support to the leader — will collapse.

WHEN AN UNREASONABLE GROUP CONFRONTS YOU in a way you can't avoid, listen — but don't negotiate and don't argue. Encourage it to form an advisory committee. (Advisory committees can blow off steam, but can't bargain.)

Group bargaining sessions are unwieldy and emotional. A group is often under the sway of a fiery leader who has his own fish to fry. He wants to preserve and magnify his status. To do this, he'll keep taking credit for all changes, and upping his demands. You should arrange private chats with him, and look for constructive ways to win him over.

One militant woman threatened to use her leaderhip role in a local church, and her connections with neighborhood gangs, to stir up trouble for a property manager. The manager offered her a small fee for contributions to the newsletter. She accepted, and as her grievances were aired in the newsletter, the other residents began to see how warped she was.

When a tenant group tries to become a bargaining agent, your best strategy is to tell each tenant privately, "I negotiated your lease with you as an individual. When you have a problem, I'll talk with you personally. Each case is different, and I want to deal with it on its merits."

Psychologists say that the way to weaken any mass of belligerent people — even a lynch mob — is to talk to individuals one at a time, rather than make a speech to the group.

IF YOU'RE FORCED INTO MEETING with a militant organization, here are guidelines:

— Don't meet on the grounds of the property, nor at any location demanded by the organization. Meet in your attorney's office if you can. As a second choice, meet in the owner's office, or in your office if you have one away from the property.

— Notify the organization that the entire discussion will be tape-recorded. Let your opponents also make their own recording if they wish. It's important to get every word on the record for future reference.

— Have a trained negotiator talk for you. Your attorney or a professional management firm might make a good representative. Such a third party will be less emotional and can more easily avoid making commitments.

— Sign nothing until your attorney studies and approves it. Make no statements to the press.

— If a real crunch threatens, seek help from realtors' and property owners' associations.

IN CASE OF MASS ACTION

SUPPOSE THE WORST HAPPENS and the tenant organization calls a rent strike, or a sit-in, or mounts a picket line around your property. What should you do then?

— Re-examine your own policies. Figure out what caused this uprising. Are your policies fully necessary? Or can you afford to be more flexible? If there are complaints that you think are unjustified, have you personally investigated them?

— Make sure your tenants are getting adequate service. And make sure they know it. Have they understood your communications? If not, you've merely been talking to yourself — or worse, you've seemed to say what you didn't mean.

— You can ignore some mass action, such as pickets. Picketing is tiresome work and seldom lasts long. Instead of discouraging prospective renters, it makes them sympathize with you unless they're red-hot activists themselves. Sit-ins can likewise be ignored unless they block traffic or prevent urgent business — in which case, you can probably get the police to remove the sitters. Ask your attorney.

— Don't try to debate through newspapers. Decline to be interviewed by reporters; they can misquote you or trap you into blurting something you'll regret. If you want to state your case, put it in writing — once only. After that, make no response at all.

— If the organization wants something you can't deliver, try to give in on other points, or offer alternative concessions. This will enable your opponents to claim a victory and call off further action.

— Consider arbitration as a way of settling a knotty dispute. It is possible if you and the other side agree that whatever the arbitrator decides will be binding on both of you. The usual procedure is to get in touch with the nearest office of the American Arbitration Association, which has more than 35,000 arbitrators across the country. The arbitrator will hear both sides informally and in private; then decide. The two opposing sides split his fee, which usually is $150 to $250.

Arbitration is probably a better bet for you than trying your case before a jury. Juries tend to be hard on owners. They figure that owners are rich. Even when an owner looks poor, they imagine that an insurance company or lending institution will be the real loser, rather than the owner.

You can appeal an arbitrator's decision if you can establish that he refused to listen to important evidence, that he denied a proper request for postponement, or that he had some personal stake in the dispute.

HOW TO HANDLE A RENT STRIKE

Now that they don't fear landlords so much, tenants sometimes band together and withhold their rent in order to put pressure on the owner. It demoralizes the building's management; the resident manager is caught between loyalty to the residents around him and loyalty to his boss. The strikers annoy tenants who don't want to join the strike, and sometimes even harass them into moving. Other people don't want to move in once they hear of the strike.

So your strategy is to act fast. Nip the strike before it cuts deep into your income. On the very day the rent is overdue — or as soon afterward as you realize there's a strike — pick out the leaders and start eviction proceedings against them, as explained in Chapter 4.

At this writing, 17 states allow tenants to withhold rent under certain conditions. The number of such states seems to be growing. But there's nothing so far that gives a group of tenants the legal right to stop paying their rent as a protest against a raise, or against management's refusal to meet with them, or against anything else except unlivable apartments.

Housing and sanitary codes often set a minimum level of required maintenance; and some statutes say that if a dwelling is below this level, tenants can legally refuse to pay the rent. If an owner doesn't make needed repairs or remodeling, a tenant can pay for the repairs or remodeling, and deduct these expenses from the rent — but only up to an amount equalling one month's rent. And he can do this only once a year.

This means that rent strikers are on shaky legal ground. Have they asked you to make repairs? Have you failed to do so? If not, they are in default and you can evict them in the usual way. Once you start the eviction process, strikers are likely to get scared. As you continue inexorably with the steps toward putting them out — and expand your legal action to include more and more of them — the strike may collapse. If not, the sooner you evict all strikers and start renting anew, the better.

A tenant union with a highly sophisticated lawyer may find ways to stall eviction. This means that an outside organization is calling the shots, and you're in for a major battle.

The outside organization probably sees you as one pawn in a larger game. It would like to drive you into bankruptcy or force you to abandon the building. But this won't necessarily make your tenants any better off. They'll be much worse off, in fact, if the property is boarded up and allowed to rot, as so many properties were in New York.

You might point this out to individual tenants in private chats, whereupon they might realize that the strike may leave them out in the street. (As noted a few pages back, one-to-one talks are your best hope of beating group action. So, it's important to be on friendly speaking terms with your residents, if possible.)

When you're a target of action by an outside organization, other owners are too. Get in touch with them and with your local apartment association. Together you can afford better legal advice than you could separately. You may also be able to obtain other kinds of help, such as favorable publicity in the press and vigorous action by somebody in government.

IF RENT CONTROL IS PROPOSED

One of the goals of radical groups is city-wide or statewide rent control. Usually, this can be imposed by action of a city council or state legislature, but these bodies hesitate to go so far without full consideration and debate. Sometimes the measure must be put to public vote. Either way, you and other property owners have a good chance of defeating it by highlighting the history of such measures elsewhere.

MANY CITIES HAVE TRIED RENT CONTROL and dropped it. Controls began as a wartime expedient in 1943 when thousands of veterans returning home had no place to live. Only people who could afford the high rents got apartments. The rest found themselves in a severe, widespread housing shortage.

To compensate for the shortage, at least a dozen cities, and four states, clamped a lid on rents. We know now that they would have done better by promoting building projects to help the supply of housing catch up with demand.

It wasn't uncommon around 1950 to see five-room apartments renting for $100. At that rate, people wouldn't move, no matter what. Where else could they get such a large apartment at such a low price? Even in 1968 a survey in New York City found 60,000 families with incomes above $15,000 who were paying no more than $150 a month — only 12% of their incomes or less — for large apartments in good condition. Meanwhile, 280,000 families who earned less than $3,000 a year were paying $75 a month rents — 30% of their income. Such are the inequities caused by rent control.

But this wasn't the worst of the story. The frantic search for a place to live turned neighborhoods upside down. People stood in line through the night to get the earliest copies of morning newspapers so they could check the obituaries and rush to the deceased's address in hope of claiming the apartment. Of course, building employees knew of each vacancy sooner and usually took it themselves or tipped off friends. When the newspaper readers arrived, they were likely to find someone already moving in.

Owners found that expenses kept rising although rents were frozen, so their cash flow dwindled to nothing. Buildings deteriorated because owners couldn't afford repairs. As years passed, tenants gave up trying to keep units livable, and moved out. Less desirable tenants swarmed in with big broods of young children who caused more damage. Whole neighborhoods became squalid; then worthless. Owners couldn't even give away their buildings. Their only alternative was abandonment. With utility bills unpaid, the utilities were turned off and the remaining tenants fled in search of places where they at least could find running water. The city boarded up the buildings.

Cities across the country dropped rent control (re-named "rent stabilization") by 1953, and tried to encourage new building. But New York kept the lid on because the voters were for it. In New York City, 70% of families live in rented multiple dwellings. Country-wide, 60% of families own their homes.

A building boom overcame the housing shortage in most parts of the country by the early 1960s, but not in New York. Few people wanted to build apartment houses there, and few lenders would invest in them. In 1969, the biggest year for apartment construction, only 6,700 units were built or rehabilitated in New York, mostly financed with government-backed loans. In that same year, owners abandoned buildings that contained 33,000 units. Altogether, 100,000 housing units in New York "disappeared" between 1965 and 1968. The city finally admitted that rent control was a failure and lifted it – partially – in July, 1971. Meanwhile, the city had lost real estate tax revenues put at hundreds of millions of dollars per year.

Elsewhere tenant anger against skyrocketing rents has recently enabled tenant organizations to get new rent control statutes passed in Miami, Baltimore, the State of Massachusetts, and a few other places – notably Berkeley, California, where a whole slate of radical candidates was voted into control of the city council in 1972. (Some 63% of Berkeley voters were renters.)

RENT CONTROL MAY SPREAD now because New Yorkers are moving around the country, and are talking up the idea of cheap rents in their new communities.

Young people are rising to power in local governments, and groups of young voters are becoming strong. These are groups who don't know the history of rent control's failures. They find the idea attractive.

"Free enterprise" is a catchword of capitalists, but it hasn't much appeal to young people on small incomes. To them, "public ownership" sounds more promising. They too are inclined to favor a rent freeze, or at lease some restrictions on rent raises.

Rent control's advocates are vocal, persistent, well organized, and growing in numbers. Nevertheless, they can be defeated by intelligent opposition.

The arguments against rent control are readily available, and need not be outlined here. The appeal of temporarily lowering living costs can be offset by case histories showing that renters soon lose because maintenance stops, and home owners lose because their taxes rise to fill the gap after rent control forces down apartment values.

RENT CONTROL WAS BEATEN IN 1977 in Berkeley, a city that seemed the most likely to love it. Berkeley's previous rent control ordinance had been thrown out by the highest court as unconstitutional. To reinstate it, the Berkeley Housing Coalition proposed a charter amendment that would have rolled back rents to the level of June 16, 1976, and would have set up a board with dictatorial power over rents. Early surveys of public opinion indicated that the measure would pass by a 60-40 margin.

However, apartment owners and other real estate interests (not just in Berkeley, but in other parts of the state where real estate investors realized that Berkeley's action might be widely copied) raised enough money to retain a political consulting firm and to buy newspaper and radio advertising. A thousand people volunteered their services or lent their names to the campaign, holding small meetings and stuffing envelopes at the campaign office. More than 250 volunteers walked precincts and telephoned voters.

The arguments against rent control were presented so effectively that the Daily California (student newspaper) came out against it; so did the Berkeley Black Council, every black city council member, and the League of Women Voters. On election day, citizens voted down the proposed charter amendment by about 22,000 to 13,000 – reversing the 60-40 edge that the amendment had held earlier. Every candidate backing it was beaten.

RENT CONTROL HAS BEEN BEATEN ELSEWHERE in recent years. The Miami city council voted to let its rent control law expire at the end of 1976. In Palo Alto, California, where many Stanford University students live, a city charter amendment similar to the Berkeley proposal was put on the ballot by petition of 6,000 voters, and a poll showed that a substantial majority of voters were in favor of it five weeks before election day. Nevertheless, it lost by 14,900 to 5,700.

STRATEGY TO BEAT RENT CONTROL AT THE POLLS would include the following elements, to judge from experiences in Berkeley, Palo Alto and elsewhere:

– Accept the premise – if it is true, and it usually is – that housing is scarce locally, and that rents are high by comparison with the past. Focus attention on the real issue – "What is the best solution to these problems?"

    — Strongly support reasonable alternatives to rent control which can (a) help reduce suffering caused to people of low and moderate incomes by inflated rents, and (b) help make local rental practices more fair.

    — Organize a broad-based campaign group. Avoid identifying with special-interest groups, such as apartment owners or real estate people. Go after endorsements from student publications, local news media, the city council, and organizations which cut across political and ideological lines.

    — Never make personal attacks on advocates of rent control. Ignore attacks on those who oppose rent control. Don't try to get sympathy for big landlords. (Call them owners.) Keep the campaign on a high impersonal level.

    — Stay away from abstract themes such as "free enterprise." Focus on the specific harm to be expected from the proposal.

    — Enlist professional advisers, including public relations and advertising experts. But avoid massive advertising, costly-looking brochures and slick slogans. Discourage inflammatory statements by owners and realtors. Insist that only one skilled person speak to the press for the organization.

    — Make intense efforts in advance to organize a professionally managed phone bank and door-to-door canvassing within the final week of the campaign.

    — Get prominent, respected local people to send well-written, non-inflammatory "letters to the Editor." These should be factual and varied.

    — Take care to comply with all provisions of the campaign financial reporting laws.

    — Tell the truth. Any inaccurate or misleading statement will give opponents an opening.

HOW TO OPERATE UNDER RENT CONTROL

Let's suppose that the opponents of rent control don't make a convincing case in your community, and a "rent stabilization" measure passes. Or suppose you live in an area where rents have been controlled for some time. Does this mean you should avoid investing in rental properties?

Not necessarily. Even under New York's harsh laws, some small investors quietly and altogether legally made profits in apartment operation. The same has happened everywhere else under regulation.

READ THE NEW LAWS CLOSELY. Almost certainly they allow rents to be raised in certain situations. Make sure you understand what you can and can't do under the ordinances in your area.

For example, they probably say that an owner who improves his property can apply for permission to increase the rent. Buy the worst, most rundown properties you can find — at bottom prices, of course — and make basic repairs. You can justify increases that will net you a nice return on your small outlay.

Or the ordinances may provide that you can raise the rent if the present occupant moves out. Under such conditions, it's worthwhile to give an occupant a bonus of $500 or $1,000 for moving.

BECOME ACTIVE IN A GROUP — the apartment association, perhaps — that deals with the rent control authorities. The people who run the controls are human beings like the rest of us — probably idealistic humans, trying to do a good job. When they know you personally and are convinced that you are ethical, they'll give reasonable consideration to whatever you ask. So, it behooves you to get acquainted, listen to discussions, learn the ropes, understand how these regulators think and work.

Maybe "you can't fight City Hall," but you can get City Hall to help you. The first step is to show that you are cooperative and understanding. Obey the regulations scrupulously, and the regulators will be more likely to rule in your favor when borderline questions come up. Most regulations are interpreted and modified in different ways for different people. Even when City Hall rules against you, it's still possible to get its ruling softened — especially if you are well known as someone who sympathizes with the need to keep rents at reasonable levels.

The worst thing you can do is to get mad at authorities, or call them stupid or inefficient or biased. Once they tab you as an enemy, they'll make your life harder by close inspection and policing.

New York hasn't entirely abandoned controls. In fact, its rules and regulations and exceptions have proliferated. According to an article in *Barron's,* "there are rent-controlled tenants, rent-stabilized tenants, tenants who were decontrolled by virtue of vacancy de-control (since rescinded), and tenants who were recontrolled or restabilized by virtue of the Emergency Tenant Protection Act of 1974." Even so, some apartment owners are doing very well, thank you.

IT'S A BUYER'S MARKET under rent control, countless sellers desperately trying to dispose of their buildings, and very few prospective buyers at any price. So if you shop around, you'll find bargains everywhere.

A group of New York rabbis bought buildings worth $700,000 for $300,000. They knew their way through the maze of regulations. In some buildings, adding furniture at above-normal profits was a permissible way to increase revenues, so they did. In others, they improved and renovated apartments, increasing values to the point where tenants as well as officials agreed that higher rent was justified. Or they raised the rent of tenants whose pay had been raised, as permitted by law. Or they refinanced to slash their mortgage payments. Or they bought out tenants; then re-rented at higher rates. It all depended on which regulation applied.

Sometimes they found that a building had been poorly managed. Just by getting an efficient manager and cutting waste, they improved the profit margin dramatically without raising anyone's rent. Altogether, they made hundreds of thousands of dollars in net profit for their churches.

In your community, the controls may exempt buildings containing less than five units. (This is a common exemption.) But few investors know this. You may find plenty of duplexes and fourplexes dumped on the market with no takers.

Or you may find that the local board is merely trying to keep rental increases within a certain range, while offering incentives for capital improvements. If you take the trouble to convince the authorities that your operating and maintenance costs have squeezed you badly, they're likely to grant your request for rent increases. Or, if you show them your bills for capital improvements, you'll get the same consideration.

Under rent control, as in other difficult situations, the whole secret of successful property management is in knowing how.

REMEMBER THESE BASIC POINTS:

* *You can minimize militancy by moving fast to take care of legitimate grievances. Good maintenance is important.*

* *Go slow in raising rents if it may trigger mass action.*

* *When you announce a rent increase, or a maintenance problem, do so in a personal letter to each resident or in personal conversation.*

* *Don't help residents organize any group get-togethers.*

* *If a group does form, try to ignore it. If it confronts you, listen but don't argue. Talk privately with each resident about his or her individual complaints.*

* *If forced into meeting with a militant organization, pick a place away from the premises. Have a trained negotiator talk for you, and tape-record the entire proceedings.*

* *If the organization makes impossible demands, offer compromises. Consider arbitration before going to court.*

* *If there is a rent strike, start immediately to evict the leaders. Keep trying for friendly one-to-one chats with individual occupants.*

* *If rent control is proposed, marshal the facts to show how it has hurt renters and home owners in other places. Avoid identifying with special interest groups.*

* *If operating under rent control, show authorities that you are cooperative. Find ways to improve profit margins.*

XIX *Your Best Is Yet to Come*

WERE YOU SCARED a little as you read a few of the foregoing chapters? I hope you were if you had been taking too lightly the possible problems you may encounter in managing real estate. You need awareness and foresight to maximize the prosperity of your properties.

Managerial work, even if done part-time from a distance, delegating to others the hard physical chores and/or dealing with difficult people, isn't always a breeze. Things can go wrong if you don't pay attention.

DON'T BE DISCOURAGED, though, by occasional trouble. If managing apartments were easy, there'd be no profit in it because everyone would be doing it. Some properties in excellent locations lose money; some of the least likely-looking places are profitable. The fact that some people can make profits in this field, while others lose money, shows that the profit-makers must be doing some things right and the losers must be doing many things wrong. Now that you've read this book, you know how to make sure that nearly everything is done right in whatever properties you own or manage. Just apply yourself, and you'll rise above difficulties in the rare cases where you can't forestall them completely.

ASK FOR HELP IF YOU NEED IT. By now you know there's always someone who can solve your problems, surmount difficulties, get work done when you can't do it yourself. All you need do is ask. Most people really like to be helpful. You needn't try to run even the smallest property single-handed.

Some obvious sources of advice are your professional service friends. Depending on the problem, your lawyer, accountant, banker or realtor may be able to help, or to steer you to someone who can.

Some managers or owners make the mistake of staying remote from their suppliers of equipment and merchandise. Owners are especially prone to shy away from suppliers with whom they have no active dealings. But suppliers (including real estate salesmen) are great sources of information. They know who's buying what; they know about new processes and new merchandise and new ideas, and they always know a lot of the latest business gossip. Tradesmen and salesmen enjoy discussing their knowledge with customers and potential customers, so eat lunch with them occasionally. Your time may be well spent.

YOU HAVE MUCH IN COMMON with other property owners and managers. Join and take an active part in the activities of local organizations such as the apartment association, property owners' association, and chamber of commerce. Membership will put you in touch with new angles on common problems, and a vast fund of technical information all filed and classified for ready reference. You'll meet and compare notes with people who share your interests. Many of them have had decades of practical experience which they're glad to pass along to newer members. Finally, subscribe and read (or at least skim through) all the apartment trade publications in your area. You'll find information worth clipping and saving.

YOUR HUSBAND OR WIFE can be a valuable partner in managing your properties. Some people have a tendency to think of owner-managers as male and of spouses as female. But even in the 1950s that would have been inaccurate — especially in the real estate field where thousands of women have done very well on their own. Many women now own thriving assemblages of residential real estate which they run efficiently. Sometimes their husbands become extremely helpful to them. And, of course, the same is true about wives of men who start a new career as owner-managers.

Spouses of either sex can do many things to help, particularly during their partner's first few years in this new occupation. But sometimes it's hard for people, especially spouses, to understand what drives a person to become a property manager. They wonder why their husband or wife would give up a comfortable life at home or in a corporation, and work energetically with no guarantee of success, especially if there are children and a mortgage involved. Why would anyone embark on such a seemingly wild venture?

Well, people start managing property for different combinations of reasons. Surely freedom, self-satisfaction, creativity, and fulfillment are important, as well as the money to be made. The attractions of self-employment must be evident to you, or you wouldn't have picked up this book and read this far. Why not explain the reasons to your spouse?

It's important for your spouse to understand why you want to be in this business. Some day soon, when you have some quiet time together, bring up the subject. Talk it over. Explain your motives and share your feelings. Your spouse is almost certain to respond with encouragement and help.

The first months of management may temporarily disrupt your household schedules now and then. Dinner can be late; plans for an evening or weekend may have to be changed at the eleventh hour. There's probably no way to eliminate all these distractions. But the partner at home can make this period a little easier on everyone involved, perhaps by assuming more than a normal share of household responsibilities, perhaps by being more flexible in his or her own routines.

Usually, there are plenty of chances for a spouse to help with management. If you haven't already done so, why not discuss the possibilities? Managers often need someone to do such things as typing, keeping records, answering the phone. I think it's a great idea to have both husband and wife actively participate in the family business.

ABOVE ALL ELSE, GIVE GOOD VALUE to the people who rent from you. Good management is the life blood of any successful building. It's important for a manager to convey a genuine concern about the problems of the people in the building.

Henry Ford, the man who first made automobile manufacturing a big business, often said, "The man who will use his skill and constructive imagination to see how *much* he can give for a dollar, instead of how little he can give, is bound to succeed." It holds true in every field of business.

Value is hard to define or measure. But renters can sense its presence. They know when they are receiving sincere service and a little more quality than their money's worth. It's a feeling, more than anything else — but it's a most important feeling. If they are satisfied, they'll continue to rent from you and they'll recommend you to others.

IF YOU'RE ONLY A MANAGER NOW, always keep in mind the goal of becoming an owner-manager, and eventually perhaps becoming solely an owner who knows how to make sure that his managers do a good job.

Right now your compensation as a manager, and whatever other income you may have, can build up the extra cash you need to get started as an owner. (If you'll read my book, *How You Can Become Financially Independent By Investing In Real Estate*, you'll see how little capital it takes, and you'll learn the foolproof step-by-step methods of expanding.)

Some people think the way to make money is to build up a big bank account. Money-wise investors have learned that the only way to make really big money is through capital gains — through building net worth, not cash. Anyone who becomes a millionaire today cannot make money in the form of cash. If he does, most of it will be taken away from him by taxation. Cash is tax as soon as it is taken out of property. When he banks it or lends it, the interest he collects is also taxed.

BUILDING YOUR WEALTH is a matter of building equity — becoming an owner, in other words. Cash burns a hole in your pocket. Capital gain doesn't. Cash is almost valueless unless you put it to work as capital, where it can multiply.

I know a few small property owners who think mainly in terms of how many shares of General Motors stock they own. Is this a hedge against their own inefficiency in managing their property? Or is it a status symbol? Why do they invest in bigger enterprises than their own?

Why invest in someone else's business, whether IBM or Xerox or some local concern, when you can invest in your own? If you think you can make more profit in someone else's enterprise, you'd better sell yours at once!

I'm sure you don't think that way, now that you've read this book. In someone else's business you have no control over management. In real estate you've bought, complete control is yours. The satisfaction of building up your holdings through personal enterprise far outweighs watching stock quotations in the newspaper.

Most important, the potential income from your own successful real estate operations can far exceed earnings you might expect from stock in the hottest company. Capital gains appreciation, expense accounts, tax advantages, estate planning — what stock pays such dividends, even if your buildings are only modestly successful?

And you realize, now that you've read this book, that your buildings can be considerably more than just modestly successful. Managing them profitably is a matter of know-how plus a little energy applied at the right times.

In the past 18 chapters, the complete guide for success in every phase of residential property management is at your fingertips. Opportunities are everywhere. Your biggest barrier is inertia. Take yourself in hand and get going! You'll always be glad you did.

REMEMBER THESE BASIC POINTS:

* *Now that you know how to manage, your main need is to apply yourself.*
* *Whenever you need help, ask for it, from people who have the skills or information you need.*
* *Be active in local organizations.*
* *Enlist the help of your husband or wife. Make sure he or she understands why you're in this business.*
* *Try to give your residents more than their money's worth.*
* *Keep your eye on the eventual goal of building your wealth by building equity.*

ABOUT THE AUTHOR

Albert J. Lowry is a nationally recognized author, instructor, counselor and platform speaker. He holds the following degrees and certificates: Ph.D. - California Western University, M.R.E. - Masters in Real Estate, M.B.A. - Masters in Business Administration, C.P.M. - Certified Property Manager, G.R.I. - Graduate of Realtors Institute, C.A.M. - Certified Apartment Manager, R.E.C.I. - member of Real Estate Certificate Institute, Certificate in Management - University of Southern California. He is a member of the Institute of Real Estate Management, the National Institute of Real Estate Brokers - Commercial and Industrial Division and the International Platform Association.

Emerging from an orphanage at 16 years of age, Al Lowry went to work as a day laborer in a Canadian steel mill and then took up the trade of butcher. He moved to the United States and began to study Real Estate in his spare time. By attending evening classes he obtained his Real Estate license. Without a fixed income, credit, or savings, he began purchasing small duplexes and triplexes in downtown Oakland with little or no down payment. He took care of his own maintenance and made improvements to enhance the value of each property. By leveraging his investments, he continuously purchased larger properties and has become a multi-millionaire in less than ten years.